The Ottoman Empire, 1300–1650

The Ottoman Empire, 1300–1650

The Structure of Power

Colin Imber

Published by
PALGRAVE MACMILLAN
Houndmills, Basingstoke, Hampshire RG21 6XS and
175 Fifth Avenue, New York, N.Y. 10010
Companies and representatives throughout the world

PALGRAVE MACMILLAN is the global academic imprint of the Palgrave Macmillan division of St. Martin's Press, LLC and of Palgrave Macmillan Ltd. Macmillan® is a registered trademark in the United States, United Kingdom and other countries. Palgrave is a registered trademark in the European Union and other countries.

ISBN-13: 978–0–333–61386–3 hardback
ISBN-10: 0–333–61386–4   hardback
ISBN-13: 978–0–333–61387–0 paperback
ISBN-10: 0–333–61387–2   paperback

This book is printed on paper suitable for recycling and made from fully managed and sustained forest sources.

A catalogue record for this book is available from the British Library.

Library of Congress Catalog Card Number: 2002070425

Printed and bound in Great Britain by
Antony Rowe Ltd, Chippenham and Eastbourne

Contents

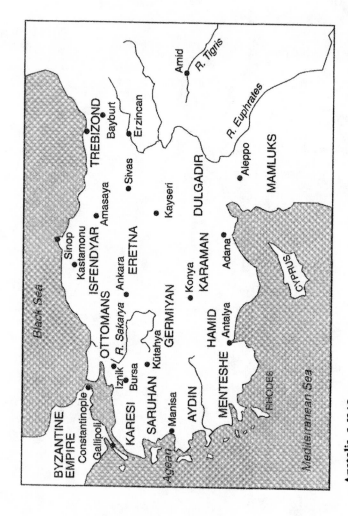

Anatolia, c. 1340

Adapted from Claude Cahen, *Pre-Ottoman Turkey*, London: Sidgwick & Jackson (1968), map IV

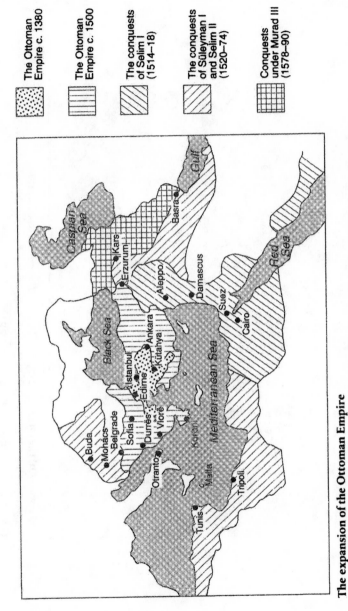

The expansion of the Ottoman Empire
Adapted from Robert Mantran (ed.), *Histoire de l'Empire Ottoman*, Paris: Fayard (1989), frontispiece

Legend:
- The Ottoman Empire c. 1380
- The Ottoman Empire c. 1500
- The conquests of Selim I (1514–18)
- The conquests of Süleyman I and Selim II (1520–74)
- Conquests under Murad III (1578–90)

x

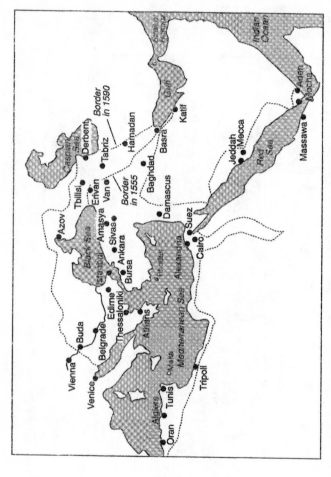

The borders of the Ottoman Empire, sixteenth/seventeenth centuries
Adapted from Palmira Brummett, *Ottoman Seapower and Levantine Diplomacy in the Age of Discovery*, New York: SUNY Press (1994), map 1

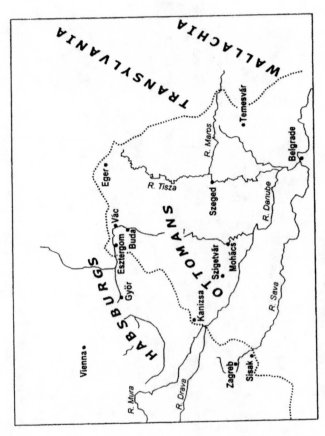

The Ottoman–Hapsburg frontier, 1600
Adapted from Rhoads Murphey, *Ottoman Warfare, 1500–1700*, London: UCL Press
(1999), map 5

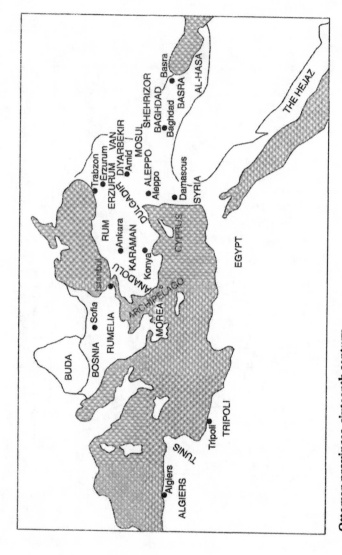

Ottoman provinces, sixteenth century
Adapted from Robert Mantran (ed.), *Histoire de l'Empire Ottoman*, Paris: Fayard (1989), frontispiece

Introduction

To write a general history of the Ottoman Empire is a foolhardy undertaking, and one that needs justification. A general history requires a solid foundation of books and articles that cover all aspects of the subject, and a tradition of debate that gives it a shape and a direction. These are things whose existence the historian of western Europe can take for granted. For an Ottomanist, however, the scene is different. It is not that books and articles on the Ottoman Empire do not exist, but rather that they are fewer and their quality more variable. Furthermore, as relatively few people work in the field, research results tend to exist in isolation, with the consequence that the subject as a whole lacks coherence. It is, for the same reason, difficult to talk of debates in Ottoman history, or to perceive an overall direction in which the field is moving. Historians of the Ottoman Empire quickly find that not only have the major questions not been answered, but that more often than not they have never been asked. The sensible thing, therefore, would probably be to wait until the subject has developed before attempting to write a general synthesis.

Nonetheless, there is, I believe, a justification for a general book. The history of the Ottoman Empire is important and, as recent events in the Balkans have shown, sometimes even necessary for understanding contemporary problems. It is, however, difficult for non-specialists to gain an entry into the field. Most of what is easily available is unsatisfactory, while much of the best work is too specialised or too technical for most readers. A general history can therefore serve to introduce the non-specialist to the field, and to provide a context which makes it possible to read the specialist works. I hope too that it might prove useful to Ottomanists, in giving the straightforward chronology of events which has hitherto been lacking – however unfashionable chronologcal narrative might be, it remains fundamental to historical understanding – and in providing a tentative account of the development of Ottoman institutions.

My approach to the subject is narrow, and arose from a tendency among Ottoman historians no longer to refer to the Ottoman 'Empire', but rather to the Ottoman 'State'. Initially, this term gained currency from its use by nationalist historians in the Republic of Turkey who have popularised the theory that the Turks have a genius for state-creation, and that the Ottoman Empire was one of a number of Turkish states established throughout history. The theory is nonsense, but it does raise a question: what kind of a 'state' was the Ottoman Empire? I have tried to answer the question – or to begin to answer it – by describing those institutions through which the Ottoman Sultan projected his power: the dynasty and the means of recruitment to dynastic service; the palace, court and central government; provincial government; the law; the army and the fleet. There should have been a chapter on taxation, but I leave this important topic to someone who, unlike me, understands figures. I have tried to show how these institutions developed and changed over three-and-a-half centuries. The study ends in the mid-seventeenth century, at the close of a period of crisis which brought to an end the Empire's expansion and brought changes to the structure of its institutions. The successive crises in the half century from about 1600 mark the end of the period in Ottoman history that it was once customary to designate as 'the rise of the Ottoman Empire'. It seemed, for this reason, to be an appropriate place to conclude this study.

It is detail and an awareness of primary sources that bring the study of history to life. A general history, however, necessarily omits details and must rely mainly on secondary materials. I have tried, nevertheless, to include some historical details, either to illustrate generalities, or to use them as evidence for assertions. I have tried, at the same time, to keep the reader in touch with the primary sources.

COLIN IMBER

1 Chronology

The Ottoman Empire in 1650

In 1650, the Ottoman Empire occupied lands in Europe, Asia and Africa. In Europe, Ottoman territory encompassed most of the Balkan Peninsula south of the rivers Danube and Sava, and the lands of central Hungary to the north. The Principalities of Transylvania, Wallachia, Moldavia and the Crimea which lay between Hungary and the Black Sea were tributaries of the Ottoman Sultan. In Asia, the Empire extended eastwards from the Bosphorus to the mountainous border with Iran, and southwards to the headwaters of the Gulf, and to Yemen in the south-west of the Arabian Peninsula. In Africa, the lands of the Empire comprised part of the western littoral of the Red Sea, the wealthy province of Egypt, and the semi-autonomous outposts of Tripoli, Tunis and Algiers. In the Mediterranean, Cyprus and most of the islands of the Aegean Archipelago were Ottoman possessions. By 1669, so too was Crete.

Europeans in the seventeenth century, as they still do, normally referred to the Empire as the 'Turkish Empire', and to its people – or at least its Muslim people – as 'Turks'. These designations are, however, only partially correct. The population of the Empire was heterogenous in religion, language and social structure. As the Faith of the sultans and of the ruling élite, Islam was the dominant religion, but the Greek and Armenian Orthodox Churches retained an important place within the political structure of the Empire, and ministered to large Christian populations which, in many areas, outnumbered Muslims. There was also a substantial population of Ottoman Jews. Following the settlement there of Jews expelled from Spain in 1492, Thessaloniki had become the city with the largest Jewish population anywhere in the world.[1] Outside these main groups, there were

1

numerous other Christian and non-Christian communities, such as the Maronites and Druzes of Lebanon. Linguistic groups were as varied and overlapping as religious communities. In the Balkan Peninsula, Slavonic, Greek and Albanian speakers were undoubtedly in the majority, but besides these, there were substantial minorities of Turks and romance-speaking Vlachs. In Anatolia, Turkish was the majority language, but this was also an area of Greek and Armenian speech and, in the east and south-east, Kurdish. In Syria, Iraq, Arabia, Egypt and north Africa, most of the population spoke dialects of Arabic with, above them, a Turkish-speaking élite. However, in no province of the Empire was there a unique language. The social structure of the Empire was also varied. The economy of the Ottoman Empire was overwhelmingly agricultural, and the glory of the sultans, as political writers frequently emphasise, rested on the labour of the peasantry. However, the types of agriculture and livestock rearing, as well as the social structure of villages and peasant households, varied with different traditions and with the variations in terrain and climate. In contrast with the peasantry, a part of the Empire's population led a semi-nomadic, pastoral existence, often at odds with the settled peoples and government. Among these groups were the Bedouin on the desert margins of Arabia, Syria and Egypt, the Vlachs of the Balkan Peninsula and the Turkish-speaking tribesmen of Anatolia, northern Syria and south-eastern Europe.

In the mid-seventeenth century, the political and military élite tended to be of Albanian or Caucasian – that is, typically, Georgian, Abkhazian or Circassian – descent.[2] The legal and religious figures who staffed the religious colleges, law courts and mosques were more likely to be Turks, in the western Balkans, Bosnians or, in the Arabic-speaking provinces, Arabs. The Ottoman Empire was, in short, multinational. Certain groups certainly enjoyed an advantage in the competition for political office, and rivalry between ethnic factions was an important element in Ottoman politics. In principle, however, discrimination existed only on grounds of religion. Muslims alone could achieve political office or pursue careers in the scribal service, but even here, Muslim descent was not necessary. Many, if not most, political office holders were first or second generation converts from Christianity. It was the judicial offices that were the preserve of old Muslim families. One vital organ of government, however, remained open to non-Muslims. Many of the men who engaged in the risky if potentially profitable activity of tax farming were Christians or Jews.

The Ottoman Empire was not, therefore, exclusively Islamic; nor was it exclusively Turkish. Rather, it was a dynastic Empire in which the only loyalty demanded of all its multifarious inhabitants was allegiance to the sultan. The loyalty demanded of those who did not hold office consisted in no more than not rebelling and paying taxes in cash, kind or services. Even these were often negotiable. It was in the end the person of the sultan and not religious, ethnic or other identity that held the Empire together.

Nevertheless, it is not wholly misguided to refer to the sultan's – in their Ottoman designation – 'Well-Protected Realms' as the 'Turkish Empire'. By the seventeenth century, literate circles in Istanbul would not identify themselves as Turks, and often, in phrases such as 'Turkish mischief makers' or 'senseless Turks', used the word as a term of abuse. Nonetheless, Turkish in a refined form was the language of government and the lingua franca of the élite. A vizier might, by origin, be an Albanian, a Croat or an Abkhaz, but for all official and most literary purposes he would use Turkish and not his native tongue. As the language of power, Turkish had prestige throughout the Empire. Furthermore, despite their abuse, the Ottoman élite seems always to have thought of Muslim Turks as the most reliable of the sultan's subjects. The settlement of Turkish colonies in the Balkans had accompanied the Ottoman conquest in the fourteenth and fifteenth centuries; and again, the years after the conquest of Cyprus in 1573 had witnessed the forcible removal to the island of Turks from Anatolia. The deportees were sometimes troublemakers at home, but the intention was that with their removal to a distant territory they would form a nucleus of loyal Ottoman subjects. It should be noted, however, that the sultans also resettled non-Turkish groups, such as the Jewish community implanted on Cyprus after 1573 in order to stimulate the commercial life of the island. The Jews, like the Turks, had a reputation for loyal endeavour.

The reason for the dominance in the Empire of the Turkish language and the important, although unprivileged position of the

Turks lies in the Empire's origins and in the history of Anatolia in the
two and a half centuries before its foundation.

Before the Ottomans

The Ottoman Empire came into being in about 1300 in north-western Anatolia to the east of the Byzantine capital, Constantinople. It
was only one of numerous small principalities which had emerged in
Anatolia in the last two decades of the thirteenth century on territory which had previously formed part of the Byzantine Empire. The
lords of these territories and their followers were Muslim Turks, and
their presence in Anatolia indicates not only a change in sovereignty,
but also a change in ethnicity and religion. From being primarily
Greek and Christian in the eleventh century, by 1300 Anatolia had
become primarily Turkish and Muslim.

The origins of this change lie in the eleventh century. In the mid-
century a confederation of Turkish tribes from Transoxania conquered Iran, and in 1055, occupied Baghdad, establishing it as the
capital of the Great Seljuk dynasty. The consequence of these events
was not simply to establish a new ruler in Baghdad, but also, with the
influx of Turks from Central Asia, to alter the ethnic balance of the
Middle East. Many of these Turkish incomers were to colonise
Anatolia.

A convenient date for marking the beginning of this phenomenon
is 1071. In this year the Great Seljuk Sultan defeated the Byzantine
Emperor at Manzikert in eastern Anatolia. The battle heralded the
rapid collapse of Byzantine rule in eastern and central Anatolia, and
the establishment in the following decades of the rule of a branch of
the Seljuk dynasty. The area of Byzantine sovereignty shrank to the
territory in western Anatolia between the Aegean and the central
plateau. The collapse of Byzantine defences and the appearance of a
Muslim dynasty undoubtedly encouraged the immigration of Turks.
So too did geography. It seems that the Turks who had migrated
from Transoxania to the Middle East were, in the main, semi-
nomadic pastoralists, and Anatolia was well suited to this way of life.
The Mediterranean coastlands and the plain of northern Syria provided them with a warm winter climate, while in the summer they

and their flocks could follow the retreating snowline to the upland pastures of the Taurus mountains and the Anatolian plateau. It was perhaps these factors more than the collapse of Byzantine rule that encouraged the first Turkish immigrants into Anatolia. Many, one may presume, were to abandon pastoralism and settle in villages.[3]

The Turks undoubtedly made up an important element in the realms of the Anatolian Seljuks. They did not, however, form a ruling class. The language of government in the twelfth and thirteenth centuries was Persian, and there was clearly a sharp divide between the Persian speaking élite of the cities and the Turks in the countryside. It was events in the thirteenth century that were to raise the political status of Turkish speakers in Anatolia. The same events were also to bring about the political fragmentation in Anatolia and the Balkan Peninsula that was to make possible the establishment of the principality that was to become the Ottoman Empire, and also to favour its rapid expansion.

The first of these crises affected the Balkan Peninsula rather than Anatolia. In 1204, the army of the Fourth Crusade conquered Constantinople and established a Latin Emperor in the city. With the capital in their possession the leaders of the Crusade divided Byzantine territory in Greece and the Aegean Archipelago among themselves, forcing the Byzantine government into exile at Nikaia (Iznik) and confining its territories to western Anatolia. During the course of the century, the Byzantine emperor recovered some lands in mainland Greece and the Peloponnesos, but the area still remained a patchwork of small principalities. The most lasting benefit of the Crusade came to Venice, which acquired strongholds in the Pelponnesos and islands in the Aegean, the most important of which was Negroponte (Evvoia) off the eastern coast of the Greek mainland. By the time of the Ottoman invasion of the Balkan Pensinsula in the fourteenth and fifteenth centuries, the lands to the north had become similarly fragmented. For a while during the fourteenth century they found political unity under the Serbian Tsar, Stephen Dushan (d. 1355), whose lands comprised Serbia itself, as well as much of Macedonia, Thessaly, Epiros and Albania. On Stephen's death, however, his successors divided the territory into small principalities. The same thing happened in Bulgaria. On the death of Tsar Alexander in

1371, his lands between the Danube and the Balkan mountains divided into three separate principalities. This fragmentation of the Balkan Peninsula, which had begun with the Fourth Crusade, was something which the Ottoman conquerors were later to exploit.

The Fourth Crusade did not, however, upset the equilibrium in Anatolia. The Byzantine Emperor retained control of western Anatolia and remained at peace with the Seljuk Sultan to the east. In the mid-thirteenth century, however, the Seljuk sultanate suffered a catastrophe. In 1243, a Mongol army – part of an invading force which, by 1258, had conquered Iran, Anatolia and Iraq – defeated a Seljuk army at Kösedağ and reduced the Sultan to the status of vassal. Henceforth, his overlord was the Ilkhan, the Mongol ruler of Iran.

The Mongol conquest did not at once affect Byzantine lands in western Anatolia. It was, however, a factor in the collapse of Byzantine rule in this area. The Mongols were a pastoral people, and needed the grasslands of the newly conquered Seljuk territory not only for their flocks, but especially for the horses that were essential for their military success. It seems very likely, therefore, that competition from the Mongols forced many Turkish pastoralists to seek new lands in the west. They found these in Byzantine Anatolia, where the river valleys lead down from the high plateau to the warmer climate on the shores of the Aegean, a feature of the landscape that was well suited to their summer and winter migration. The Turkish migration to the west became easier after 1261.

In this year, the Byzantine Emperor, Michael VIII Palaiologos, reconquered Constantinople. It was, as it turned out, a victory with some unhappy consequences. Once established in Constantinople, the Emperor used his resources against enemies in the west, ignoring his apparently secure eastern frontier. As Byzantine fortresses and military organisation fell into disrepair, invasion from the east became easier, and there was a Turkish migration, through the crumbled defences, to the sea. Thus, in the last decade of the thirteenth century, western Anatolia experienced the same transformation in its ethnic composition as central and eastern Anatolia had experienced in the last decade of the eleventh. As in the eleventh century, this change in ethnicity from primarily Greek to primarily Turkish had important political consequences.

These to a large extent mirrored the political changes in the former Seljuk realms. After 1243, the Seljuk sultans lost their power to Mongol governors, their formerly sovereign territory becoming the western outpost of the lands of the Ilkhans of Iran. In 1302, the last Seljuk sultan died. His death coincided with a period of weakening Ilkhanid control over Anatolia, making it possible for local governors, lords and bandits to establish themselves as independent rulers. Thus, in the early fourteenth century, what had been Seljuk and Ilkhanid Anatolia broke up into a kaleidoscope of principalities. Of these, the largest, the longest lived and the most fearsome rival of the Ottoman Empire was the emirate of Karaman in south-central Anatolia, with the old Seljuk capital of Konya as a principal city.

The same phenomenon occurred in the former Byzantine lands in western Anatolia. Byzantine rule did not survive the Turkish immigration of the late thirteenth century, and by 1300 Turkish rule had replaced Greek, with a series of Turkish principalities on the former territory of the Emperor. On the south coast, around Antalya, lay the principality of Teke. To the north of Teke and lying inland were the territories of Hamid, around Isparta, and Germiyan, with its capital at Kütahya. At the southernmost tip of the Aegean coast lay the principality of Menteshe. To the north of Menteshe were Aydın and Saruhan, with Tire and Manisa as their respective capitals. To the north of Saruhan, with part of its shoreline along the Dardanelles, lay the emirate of Karesi. North-west of Karesi, in the former Byzantine province of Bythinia, was the emirate of Osman, the founder of the Ottoman dynasty. His lands were to form the nucleus of the Ottoman Empire.[4]

One feature in particular distinguished the principalities that had emerged on former Byantine and Seljuk territories from the polities which they had replaced. Now the rulers and their followers, and not simply the subject people, were Turks. They were also Muslims. The mosques which they built during the course of the fourteenth century bear witness to their Faith, while the grandiose titles which they adopted for their mosque inscriptions show their wish to emulate the Seljuk sultans and the rulers in the old Islamic world. Nonetheless, the literary fragments which survive in Turkish from fourteenth-century Anatolia suggest that these new Turkish lords were 'a rude, unlettered folk', largely ignorant of the tenets of the orthodox Islam which they outwardly professed. This was the world into which the future Ottoman Empire[5] emerged: strongly Turkish and tentatively Islamic. As the Empire expanded it became increasingly multinational, both in its subject populations and in its body politic. At the same time, the Islam of the rulers, which expressed itself through the adoption of Islamic law and the imposition of formal Islamic ritual, became increasingly orthodox. Nonetheless, the use of Turkish as the language of government and the Turkish element in the population – both a reflection of the Empire's origins – gave the state a Turkish character.

The Ottoman Emirate: from triumph to disaster, 1300–1402

Ottoman tradition names Osman son of Ertughrul as the founder[6] of the Ottoman Empire, and relates how he declared himself a sovereign ruler at Karajahisar, a place which probably corresponds with Byzantine Malagina[7] in the lower Sakarya valley. This much of the tradition appears to be true. How Osman and his followers came to settle in this area is a matter for speculation, since later Ottoman accounts are almost certainly myths. It is possible, however, that a natural disaster provided the first impetus. The Sakarya valley was a strategically important area, since it controlled the approach to Constantinople from the east. Despite his preoccupations in the west, the Byzantine Emperor Michael VIII reorganised this frontier and, by 1280, had completed a new series of fortifications along the river bank. However, in the spring of 1302 the Sakarya flooded and, as a result of the indundations, changed its course, rendering the new defences useless. It was possibly this event that allowed Osman's men to cross the river and settle in the Byzantine province of Bythinia.[8]

Within a very short time, Turkish raiders had reached the Sea of Marmara. The contemporary Byzantine chronicler Pachymeres describes how news of Osman's victories spread and attracted Turks from other areas of western Anatolia to join his following, and how his force was strong enough to defeat a Byzantine army near Nikomedia (Izmit), exposing all Bithynia to his raids. From their base in the Sakarya valley, where Osman had occupied the old Byzantine fortified places, his men plundered the countryside to the west, forcing the inhabitants into the walled towns. These remained secure, since Osman obviously lacked the military skills to undertake formal sieges: his assault on Nikaia failed. At the time of his death in the mid-1320s, Nikaia, Prousas (Bursa), Nikomedia (Izmit) and Pegai had still not fallen.

It was Osman who was the founder of the Ottoman Empire, and who was to give his name to the Ottoman – or Osmanlı – dynasty, but it was under his son Orhan (1324?–62) that the little principality began to acquire a more settled aspect. Osman's territory had contained no large towns. In 1326, however, the city of Bursa succumbed to starvation and became, from this date, the first capital of the Ottomans. In the next year, following an earthquake which damaged its fortifications, Orhan's men occupied the Byzantine town of Lopadion (Ulubat), towards the Dardanelles. These disasters persuaded the Emperor Andronikos III to lead an army to Bithynia in 1328, but he turned back when Orhan checked his advance at Pelekanon, two days' march from Constantinople. With the land route between the city and Bythinia now impassable, the fall of the remaining Byzantine cities was inevitable. Nikaia was the first to succumb, in 1331. Nikomedia followed in 1337, confining Byzantine territory in Asia to a few miles to the east of Constantinople. Ottoman expansion, however, was not only at the expense of Byzantium. In 1345–6, Orhan annexed the Turkish emirate of Karesi, whose lands along the Dardanelles provided a crossing point from Asia into Europe. Less than ten years later, in 1354, Orhan's son Süleyman Pasha occupied Ankara to the east of his father's territory but such is the obscurity of this period, that it is not clear from whom he took the city.[9]

It was Orhan, too, who first established an Ottoman bridgehead in Europe. He achieved this by exploiting a civil war in Byzantium between the rival Emperors John [VI] Kantakouzenos and John [V] Palaiologos. Kantakouzenos sought allies among the Turkish rulers of western Anatolia and, in 1346 formed a pact with Orhan by marrying him to his daughter Theodora. The strategy was successful and, in 1347, Kantakouzenos entered Constantinople and proclaimed himself Emperor, with John V as his co-regent. It was, however,

Orhan who gained most from this arrangement. In 1352, as war raged between John V and Kantakouzenos' son Matthew, the father summoned help from Orhan, granting his troops under Süleyman Pasha a fortress on the Gallipoli peninsula.This was the first territory that the Ottomans occupied in Europe. Further conquest followed a natural disaster. In March 1354, an earthquake destroyed the walls of Gallipoli and other towns along the Dardanelles, which Süleyman at once occupied, bringing in as settlers Turks from Anatolia.

In 1354, Kantakouzenos abdicated, leaving John V as sole Emperor. Orhan had no family ties with John V, despite the Emperor's wish to form a marriage alliance, and so had no obligation to relinquish his new European possessions. Instead, he continued for a while to support the claims of Matthew Kantakouzenos to the Byzantine throne, while his men raided and eventually conquered much of eastern Thrace. In 1359 or 1361 – the date is unclear – Orhan captured Dhidhimoteichon (Dimetoka), clearing a passage along the northern shore of the Aegean towards Thessaloniki.

By the time of Orhan's death in 1362 his realm had taken on characteristics which were to distinguish the Ottoman Empire into the twentieth century. It comprised lands in both Asia and Europe, cities as well as rural settlements; and the ruler had constructed the first mosques and religious establishments that distinguished his principality as a Muslim polity.

It seems from a short literary reference that Orhan's son, Murad I (1362–89), came to the throne after a civil war.[10] By the end of the 1360s, he was clearly secure in his rulership and his realms in Anatolia and in Europe began to expand rapidly. In the east he annexed the Turkish principalities that lay in an arc between his own lands in north-western Anatolia and Antalya on the Mediterranean coast. Ottoman chronicles present these annexations as entirely peaceful. Murad acquired, they say, part of the principality of Germiyan as a marriage portion which came with the betrothal of a Germiyanid princess to his son, Bayezid. Hamid to the south of Germiyan, Murad acquired by purchase. In fact, the Germiyanid marriage and the annexation of Hamid probably followed a military campaign. A chronology of 1439–40 tells us that in 1375–6 'The Germiyanid and Tatar armies were routed, and Kütahya, some of the fortresses of Germiyan and the land of Hamid were conquered.' Eastwards expansion brought Murad into contact with Karaman, the most powerful of the Anatolian emirates, and contact led to war. In 1387, to avenge himself for a previous Karamanid attack, Murad invaded and reduced the lord of Karaman, Alaeddin Ali, to submission.

The control of Germiyan, Hamid and territory to the south gave Murad control of a trade route leading from his capital at Bursa to Antalya, and most probably enhanced his treasury as much as it expanded his realms, but his conquests in Europe were more spectacular.

His reign, however, began with a defeat which might have halted Ottoman conquests in Europe altogether. In 1366, Amadeo of Savoy, the cousin of the Byzantine Emperor John V, captured Gallipoli on the European shore of the Dardanelles, a conquest which should have enabled the Byzantines to block the passage of the Turks across the Straits. Then, in 1369, the Emperor travelled to Rome to procure the assistance of the Pope. Nonetheless, Byzantine success was temporary. The continuing Ottoman advance into the Balkan Peninsula suggests that reinforcements continued to cross from Asia Minor, and no assistance came from Europe. Whatever advantage the Byzantines possessed they lost again in 1377, when the Emperor Andronikos IV ceded Gallipoli to Murad in return for his assistance in a civil war against his father and brothers.

The first of Murad's great victories in Europe came, probably, in 1369,[11] when Turkish forces occupied Adrianople (Edirne). The city occupies a strategic position at the confluence of the Maritsa and Tundzha rivers, giving access to central and eastern Bulgaria, and to western Thrace. It was probably, therefore, the imminent danger to the lands lying to the west of Edirne that motivated the two Serbian lords of Macedonia to form an alliance against Murad and to attack his forces on the Maritsa river in 1371. Both men lost their lives in the rout which followed and, in the words of a Greek Short Chronicle: 'From then on the Muslims began to overrun the Empire of the Christians.'

The pressure which these Muslims exerted was both political and military. The Tsardom of Bulgaria became a vassal of Murad following his marriage, at an uncertain date, to Thamar, the sister of Tsar Shishman. The conquest of Thrace and Macedonia, however, was by war. Turkish raids began immediately after the battle of the Maritsa, with Thessaloniki suffering its first attack in 1372. In the same year, Pope Gregory XI tried unsuccessfully to form an anti-Turkish alliance, suggesting that the Latin colonies in central and southern Greece also felt under threat of attack. What had begun as raids, led to permanent conquests. In 1383, an Ottoman army under the Vizier Hayreddin Chandarli captured Serrai and laid siege to Thessaloniki. Four years later, in 1387, the city fell. The blockade of Thessaloniki, however, occupied only a fraction of Murad's forces. Verroia fell, probably, in 1385–6 and Bitola shortly afterwards, bringing all of southern Macedonia under Ottoman control by 1387. By the 1380s, too, the Turks had begun to make raids south-westwards into Epiros – by 1386, Esau Buondelmonti, the Despot of Epiros, was Murad's vassal – and southwards to the Peloponnesos. In 1387, in response to an invitation from Theodore, the Byzantine Despot of Mistra, the Turkish lord Evrenos harried lands in the Peloponnesos, attacking not only the rebels against the Despot, but also the Venetian settlements in the peninsula. Meanwhile, to the north, Ottoman expansion continued in the direction of Serbia.

In, probably, 1385 Sofia fell. Nish followed in the spring or summer of the next year, enabling Murad to enter the territory of the Serbian lord, Prince Lazar. This invasion was a failure. Lazar checked Murad's advance at Ploc̆nik, possibly in the summer of 1386, and forced his withdrawal. For three years Murad did not return to Serbia. His advance in the west had given the emir of Karaman, Alaeddin Ali, the opportunity to attack his lands in Anatolia, and it was against Karaman that Murad campaigned in 1387. Then, during the same year, the Bulgarian Tsar Shishman renounced his allegiance to Murad, unleashing a campaign under the Vizier Ali Chandarli to reduce him to submission. By the summer of 1388, Shishman had again accepted Murad's overlordship.[12] But it was another event in 1388 that drew Murad back to Serbia in the following year.

It seems feasible that Murad's vassal George Stracimirović Balšić, lord of Zeta to the south of Bosnia, asked Murad for troops to attack Tvrtko, King of Bosnia, and that Murad responded by sending a certain

Shahin. In August 1388, Bosnian troops routed Shahin's men at Bileća, near the Adriatic, and it was perhaps with a view to striking ultimately against King Tvrtko that Murad marched westwards in 1389. His route, in any case, led him into Serbia, and here, on 15 June 1389, he encountered the army of Prince Lazar at Kosovo Polje.[13] The outcome of the battle seems to have been a Turkish victory insofar as the Turks held the field, but with great losses. Both Murad and Lazar lost their lives in the battle. According to Ottoman tradition, Murad's son, Bayezid, succeeded his father in a coup on the battlefield of Kosovo.[14]

Fourteenth-century sources suggest that Murad styled himself modestly as 'emir' and not yet as 'sultan'. The emirate that he had established on the basis of his inheritance from Orhan consisted of a federation of lords under Ottoman suzerainty. The lands which he had inherited around Bursa in Anatolia and the lands in Thrace around Edirne probably came directly under the rule of Murad himself or of his appointees. After the Germiyanid marriage of 1375–6, much of Ottoman Anatolia probably came under the rule of his son, Bayezid. Political power in the Balkan Peninsula lay largely with the Muslim marcher lords, whether these, like Evrenos in Macedonia, were of Turkish origin, or whether, like the Mihaloghlu family in north-eastern Bulgaria, they were converts from Christianity. In addition, many of the Christian dynasts of the Balkan Peninsula, such as Esau Buondelmonti of Ioannina, George Stracimirović of Zeta, Shishman and Ivanko in Bulgaria, and the Byzantine Emperor and his son Theodore of Mistra, were Murad's vassals. They owed him tribute and provided him with troops, but in return received support against their enemies. The Ottoman Empire was to retain a similar political structure until after 1450.

News of Murad's death at Kosovo had, in all probability, reached Anatolia in the months after the battle and encouraged neighbouring powers to seize Ottoman lands. A contemporary source mentions in particular that Alaeddin of Karaman had recovered Beyşehir, and that the lord of Germiyan had also tried to regain his lost lands. Bayezid's response came in early 1390. By March of that year he had conquered the three principalities on the Aegean shore of Anatolia – Saruhan, Aydın and Menteshe, retaken Beyşehir from Karaman and in this, or a later campaign, seized the lands that remained to Germiyan. The campaign, while extending Bayezid's territories, did not secure peace. During its course, one of Bayezid's Anatolian vassals, Süleyman Pasha of Kastamonu, transferred his allegiance from Bayezid to Burhaneddin, the ruler of much of central Anatolia, and Bayezid's next campaign was against Süleyman Pasha. Its outcome was his execution in 1391 and the annexation of his realms. Next, Bayezid continued eastwards against Burhaneddin, his army strengthened as local lords from northern Anatolia attached their forces to his. He suffered a defeat at Çorumlu, but this was clearly not so severe as to prevent his further advance. In December, however, weather, terrain and events in Europe forced him to return westwards. During the course of the campaign he had annexed Kastamonu, and perhaps obtained the allegiance of the lords and clan chiefs of northern Anatolia. The army that he led was very different from that of the first two Ottoman rulers. He now had in his following his vassal, the Byzantine Emperor Manuel II with a contingent of Byzantine troops and also, on Manuel's testimony, contingents of Serbs, Bulgarians and Albanians.[15]

In 1392, Bayezid's main concern seems to have been with Serbia. After the battle of Kosovo, Serbia faced a threat of invasion from the Kingdom of Hungary to the north, and from the Ottomans to the south and east. It clearly had to accept the overlordship of one in order to gain protection from the other. A faction in Serbia preferred, it seems, Bayezid to King Sigismund of Hungary, and to formalise the arrangement Bayezid married Olivera, the sister of Lazar's son and successor, Stephen Lazarević. Stephen was henceforth Bayezid's vassal. At the same time Bayezid asserted his suzerainty over George Stracimirović of Zeta and Vlk Branković, lord of Priština. Bayezid's next concern was Bulgaria. Why he should have invaded Tsar Shishman's territory in 1393 and captured his capital of Tarnovo is not clear: Shishman had perhaps, for a second time, broken his allegiance to the Ottoman ruler. This was, however, only a preliminary engagement. Two years later, in order presumably to pre-empt the consequences of an anti-Turkish alliance between King Sigismund of Hungary and Voyvoda Mircea of Wallachia, Bayezid led his army to the north of the Danube and encountered the Wallachians in a violent but indecisive battle. On his return he entered Tarnovo and executed Tsar Shishman, exiling other members of the dynasty to governorships in Anatolia.

The establishment of Ottoman suzerainty over Serbia, the extinction of the Tsardom of Bulgaria, and Bayezid's invasion of Wallachia posed a threat to the Kingdom of Hungary, lying to the north of the Danube. In the face of this danger, King Sigismund renewed his efforts to form an anti-Turkish league. It was not difficult to find allies among those whose lands Bayezid threatened, the first of whom was the Byzantine Emperor Manuel II. In 1394, Bayezid had placed Constantinople under siege,[16] and it had become clear that the city could not survive without assistance from foreign powers. The Emperor's main hope was Venice whose possessions in mainland Greece suffered from Turkish raids, and whose Aegean strongholds were coming under attack from Bayezid's ships at Gallipoli. By 1396, Sigismund, the Emperor Manuel and Venice had agreed to contribute troops and ships to a war against Bayezid. A more significant contingent came from France and Burgundy. In 1395, a truce between France and England had released the Franco-Burgundian knights for adventures elsewhere, and a contingent under John of Nevers, the son of the Duke of Burgundy, travelled to Hungary to join Sigismund's Crusade against Bayezid.

Bayezid encountered the Crusaders in 1396 at Nicopolis (Nikopol) on the Danube in Bulgaria. His lightly armed cavalry, including a contingent under Stephen Lazarević, outmanoeuvred the heavily armed western knights, drawing them into a trap and inflicting a total defeat. The survivors whom Bayezid did not execute, he kept for ransom. Following his victory, Bayezid removed the last independent Bulgarian lord, Sratsimir of Vidin, consolidating Ottoman domination of the lands south of the Danube. Hungary, however, while exposed to raids, did not face the invasion which King Sigismund had evidently feared. In 1397, Bayezid instead led his army to Anatolia.

The reason for his departure from Europe into Asia was the action of the emir of Karaman, Alaeddin, who, while Bayezid encountered the Crusaders at Nicopolis, had attacked and taken prisoner his Governor-General in Anatolia. Bayezid's response was decisive. In 1397 he invaded Karaman, occupied Konya, its major city, and executed Alaeddin.

Alaeddin was also his brother-in-law and, when he marched south to lay siege to Larende, his sister, Alaeddin's widow, ordered the garrison to open the gates to Bayezid. With the death of Alaeddin and the removal of his widow to Bursa, Karaman became an Ottoman territory, and a base for further conquest in the north-east. This involved Bayezid in further conflict with Burhan al-Din of Sivas, whom he had first encountered in his Anatolian campaign of 1391. In 1398, he expelled Burhan al-Din from Sivas, annexed the small principalities near the Black Sea coast and then, following Burhan al-Din's death, occupied Sivas itself. Soon afterwards, probably in 1399, he seized Malatya to the east of Sivas, a northernmost outpost of the Mamluk Sultans of Cairo. By 1401, he had advanced along the Upper Euphrates valley to take Erzincan from its lord, Taharten.

Bayezid's ambitions in eastern Anatolia had a fatal consequence. The period of his conquests had coincided with the growth of another Empire to the east. Between the 1370s and 1400, Timur[17] – or Tamburlaine – had from humble beginnings overrun lands in Central Asia, southern Russia, Iran and Azerbaijan, and out of these created an Empire of vassals, with its capital at Samarkand. By 1400, the westward expansion of Timur's Empire and the eastward expansion of Bayezid's led to conflict. The first blow fell in 1400, when Timur sacked Sivas. In 1401, he led his army into Syria, plundering Aleppo, Homs, Hama, Baalbek and Damascus, returning to spend the winter of 1401–2 in Karabagh in the Caucasus. Disputes with Bayezid over the allegiance of vassals provided Timur with an excuse for war and, in 1402, he invaded Bayezid's realms, camping in July outside Ankara.

Timur's strategy was as much political as military, exploiting the fragile loyalties of Bayezid's subjects in Anatolia. In 1390, the lords of the old emirates of Germiyan, Saruhan, Aydın and Menteshe had sought the protection of Timur after Bayezid had annexed their lands. He now placed these men in prominent positions in his army. At the same time, his envoys had negotiated with the tribal chiefs of Anatolia, whose men fought in Bayezid's army, to desert Bayezid on the battlefield. Furthermore, before the battle began, he had occupied a position which controlled access to the water supplies, exhausting Bayezid's men even before the conflict. His strategy succeeded. When the battle opened, the cavalrymen from the old emirates, seeing their former lords in Timur's army, deserted Bayezid. So, as pre-arranged, did the tribal levies. When these men changed sides, the forces under the command of his elder and younger sons, Süleyman and Mehmed, abandoned the field, leaving Bayezid with only his Janissary bodyguard and the contingent from Serbia under Stephen Lazarević. He ended the battle a prisoner of Timur. He died a year later, still in captivity. Timur followed the battle with a campaign of massacre and plunder in western Anatolia, which lasted until the summer of 1403.[18] He died in 1405, in the early stages of a campaign against China.

The Ottoman Emirate: civil war and recovery, 1402–1451

Timur's campaign spread devastation in Anatolia, especially in the west. It also altered the political configuration. After the battle of Ankara, Timur re-established the old emirs of Germiyan, Saruhan, Aydın and Menteshe in their former realms, and reinstated the dynasty of Karaman, confining Ottoman rule in Anatolia to the strip of territory running from Amasya in the east to Bursa and the Sea of Marmara in the west. Timur had not touched Ottoman lands in the Balkans, but it was in the aftermath of Ankara that the Christian powers in the region – the Byzantine Emperor, Venice, Genoa and the Knights of St John – forced Bayezid's son, Süleyman, in a treaty concluded at Gallipoli, to relinquish Thessaloniki to the Emperor and to make some other, less significant concessions.[19] The Ottoman lands themselves were divided; Bayezid's eldest son, Süleyman, ruled in Europe, his youngest son, Mehmed, in Amasya to the north-east of Ankara. A third son, Isa, tried to establish himself in western Anatolia. Another son, Musa, after Timur had released him, came into the custody of Mehmed. Another, Mustafa, disappeared, conceivably as a captive to Samarkand. With no agreed succession to Bayezid, a civil war was inevitable.

In 1403, Süleyman was the most powerful of Bayezid's successors. He had, in the Treaty of Gallipoli, ceded Thessaloniki and some other territories, but otherwise had inherited his father's European domains intact. An alliance which Sigismund of Hungary had proposed in

1406 between himself and Stephen Lazarević of Serbia never materi-alised. Instead, in 1409, Süleyman's forces assisted Stephen's brother, Vlk Lazarević and George Branković in devastating Stephen's realms and establishing themselves as rulers in southern Serbia. Süleyman's action made him overlord of all three Serbian principalities. In Anatolia, Prince Mehmed faced more opposition to his rule. From the battlefield of Ankara, he withdrew to Tokat in the north-east, where he faced the attacks and rebellions of local dynasts and tribal leaders. It was only when he had averted these dangers that he could travel westwards to challenge his brother Isa for possesion of the old capital of Bursa. Isa offered no effective resistance. He fled to Karaman and 'disappeared there'. Isa's flight did not, however, put an end to Mehmed's troubles. In 1404, feeling his European territories to be secure, Süleyman crossed the Straits to Anatolia and, with his superior forces, occupied Bursa, driving Mehmed back to Amasya and confining his rule to the Ottoman territories to the east of Ankara. For the next five years, Süleyman was master of part of west-ern Anatolia and of the Ottoman Balkans.

The decisive move which Mehmed made against Süleyman was political rather than military. He had in his custody his brother Musa, and in 1409 he set him free. Released from captivity, Musa crossed the Black Sea to Wallachia where he entered into a marriage alliance with the Voyvoda Mircea. Then, with troops from his father-in-law, he crossed the Danube into Süleyman's territory and, in his brother's absence, overran eastern Bulgaria and Thrace and occupied Gallipoli. The result of Musa's success was exactly as Mehmed had intended. The need to re-establish his rule in his European territories forced Süleyman's withdrawal from western Anatolia, allowing Mehmed to occupy the territories which Süleyman had conquered. His victory was complete when, in the summer of 1410, the Byzantine Emperor ferried Süleyman and his men across the Straits to confront Musa.

Süleyman rapidly gained the upper hand, forcing Musa to live 'like a brigand in the mountains'. Six months later, Süleyman was dead. The cause of his downfall was drunkenness. Early in 1411, Süleyman was in Edirne and as, to quote a Greek Short Chronicle, 'he lay in stews and drank great cups of wine', his brother's army approached. Süleyman ignored all warnings until it was too late. As Musa's faction occupied Edirne, he fled towards Constantinople. Musa's men caught up with him and strangled him on the road.[20]

Musa's reign was brief. He faced the hostility not only of his brother Mehmed in Anatolia, but also of the Serbian despot who harried his lands in the Morava valley, and of the Byzantine emperor, who set free Süleyman's son, Orhan, to oppose his rule. It was this hostile act that led Musa, briefly and unsuccessfully, to lay siege to Constantinople in 1411. While facing these enemies, Musa also suffered the desertion to Mehmed of several of the powerful marcher lords, apparently because he had seized their money and property, in an effort, presumably, to replenish his treasury at a time when the uncertainties of war and politics had cut off the flow of taxes. Nonetheless, in 1411, he defeated his brother Mehmed and in the following year carried out reprisals against Serbia. In late 1412, when Mehmed attempted to invade for a second time, foul weather forced him to retreat. In 1413, however, after receiving the friendship of Stephen Lazarević in Serbia and securing his eastern border by a marriage alliance with the lord of Dulgadir, he crossed the Bosphorus for the third time. In July he defeated and killed his brother outside Sofia.

The death of Musa left Mehmed I (1413–21) as the sole ruler of Ottoman territories in Europe and Asia. His inheritance, however, was fragile, with enemies determined to destroy his fractured domains. The first to attack was the emir of Karaman, who had laid siege to Bursa already during Mehmed's last campaign against his brother. When the Karamanids had withdrawn on Mehmed's return to Anatolia, the Emperor Manuel tried unsuccessfully to negotiate with Venice for a subvention against the Turks. When this plan failed, he again released from his captivity Süleyman's son Orhan, with the intention that, in alliance with Mircea of Wallachia, he should overthrow Mehmed. This scheme too was a failure, but in 1414 another possibility arose when a Venetian galley captain at Trabzon took on board the envoy of a man who claimed to be Mustafa, the son of Bayezid who had disappeared at the battle of Ankara in 1402. The Venetians refused to cooperate, as to support Mustafa would upset their relationships with Mehmed. Mustafa, however, was to be useful to other of Mehmed's enemies.

These, however, did not act immediately, giving Mehmed the opportunity to take vengeance on the emir of Karaman. In 1415, he besieged Konya, forcing the emir to cede the lands in western Karaman which he had taken from the Ottomans after their defeat at Ankara. From Karaman, Mehmed began the pacification of the old western Anatolian emirates, re-establishing his suzerainty and annexing Saruhan and part of Aydın. As governor he appointed Alexander Shishman, a scion of the old Bulgarian dynasty. The year 1415 was thus a year of renewed Ottoman advances.

In the following year, however, Mehmed faced three crises. The first was the consequence of the aggression of his ships at sea, which had begun to attack Venetian and other settlements in the Aegean Archipelago. In April 1416, after diplomacy had failed, a Venetian squadron destroyed the Ottoman fleet outside the Dardanelles. The Ottoman fleet did not present a danger again until after 1450. The second crisis came in August, when the man who had contacted Venice in 1414, claiming to be Mehmed's brother Mustafa, landed in Wallachia and then, at the head of a force of Turks and Vlachs, crossed the Danube into Mehmed's realms. The invasion failed. Mehmed defeated Mustafa's army, compelling Mustafa himself to take refuge in Byzantine Thessaloniki. In response Mehmed laid siege to the city.

It was when he was here that he faced the greatest challenge to his rule, when two revolts broke out simultaneously, the one in the Dobrudja in north-eastern Bulgaria and the other on the Karaburun peninsula, on the Aegean shore of Anatolia opposite Chios. The leader of the Bulgarian revolt was Sheikh Bedreddin, a jurist and mystic, who had served as Musa's Military Judge in Rumelia between 1411 and 1413.[21] The leader in Karaburun was Börklüje Mustafa, a charismatic dervish. Ottoman sources plausibly claim that the two men were in collusion. Both rebellions were the consequence of the instability and insecurity that had followed the Ottoman defeat at Ankara in 1402. Ottoman accounts of the rebellion are partisan, but entirely credible in their claim that Bedreddin found much of his support in the Dobrudja from among the officers and fief holders whom Musa had appointed during his reign in Rumelia, and whom Mehmed had dismissed on his accession to power. Bedreddin, who appears to have claimed the sultanate on the basis of his alleged descent from the Seljuks, anounced that, as Sultan he would reinstate the dispossessed. The revolt of Börklüje Mustafa had a different character. It was, it seems, a popular, millenarian rebellion around the person of Börklüje, who preached, according to the Greek chronicler Doukas, the equality of Muslims and Christians and the common ownership of property. Börklüje's followers, Doukas leads us to believe, were 'simple country folk'.

Both rebellions failed. The revolt in the Dobrudja collapsed when an agent of the Sultan seized Bedreddin and brought him before the Sultan at Serrai, where, in accordance with the fatwa of a Persian *molla*, he was hanged in the marketplace. The resistance of Börklüje's followers was fiercer. They defeated first the army of Shishman, the governor of Saruhan, and then the army of Ali Bey, another Ottoman governor in western Anatolia. It was only when Mehmed sent against them an army under the Vizier Bayezid Pasha that he was able to crush the rebellion. 'Bayezid Pasha', writes Doukas, 'killed everyone in his path without sparing a soul, young or old, men and women.' Börklüje Mustafa and his dervishes he brought to Ephesus and executed. Despite the defeat, memories lingered, and a sect named after Bedreddin survived in the Dobrudja for at least two centuries after his death.

A beneficiary of Mehmed's troubles had been the emir of Karaman who, when Mustafa invaded the Ottoman realms in Europe, had pillaged Ottoman Anatolia as far as Bursa. As a reprisal, in 1417 Mehmed invaded Karaman, bringing his army almost to Konya. He refrained, however, from attacking the city. Instead, in the same year, he led a second expedition in Anatolia against Isfendyaroghlu of Sinop, a campaign which left him in control of Kastamonu and its copper mines, and confined Isfendyaroghlu to the lands around Sinop. Three years later, in obscure circumstances, the Ottomans also occupied the Genoese colony of Samsun on the Black Sea coast. Mehmed's conquests in the Balkan peninsula matched those in Anatolia. In 1417, the Venetians were alarmed to hear that an Ottoman force had seized Vlorë on the Adriatic coast from Rugina, the 'Lady of Valona', and feared that Ottoman ships might appear in the Adriatic to harry Venetian commerce. Instead, in the same year,

Hamza Pasha conquered Gjirokastër, the stronghold of the Zenevis clan, Vlorë and Gjirokastër together giving the Sultan a substantial territory in southern Albania. This was in 1418. In the same year Mehmed led in person an expedition against Mircea of Wallachia, forcing him into submission and occupying the fortresses which controlled the crossing points on the Danube.

In 1421, Mehmed died. His son, Murad II (1421–51), did not, however, take possession of an undivided realm. In order to exploit the uncertainties of the succession, the Byzantine Emperor Manuel II released Murad's uncle, Mustafa, from custody in Thessaloniki, and it was to take vengeance on the Emperor for this act that in 1422 Murad laid siege to Constantinople. The siege lasted until September, when the Sultan withdrew, not so much in despair at Byzantine resistance, as in consequence of renewed dynastic strife.

The cause was the appearance in October 1422 of his younger brother 'Little' Mustafa, and it was only after his defeat that Murad could turn against external enemies. During the time of Murad's struggles with the two Mustafas, Drakul, the Voyvoda of Wallachia, had crossed the Danube and harried Ottoman Rumelia. At the same time, Isfendyaroghlu of Sinop had recovered the territories in Kastamonu which Mehmed I had seized. After the death of the younger Mustafa, Murad personally led his army to Kastamonu to recover the lost territory and its copper mines, while a Rumelian marcher lord led a destructive expedition into Wallachia. The outcome of both campaigns was to reduce both Drakul and Isfendyaroghlu to vassalage, with Murad marrying an Isfendyarid Princess.

These campaigns restored stability to Murad's realms, and within twenty years he had, with the exception of Karaman and the upper Euphrates valley, recovered the territories lost after the Battle of Ankara. The most significant loss in Europe at this time had been Thessaloniki and, in 1422, Murad's forces blockaded the city. A year later, the Byzantines could no longer withstand the assault and ceded Thessaloniki to Venice. In the same year, a series of raids into the Peloponnesos by the Turkish marcher lord Turahan reminded the Christian signatories of the 1403 Treaty of Gallipoli that their political advantage over the Ottomans had evaporated.

While Thessaloniki was under siege, Murad directed his forces against the remaining emirates of western Anatolia. In 1424, he sent an army against Juneyd, the lord of Aydın, obliging him to take refuge in a coastal fortress and to seek assistance from the Venetians in Thessaloniki and from Karaman. These efforts failed. With the help of Genoese ships, the Ottoman besiegers captured the fortress and executed Juneyd with his entire family. By 1425, Murad had in addition annexed Menteshe, bringing all the Aegean coastline of Anatolia under his rule. Three years later, he completed his conquests in Asia by annexing the thickly wooded and mountainous areas along the Black Sea coast to the east of Samsun, and then, in 1428, occupying Germiyan after the death of its last dynastic lord.

During these years, the siege of Thessaloniki continued, forcing the Venetians to seek allies against the Sultan. When they received overtures from the Duke of Athens, Antonio Acciajuoli, and from Theodore, Despot of Mistra, the Venetians procrastinated. Their hope was for an alliance with King Sigismund of Hungary. These plans did not materialise, even though Sigismund and Murad had come into conflict. The cause was the disputed overlordship of Serbia. The elderly Stephen Lazarević had, it seems, transferred his allegiance from the Ottoman Sultan to Sigismund and had, furthermore, promised to bequeath the Danubian fortress of Golubats to the Hungarian King. An Ottoman advance to the Serbian border seems to have forced Stephen into submission but, in 1427, the old Despot died. This unleashed a war, with Sigismund seizing Belgrade, and Murad retaliating with the capture of Golubats. The Serbian Despot, George Branković, found himself squeezed between the King and the Sultan.

By 1430, it had become clear that Venice could expect no help from Hungary in relieving the siege of Thessaloniki, and in March of that year, the Sultan himself encamped before the city. At the end of the month, Thessaloniki fell to a general assault. In the subsequent treaty, Venice ceded the city and agreed to pay Murad an annual tribute for Venetian possessions in Albania. In the same year, the Ottomans conquered Ioannina in Epiros. The occasion for this was the death of the Despot Carlo Tocco in 1429, with no legitimate heirs. The Despotate passed therefore to his nephew, Carlo II, a protégé of the

Angevin King of Naples. Murad clearly did not wish to see the implantation of Angevin influence in Greece, and found a reason to oust Carlo II. Carlo I Tocco had no legitimate heir, but he had had six illegitimate sons, who had resided in turn at Murad's court, and it was in answer to the call of the eldest, Hercules Tocco, that Murad sent Sinan Pasha against Ioannina in 1430. Sinan Pasha occupied the city, but instead of installing Hercules, he placed it directly under Ottoman rule. He next harried Carlo II's domains in Arta, as a reminder no doubt that he ruled there as a vassal of Murad.

The years after 1430 saw the uncertain establishment of Ottoman rule in central and southern Albania. This began with the seizure of territories to the north of Gjirokastër belonging to the Arianit and Kastriote clans, and then a successful rebellion of the defeated lords and an Albanian siege of Gjirokastër. Ottoman reprisals came early in 1433,when an army under the marcher lord Ali, the son of Evrenos, entered Albania, raised the siege of Gjirokastër and 'destroyed John Kastriote's domains'. John Kastriote was to continue to rule at Krujë as an Ottoman vassal, with his son George – the famous Scanderbeg – a hostage at the Ottoman court. With much of Albania under his control, Murad next extended his dominion over Serbia, not this time by force, but by marriage. In 1435, he wed Mara, the daughter of the Despot George Branković, establishing her father as his vassal.

The marriage was the first step in the conquest of Serbia. Despite Branković's protected status as a vassal, in 1438 Murad led a campaign which first captured Borač in the north of Serbia, before crossing the Danube and making a devastating raid into Transylvania. In 1439, he took Zvornik and Srebrenica on the border with Bosnia and, most importantly, the fortress of Smederovo on the Danube, bringing northern Serbia under his control. His final goal, however, was the Kingdom of Hungary. By 1439, with Serbia under his dominion and his eastern border secure after defeating Ibrahim of Karaman in 1437, he was free to act. The moment was propitious. In 1437, soon after the death of King Sigismund, a peasants' revolt had shaken Hungary. In 1440, Sigismund's successor, Albert II, died, leaving an infant as his heir. It was at this moment that Murad attacked, laying siege to the strategically vital fortress of Belgrade and sending raiders into the Kingdom.

The siege of Belgrade was a failure, and the defeat marked the beginning of a crisis in Ottoman rule. This was not at first evident. Civil war in Hungary over the succession to King Albert allowed Murad to launch a new raid in 1441, and civil war in Byzantium allowed him to intervene on behalf of the pretender Demetrios. Demetrios, however, failed to secure the Imperial title, and the lord of Transylvania, John Hunyadi, defeated the Ottoman incursion of 1441 and another in the following year. These small victories, together with the election of King Vladislav III of Poland as Vladislav I of Hungary, clearly raised Christian morale. But what threatened Murad most was a new crusading alliance.

In 1439, as the price of receiving military aid from Catholic Europe, the Byzantine Emperor, John VIII, had accepted the union of the Greek and Latin Churches under the primacy of Rome. Pope Eugenius IV had a strong motive for fulfilling his side of the contract and organising a Crusade on the Emperor's behalf. His position as head of the Church was not secure, but a successful Crusade would make his position unassailable. Nor did he have difficulty in raising support for the project. Above all, he was able to enthuse King Vladislav whose kingdom was under attack from the Ottomans. Venice, too, was ready to participate, since a successful Crusade could lead to the reoccupation of Thessaloniki and the acquisition of other territories. So, too, was the Duke of Burgundy. Credentials as a Crusader could lead to his recognition as a king. The other willing participant against his Ottoman enemy was the emir of Karaman. If the emir could attack Murad in the east and draw him into Anatolia, the Venetian, Burgundian, Pontifical and Byzantine galleys could block the Bosphorus and the Dardanelles and prevent Murad from crossing the Straits to meet the Hungarian army as it invaded his territories in Europe.

The difficulty with this plan was coordination. In 1443, before the allied fleet was ready, Ibrahim of Karaman attacked Murad's lands in Anatolia. With no opposition at the Straits from the Byzantine Emperor, Murad crossed to Anatolia and forced Ibrahim into submission before returning to Edirne. Here he learned first of the death of his favourite son, Alaeddin, and then, in late autumn, of an invasion. A Hungarian army under John Hunyadi had entered and devastated

Serbia and was advancing towards Sofia, destroying or forcing back the Ottoman forces in its path. The Hungarians had the advantage not only in the size of their army, but also in the new battlefield tactic of creating mobile fortresses out of carts and field artillery, which the Ottoman cavalry were unable to approach. In the end, despite the desertion of his cavalry army, Murad and his Janissaries stopped the Hungarian advance at the Zlatitsa Pass in the Balkan Mountains. In bitter winter weather, both armies retreated.

It was probably the horrors of the winter war that persuaded Murad and Vladislav to make peace. In the summer of 1444 in Edirne, the negotiators agreed on a ten-year truce between Murad and Vladislav,[22] and the cession of Golubats, Smederovo and other fortresses to George Branković. In August an Ottoman envoy travelled to Hungary to ratify the terms. Then Murad made an extraordinary decision. Saddened, no doubt, by the death of Alaeddin and the events of the winter war, and with all his borders apparently secure, he abdicated in favour of his twelve-year-old son, Prince Mehmed.

This was an opportunity that the Pope did not let pass. To allow the Crusade to continue, he absolved the King of Hungary from his oath and, in the autumn of 1444, King Vladislav and John Hunyadi led the Hungarian army on a destructive march to Varna, on the Black Sea coast of Bulgaria. In the crisis, the Viziers recalled Murad from his retirement in Manisa. This time, however, the allied fleets did block the Straits. The Sultan, however, chose to cross at the Bosphorus and, as he set up cannon on the Asian shore, the Genoese of Pera established a shore battery on the European side. Under the cover of these guns, and in boats which the Genoese had supplied, his army crossed the Straits. On 10 November 1444, the armies met at Varna, with the Hungarian cannon again driving the Ottoman cavalry from the field. At a crucial point, however, the King broke loose from the ranks, allowing one of the Janissaries around the Sultan to unhorse and kill him. The death of the King decided the battle. The Ottoman victory, in turn, ensured that the largely Orthodox Balkan Peninsula came under the rule of the Muslim Ottomans rather than the Catholic Hungarians.

From Varna, Murad returned to Manisa, but not to a peaceful retirement. During the crisis of 1443–4, Constantine, the Byzantine Despot of Mistra, had seized Ottoman lands in southern Greece and was continuing his raids, while George Kastriote, or Scanderbeg, had recovered the old Kastriote domains in central Albania. However, it was a crisis in 1446 that brought the old Sultan out of retirement. First, a fire devastated Edirne. Next, a Janissary rebellion, which Prince Mehmed could not control, terrorised the city, persuading the Grand Vizier, Halil Chandarli to recall Murad.[23]

On his reaccession, Murad turned against his rebellious vassals. In 1447, he invaded the Peloponnesos and reduced Constantine to submission. Next year he attacked Scanderbeg in Albania, but in mid-campaign received news that John Hunyadi had again invaded his lands with an army of Hungarians and Vlachs. Abandoning the Albanian campaign he marched northwards and, in October 1448, encountered Hunyadi on the Plain of Kosovo. After a two-day battle, Hunyadi fled the field. The removal of the danger from Hungary left Murad free, in the winter of 1448–9, to seize Arta, the last of the Tocco domains on mainland Greece and, in 1449, once again to attack Scanderbeg, confining him to the fortress of Krujë. Against this stronghold, however, his attacks were unsuccessful.

This was Murad II's last campaign. He died early in 1451.

The Ottoman Empire: conquest and consolidation, 1451–1512

In 1450, the Ottoman Empire was an important local power, dominating western and northern Anatolia and a large part of the Balkan peninsula. In much of this area, however, the sultan exercised his power through vassals or semi-independent marcher lords. In the context of the Middle East, the Mamluk Sultanate of Cairo was probably more powerful and certainly more prestigious. As rulers of the Holy Cities of Mecca, Medina and Jerusalem, the Mamluk sultans could claim first place among all Islamic monarchs. In the context of south-eastern Europe, the Kingom of Hungary still counterbalanced Ottoman power. At sea, Ottoman strength was negligible. By 1512, the Ottoman Empire had acquired an imperial capital. Its territories in both Anatolia and the Balkan Peninsula had expanded greatly. The power of the marcher lords had diminished, and they were no longer present in the central councils of the Empire. In Europe, south of the Danube, the sultan ruled through his own appointees rather than through vassals, although former Christian dynasties in the area often came, after conversion to Islam, to form part of the Empire's ruling élite. In Anatolia, it was only in the borderlands that the authority of the sultan still depended on the allegiance of vassals. The institutions of the Empire had also begun to take the forms that would be familiar in later centuries. By now too, the Empire enjoyed a military superiority over the neighbouring powers – Hungary in the north, the Mamluk Sultanate in Egypt and Syria, and the Safavid dynasty in Iran – but as yet the Ottoman army had not demonstrated this advantage in war. The Empire had also emerged as a naval power, albeit on a small scale.

At the time of Prince Mehmed's second accession to the throne in 1451 as Mehmed II (1451–81),[24] his immediate goal was to conquer Constantinople. In order first to secure his borders, in 1451 he led a campaign against Karaman whose emir, on Murad's death, had seized some castles on the Ottoman frontier. The campaign once more forced Karaman to accept Ottoman suzerainty. At the same time, Mehmed concluded treaties with George Branković of Serbia, and John Hunyadi, the Hungarian regent. To secure his southern border, in 1452 he sent the marcher lord Turahan on a raid against the Byzantine Despots of the Peloponnesos, Thomas and Demetrios. In the same year, with his borders safe, he began to prepare for the siege by building a castle on the European shore of the Bosphorus, opposite another on the Asian side, which Bayezid I had constructed during the siege of 1394–1402. The cannon from the two fortresses prevented the passage of shipping. In early spring. 1453, Mehmed's army encamped before the double walls of the city, while his ships anchored in the Bosphorus. Most of the assaults the defenders were able to repel, despite their depleted numbers. They thwarted Ottoman attempts to mine beneath the walls, or to use siege towers to bring the assailants to the level of the ramparts. The Ottoman fleet was unable to prevent Genoese reinforcements coming by sea, or to break the boom which blocked the entrance to the Golden Horn, the estuary that formed a natural moat on one side of the city walls. In the end, the besiegers dragged the ships overland from the Bosphorus to the Golden Horn, but again this did not break the siege. What in the end determined its outcome was the power of the

Ottoman artillery against the land walls. On 29 May, with the Janissaries in the vanguard, Mehmed's army entered the city through a breach in the wall and began a three-day pillage. On the day after the conquest, the Sultan entered the city.[25] The repopulation and refurbishment of the ruined metropolis was to be a major preoccupation throughout his reign.[26]

The conquest of Constantinople gave the Ottoman Empire a capital city at the juncture of its European and Asian territories, on the Straits which linked the Black Sea to the Mediterranean. It was a city too which enjoyed a special position in Muslim eschatology, and which had been the seat of the Roman Emperor. The imperial, eschatological and geographical prestige of the city enhanced the status of its conqueror in both the Muslim and Christian worlds, and it is for this conquest that Mehmed II remains famous. It was, however, only the beginning of the incessant warfare that marked his reign.

After the fall of Constantinople, Mehmed secured the surrender of Pera, the Genoese city opposite the Byzantine capital, across the Golden Horn. In the following year he attacked Serbia. In two campaigns, in 1454 and 1455, he seized Novo Brdo and the silver mining districts of southern Serbia, confining the Despot George Branković's territory to the north of the country. In 1456, he besieged the Hungarian city of Belgrade, but this time he was unsuccessful. John Hunyadi's forces not only repelled the attack, but came close to overrunning the Ottoman camp. The victory saved Hungary from a full scale invasion, but did not prevent the final extinction of Serbia. In 1457, George Branković died, and his son Lazar soon afterwards, exposing his territory to invasion by King Matthias Corvinus of Hungary, or by Mehmed II. Mehmed was the first to act. In 1458, an army under the Serbian Vizier, Mahmud Pasha, invaded and, by virtue of Mahmud's political guile as much as by military force, captured Golubats, Smederovo and other key fortresses, bringing Serbia under Ottoman control, and establishing the Danube as the border between Hungary and the Ottoman Empire.

The conquests which the Sultan made in the Aegean region during the same years were less extensive but probably more lucrative. The fall of Constantinople had alarmed the Latin rulers in the Aegean region, who rightly feared that their own possessions were now under threat. Venice in particular, fearing for the safety of Negroponte, had annexed the islands of the northern Sporades to form a northern line of defence and, at the same time, pursued negotiations with Mehmed. These resulted in a treaty which allowed them to trade freely and to maintain a colony with a *bailo* in Istanbul.

It was rather the Genoese colonies that came under attack. In 1455, Mehmed despatched a fleet which seized the two Genoese settlements of Old and New Phokaia on the Anatolian coast, having an eye no doubt on the revenues from the alum mines in the district. Then, in the bitter weather of January 1456, he himself led an army to Enez, a Genoese colony in western Thrace, forcing its lord, Dorino Gattilusio to surrender Enez and its salt-pans, together with the islands of Samothrace, Imbros and Limni. These attacks were clearly premeditated. The capture of Athens, however, was opportunistic. In 1451, the Florentine Duke of Athens, Nerio II Acciajuoli, had died, and both Nerio's nephew and his widow's new husband called on the Sultan to support their claims to the city. Mehmed's response was, in 1456, to send Turahanoghlu Ömer to occupy Athens. By now the the Catholic powers in the Aegean were so alarmed at Mehmed's aggression that, in 1456, Pope Calixtus III and his former employer, King Alfonso of Aragon, assembled an anti-Ottoman fleet that in 1457 captured Imbros and Limni.

The success of Pope Calixtus's fleet had already alerted Mehmed to the dangers of Latin intervention in Greece and the Aegean, when the possibility of further Latin action grew with the proposed marriage alliance between the daughter of Demetrios Palaiologos, one of the Byzantine Despots of the Peloponnesos, and a grandson of King Alfonso of Aragon. In 1458, Mehmed invaded. By the end of the campaign, much of the Peloponnesos was under his control, while Demetrios had agreed to marry his daughter to Mehmed, and to leave the Peloponnesos, accepting as an appanage lands in Thrace and the recaptured islands of Imbros and Limni. However, he did not move. Instead, he fought with his brother Thomas, provoking another Ottoman attack in 1460. By the end of the year, all of formerly Byzantine Peloponnesos was in Mehmed's hands, Demetrios had left for his new territory, and Thomas had fled to Rome. Only the Venetian colonies remained independent of the Sultan.

Mehmed's next targets were the independent enclaves that remained along the southern shores of the Black Sea, divided by mountains from the Ottoman territory to the south. The first of these was the Genoese colony of Amasra, which succumbed without a fight in 1459. Two years later, Mehmed launched a second campaign, sending a fleet along the Black Sea coast, while he led his army overland. His first goal was Sinop, the territory of Isfendyaroghlu Ismail. As at Amasra, the fleet at sea and the army beneath his walls persuaded him to surrender. In exchange for Sinop, he received lands near Bursa. Mehmed meanwhile continued the difficult march to Trabzon, a Greek enclave under the rule of an Emperor of the Comnenes, the dynasty that had ruled in Constantinople before 1204. The fall of Trabzon in 1461 brought to an end the last relic of the Byzantine Empire.

The Sultan's next campaign, in 1462, was against the rebel lord of Wallachia, Vlad the Impaler, who had refused to pay tribute to the Sultan, killed his agent and terrorised Ottoman lands in Bulgaria. Vlad's flight and the submission of Wallachia brought much of the western shoreline of the Black Sea under Ottoman control, making the Ottoman Empire the dominant power in the area, a position which Mehmed enhanced in the same year with the construction of two fortresses at the Dardanelles to control the passage of shipping between it and the Mediterranean. It was also in 1462 that Mehmed continued his war on the Genoese by conquering the Genoese island of Lesbos and bringing it under direct Ottoman rule.

His next goal was the Kingdom of Bosnia. In 1463, he led his army westwards, and within the year the Kingdom had fallen. The first large fortress to capitulate was Bobovac, and from here the army proceeded to Travnik. Hearing that the King had fled to Jajce, the Sultan sent Mahmud Pasha in pursuit. Mahmud Pasha eventually captured King Stephen at Kljuć and, with his execution, the old Kingdom of Bosnia became extinct. Mahmud Pasha continued the campaign by seizing part of the lands of Duke Stephen Vukčić-Kosača in Hercegovina.What lands remained to the Duke, Mehmed seized in 1466. The conquests of Serbia, Bosnia and Hercegovina now brought the Ottoman border with Hungary along the Sava, and southwards along the Vrbas to the Adriatic.

In 1463, while the Bosnian campaign used most of Mehmed's resources, war broke out in the Peloponnesos. Early in the year, Turahanoghlu Ömer had seized the Venetian town of Argos, and it was this incident that finally led the Venetian Senate, alarmed for some time by Mehmed's conquests in the Peloponnesos and the Aegean, to declare war.

At first, events seemed to justify Venetian calculations. By the end of 1463, Venice had retaken Argos, occupied Monemvasia and gained control of much of the Peloponnesos. In the Aegean, the Venetian fleet captured Limni. Diplomatically, Venice had constructed an alliance which included the King of Hungary, the Pope, the Duke of Burgundy and, in the east, the Karamanids. The involvement of Hungary produced immediate results. On Mehmed's withdrawal from Bosnia, King Matthias Corvinus invaded and captured the fortresses of Zvečaj and Jajce, and next year, a Venetian fleet attacked Lesbos. In 1464, however, Venetian plans collapsed. The attack on Lesbos was unsuccessful and, although the Sultan's expedition to Hungary failed to retake Jajce, his army under Mahmud Pasha thwarted a Hungarian attempt to capture Zvornik. In the same year, too, the emir of Karaman died, undermining Venetian plans for an eastern alliance. So, too, did Pope Pius II, and with him the plans for a Crusade. Nonetheless, the Venetian Senate refused a peace overture from Mahmud Pasha, trusting perhaps that a new ally in the east would destroy the Ottoman Sultan.

This was Uzun Hasan, the ruler of the Akkoyunlu Empire that during the fifteenth century had risen to become a great power in Iran, Iraq and south-eastern Anatolia.[27] In 1464, Uzun Hasan had revealed himself to be an enemy of the Ottoman Sultan. The cause of hostility was the succession to the emir of Karaman, who had died leaving six sons by an Ottoman Princess and one, Ishak, by a different mother. In order to block a relative of Mehmed II from the Karamanid succession, Uzun Hasan intervened and established Ishak as emir. At the same time, he sent an embassy to Venice, proposing an anti-Ottoman alliance. This proposal Venice accepted, leaving Mehmed to face an alliance of Venice and Hungary in the west and Uzun Hasan in the east. When, in 1465, he prepared an expedition to salvage his position, his troops refused to fight. Constant war had left them exhausted and impoverished.

Nevertheless, the allies did nothing. Instead, in 1465, Mehmed sent a small force to Karaman and ousted Ishak, placing his own cousin, Pir Ahmed, on the throne. With the danger to his eastern border lifted, in 1466, the Sultan led an expedition to the west. His target was Scanderbeg – George Kastriote – who had reoccupied his father's domains in 1444, and since then resisted Ottoman attempts to recapture his lands. By the end of 1466, Mehmed's army had confined him to the stronghold of Krujë. In the winter, however, he travelled to Italy and, having obtained troops from King Ferrante of Naples, was able to break the siege of Krujë and recapture his lost territory. In 1467, Mehmed invaded again, forcing him to flee. He died in 1468, leaving Krujë to Venice. The Venetians were, in fact, the beneficiaries of Mehmed's engagement in Albania, using the opportunity in 1466 to seize the island of Imbros and lands around Athens. Mehmed's response had been to begin the construction of a fleet, perhaps to attack Negroponte, but Scanderbeg's counter-attack in 1467 undermined these plans.

Nor did he attack the Venetians in 1468. Instead, he prepared a campaign in Asia, whose original goal was perhaps the lands of the Mamluk Sultan in Syria. It transpired, however, that his Karamanid cousin, Pir Ahmed, refused to join the campaign or to act as guide, thwarting any plan to attack the Mamluks, since Karaman lay between their territory and the Sultan's Anatolian realms. Instead he attacked Karaman, occupying most of Pir Ahmed's domains to the north of the Taurus mountains, and appointing his son Mustafa as governor. A second campaign in 1469 consolidated his position.

Much as Mehmed's absence in Albania in 1466 had given Venice the opportunity to seize Imbros and part of Attica, the Karamanid campaign gave the Venetian Captain-General Niccolò da Canal the the opportunity in July, 1469, to pillage Enez on the coast of Thrace. This time, however, the reprisal was quick. In June, 1470, a fleet, which an observer estimated as consisting of four hundred ships, left the Dardanelles, while the Sultan led an army overland. The destination of both was Negroponte, the Venetian island off the east coast of Greece. The Ottoman fleet was too large for da Canal to engage, and he remained an observer as the Ottoman troops crossed a bridge from the mainland, pillaged the island and captured its capital,

Chalkis. With the fall of Negroponte, Venice had lost her most important strategic and commercial centre in the Aegean, but this was not the only blow. After the conquest of the island, an Ottoman force under Hass Murad Pasha – a scion of the Byzantine Imperial dynasty – recaptured most of the fortresses in the Peloponnesos that Venice had conquered since 1463.

Nonetheless, despite these disasters, Venice rejected a peace offer which Mehmed made in 1471, hoping no doubt that an alliance with Uzun Hasan would bring a victory over the Sultan. Conflict between Mehmed and Uzun Hasan was indeed inevitable, the issue being who was to dominate Karaman. Despite the Ottoman campaigns of 1468 and 1469, one of the Karamanid Princes, Kasim, had rebelled and, at the time of the Ottoman siege of Negroponte, had attacked Ankara. In reply, in 1471 and 1472, Mehmed sent two expeditions to Karaman, subduing not only the north of the country, but also the mountainous interior down to the Mediterranean coast. It was during the second of these campaigns that Uzun Hasan attacked, claiming that he would restore the fugitive Pir Ahmed to the throne of Karaman, and Kizil Ahmed, son of Isfendyaroghlu Ismail, to Sinop. To coincide with his incursion, the Venetians made destructive raids on the Ottoman ports of Antalya and Izmir. Mehmed's son, Prince Mustafa, repelled the Akkoyunlu incursion, but only after it had caused much damage and captured the city of Kayseri.

In anticipation of another Akkoyunlu attack in Anatolia, the Venetians, in early 1473, organised a partially successful sabotage of the the Ottoman naval arsenal at Gallipoli, and in the summer landed artillery on the Mediterranean coast ready for Uzun Hasan's agents to collect. On behalf of the Karamanids, they captured Silifke at the foot of the Taurus mountains. In the meantime, Mehmed prepared an army to fight Uzun Hasan and marched eastwards. In their first encounter, on the upper Euphrates, in early August 1473, the Akkoyunlus defeated a detachment of the Ottoman army but, in a battle near Bayburt, Uzun Hasan fled, terrified by the Ottoman artillery. He had no guns himself, and had never collected the ones which the Venetians had left on the Mediterranean shore.

The defeat of Uzun Hasan allowed Mehmed to attack the allies of the Akkoyunlu Sultan. In 1474, he directed raids from Bosnia into the

Venetian mainland, and began a campaign against Venetian strong-holds in Albania with an assault on Shkodër (Scutari) in the north of the country. The siege failed, probably through fear of a Hungarian attack. In the same year, Gedik Ahmed Pasha led a campaign against the last Karamanid stronghold within the Taurus range. By 1474, the emirate of Karaman was extinct.

Venice in the meantime continued to believe that it might still be possible to conclude a peace with the Sultan, or to construct an anti-Ottoman alliance involving the Princes of Italy, the King of Poland, the King of Hungary, or the Grand Duke of Moscow. Hopes increased in early 1475, when Süleyman Pasha, the Ottoman commander at the siege of Shkodër, led his already exhausted men to Moldavia to pun-ish its ruler, Stephen, for not paying the tribute due to the Sultan. Stephen routed Süleyman Pasha's army, inflicting heavy losses and raising the hopes of the Venetian ambassador to the Sultan that he could negotiate a peace. All he received was a promise that the Ottoman fleet would not engage the Venetians for six months. The Ottomans kept this promise since, in 1475, the fleet sailed against the Genoese town of Caffa (Feodosiya) in the Crimea. The occasion for this was a call for assistance from the Tatar Khan of the Crimea, whose lands surrounded Caffa and who now, as a result of a feud within the ruling family, found himself a refugee in the city. The fleet under Gedik Ahmed Pasha captured first Caffa, and then the Genoese town of Tana (Azov) at the mouth of the Don, and other fortresses in the Crimea. The refugee Khan, Mengli Girey, was restored to the Khanate, but as a vassal of the Ottoman Sultan.

The capture of the Genoese towns in the Crimea and the submis-sion of the Tatar Khan confirmed Mehmed's already dominant posi-tion in the region of the Black Sea, and it was presumably in order to reinforce his control of this area that he led his army in 1476 on an inconclusive campaign against the rebellious Stephen of Moldavia. When his army returned to Edirne in the autumn, he heard that dur-ing his absence, the Hungarians had built three fortresses between the Danube and the Morava in order to block access to Smederovo. Despite a threatened mutiny, the Sultan forbade his army to disband, and instead led it through the snow to the Morava. The moats of the forts had frozen, and it was by approaching them over the ice to lay brushwood against the walls, and threatening to set fire to it, that the besiegers forced the garrison to surrender, and so lifted the threat to Smederovo. The campaigns against the Crimea, Moldavia and the Hungarian fortresses had diverted Ottoman resources away from Venice. In 1477, however, the Sultan attacked the Venetian town of Lepanto (Navpaktos) on the Gulf of Corinth and Scanderbeg's old citadel at Krujë. Both sieges failed, but the same year saw a raid into the Venetian mainland itself. In 1478, there were renewed assaults in Albania, where the first place to come under siege was Shkodër. It was also the last to fall. Before the Sultan arrived at the town in person, he had already secured the surrender of Krujë. At Shkodër itself, he realised that the citadel would not succumb until he had taken the surrounding places. To this end he sent detachments to capture Zhabljak, Drisht and Lezhë. In the early autumn, the main body of the army departed, leaving Evrenosoghlu Ahmed to continue the blockade. Venetian attempts to send reinforcements to Shkodër failed.

By the beginning of 1479, the Venetian Senate understood that there was no choice but to make peace with the Sultan. Its efforts to form an effective anti-Ottoman alliance had failed, and Venice alone lacked the resources to continue the war. In January it took the decision to surrender Shkodër, and in negotiation which followed, ceded the island of Limni and agreed to an annual tribute of 10,000 gold ducats. The ratification of the treaty in April 1479, brought the sixteen-year war to an end.

It did not, however, end Mehmed's ambitions of conquest. His thoughts by now had probably turned to the invasion of Italy itself, since his next goal was the seizure of the Ionian islands of Levkas, Cephalonia and Zante. The lord of these islands was Leonardo Tocco, whose wife was a niece of King Ferrante of Naples. His removal therefore was necessary if Ottoman troops were to make an attack on Ferrante's kingdom in southern Italy. In 1479, therefore, Gedik Ahmed Pasha seized control of the islands and, in the following year, crossed the Adriatic to Otranto on the heel of Italy, where he captured and occupied the fortress. At the same time as Gedik Ahmed's operations in Italy, the Vizier Mesih Pasha led an attack on Rhodes, the stronghold of the Knights of St John, which enabled them to prey on shipping passing between the Aegean and the Mediterranean. One aim of the attack was perhaps to prepare the way for an invasion of the Mamluk domains in Syria and Egypt, an operation which would be more secure if the Sultan could control the sea lanes between Istanbul and the Levant coast and Egypt.

The siege was a failure. Nonetheless, in 1481 the Sultan set out with his army on a campaign to the east, apparently against the Mamluks. A few days march from Istanbul, he died. His army did not mourn. Instead, the Janissaries returned to Istanbul and subjected the city to several days' looting until, as a temporary measure, the Viziers placed Mehmed's grandson Korkud on the throne.

By the end of his reign, Mehmed had consolidated or extended Ottoman territory to comprise, in Europe, most of the lands between the Danube and the Sava in the north and the Peloponnesos in the south. In Asia Minor, he had added to the Ottoman domains parts of the Black Sea coast, the upper Euphrates valley and the old emirate of Karaman. These two blocks of territory in Europe and Asia were in later centuries to form the core of the Ottoman Empire.

The reign of Mehmed II's son, Bayezid II (1481–1512) was to be very different from his father's thirty years of ceaseless conquest.[28] One of the reasons for the difference was the personality of the new Sultan. In contrast to his father, whom he reputedly hated, Bayezid clearly disliked war. Indeed, some of his subjects discreetly criticised him for his reluctance to lead his army in battle. However, there were also social and political reasons. In the prosecution of his wars, Mehmed had not only driven his men to exhaustion, he had also strained the fiscal resources of the Empire. He had raised taxes on peasant holdings, he had debased the silver coinage and, most controversially, he had seized some private properties and properties belonging to charitable trusts, and redistributed their income as military fiefs. This measure had caused such discontent that one of Bayezid's earliests acts was to return the properties to their original owners.[29] Finally, the survival and captivity in Europe of his brother Jem meant that the European powers held a hostage who guaranteed Bayezid's nonaggression against the west.

The new Sultan's reign began with a civil war between Bayezid and Jem.[30] The fighting ended with the flight of Jem to the custody of the

Knights of St John, first on Rhodes and later in France, where his presence as a political hostage in the hands of the Knights was to dominate Bayezid's foreign policies for the first half of his reign. In 1483, he agreed to pay an annual tribute to Rhodes for Jem's safe-keeping, transferring this payment to Rome when, in 1489, Jem came into the custody of the Pope. This agreement with the Knights, and subsequently with the Pope, was crucial in securing Bayezid's realms from both civil strife and war with Catholic Europe. At the same time, he took other measures to ensure peace. He refused to allow Gedik Ahmed Pasha to return to Otranto, and he ratified the 1479 treaty with Venice, at the same time releasing the Venetians from the obligation to pay tribute. In 1483, after a series of raids and counter-raids across the border, he concluded a five-year truce with King Matthias Corvinus of Hungary. In 1490, he undertook not to attack Venice, the Papal States or Rhodes. These measure, he hoped, would ensure that Hungary, the Italian states and the Knights of St John did not use Jem as a weapon against the Ottoman Empire. By these means he hoped that his throne would be safe.

The need to secure peace in the west did not, however, mean an absence of war. In 1483, the Governor-General of Rumelia invaded and finally annexed Hercegovina, and in the following year Bayezid led an expedition to Moldavia. The pretext was Voyvoda Stephen's raids into Bulgaria, his efforts to detach Wallachia from loyalty to the Sultan, and the attacks on Ottoman shipping by pirates operating from the Danube delta. Bayezid's army captured first Kilia and then Akkerman, both important commercial centres. Stephen counter-attacked in 1485, but did not recapture the fortresses, a failure which confirmed Ottoman domination of the Black Sea. The year 1485 also saw the outbreak of a war with the Mamluks.

A conflict between these two Islamic Empires was probably inevitable. The Ottoman annexation of Karaman had brought the Ottomans and the Mamluks into direct confrontation, with the Taurus mountains forming an ill defined boundary between the two powers. The question of who was to secure the loyalty of the Turcoman tribes in the region was to be a source of conflict between them, as was the aid which Bayezid sent to his vassal Alaeddevle of Dulgadir, whose lands abutted on both Ottoman and Mamluk territory. In 1485, war broke out when Bayezid rejected Mamluk peace overtures and the Ottoman Governor-General of Karaman occupied Adana and Tarsus in the Çukurova.[31] In the following year, the Mamluks reversed this success. A Mamluk army recaptured Adana and then, in the battle which followed, captured the Governor-General of Anatolia, Hersekzade Ahmed Pasha, and other Ottoman notables. It was perhaps this defeat that encouraged the Turcoman tribes of the Taurus mountains to raise an anti-Ottoman rebellion around the figure of a Karamanid pretender. This rebellion, the Ottoman Grand Vizier, Daud Pasha, was able to suppress in 1487, but the Ottoman position had nonetheless become precarious. Aware that the Mamluks were seeking Christian allies and also attempting to secure the release of Jem, Bayezid set about preparing a new campaign for 1488. In this year, as Hadim Ali Pasha led an army into the Çukurova, Hersekzade Ahmed – released from captivity in Cairo – prepared to support it with a fleet. This expedition, too, was a disaster, with the Mamluks securing a major victory in the plain between Adana and Tarsus. In the same year, Bayezid's vassal, Alaeddevle of Dulgadir, defected to the Mamluks. Then, in 1490, as the Mamluks laid siege to Kayseri, Bayezid prepared to go to war in person. This threat, it seems, was enough to persuade the Mamluks, who had never had the resources to exploit their military advantage, to negotiate. By the peace concluded in 1491, the Ottomans renounced their claims to the Çukurova and its towns, restoring the pre-war border between the two powers.

With the end of the war against the Mamluks, Bayezid hoped to take advantage of political instability in Hungary following the death of King Matthias Corvinus and the apparent willingness of the garrison at Belgrade to defect. This plan came to nothing. When he arrived in Sofia in 1492, the political crisis in Hungary had ended with the enthronement of the new king. Instead, he sent raids into Hungary and Transylvania, while he led the army to Albania to suppress the rebellion of John Kastriote who, in the tradition of his family, had not recognised Ottoman overlordship since the death of Mehmed II. The expedition was not wholly successful: the Albanian rebellion continued until shortly after 1500. The expedition did, however, have an unforeseen consequence. As the army returned through Prilep, a 'naked dervish, bare-footed and bare-headed' tried to assassinate Bayezid. The terrified Sultan ordered – in vain, as it turned out – the expulsion of all such dervishes from his realms and, more importantly, withdrew to some degree from the public eye. The incident marked a stage in the gradual process of the sultans' withdrawal from contact with their subjects.

Three years later, in 1495, Bayezid faced the crisis which he had been dreading for fourteen years. In 1494, the French king, Charles VIII, invaded Italy, capturing Rome and taking custody of Jem. In January 1495, with Jem as his most potent weapon, he announced a Crusade against the Turks, provoking a panic in Istanbul as Bayezid ordered the strengthening of the city's fortifications. To protect himself in the west, Bayezid negotiated a three-year treaty with Hungary, and waited for the invasion.

This never happened. In February, Jem died and events forced Charles to evacuate Italy, leaving Bayezid to deal more freely with the European powers. To begin with, he ignored the truce with Hungary, allowing the Ottomans to capture some Hungarian forts in Bosnia. He also responded to the call from his former enemy, Stephen the Great, when King John Albert of Poland, refusing to accept Ottoman suzerainty over Moldavia, tried to replace Stephen with his own brother, Sigismund. At Stephen's request, Bayezid's men expelled the King's troops, and in 1498, Ottoman and Tatar raiders made a devastating razzia into Poland. Bayezid also re-opened hostilities with Venice. He was aware, however, of deficiencies in Ottoman naval power: such successes as his father had achieved at sea had depended on overwhelming superiority in numbers of ships and men. In 1498, therefore, Bayezid both increased the size of the fleet and engaged experienced corsairs as naval captains. Piracy was, in the succeeding centuries, to act as the most important school of seamanship and naval warfare for Ottoman mariners, and the corsairs were to provide the most successful Ottoman admirals. It was Bayezid who established the close link between piracy and the Imperial Ottoman fleet.

Piracy on both sides was also one of the causes of friction which led to war with Venice. In 1499, the repatriation of Jem's body from Italy and its public burial removed a lingering fear that rumours of the Prince's survival might still encourage dissent, and in this year, Bayezid declared war. The first Ottoman victory came at the end of August, with the fall of Navpaktos on the Gulf of Corinth. At the same time the Sultan sent raiders into Venetian territory in Dalmatia, and later into Friuli, convincing the Venetians that they should try to end the war by diplomacy. However, the embassy to Bayezid failed and, in 1500, they suffered serious losses with the fall in August of the coastal fortresses of Methoni, Koroni and Navarino in the Peloponnesos. The losses spurred Venice to further diplomatic action, this time successful. By the end of May, 1501, negotiators had constructed a triple alliance between the Papacy, Venice and Hungary and, in addition, persuaded the Kings of France and Spain to contribute to the war. With the help of these allies Venice began to win victories. In December, 1500, with Spanish reinforcements, she occupied Cephalonia. In 1501, a joint Franco-Venetian attack on Mitylene, the main fortress on Lesbos, failed, but in 1502, with the armed assistance of the Papacy, Venice took the island of Lefkada, establishing, temporarily at least, a dominance in the Ionian islands, with control of Corfu, Lefkada, Cephalonia and Zakynthos. Bayezid, however, offset this loss with the capture in the same year of the Venetian port of Durrës on the Adriatic.

By 1502, the war had ruined Venice, and since Bayezid had achieved his goals, he was prepared to conclude a peace. By the treaty of 1503, while retaining commercial privileges, Venice abandoned Methoni, Koroni, Navpaktos and Durrës, and ceded Lefkada to Bayezid. In the same year, the Sultan concluded a seven-year truce with Hungary. The war had brought Bayezid important gains of territory in Greece. Their encounter with French gunners at the siege of Mitylene had taught Ottoman artillerymen the most up-to-date artillery techniques. Above all, it had established the Ottoman Empire for the first time as a naval power.

The treaty of 1503 marked the beginning of an Ottoman disengagement from Europe that was to last until 1521. In the first two decades of the sixteenth century, it was events in the east that were to preoccupy the sultans. The first sign of these troubles was a revolt in 1500 of the Turgut and Varsak Turcomans of the Taurus mountains, around a Karamanid pretender. The Grand Vizier, Mesih Pasha, was able to suppress the uprising without, it seems, much trouble. This, however, had been a local incident, whereas future revolts in Anatolia were to acquire a far more dangerous, international aspect. The reason for this was the establishment of the Safavid dynasty in Iran.[32]

The dynasty takes its name from its ancestor, Safiy al-Din, the leader in the early fourteenth century of a religious order at Ardabil on the Caspian Sea. During the course of the fifteenth century, the nature of the order changed, as the descendants of Safiy al-Din began to claim divinity for themselves and, at the same time, adopted the tenets of Shi'i Islam. With a claim to divinity went a claim to political power and an active programme of proselytisation not only in Iran, but also in Syria and, above all, in Anatolia. The most active supporters of the Safavid Order were the Turcoman tribesmen of Anatolia, many of whom migrated to Iran. It was the support of these men, known as *kizilbash* ('red head') from their distinctive red headgear, that brought Shah Ismail I to power in Tabriz in 1501. It was they too who fought in the armies which defeated his enemies in Iran and Iraq. In 1501, Ismail took Tabriz and all Azerbaijan; in 1503, he defeated the last Akkoyunlus at Hamadan, and extended his rule into central and southern Iran. In 1504, he conquered the Caspian provinces of Mazendaran and Gurgan. Between 1505 and 1507, he annexed Diyarbekir to the north of Syria. In 1508, he conquered south-western Iran and Baghad. Shirvan followed in 1509, and Khurasan in 1510.[33] Within ten years, therefore, Ismail had established a polity which matched the Ottoman Empire in its resources; which, in its adoption of shi'ism, professed a religion which was hostile to the sunnism of the Ottoman sultans; and whose messianic leader claimed the allegiance of many thousands of the Sultan's subjects.

Bayezid's reaction to this new danger was extremely cautious. When Ismail summoned his adherents to Erzincan in eastern Anatolia before his entry into Tabriz, Bayezid sent an army to his eastern border but did not intervene. After Ismail had proclaimed himself Shah in 1501, Bayezid ordered the arrest of Safavid sympathisers in his realms and their deportation to the Peloponnesos. Also, insofar as such a thing was possible, he closed his eastern border.

However, since he did not also stop the caravan trade, Safavid missionaries were able to enter his realms by this route. Bayezid was anxious, however, not to provoke war. He was ready, in 1505, to receive an embassy from Ismail which laid claim to Trabzon and to listen to protests against the raids which the current governor of Trabzon, Bayezid's son Selim, had made into Safavid territory. In 1507, too, Bayezid allowed Shah Ismail to cross his territory in a campaign against Dulgadir, again simply sending an army to the border as a precaution.

Bayezid's timidity in the face of the danger from the Safavids was a product in part of his age and infirmity. These too were the causes of another crisis in his later years, the struggle for the succession between his sons, Korkud, Ahmed and Selim.

It was during the course of this conflict, in April 1511, that a terrifying rebellion broke out in Teke, in south-western Anatolia, the area under the governorship of Prince Korkud. Its leader was a certain Shah Kulu – 'slave of the Shah', whose father had been in the service of Shah Ismail's grandfather, Sheikh Hayder. On the death of his father, Shah Kulu had sent agents to proselytise the Safavid cause in the eastern part of Rumelia, while his local adherents in Teke claimed, according to a report to Prince Korkud: 'He is God, he is a Prophet. The Day of Judgement will be before him. Whoever does not obey him is without Faith.'[34] It was not, however, only true believers who joined the rebellion. According to reports, many of his followers were cavalrymen, who claimed that tricksters had defrauded them of their fiefs, leaving them destitute. In the face of the rebellion, Prince Korkud retreated to Manisa, while the rebels defeated a force which he had sent against them and occupied Antalya. Shah Kulu's next victory as he advanced northwards was against the Governor-General of Anatolia, Karagöz Pasha. As he approached Kütahya, Karagöz Pasha attacked again but, in a counter-attack, Shah Kulu, defeated and killed him, impaling and – according to Prince Korkud's report to Bayezid – roasting his corpse. From Kütahya he advanced to Bursa. It was at an urgent request from Bursa that finally, in June, the Grand Vizier Hadim Ali Pasha and Prince Ahmed led a force against the rebels, forcing Shah Kulu to retreat to Karaman and then to Sivas. Hadim Ali, in the meantime, left Prince Ahmed and went in pursuit with a small detachment of Janissaries. The encounter near Sivas was Shah Kulu's last victory. He defeated and killed Hadim Ali, but seems himself to have lost his life, leaving the now leaderless rebels to flee across the border into Iran.

The Shah Kulu rebellion had discredited both Bayezid's rule and the claims to succession of Korkud, who had abandoned Teke to the rebels, and Ahmed, whose pursuit of the rebels had been ineffective. It was clearly with this knowledge that Selim rose in rebellion. In April, 1512, he arrived in the capital, and twelve days later Bayezid abdicated in his favour. The old Sultan died in the following June.

His reign, despite the civil strife at its beginning and end and the defeats in the Mamluk war, marked an important stage in the evolution of the Empire. Ottoman failure against the Mamluks had led the Sultan to improve the weaponry of the Janissaries and to tighten his control over the cavalrymen in the provinces. His reconstruction of the navy and encouragement of corsair captains had produced a fleet that was the equal of Venice's and had extended Ottoman naval power into the Mediterranean. His conquests, in comparison with his father's, were limited, but nonetheless significant, extending Ottoman control over the littoral of the Black Sea and the Peloponnesos and pacifying Albania. More important, however, were his institutional innovations. It was Bayezid who initiated the systematic codification of Ottoman customary law which, in essence, regulated the relationship between fief holders and the peasants on their land, and the military obligations of fief-holders. It was thus in Bayezid's reign, that what have come to be regarded as 'classical Ottoman institutions' came to receive their 'classical' formulation.

The apogee of Empire, 1512–1590

The first concern of Selim I (1512–20), after securing his throne, was to defeat and kill his brothers. His next goal was the destruction of the Safavids and of their followers within his own realms. His campaign began with an investigation of the regions where Shah Kulu and lesser rebels had recruited followers, and continued with the execution of ringleaders and the removal of fief holders who had acted disloyally. Then he prepared to attack Shah Ismail. The immediate sources of provocation had been a Safavid attack on Tokat in 1512, Shah Ismail's support for Prince Ahmed in the civil war, and his providing refuge in its aftermath to Ahmed's son, Prince Murad. Selim also, in a move which clearly defined a new Ottoman claim to be defenders of sunni Islam, obtained a fatwa declaring Ismail and his followers to be heretics, whose destruction was not merely legitimate but obligatory.[35] With this legal backing for his action, Selim left Istanbul on a campaign against Shah Ismail.

In August, 1514, Selim's army won an overwhelming victory at Chaldiran in Azerbaijan. The Safavid cavalry, like Uzun Hasan's in 1473, could not withstand the artillery fire from the fortified encampment at the centre of Selim's battle line. From Chaldiran, Selim marched eastwards and entered Tabriz, intending to continue the campaign in the following year. The Janissaries, however, refused to spend the winter in Tabriz, forcing Selim to retreat to Amasya.

Despite this setback, Selim did not abandon the war against the Safavids, but in the two years following the battle of Chaldiran expelled them from south-eastern and much of eastern Anatolia. He achieved this partly by force and partly by persuasion. His envoy was a Kurdish scholar and notable, Idris of Bitlis, who had previously served the Akkoyunlu sultans. In 1515, Selim sent him to secure the allegiance of the Kurdish chieftains of south-eastern Anatolia and northern Iraq, and by the end of the year, all except one had recognised Selim's overlordship. The loyal Kurdish chiefs included Sharaf al-Din, who offered his allegiance to Selim in return for recognition of his hereditary rights as ruler of Bitlis.

The commander of the military operations was Biyikli ('the Moustachioed') Mehmed Pasha, the conqueror of Bayburd and Kigi, whom Selim had installed as governor of Erzincan after the victory at Chaldiran. Mehmed Pasha's first action in 1515 was to lay siege to the important fortress of Kemah on the upper Euphrates. Kemah fell in May and, at about the same time, emboldened by the Ottoman victories and Idris's propaganda, the inhabitants of Amid (Diyarbakır) rebelled against their Safavid governor. The Safavid response was to subject them to a siege, which lasted until September, when Mehmed Pasha arrived with a largely Kurdish force and took possession of the city. From here he proceeded to Mardin and took the town, but not the citadel. In the summer of 1516, his defeat of the last Safavid army to remain in Anatolia led the way to the submission of Sincar, Ergani, Siverek, Birecik and Urfa. At the very end of the year, the citadel of Mardin capitulated, completely extinguishing Safavid rule in southeastern Anatolia, and giving the Ottoman Empire an extended border with the Mamluk realms in Syria.

By this time, Selim had also extended his sphere of influence to include Dulgadir and the Adana region, the scene of Ottoman defeats in the war of 1485–90. In Dulgadir, he exploited a rift between members of the ruling dynasty. In 1514, Alaeddevle of Dulgadir had refused to participate in the Chaldiran campaign, but his rebellious nephew, Ali, had fought with the Ottoman army and, as a reward, Selim had appointed him Governor of Kayseri, a district whose territories abutted on Dulgadir. In 1515, with the assistance of an Ottoman army under the Governor-General of Rumelia, Ali attacked and defeated Alaeddevle and, in recognition of the victory, Selim made him ruler of the principality. In the same year, Selim clearly also won the allegiance of Ramazanoghlu Piri, the hereditary governor of Adana, since he nominated him as Ottoman Governor of Adana and its surrounding districts.

The territories of the Ramazanoghlu and Dulgadir dynasties had formed a buffer zone between the Ottomans and Mamluks,[36] and the establishment of Ottoman suzerainty over both, together with the Ottoman occupation of Diyarbekir, was certain to strain relations between Selim and the Mamluk Sultan, Qansuh Ghawri, and to persuade Qansuh to receive favourably an embassy which arrived from Shah Ismail, proposing an alliance against the Ottoman Sultan. Aware of the possibility of a Mamluk–Safavid alliance, in 1516 Selim prepared to lead an expedition to the east.[37] In June, he finally left Istanbul, joining the main part of the army at Elbistan in the territory of Dulgadir. It seems that, at this stage, Selim was uncertain whether to proceed eastwards against Ismail, or to attack the Mamluks in Syria. It was, in the end, the actions of the Mamluk Sultan that forced him to a decision. Fearing an Ottoman invasion, Qansuh had led his army from Cairo to Aleppo and also, as Selim discovered, sought help from Shah Ismail. Selim clearly could not attack Ismail with a Mamluk army on his border.

At the beginning of August, therefore, he began the march against Qansuh. On 24 August, the armies met at Marj Dabiq, north of Aleppo and, again, it seems to have been Ottoman superiority in artillery that led to the rout of the Mamluks. The death of the Mamluk Sultan in battle, and the flight of the Egyptian army, allowed Selim to occupy Syria almost without resistance. At the beginning of October, 1516, he entered Damascus and, with no Egyptian troops north of the Sinai peninsula, he was able to appoint Ottoman governors to Aleppo, Damascus, Tripoli, Jerusalem and other districts of Syria, Lebanon and Palestine. At this stage, it seems that he had not yet determined to invade Egypt. The perils of crossing the Sinai desert and the danger of an attack from Ismail advised caution. In the end, however, the urgings of Khairbay, a former Mamluk commander in his entourage, and the action of Qansuh's successor, Tumanbay, in mounting a counter-attack in Gaza and in executing an Ottoman ambassador, led Selim to abandon caution. At the beginning of January 1517, he left Gaza, crossed the desert with his army and, at the end of the month, defeated Tumanbay's army at Raydaniyya, outside Cairo. He remained in Cairo until the end of the year. He spent the winter of 1517–18 in Damascus, planning a new campaign. When, however, the army assembled on the Euphrates in May, it refused to move further. For the second time, Selim's ambition had outstripped the capacity of his troops.

He continued, however, to plan, extending the naval arsenal in Istanbul and preparing a large fleet, whose destination Venetian observers assumed to be Rhodes. This assumption was entirely reasonable since, so long as Rhodes remained in the possession of the Knights of St John, the sea route between Istanbul and the newly conquered province of Egypt would never be secure. These naval preparations marked an important stage in the emergence of the Ottoman Empire as a maritime power, coinciding as they did with an expansion of Ottoman territory into the western Mediterranean. This was the result of a private enterprise. In the first decade of the sixteenth century, two brothers, Hayreddin Barbarossa and Uruj, had been active in piracy off the southern and western shores of Anatolia, enjoying the patronage of Bayezid's son, Korkud. Selim I's execution of Korkud and pursuit of his followers in 1513 forced the brothers to flee to the North African coast, where they established themselves not simply as pirates, but eventually as rulers of Tunis and Algiers.[38] By 1519, however, Hayreddin found himself in a difficult position. His brother was dead; on land he faced local political opposition; and at sea he faced the maritime power of Spain. He needed therefore to seek a protector and found one in the Ottoman Sultan. Tunis and Algiers became semi-autonomous Ottoman provinces, extending the Sultan's power into the western Mediterranean and marking the beginning of a long conflict with Spain.

Selim died in 1520. His eight-year reign had doubled the size of the Empire that he had inherited by adding to it the former Safavid territories in eastern and south-eastern Anatolia; all the territories of the Mamluk Empire in Egypt, Syria, Lebanon, Palestine and the Hejaz; and, in addition, Tunis and Algiers in North Africa. The acquisition from the Mamluks of the three Holy Cities of Mecca, Medina and Jerusalem gave the Ottoman Sultan primacy among Islamic monarchs, and bolstered his claim to be the sole defender of Islamic orthodoxy against Safavid heresy. However, in the face of this glory came a reminder of the strength of Safavid propaganda and of the opposition to Ottoman rule in Anatolia, especially among the tribal peoples. In 1519 came the appearance in central Anatolia of a religiously inspired rebel called Jelal, whose claim to divinity recalled Shah Kulu's. Ottoman troops quelled the insurrection only with the greatest difficulty.

The succession to Selim I was peaceful, since his only son, Süleyman I (1520–66)[39] had no brothers to dispute the throne. In Syria, however, he faced an immediate challenge, when the Governor-General of Damascus, Janberdi Ghazali, a former Mamluk who had allied himself with Selim, declared himself an independent ruler. A campaign by Shehsuvaroghlu Ali of Dulgadir and the Governor-General of Rumelia immediately suppressed Janberdi's rebellion, while the new Sultan prepared for his first campaign. On his accession, Süleyman had sent an ambassador to King Lajos of Hungary to renew the treaty which his father had concluded with the King. Lajos, however, perhaps expecting Janberdi to be successful, treated the ambassador with disrespect. In 1521, therefore, Süleyman led his first campaign against Hungary.

The goal of the expedition was Belgrade and, in July, the Sultan sent the Grand Vizier ahead with a small force to besiege the city. He himself, instead of going straight to Belgrade, besieged and captured Šabac on the Sava to the west, sending a force across the river to plunder the land between it and the Danube. This diversionary action had no purpose, and had the Grand Vizier not disobeyed an order to join Süleyman at Šabac, it is unlikely that Belgrade would have fallen. However, the city had a garrison of only seven hundred and, with no relief from the King, it fell at the end of August 1521.[40] This was Süleyman's first major victory. For the second campaign of his reign, Süleyman was able to make use of his father's navy. In the summer of 1522, a fleet and army departed for Rhodes, the Sultan himself travelling overland to Marmaris. In December 1522, after a five-month siege, and despite the strength of its fortifications, Rhodes capitulated. On 1 January 1523, the Knights of St John left the island.[41] Their Order, however, continued intact and, from their new base on Malta, continued to harry Muslim shipping.

The conquests of Belgrade and Rhodes were doubly important. In the first place, they established Süleyman's reputation as the Sultan who had succeeded where his great ancestor, Mehmed the Conqueror, had failed. Secondly, both places were strategically important. Belgrade at the confluence of the Danube and the Sava was the key to the conquest of Hungary from the south. Rhodes occupied a position commanding the sea lanes leading from the Mediterranean into the Aegean and, in particular, the route between Istanbul and Egypt.

Süleyman's next expedition exploited his victory at Belgrade. Diplomatic relations with Hungary had not improved and then, in 1525, the Janissaries rebelled, with the complaint that the lack of campaigns had deprived them of the opportunity for bonuses and plunder. In 1526, Süleyman led his army into Hungary and, on 29 August, routed the Hungarian army at Mohács. Ottoman artillery fire had proved fatal to the Hungarian heavy cavalry. In September, Süleyman entered Buda, the Hungarian capital, leaving it ten days later and precipitating a crisis which was to occupy him throughout his reign. It was a crisis, too, in Anatolia that had forced his quick return to Istanbul. At the moment when the imperial army was victorious in

Hungary, a rebellion had exploded in central Anatolia, requiring a major force to bring it under control. Then, in 1527, a second and more ferocious uprising under the leadership of a millenarian dervish called Kalenderoghlu defeated the army that Süleyman had sent for its suppression. It required the political skills of the Grand Vizier, Ibrahim Pasha, to defeat the rebels. The problem was that 1522 had seen the Ottoman annexation of Dulgadir, and the execution of its last independent ruler, Shehsuvaroghlu Ali. At the same time, the fief holders of Dulgadir had lost their fiefs, leading many of the dispossessed to join Kalenderoghlu's rebellion. By promising them the return of their fiefs, Ibrahim Pasha detached them from the core of the rebels, whose depleted ranks he overcame in battle. This was not the last rebellion. There were further uprisings in the Çukurova in 1528 and, for the rest of the century, it was only by establishing a network of informers, particularly against Safavid sympathisers, that Süleyman and his successors maintained order in Anatolia.[42]

The major political crisis, however, was in Hungary. King Lajos had lost his life at the battle of Mohács and, when Süleyman left the country in 1526, the Hungarian throne was vacant. In November, the Hungarian Estates elected John Szapolyai as his successor. However the Habsburg Archduke Ferdinand of Austria – brother of the Holy Roman Emperor and King of Spain, Charles V, and brother-in-law of King Lajos – did not accept the decision and, in December, had himself crowned King of Hungary. The arbiter in the dispute was the victor of Mohács and, in 1528, Süleyman unsurprisingly accepted Szapolyai as King. Ferdinand rejected the decision and occupied Buda. Süleyman's campaign of 1529 was the beginning of an Ottoman–Habsburg conflict that was to last into the twentieth century. The Sultan marched to Hungary, reoccupied Buda and, in the autumn, laid siege to Vienna. Hampered by the weather and the determined defence, on 14 October, Süleyman withdrew. In 1530, Ferdinand besieged Buda again. He was unsuccessful, but his occupation of the western part of the Kingdom of Hungary and his continuing claim to the Hungarian crown made it necessary for Süleyman to intervene once again on behalf of King Szapolyai. The campaign was not one of conquest: the Ottoman army succeeded only, after a long siege, in capturing Köszeg and carrying out raids into Styria, but it was sufficient to force the Habsburgs to seek a truce. An agreement of 1533 confirmed the existing division of Hungary, with Ferdinand and Szapolyai ruling their respective territories as Ottoman tributaries.

The truce made it possible for Süleyman to undertake a campaign against the Safavids, for which two events had supplied a pretext. First, in 1528, a Safavid governor of Baghdad had offered the city to the Ottomans and, although Shah Tahmasb I had executed him shortly afterwards, the offer formed the basis for a continuing claim. Second, the Safavid governor of Azerbaijan, Ulama Tekelu, had defected to the Ottomans in 1530 and, at the same time, engineered the disgrace of Sharaf al-Din of Bitlis, who then offered his allegiance to Tahmasb. Ordering Ulama to capture Bitlis – which he never did – Süleyman prepared a campaign. In 1533, the Grand Vizier Ibrahim Pasha retook Bitlis and, in 1534, occupied Tabriz with no resistance from the Shah. In the same year, Süleyman joined Ibrahim Pasha in Tabriz , and then led the army to Baghdad which surrendered at the end of November, again with no resistance.⁴³ From Baghdad, the army undertook a difficult march across the Zagros mountains to Tabriz. By the time of the Sultan's return to Istanbul in 1536, he had added to the Empire Baghdad, Erzurum and, temporarily, Van.

Despite his success on land in securing his western border and in expanding his territories in the east, Süleyman clearly realised that his seapower was not equal to that of the combined Christian navies. In particular, the Spanish fleet based at Messina and the ships of the Knights of St John remained a constant danger, and it was presumably with this in mind that he invited Hayreddin Barbarossa to come from Algiers to serve as Admiral. The threat from Spain materialised two years later when, in 1535, Charles V – Holy Roman Emperor and King of Spain – personally led an expedition against Tunis. This Spanish victory, together with the outbreak of war with Venice in the following year, led Süleyman to accept the proposals for an alliance coming from the French King, Francis I, who needed an ally against his arch-enemy, Charles V.

In 1537, Süleyman and Francis planned a combined attack on Habsburg territories in Italy. Francis was to invade Lombardy, while Süleyman launched a seaborne attack from Albania on the Kingdom of Naples, with assistance from the French fleet. The plan failed. Francis did not invade Italy and in August, instead of invading Naples, the Sultan laid siege to the Venetian island of Corfu, sending raiders against Brindisi and Otranto which he withdrew when there was no news from the French King. The siege of Corfu was also a failure, and in September, Süleyman retreated. Nonetheless, the war with Venice continued. In 1538, Barbarossa captured most of the Venetian islands in the Aegean which had remained in Venetian hands, including Naxos, Paros, Santorini and Andros. The Venetian response was to seek allies and, in February 1538, the Holy League of Pope Paul III, Charles V, Ferdinand of Austria and Venice came into being. Its moment came later in the same year when, after the Spanish capture of Kotor on the Dalmatian coast, its combined fleet under Andrea Doria trapped Barbarossa's ships in the Gulf of Prevesa. The battle which followed was Barbarossa's most famous victory. After defeating the allies, he recaptured Kotor, forcing the war to a conclusion in 1540. By the treaty of that year, Venice ceded to Süleyman the islands which Barbarossa had captured in the Aegean, as well as Monemvasia and Navplion in the Peloponnesos.

Süleyman in the meantime had led his troops in 1538 against the Voyvoda of Moldavia, Petru Rareş, who had not paid the tribute due to the Sultan, and whom Süleyman suspected of collaborating with Ferdinand and inciting the King of Poland. In consequence of the invasion, Süleyman annexed south-eastern Moldavia, including the port of Bendery on the Dniestr, so completing the land link between Istanbul and the Crimea.

The 1540s saw a renewal of Ottoman–Habsburg conflict and again, as in the previous decade, its focal point was Hungary, with a subsidiary theatre of war in the Mediterranean. The source of the conflict was a treaty which Ferdinand of Austria had concluded with King Szapolyai in 1538. By its terms, each recognised the other's territory, but Szapolyai's lands were to pass on his death to Ferdinand, making him the sole ruler of Hungary. In 1540, King Szapolyai died, leaving an infant son whom the Bishop of Varad, George Martinuzzi, contrived to have elected as King at Buda. Ferdinand at once tried to make good his own claims and, in September, laid siege to Buda. The operation was a failure, but nonetheless his army captured Vác,

Visegrad and Székesfehérvár. In 1541, he tried again, but Martinuzzi resisted for long enough for the Sultan's army to rout the besiegers. At the end of August, however, when the Janissaries occupied the citadel of Buda, it became clear to Martinuzzi that Süleyman did not intend to make him regent in Hungary. Instead, the Sultan appointed an Ottoman Governor-General to the central part of the old Kingdom of Hungary, and nominated the infant John Sigismund as King of Transylvania – the eastern part of the old Kingdom – under the tutelage of Martinuzzi who, thwarted in his ambition, made contact with Ferdinand.

Ferdinand's siege of Buda was only one of the Habsburg actions against Süleyman in 1541. In the same year, to coincide with the assault in Hungary, and hoping no doubt to repeat the success that he had gained at Tunis in 1535, Charles V led an attack on Algiers. The enterprise ended in disaster. Following Hasan Agha's repulse of the besiegers, a violent storm destroyed much of the Spanish fleet. The Habsburg offensive of 1541 led not only to defeat in the field, but also encouraged Francis I of France to renew the alliance with Süleyman against their common Habsburg enemy. In the late summer of 1542, as Ferdinand's army attacked Buda for the third time, a French ambassador was conducting negotiations in Istanbul. He returned with the agreement for a joint action in 1543. In the spring of this year, Süleyman led his army into Hungary, extending his border to the west of the Danube with the capture of Valpo, Siklos, Pécs, Székesféhervár and Esztergom. In the meantime, his fleet under Hayreddin Barbarossa's command stormed Nice and spent the winter in the French port of Toulon.

However threatening the appearance of Süleyman's fleet in the western Mediterranean may have seemed to the Habsburgs, the danger was momentary. Barbarossa had relied on French support, and a peace between Charles V and Francis I temporarily put an end to Franco-Ottoman cooperation. In Hungary, however, the war continued. Süleyman himself led no more expeditions, but in 1544, the Governor-General of Buda captured more Habsburg fortresses, including Nógrad, Hatvan and Simontornya to the north-east of Buda. In the same year, Ferdinand made the first moves towards peace. In 1545, he and his brother Charles V sent ambassadors to

Istanbul. In 1547, they concluded a five-year treaty with Süleyman, which confirmed the territorial status quo. Ferdinand, however, renounced his claim to the kingdom of Hungary, and agreed to pay 30 000 ducats each year for the Hungarian territory which he continued to rule. For Süleyman, the treaty also had a symbolic significance, since the text no longer refers to Charles as 'Emperor', but simply as 'King of Spain', and it was from this moment that the Ottoman Sultan considered himself to be 'Emperor of the Romans' or 'Caesar'.[44]

The peace with the Habsburgs, like the earlier peace in 1533, left Süleyman free to lead an expedition against Iran, the pretext for the action being the revolt of Shah Tahmasb's brother, Alqass Mirza, who had found refuge in the Ottoman court. Early in 1548, the Sultan sent Alqass to the border. He himself followed in April and, in July, again occupied Tabriz without resistance. However, after only five days, he returned westwards and laid siege to Van, a fortress which the Safavids had recaptured after Süleyman's expedition of 1533–6. Van fell in August, and the Sultan retired to Aleppo for the winter. In 1549, his troops undertook an expedition to secure the Empire's north-eastern border against raids from Georgia, but in its main objective, the campaign was a failure. Shah Tahmasb captured his brother Alqass Mirza, ending any hope that Süleyman could profit from the rebellion. At the end of 1549, the Sultan returned to Istanbul.

During his absence, events in Hungary had again led to conflict with the Habsburgs. Ferdinand did not contravene the treaty of 1547 by launching a direct attack but, instead, opened negotiations with Martinuzzi who, in 1549, agreed to cede to him Transylvania. Süleyman heard of these developments through the French ambassador and ordered the Governor-General of Buda to intervene. However, neither the Governor-General nor the appeal by John Sigismund's mother, Queen Isabella, could deflect Martinuzzi who, in 1551, forced her to give up the crown of Transylvania. As had been the case a decade earlier, these events had international consequences. Taking advantage of the Sultan's preoccupation with Transylvania, Charles V's admiral, Andrea Doria, in 1550 captured Mahdia and Monastir on the Tunisian coast, the strongholds of the Turkish corsair, Turgud Reis. In turn, this growth in Habsburg power so alarmed the French that, in early 1551, the French King, Henry II, proposed that he and the Sultan form an alliance. Their fleets, he suggested, should cooperate in the Mediterranean, while the French invaded Piedmont and the Turks attacked Transylvania. The alliance proved as unsuccessful as earlier attempts at cooperation. In 1551, the Pope negotiated a peace in Piedmont, the French fleet remained at anchor in Marseille, and an invasion of Transylvania by the Governor-General of Rumelia, Sokollu Mehmed Pasha, failed. The mobilisation of the Ottoman fleet did, however, have an important consequence. After his success against Mahdia and Monastir, Andrea Doria attacked the island of Jerba, off the Tunisian coast, almost taking Turgud prisoner. As a reprisal, Süleyman ordered the Admiral, Sinan Pasha, to attack Malta. After making a raid on Sicily, Sinan anchored before Malta, but all assaults on the island failed, and the French fleet did not appear. Instead, a section of the Ottoman fleet left for North Africa and laid siege to Tripoli, which the Knights of St John had occupied in 1530. Tripoli fell in August 1551. In the meantime, the warring parties continued unsuccessfully to seek alliances, Charles V with Shah Tahmasb, and Süleyman and Henry II with the Protestant Princes in Germany.[45]

Nothing came of these overtures, and attempts at joint Franco-Ottoman action in 1552 were no more successful than in the previous year. The Ottoman fleet put to sea in April[46] and cruised off the western coast of the Kingdom of Naples, but did not make contact with the French until September at the end of the sailing season. By this time, too, Charles V and Henry II had temporarily made peace.

The same year as this abortive naval campaign saw another crisis in Transylvania. In December 1551, Martinuzzi was murdered, and a Spanish mercenary general seized power in his place. Shortly afterwards, there was a rebellion in Szeged. To overcome the two crises required two campaigns. First, the Governor-General of Buda suppressed the rebellion, and then in May, the Second Vizier, Kara Ahmed Pasha, led an expedition to Hungary. On learning of this campaign, the Governor-General too began an offensive, capturing Veszprem and then a number of smaller fortresses to the north of Buda. Kara Ahmed Pasha in the meantime took Temesvár and Lipova in Transylvania, and then, joining forces with the Governor-General, took Szolnok. The campaign ended with an unsuccessful siege of Eger.

The campaign of 1552 was only a partial success. It led to the Ottoman occupation of Temesvár and the conquest of part of Transylvania, but it did not reinstate John Sigismund and his mother, nor did it extinguish Ferdinand's claim to the kingdom. However, it convinced Süleyman that his western border was secure enough to allow him to undertake his third campaign against Iran, sparked by Safavid raids in 1551. The expedition was as unsuccessful as the campaign of 1548–9. Süleyman advanced as far as Nakhichevan, but once again Tahmasb's scorched earth tactics forced a retreat. Furthermore, Shah Tahmasb on this occasion offered some military resistance, defeating the Governor-General of Erzurum outside the city, and capturing some fortresses on the the frontier. The outcome of the campaign was the Treaty of Amasya in 1555, which confirmed the existing frontiers between Iran and the Ottoman Empire.

The major negotiations at Amasya were between Süleyman and Shah Tahmasb. Subsidiary to these were discussions between Süleyman and Ferdinand. In these, Süleyman made it a condition that, if he wished for peace, Ferdinand should abandon his claim to the crown of Transylvania, and this Ferdinand was reluctant to concede. Süleyman's response was, in the next year, to order the Governor-General of Buda to capture the border fortress of Szigetvár in southern Transdanubia. The siege failed, but it caused sufficient alarm for the Estates of Transylvania to vote in June to reinstate Sigismund and Isabella. Their return to Cluj in September 1556 brought an end to the crisis of the Transylvanian crown.

The same year also saw a change in the political configuration of western Europe. In 1556, Charles V abdicated. His son Philip II inherited the Kingdom of Spain and the Spanish Netherlands, but not the crown of the Holy Roman Empire. Philip also opened negotiations with Henry II to bring an end to the hostilities between France and the Habsburg monarchy, which had brought the Ottoman Sultan into an alliance with France, and whose last manifestation had been a Franco-Ottoman naval campaign against the Spanish Kingdom of Naples in 1555. The allies had captured some fortresses but not garrisoned them permanently. In 1559, however, Philip II of Spain and

Henry II of France concluded a peace at Cateau-Cambrésis, depriving Süleyman of an ally against Spain, and allowing Philip to prosecute a war against the Ottomans in the Mediterranean without fear of France. The focal point of these hostilities was the coast of North Africa. In 1556, the Ottoman Admiral, Piyale Pasha, in cooperation with the Governor-General of Algiers had captured the Spanish fortress of Wahran to the west of Algiers. Next year, Piyale took Bizerta near Tunis and, in 1558, plundered Ciudadela on Minorca. Philip's response was to occupy the island of Jerba, off the Tunisian coast. His success was transitory since, in 1560, Piyale defeated the Spanish garrison and reoccupied the island.

While the major Ottoman naval actions took place in the Mediterranean, the maritime engagements in the southern ocean were perhaps, in the end, as significant.[47] With the conquest of Egypt in 1517, Selim I had acquired an outlet into the Indian Ocean and access to the trade, especially in spices, coming from south Asia to the Mediterranean. Some years before the conquest, however, the Portuguese had established a new route from the Indies, via the Cape of Good Hope, to Lisbon, and were attempting, by force of arms, to establish a trading monopoly. Already during the last years of Mamluk rule in Egypt, they had seized merchant vessels coming through the Red Sea and then, in 1517, attacked the Red Sea port of Jedda. The threat from the Portuguese and, equally, the opportunity for the Sultan to gain control of the Indies trade was the subject of a memorandum which the governor of Jedda, Selman Reis, submitted in 1525. The Sultan, however, paid no attention, and it was not until the 1530s, when trade in spices through the Mediterranean had reached a low point and there were shortages of pepper in the palace, that the Sultan took action. In 1531, the Portuguese received reports of the construction of an Ottoman fleet at Suez. In 1538, the fleet finally emerged under the command the Governor-General of Egypt, Süleyman Pasha, and sailed to India to lay siege unsuccesfully to the Portuguese fort of Diu on the coast of Gujarat. In 1541, the Portuguese responded by making an unsuccessful attack on Suez. Süleyman Pasha's expedition did, however, have important consequences. On the journey to Diu the fleet had garrisoned the coastal areas of Aden and Yemen, marking the first stage in the formation of a land frontier against the Portuguese. In 1547 and 1552, the Ottomans established themselves in highland Yemen with the capture of Ta'izz and San'a respectively.

By the early 1540s Süleyman was attempting to negotiate with King John of Portugal for the safe passage of Muslim merchant ships, for the establishment of the line Shihr-Aden-Zeila' as the frontier between the Portuguese and Ottoman fleets, and for the exchange of Ottoman wheat for Portuguese pepper. These negotiations produced no results and, unable to sail safely in the ocean, the Ottoman ships could not dislodge the Portuguese from from their shipping routes and coastal fortifications. However, the operations off the shores of Arabia may have been a factor in the recovery of the Mediterranean spice trade from the mid-sixteenth century.

The conquest of Iraq gave the Ottomans a second outlet to the Indian Ocean, through the Gulf. In 1538, four years after the occupation of Baghdad, the local ruler of Basra, the port at the head of the Gulf, received formal recognition as an Ottoman Governor-General, but it was not until 1546 that Basra became in reality an Ottoman province. However, despite its position, it could not flourish as a centre of maritime trade, as the Portuguese had, since 1515, occupied Hormuz and were able at will to prevent ships from passing between the Gulf and the Indian Ocean. In 1546, the Governor-General of Basra, Ayas Pasha, tried to establish Basra as a trading port and, presumably with a view to confronting the Portuguese in Hormuz, occupied al-Hasa on the western shore of the Gulf. In 1550, the Ottomans occupied Katif and, two years later, attempted to break the blockade at Hormuz. In 1552, Piri Reis set out from Suez to the Gulf with a squadron of thirty vessels. His first action was to capture the small Portuguese fortress at Muscat. The siege of Hormuz, however, failed, and instead Piri plundered the island of Qeshm, returning to Basra with the spoils. On his return to Egypt, the Sultan had him executed for his failure. The first attempt to bring the ships back from Basra to Suez also failed, as the Portuguese blocked the Straits. Then, in 1554, Seydi Ali Reis broke through the blockade, but once in the ocean, a storm drove him away from the Red Sea to the coast of India.

The conflict with the Portuguese continued intermittently. In 1555, in order to strengthen the Ottoman position in the Red Sea, the Sultan ordered Özdemiroghlu Osman Pasha to organise the province of Abyssinia, including the ports of Sawakin and Massawa. As with the provinces of Al-Hasa and Yemen, the revenues of Abyssinia did not cover the costs of maintaining the garrisons. Nevertheless, it contributed to the defensive frontier against the Portuguese. It was presumably, too, to strengthen the Ottoman position in the Gulf, as well as to secure control of the lucrative pearl-fishing that, in 1559, the Governor-General of Al-Hasa invaded the island of Bahrain, provoking in turn a Portuguese attack on his forces and a humiliating retreat. By 1560, it had become clear that the Portuguese could not evict the Ottomans from Basra, Al-Hasa and Katif at the head of the Gulf, nor from the Red Sea. The Ottomans, however, could not break the blockade at Hormuz, nor defeat the Portuguese in the ocean. Instead, to ensure the continuation of trade, they resorted to negotiation. In 1562, the Governor-General of Basra sent an envoy to Hormuz to discuss with the Portuguese the resumption of trade through the Gulf, while in 1564 the Sultan himself wrote to the King of Portugal, demanding that he 'ensure the passage on land and sea for the people and merchants of the Ottoman Empire trading to and from the lands under Portuguese domination'. Small scale hostilities nonetheless continued. The Ottomans, however, were never able to control the sea-routes from south Asia, and the revival of the spice trade probably had as much to do with the limitations of Portuguese resources as with Ottoman strength.

To the Sultan, these events on the fringes of the southern ocean probably seemed unimportant next to his major concerns with Iran, Hungary and the Mediterranean, and it was Hungary and the Mediterranean that were to dominate his final years. He had first, however, to face a civil war within his own realms. From about 1550 the death of the elderly Süleyman had seemed imminent, leading inevitably to a competition for the succession. In 1553, he pre-empted what he believed to be a plot against his throne by executing his son, Prince Mustafa. This left two challengers, the Princes Bayezid and Selim. In 1558, believing that his father favoured Selim, Bayezid rebelled, forcing Süleyman to confront him with an army effectively under the command of the Vizier Sokollu Mehmed Pasha. The

Sultan's men defeated Bayezid near Konya in May 1559, compelling the Prince to take flight to Iran, where he became the subject of negotiations between Shah and Sultan. Finally, in 1562, when Tahmasb had secured a treaty of peace and financial compensation from the Sultan, he allowed an Ottoman executioner to enter the Prince's cell and end his life.

The agreement with Tahmasb in 1562 coincided with the conclusion of an eight-year peace with Ferdinand and left Süleyman free to prepare his final campaigns. Piyale Pasha's incursions into the western Mediterranean in the 1550s had extended the reach of his fleet and offered the vision of further conquest. An essential preliminary, however, was the conquest of Malta which, at the sea's narrowest point, dominated the passage from the eastern to the western Mediterranean. The siege of 1565 was, however, unsuccessful, and in 1566, as if in compensation for the defeat at Malta, Piyale Pasha took the Genoese island of Chios. It is, however, significant that Chios is in the Aegean and lay off the Ottoman coastline: its conquest marked the end of Ottoman maritime expansion towards the west.

Süleyman's last campaign was against Hungary. In 1564, Ferdinand died. His son, Maximilian, wished to renew the peace, but largely in order to leave himself free to pursue his claim to Transylvania. In 1565, with most of his forces engaged in the siege of Malta, Süleyman could only order the Governor-General of Temesvár to undertake a limited incursion into Transylvania. A major campaign followed in 1566. In April, the elderly Sultan left Istanbul, carried for the most part in a litter. Sending the Vizier Pertev Pasha to occupy the disputed lands to the east of the Tisza, the Sultan himself laid siege to Szigetvár. He died on the field of battle in 1566, two days before the fortress capitulated.

During his forty-six year reign, Süleyman had added to the Empire territory in eastern Anatolia, Iraq, the Gulf and the Red Sea, the Aegean, Moldavia and Hungary. Some of these territories cost more in defence than they provided in revenue, but all served to emphasise Süleyman's status as the ruler of one of the world's greatest Empires. Ottoman territory was to expand further during the reigns of his two successors, but the Empire was never again to play the international role that it had done at the height of Süleyman's power. The French

Kings Francis I and Henry II had sought him as an ally, as had, briefly, the Protestant Princes of Germany. He had provided artillery and gunners to the Muslim rulers of India and Ethiopia, and even, at the end of his reign, despatched ships, artillery and artillerymen to Aceh in Sumatra. At the same time, the campaigns of Süleyman's reign had shown that there were geographical constraints to imperial ambition. Süleyman's campaigns against the Safavids in 1548–9 and 1553–4 had shown that the hostile terrain in the borderlands between the two Empires was sufficient to frustrate Ottoman aggression, even when the Safavids offered no military resistance. In the south, the isthmus of Suez was a barrier to the import of Mediterranean timber and other materials for the construction of ships in the Red Sea, and to the passage of ships from one sea to the other. More importantly, ignorance of how to construct armed, ocean-going vessels made it impossible for the Ottomans to challenge the Portuguese in the Indian Ocean. These were problems that were to confront Süleyman's successors.

Selim II (1566–74) was Süleyman's only surviving son and so enjoyed an undisputed succession. He was very different from his father having, it seems, a peaceable disposition and a distaste for affairs of state. Throughout his reign, he delegated much of the responsibility of government to his Grand Vizier and son-in-law, Sokollu Mehmed Pasha. At the time of Selim's accession, Sokollu faced three immediate problems: the war in Hungary, a revolt by the Zaydi Imam of Yemen which had deprived the Ottomans of control of most of the province,[48] and an Arab revolt in the marshes to the north of Basra. Sokollu acted decisively in all three cases. In 1567, a river-borne expedition at last pacified the leader of the marsh Arabs, Ibn 'Ulayyan. The rebellion ended when the Sultan formally bestowed on him the title of Governor, a device which the Ottomans used to secure the loyalty of local dynasties on the fringes of the Empire. The revolt in Yemen took three years to suppress. The operation began with the dismissal of its commander, Lala Mustafa Pasha, and his replacement by the Governor-General of Egypt, Koja ('the Elder') Sinan Pasha. Sinan Pasha captured first Ta'izz, and then Aden, in an assault by land and sea. In 1569, the Imam's stronghold at San'a fell, and the campaign ended in the following year with the capture of Kawakaban. In Hungary, Sokollu in 1568 concluded an eight-year peace with Maximilian, on condition that the Emperor pay a yearly tribute of 30 000 ducats.

It was perhaps the war in Yemen that led Sokollu, in 1568, to order the construction of a canal linking Suez with the Mediterranean. The project would have made possible the despatch of ships, troops and war materials directly from the Mediterranean to the Red Sea, and the easy transport of supplies to the naval arsenal at Suez. This would have benefitted the Ottomans both in the war in Yemen, and in the continuing hostilities with the Portuguese. The plan, however, failed, as did a similar project in 1569.[49] The immediate stimulus for this was the Russian occupation of Astrakhan on the Volga, near the point where the river empties into the Caspian. The Russians did not directly threaten Ottoman territory, but rather presented an alternative focus for the loyalty of the Khan of the Crimea, who was a vassal of the Ottoman Sultan. Sokollu planned, therefore, to cut a canal between the Don and the Volga at the narrowest point between the two rivers, enabling him to send a fleet directly from the Black Sea to Astrakhan and the Caspian Sea. The project would also permit the despatch of troops against Iran, bypassing the mountain barriers in eastern Anatolia and the Caucasus. In August 1569, the Ottoman–Tatar army camped at Perevolok and began work. However, they had completed only one third of the canal, when the shortening days and increasing cold began to hamper the excavation. In the meantime, the commander of the expedition, Kasim Pasha, had raided the district of Astrakhan, but the city itself had been too strong to attack. In September, Kasim Pasha ordered a retreat. About half his army perished in the swampy steppe lands, and then a fire in the provisions depot at Azov meant that there was no possibility of continuing the campaign in the following year. The Viziers had conceived both canal schemes as a way of overcoming the geographical barriers to further conquest. With the failure of both projects, Ottoman military and maritime power continued to operate within the old constraints.

The major campaign of Selim's reign was therefore more conventional. Since 1489, Cyprus had been a Venetian colony. In 1570, despite an unexpired peace treaty with Venice, an Ottoman fleet attacked the island. The invasion, it seems, was the personal wish of the Sultan, and had gained the support of two of his Viziers, Piyale Pasha and Lala Mustafa Pasha, who were to command respectively the naval and land forces. Sokollu, fearing an alliance of Venice, Spain, the Knights of St John and the Pope, had opposed the war. In 1570, Lala Mustafa captured Nicosia. In 1571, after a prolonged siege, he took Famagusta, on the east coast. The war, however, had produced the result that Sokollu had feared and, in October 1571, the Ottoman fleet encountered the ships of the Holy League off Lepanto (Navpaktos) in the Gulf of Corinth. In the ensuing battle, the Christian allies destroyed most of the Ottoman fleet. Of the Ottoman commanders, only Uluj Ali, the Governor-General of Algiers, had fought successfully, and it was he who returned with the remaining ships to Istanbul. Lepanto, however, was a battle without strategic consequences. As it occurred in the autumn, the allied fleet immediately returned to its bases. During the winter of 1571–2, under Sokollu Mehmed's direction, the Ottoman arsenals constructed a new fleet which emerged in 1572 under the command of Uluj Ali. In 1573, the war ended with the cession of Cyprus to the Ottomans.[50] To add to the discomfiture of the victors of Lepanto, in 1574 another naval expedition under Uluj Ali and Koja Sinan Pasha took Tunis from the Spaniards, leaving much of the North African coast to the east of Wahran under Ottoman control.

In the same year as the conquest of Tunis, Selim II died, and his son Murad III (1574–95) ascended the throne. Since he was Selim's only adult son, the succession passed with no civil strife.

For the first years of his reign, Murad retained Sokollu Mehmed Pasha as Grand Vizier. However, the Sultan had brought to Istanbul his own entourage from his days as a princely governor in Manisa and these, in alliance with Sokollu's enemies, began to undermine the Grand Vizier's authority. In 1579, perhaps with the encouragement of these men, a petitioner in the garb of a dervish stabbed Sokollu to death in his mansion. His demise brought with it a change of policy from peace to war.[51] The death of Shah Tahmasb had occurred on 1576 and the following year the death of his succcessor, Ismail II. Ismail's brother, Khudabanda, had succeeded. This instability in the Safavid realms encouraged the Uzbeks to invade from the east, and this in turn provided the Ottomans with an opportunity to launch an invasion from the west. The continuing activities of Safavid propagandists and a series of defections by the Kurdish lords on the Ottoman frontier allowed the Sultan to claim that the Safavids had broken the terms of the Treaty of Amasya. In 1578, Lala Mustafa Pasha received the command to conquer Shirvan on the Caspian Sea, passing through Georgia. Sokollu, it seems, had opposed the war, which would inevitably be fought in mountainous and inhospitable terrain, but his rivals had prevailed, and his death in 1579 brought the war party into power.

Lala Mustafa's campaign of 1578 brought a series of victories. After defeating a Safavid army at Çıldır, he received the submission of Minuchehr, Prince of Meskhetian. In August, he entered Tblisi and received the submission of Alexander Khan, Prince of Kalkhetia. Then, as he marched eastwards, the army began to suffer food shortages, leading to a demand from the Janissaries that they return home.[52] Receiving news of this, the Safavid governor of Tabriz launched an attack on the Kur river, but suffered a defeat at the hands of Özdemiroghlu Osman Pasha. In mid-September, with the supply problem eased, the army reached Eresh. By the end of the year, the other towns of Shirvan had fallen, and Lala Mustafa had appointed governors to both Shirvan and Daghestan. The weakness of the Ottoman position, however, soon became clear when the Safavids began to assemble an army south of the Kur, and the new governors refused to spend the winter in their provinces. Instead, Özdemiroghlu Osman remained with a reduced force and, to gain the confidence of the Daghestanis, married the daughter of the Shamkhal. This, however, merely emphasised the dangers of involvement in the politics of the Caucasus. As an enemy of the Shamkhal, Alexander Khan defected to the Safavids, as did Simon Khan, the Prince of Kartli. This was the situation when Lala Mustafa Pasha undertook the difficult return to Erzurum in the winter of 1578–9.

In 1579, the Safavids counter-attacked, laying siege to the Ottoman garrisons in Derbend and Tblisi, and forcing Özdemiroghlu to abandon Shamaxi. Neither siege was successful. The Khan of the Crimea came to the relief of Derbend, and an army under the Governor-General of Dulgadir compelled the Safavids to retreat from Tblisi, despite the attacks of their Georgian allies on the relief force.

In 1580, Koja Sinan Pasha was appointed army commander and, in April, departed to the east to reinforce the garrison at Tblisi. Believing, however, that peace negotiations with the Safavids would be successful, he abandoned the campaign that was in preparation for 1581. This was a decision that severely weakened the Ottoman position in the Caucasus. In 1582, a Safavid and Georgian army prepared to besiege Tblisi and routed an Ottoman force carrying pay and supplies to the garrison. In Shirvan, too, the Safavids exploited false rumours of peace to overwhelm Ottoman garrisons when they were off their guard, while the Daghestanis at the same time turned against Osman Pasha. From his stronghold of Derbend, he sent an envoy to demand assistance from Istanbul. By May 1583, his position seemed hopeless. The Shamkhal of Daghestan had allied himself with the Safavid governor of Gänjä, with a view to annihilating Osman Pasha's army and ending the Ottoman occupation of Shirvan. The result of his action was a remarkable Ottoman victory after a four-day battle at Meshale on the Sana river, consolidating Ottoman sovereignty in Shirvan and Daghestan. After the battle, Özdemiroghlu fortified Shamaxi and returned to Istanbul.

The battle of Meshale marked a revival in Ottoman fortunes. In 1583, a new commander, Ferhad Pasha led an army to the east, occupied Erivan, repaired and built fortresses in Georgia, and gained the allegiance of the Georgian Prince, Simon Khan. At the same time, he reported to the Sultan that the troops were exhausted and that Ottoman subjects were suffering from the weight of taxation. He received the reply that the army should not depart until it had forced the Safavids to sue for peace. The aim of the government was, it seems, to capture and occupy Tabriz. This objective Özdemiroghlu Osman Pasha achieved in 1585. He defeated a Safavid army under the Crown Prince, Hamza Mirza, at Sufian and then, taking advantage of a dispute among the Safavid factions, in September captured Tabriz, with resistance only from the garrison. Within a month, the occupying troops had constructed a new fortress.

Once again, however, after Hamza Mirza had lured out and defeated part of the garrison, Osman Pasha found himself facing defeat in an isolated Ottoman outpost. In October 1585, Osman Pasha died, leaving the garrison under the command of the Governor-General of

Diyarbekir, Jafer Pasha. For eleven months, until the arrival of a relieving force under Ferhad Pasha, he withstood a Safavid siege and, during his eight years as commander at Tabriz, resisted Safavid attempts to recapture the city. In Georgia, too, Ottoman fortunes advanced. In the summer of 1587, Ferhad Pasha led an expedition against Minuchehr, who had abandoned his allegiance to the Ottomans, and against Minuchehr's father-in-law and erstwhile Ottoman ally, Simon Khan. After defeating them both, he occupied and garrisoned Gori, Simon Khan's capital, and departed to reinforce Tblisi. Here he won the submission of Simon Khan, effectively making Georgia an Ottoman dependency. In the following year, a new Shah, Abbas I, came to the throne in Iran.

The war with the Ottomans was only one of Abbas's problems. He faced factional strife within his own realms, and an Uzbek invasion. In 1589, the Uzbeks captured Herat and advanced westwards to Mashhad. Abbas's preoccupation with this war allowed the Ottomans to extend their front on the western borders of Iran. In 1588, while Ferhad Pasha occupied Gänjä in Azerbaijan and received the tribute of the Georgian Princes, to the south, Jigalazade Sinan Pasha led an army from Baghdad and took Nihavend. With a war on two fronts, Shah Abbas had no choice but to sue for peace. In January 1590, a Safavid ambassador arrived in Istanbul. The treaty of the same year left the Ottomans in possession of all the territories which they had conquered in Azerbaijan and the Caucasus, and Nihavend, Luristan and Shehrizor in western Iran.

With this treaty the Ottoman Empire attained its maximum size.

The Ottoman times of trouble, 1590–1650

The war with Iran had added vast territories to the Ottoman Empire, but at great cost. To bring the war to a victorious conclusion had required a decade of fighting in the harsh terrain of the Caucasus and Azerbaijan. The continuous warfare had led to unrest and desertion among the troops, and the burden that it placed on the resources of the treasury had in turn strained the social fabric of the Empire, with growing unrest and brigandage that was to worsen in the coming decades. It was not a war that had produced an abundance of plunder, and it is unlikely that the tax yield of the new provinces covered the cost of their garrisons. Furthermore, the victorious conclusion was not simply a result of Ottoman military superiority. It owed much to the internal troubles of the Safavids and to the invasion of the Uzbeks, which left the Iranians fighting on both fronts.

This much was clear to Ferhad Pasha, who had been largely responsible for the Ottoman victory. When a new war threatened in Hungary, Ferhad was one of its opponents. In the early 1590s, Ottoman raids from Bosnia across the border into Austria and Austrian reprisals strained relations between the two powers, and raised the possibility of war. The chronicler Ibrahim Pechevi reports a meeting in the presence of the Sultan, where Ferhad Pasha opposed the declaration of war, on the grounds that the troops were already exhausted after the Iranian campaign. It was, Pechevi claims, the Grand Vizier, Koja Sinan Pasha, who, in his ambition to eclipse Ferhad Pasha's fame as a commander, was its chief advocate.

Sinan Pasha had his wish and, in 1593, departed to Hungary as commander-in-chief. The campaign began auspiciously enough with the capture, in early autumn, of Veszprem and Paluta in western Hungary. Shortly afterwards, however, it became clear that the Ottoman army could no longer boast the superiority that it had enjoyed thirty years earlier. In November 1593, the Austrians counter-attacked, laying siege to Székesfehérvár, and routing an Ottoman force sent to relieve the fortress. Abandoning Székesfehérvár on the approach of winter, they nonetheless captured a series of small fortifications in the district. The Austrian offensive continued in 1594, with the capture of Novigrad and the sieges of Esztergom, on the Danube to the west of Buda, and of Hatvan, to the north east. The besiegers again routed an Ottoman force coming to the relief of Hatvan. It was only when Sinan Pasha approached with a large force that the Austrians withdrew, and the Ottoman offensive continued with the capture first of Tata and then of Györ on the road between Buda and Vienna. Pechevi stresses, however, that it was only 'by the grace of God' that Györ fell. The overflowing river had flooded the ditch around the fortress, and the besiegers could approach the wall only in single file across a bridge. The Austrians, he claims, had no reason to surrender. The victory, nevertheless, redeemed some of the earlier defeats.

The following year brought disaster. In 1595, at the instigation of the Austrian Emperor, the King of Transylvania, Stephen Bathory, transferred his allegiance to the Habsburgs. At the same time, the Voyvodas of Moldavia and Wallachia rebelled, opening a new theatre of war, and threatening Ottoman control of the Danube, a major route for the transport of provisions and war materials to Hungary. The Voyvoda of Moldavia defeated an Ottoman force sent against him and, in the winter of 1594–5, Voyvoda Michael of Wallachia crossed the Danube and devastated an area of northern Bulgaria. The Ottoman campaign to suppress his rebellion started badly, with the dismissal of the commander, Ferhad Pasha, and his replacement by his rival, Koja Sinan Pasha. Sinan Pasha, despite forests, swamps and the harrying tactics of the Wallachians, reached Bucharest and then Tirgovişte, fortifying both places. Soon afterwards, however, Michael counter-attacked, slaughtering the garrison at Tirgovişte and forcing an Ottoman retreat to the Danube. At Giurgiu, Michael cut off the bridge across the river, and killed in their thousands the Ottoman troops left on the northern bank. Meanwhile, events in Hungary were no more fortunate. In August, the Austrians laid siege to Esztergom. The fortress fell when its commander, Sinan Pasha's son, Mehmed, fled to Buda.

In 1595, Murad III died. The accession of his son Mehmed III (1595–1603) came at a time of severe crisis on the battlefield and, at the urging of Sinan Pasha and others, in 1596 the new Sultan accompanied the army to Hungary in person. It was a campaign of mixed fortunes. As the army marched towards Eger in the north of Hungary, news came that the Austrians had captured Hatvan. To counterbalance this loss, the siege of Eger was a success and, shortly afterwards, the Ottomans won an unexpected victory. Soon after the fall of Eger, they encountered a large Austrian army near the fortress, on the plain of Mezö-Keresztes. In the face of superior Austrian artillery and of volley fire from arquebusiers sheltering under the protection of pikemen, the battle turned to a rout as the Ottoman cavalry fled the field. With very little resistance, the Austrian troops reached the central Ottoman encampment and abandoned themselves to plunder. It was at this moment that the horse grooms, cameleers, cooks and other palace servants that had accompanied the expedition attacked, shouting 'The infidel's fled!' Their shouts encouraged the defeated Ottoman troops to return to the attack. By nightfall, Pechevi estimates, they had slaughtered about 5000 Austrians. The victory was total. It did not, however, lead to further success. In 1597, the Vizier Satirji Mehmed Pasha left Istanbul for Hungary. His one success was to recapture Tata. He could not even come near, let alone defeat the entrenched Austrian artillery at Vác on the northern approach to Buda, and in the same year the Austrians recaptured Györ, blowing in its door with a new weapon, the petard. Despite these failures, Satirji Mehmed remained in command. In 1598, he received a command to attack Transylvania and restore the king to obedience. He took Csanad and then, in heavy rain, laid siege to Varad. At Varad came the news that an Austrian army with forty guns was laying siege to Buda. Satirji Mehmed at once withdrew, but foul weather, swollen rivers and swamps hampered the journey to the Hungarian capital. Hunger, disease and mutiny followed, together with the news that the Austrians were besieging Veszprem, Tata and Paluta. In the end no relief reached the besieged city, and Satirji Mehmed, on the Sultan's orders, lost his life. The disasters which threatened did not, however, materialise. Buda survived the siege and, in 1599, as the Ottoman army under the Grand Vizier Ibrahim Pasha approached Vác on the Danube, the Austrians retreated. There were other small Ottoman successes. A force under Kuyuju ('the Well-Digger') Murad Pasha took Bobovac, and the expedient of offering money to an unpaid French garrison at Papa persuaded them to change sides, and for a while the fortress came under Ottoman control.[53]

The year 1600 brought a larger prize when the Governor-General of Buda, Mehmed Pasha, took Kanizsa in south-west Hungary. The victory, however, like the battle of Mezö-Keresztes, was, as Pechevi describes it, 'a grace of God.' First, a powder magazine exploded in the fortress and when, in the face of superior Austrian gunfire, the Janissaries fled, the Austrian troops outside the fortress believed this to be a trick. Instead of attacking, they departed, leaving Kanizsa under siege. With their departure, the fortress surrendered. In 1601, the Austrians counter-attacked, taking first Székesfehérvár, and then sending an army to recapture Kanizsa. An Ottoman force under Yemishchi ('the Fruiterer') Hasan Pasha, who had succeeded to the command after the death of Ibrahim Pasha, could not dislodge the entrenched Austrian force that blocked his path to Székesfehérvár. Kanizsa, however, under the command of Tiryaki ('the Addict') Hasan Pasha, resisted a siege that lasted into the winter when, in the face of stubborn resistance and severe cold, the Austrians withdrew.

In the year after the defence of Kanizsa, Yemishchi Hasan Pasha reconquered Székesfehérvár, while in Transylvania, Szekely Mózes, a lord who resented his treatment at the hands of the Austrian general Basta, rebelled against the King and asked the Ottoman commander for assistance. Both events seemed to herald a revival in Ottoman fortunes. As it turned out, Szekely's rebellion led directly to disaster. In 1602, Yemishchi Hasan prepared to invade Transylvania, claiming that the Austrians lacked the resources to invade Hungary. Soon after the army's departure came news that the Austrians had captured Pest, on the banks of the Danube, opposite Buda. Yemishchi Hasan turned back, to find Pest in Austrian possession, and Buda under siege. He returned to Istanbul in disgrace but, enjoying the favour of the Sultan, he escaped execution and then, when he resigned, the Janissaries rebelled on his behalf. The Agha of the Janissaries, however, calmed the rebels, and soon afterwards Yemishchi Hasan was murdered.

Before leaving Hungary, Yemishchi Hasan had appointed Lala Mehmed Pasha as commander. His first success was to drive the besieging Austrian forces from Buda, enabling him to plan the reconquest of Pest on the opposite bank of the Danube. To do this, he had to dislodge the enemy from the island of Csepel, which blocked the approach to the city by river. Lala Mehmed clearly understood that to defeat the Austrians on the island required infantry in entrenched positions and planned accordingly. The Janissaries, however, disobeyed the command, refusing to entrench and demanding cavalry reinforcements. Lala Mehmed bowed to their demands, with the result that, in July 1603, the Austrians annihilated the attacking force, and remained in possession of Pest. In the following year, however, the Ottoman position began to improve.

One factor in this was the reversal of Austrian fortunes in the

Danubian principalities. The revolt of Voyvoda Michael in 1595 had benefited Austria by diverting Ottoman resources from the Hungarian front. By 1600, however, Michael was claiming the rulership not only of Wallachia, but also of Moldavia and Transylvania, an accession in power which harmed rather than benefited Austrian interests. The Austrian general, Basta, solved the problem by having Michael murdered, as much to the advantage of the Ottomans as to himself. Then, in 1603, there was a renewed rebellion in Transylvania, under the leadership of Stephen Bocskay, against the rule of the Austrian Emperor. Another factor in the Ottoman recovery was the military prowess of Lala Mehmed Pasha, who by now combined the offices of Grand Vizier and commander-in-chief in Hungary. In 1604, he left Belgrade for Hungary and, on the approach of his army, the Austrians abandoned Hatvan and Pest, and surrendered Vác following a blockade. In the autumn of 1604, he undertook an unsuccessful siege of Esztergom before returning to Istanbul. Here he received from the new Sultan, Ahmed I (1603–17), permission to crown Bocskay King of Transylvania, with the title 'King of Hungary.' In 1605, he returned to the front and this time conquered the modernised fortress of Esztergom. This was the last major encounter of the war.

In 1606, peace negotiations began at Zsitvatorok in the no-man's-land between the Habsburg and Ottoman Empires, focusing on the territorial arrangements, the tribute due to the Sultan and the settlement of cross-border disputes. Some issues the negotiators could not settle, with the curious result that both sides signed slightly different versions of the treaty. When Habsburg negotiators travelled to Istanbul in 1608 to ratify the text, they rejected it since they found that parts of it had been changed and that the clause on the equality of the Emperors had been dropped. It was not until 1612 that they ratified the final version.[54] The treaty nonetheless worked. There were no hostilities between the two sides until the 1660s, while the clause forbidding raids across the border and introducing a procedure for the settlement of cross-border disputes gave a formal expression to the concept of a fixed and peaceful frontier. The *kleinkrieg* of former centuries had finally come to an end.

The thirteen-year war with Austria had brought Kanizsa, Eger and some other fortresses to the Ottomans, but also some loss of territory. It had opened with Sinan Pasha's boast that he would 'bring the King of Vienna captive to Istanbul', and ended in compromise. It had shown that the Austrians were by now superior to the Ottomans in weapons and tactics. Nonetheless, in their ability to continue the war and, in its last two years, to win a series of victories, the Ottomans had shown an extraordinary resilience,[55] particularly since, in these years they were fighting not on one front, but three.

The second front was in the east. In 1590, Shah Abbas had, in the face of Uzbek attacks in Khurasan, conceded territory to the Ottomans. In 1598, however, he won a victory over the Uzbeks and, soon afterwards, occupied Herat. Then, using the defection to him of a Kurdish lord as a justification for war, in 1603 he entered Tabriz. The city's Ottoman garrison was absent in pursuit of the rebel Kurd and, on its return, suffered a defeat outside the city. From Tabriz, Abbas marched to Nakhichevan. After the surrender of the garrison there, he proceeded to Erivan. The fortresses of the city withstood a Safavid siege for more than nine months, but facing illness and starvation, and with no hope of relief, they capitulated in 1604. With the loss of the fortresses, it became clear that there was a need to mount a campaign in the east, despite the demands of the Hungarian front. In the second half of 1604, therefore, Jigalazade Sinan Pasha led the army initially in the direction of Shirvan, until, at the river Aras, the troops forced him to change his direction to Tabriz. Marching south from the Aras he wintered in Van. The Shah's forces, however, had made raids in the region of Kars, and defeated an Ottoman relief force from Sivas, forcing Sinan Pasha to abandon Van. In 1605, he continued towards Tabriz, with Safavid forces shadowing him in the mountains. Then, deceiving Jigalazade as to the direction of the attack, Shah Abbas routed his army at Sufian. Following the victory, he captured Gänjä in Azerbaijan, Tbilisi in Georgia and laid siege to Shirvan. With the fall of Shirvan seven months later in 1606, Shah Abbas had recovered all the territory that the Ottomans had won in the war of 1578–90.

The third front on which the Ottomans found themselves at war was in Anatolia.[56] Unrest in the area had been endemic throughout the sixteenth century but, in 1596, a rebellion erupted on such a scale as to threaten the rule of the Sultan. It was an event which the Ottoman chroniclers link directly to the battle of Meszö-Keresztes. In 1596, immediately after the battle, the Grand Vizier, Jigalazade Sinan Pasha, had dispossessed the fief-holding cavalrymen who had fled the field of battle. Deprived of their livelihoods, they joined the first of the great rebel leaders, Kara Yaziji, himself a former deputy of a governor. When the Sultan ordered the Governor-General of Karaman to attack the rebels, he defected to Kara Yaziji, who retired to Urfa. Here he withstood a two-month siege. The government next resorted to appeasement, appointing Kara Yaziji as Governor, first of of Amasya and then of Çorum. As Governor, however, he continued to plunder Anatolia, provoking another government campaign. In 1601 Hasan Pasha, the son of Sokollu Mehmed Pasha, finally defeated the rebels near Elbistan. In 1602, Kara Yaziji died.

This did not, however, put an end to the rebellion. Command of the Jelalis, as the rebels came to be known, passed to Kara Yaziji's brother, Mad Hasan who, in May 1602, besieged and eventually killed Hasan Pasha in Tokat. In August, he defeated another government force and laid siege to Ankara, extorting a huge sum from the inhabitants. Then he moved westwards and besieged another government force in Kütahya. The Grand Vizier, Yemishchi Hasan Pasha's response was again to offer the rebel a governorship, appointing him Governor-General of Bosnia. This removed the problem from Anatolia, as his rebels accompanied him to Bosnia and then to the Hungarian front, where 2000 of them perished in the disastrous attack on the island of Csepel in 1603. In 1606, the commander-in-chief in Hungary ordered Mad Hasan's execution. The departure of Mad Hasan and his men did not, however, end the disturbances in Anatolia, as new groups of rebels combined to assault towns and villages and to extract illegal taxes, provoking a 'great flight' from farms and villages to Istanbul and other large towns. At the same time, severe weather exacerbated the plight of the population.

Government attempts to defeat the rebels continued to fail. On his march to the east in 1605, Jigalazade received a command to confront the Jelalis before attacking the Safavids. He failed to do so and, in the same year, the rebel Tall Halil defeated a former Governor-General of Aleppo at Bolvadin, provoking Sultan Ahmed to the belief that he should lead an expedition in person. This plan, too, was a fiasco. In November 1605, he travelled to Bursa. Tall Halil retreated, and the Sultan returned. Instead, he offered the rebel the governor-generalship of Baghdad, and Tall Halil left Anatolia. His presence in Baghdad, however, merely caused instability in Iraq, while in western Anatolia, a new figure, Kalenderoghlu Mehmed, had emerged as leader of the rebels. A government campaign in 1606 failed altogether. It was uncertain whether its objective was the defeat of Kalenderoghlu or of Shah Abbas, and it eventually turned back when the unpaid troops mutinied. By 1607, Ottoman power in Asia seemed to be on the verge of collapse. In January, Kalenderoghlu defeated a government force near Nif, encouraging other Jelali leaders to join their forces to his. In the summer he besieged Ankara. A relieving force drove him off, but then itself suffered defeat at Ladik. Announcing that he was going to occupy Üsküdar and causing panic in the capital, Kalenderoghlu advanced towards Bursa. In 1607, he occupied the city, leaving only the citadel in government hands. In the south-east, Adana and the Taurus passes were in the hands of a rebel called Jemshid, but most dangerous of all was the rebellion of Ali Janbulad in Syria.

Members of the Janbulad family had served as hereditary governors of Kilis since 1571. In 1603, a member of the family, Hüseyn Janbulad, had, by force of arms, established himself as Ottoman Governor-General of Aleppo. Two years later, when Jigalazade Sinan Pasha had ordered him to serve on the Iranian campaign, he stayed in Aleppo. In revenge, Jigalazade had him executed, and this seems to have sparked the revolt of his son, Ali. The government tactic to defeat Ali was to appoint a rival lord, the Lebanese Yusuf ibn Sayf, governor in Damascus, with orders to overthrow the rebel. Ali Janbulad, replied with a similar tactic, allying himself with a certain Fakhr al-Din and other lords in Syria and Lebanon, in order first to defeat Yusuf, and then to divide Syria and Lebanon among themselves. By May 1606, he was demanding from the Sultan a vizierate and the right to appoint his own nominees to a large and strategically vital area around Aleppo. At the same time, he sought an alliance with Kalenderoghlu and other Anatolian rebels, and with sympathetic Ottoman governors. Ali's goal, it became clear, was to declare himself an independent ruler.

What thwarted Ali's ambitions was the appointment in 1606 of Kuyuju Murad Pasha as Grand Vizier. In contrast with the earlier improvised campaigns, Kuyuju Murad planned his expedition with great care, finally leaving Üsküdar in July 1607. In order to neutralise Kalenderoghlu during the campaign, he appointed him Governor of Ankara. It was when the inhabitants refused to accept him that Kalenderoghlu laid siege to the city. Then Kuyuju Murad crossed the Taurus mountains and occupied Adana, executing five hundred of the rebel governor's followers. From Adana, choosing the route that was least expected, he approached Aleppo, routing Ali Janbulad's forces in October 1607, and massacring his adherents. In November, he entered Aleppo and executed most members of the Janbulad family, and during the winter received the submission of Ali's Syrian and Lebanese confederates. Ali Janbulad himself fled westwards, making contact with the Jelali Kalenderoghlu at Bursa but, reaching no agreement with him, accepted instead the pardon of the Sultan, who appointed him Governor-General of Temesvár. Here, however, the populace rejected him and, in 1610, Kuyuju Murad ordered his execution.

The defeat of Ali Janbulad still left the rebels in control of much of Anatolia. In January 1608, Kalenderoghlu defeated a force under Nakkash ('the Artist') Hasan Pasha near Mihaliç, and in the summer blocked the passage of another army carrying the Treasure to Kuyuju Murad in Aleppo. Kuyuju Murad in the meantime faced severe problems in preparing for a new campaign. Kalenderoghlu had blocked his supply of cash; following a severe winter and late spring, and in consequence of the impoverishment of the countryside, his full quota of troops had failed to come from Anatolia; and supplies from Egypt were slow to arrrive. In the meantime, however, he detached some of the lesser Jelalis from Kalenderoghlu by awarding them governorships. Finally, in August 1608, he encountered and defeated Kalenderoghlu to the west of Malatya. The rebel and his followers fled to Iran, while Kuyuju Murad, ignoring the Sultan's command to stay in the field, returned to Istanbul. In 1609, the army mustered in Üsküdar, but Kuyuju Murad did not move. Instead, he sent a former Jelali, Zulfikar, to attack the rebel Musli Chavush, whom he himself had appointed Governor of İçel during the campaign against

Kalenderoghlu. During Zulfikar's absence, another rebel, Yusuf Pasha, appeared with his followers to seek a pardon, which Kuyuju Murad granted until Zulfikar had returned with news of the defeat of Musli Chavush. Then Kuyuju Murad had him executed inside his tent. With the death of Yusuf Pasha, Kuyuju Murad dismissed the army, although campaigns against the rebels in Anatolia and Iraq continued in 1610 on a smaller scale.

The defeat of the Jelalis left the Grand Vizier with two concerns. The first was to restore Ottoman fiscal and provincial administration after the Austrian war and the devastation of the Jelali rebellions in Anatolia. The result was a memorandum by a chancery clerk, Ayn Ali, which lays out, on the basis of archival registers, an idealised scheme of fiscal, provincial and military organisation. The Sultan, for his part, wished for a more visible monument to the victory over the rebels, and ordered the construction in Istanbul of the mosque that bears his name, the Sultan Ahmed Mosque or 'Blue Mosque'. In reality, however, rural life and the rural population of Anatolia were slow to recover. Fiscal surveys from over thirty years after the campaigns of Kuyuju Murad Pasha show that the population had still not recovered to its sixteenth-century level.

Kuyuju Murad's second concern was to renew the war with Iran. His campaign, however, was inconclusive. In 1611, he died in Diyarbekir, and in the following year, Nasuh Pasha, his successor as Grand Vizier, concluded a peace with Shah Abbas. This lasted only four years. In 1615, on the pretext that the annual tribute of silk due from the Shah had not arrived, the Grand Vizier, Öküz ('the Ox') Mehmed Pasha, renewed the war and unsuccessfully laid siege to Erivan.

In the west, meanwhile, there was a peace, the only engagements occuring at sea between the Ottoman fleet on its annual tour of the eastern Mediterranean and corsairs operating under the aegis of the Knights of St John, and of the Duke of Tuscany, with whom the rebels Ali Janbulad and Fakhr al-Din had established contact. More dangerous than these were the attacks of the Cossacks from their bases along the Don and the Dniepr on settlements along the Black Sea coast. These grew in intensity as the seventeenth century advanced, culminating in a raid on Sinop in 1614. In the following year an Ottoman counter-attack failed when the Cossacks, in their shallow vessels, lured the Admiral Jigalazade Mahmud so close to the shore that his galleys ran aground. In 1623, they attacked Yeniköy on the Bosphorus, near the capital, and for four years, between 1637 and 1641, even occupied Azov at the mouth of the Don, forcing the Ottomans to refortify Ochakov, a fortress occupying a similar strategic position on the Dniepr. For half a century, the war with the Cossacks required a series of maritime expeditions, using new strategies against their flat bottomed boats, and constant vigilance along the coasts of the Black Sea. These encounters with the Cossacks were the major Ottoman naval engagements until 1645.

The conclusion of the Austrian war and the defeat of the Jelalis did not end the Ottoman 'times of trouble'. In 1617, Ahmed I died, precipitating a crisis within the dynasty. Since Ahmed's sons were not yet adults, a faction within the Palace secured the succession of his brother, Mustafa I (1617–18, 1622–3). This Prince, however, was mentally disturbed and, during the absence of the Grand Vizier on an unsuccessful campaign to recapture Tabriz, the faction that had opposed Mustafa's succession secured his dethronement and replacement in 1618 by Ahmed I's eldest son, Osman.

The first year of Osman's reign saw the conclusion of a peace with Iran, which confirmed the frontier in Georgia and made some slight adjustments, in Shah Abbas's favour, to the Ottoman–Safavid border in Iraq. By contrast, there was a major crisis in relations with Poland.[57] Cossack raids from Polish territory on the coasts of the Ottoman Empire and Tatar raids into Poland had led to tension between the two powers. Moldavia, too, provided a haven for the Cossacks, and it was events here that led to war. When Caspar Gratiani succeeded as Voyvoda of Moldavia, he intercepted letters from the King of Transylvania, Bethlen Gabor, and revealed them to the Polish King, Sigismund. When the Sultan replied by deposing Gratiani, the Voyvoda rebelled and took refuge in Poland. The Ottoman response was decisive. In August 1620, the Governor-General of Ochakov, Iskender Pasha, assembled his forces and, in September, routed the combined armies of Poland and Moldavia at Iaşi. A second Polish defeat followed. King Sigismund, by this time, wished for peace, but the Sultan, despite opposition from the Janissaries, determined to continue the war, and did not allow the

Polish envoy to enter Istanbul. In May 1621, he left the capital at the head of an army and, at the end of August, reached Chotin on the Dniestr. By early October, all assaults on the fortress had failed and, despite Osman's determination to stay in the field throughout the winter, mutiny in his army forced him to accept the terms that King Sigismund was proposing. In early November, the army left Chotin with nothing achieved.

Osman's next decision was to cost him his life. His ambition, it seems, was to restore the Empire to its former glory by reforming its institutions and reversing the humiliations which Shah Abbas had inflicted. An element in his plan was to abolish the Janissary Corps. This, at least, is what the Janissaries believed. When, in 1622, he crossed the Bosphorus on the excuse of leaving for the Pilgrimage, they rebelled, in the belief that his intention was to collect an army in Syria and use it for their annihilation. Under pressure from the Janissaries, Osman returned to the Palace, but refused to order the execution of the six men whom they accused of leading him astray. His refusal provoked the Janissaries to a rebellion which ended in his execution and the reaccession of Mustafa.

The murder of one sultan and the enthronement of another who was mentally incapable ensured that political stability did not return. The Janissaries themselves, in order to expiate their guilt, demanded the execution of Davud Pasha, the Grand Vizer who, in his brief term of office, had condoned the murder of the Sultan. He and the Agha of the Janissaries lost their lives, but this unleashed a competition for the vizierate between the Georgian, Mehmed Pasha, and the Albanian, Mere ('Come here!') Hüseyn Pasha. The provinces, too, experienced unrest. In eastern Anatolia, claiming that he was avenging Osman's blood, the Governor-General of Erzurum, Mehmed Pasha the Abkhaz, rebelled, seizing Şebin Karahisar, Sivas, Ankara and eventually Bursa. In the Lebanon, Yusuf ibn Sayf asserted his independence and, in Iraq, Shah Abbas captured Baghdad.[58] His opportunity had come in 1622, when Bakr al-Subashi seized power in the city, and defeated a force sent against him under the Governor-General of Diyarbekir, Hafiz Ahmed Pasha. However, fearing another Ottoman army which was approaching, he sent the keys of Baghdad to Shah Abbas. In the same year, the Cossacks attacked Yeniköy.

The first step to prevent the disintegration of the Empire was to remove the Sultan. In 1623, after a group of ulema had taken the decision to depose Mustafa, a deputation went to the Palace and bargained with the Sultan's mother. Mustafa was dethroned, but his life was spared.

His successor was Murad IV (1623–40), the twelve-year-old son of Ahmed I. He – or rather his mother, Kösem Sultan, who was effectively ruler of the Empire during her son's minority – inherited political turbulence, the revolt of Mehmed Pasha the Abkhaz and the war with Iran. The loyalty of the Janissaries and the other salaried troops, he purchased with an accession bonus, at great cost to the Inner and Outer Treasuries. At the same time, he at once ensured that the Grand Vizier was his own nominee by executing Kemankesh Ali Pasha, ostensibly for his delay in reporting to the palace the loss of Baghdad. In 1624, Ali's successor as Grand Vizier, Mehmed Pasha the Circassian, left Istanbul with orders to defeat the rebel governor of Erzurum, and then to proceed to Baghdad. Mehmed Pasha the Abkhaz suffered a defeat near Kayseri and withdrew to Erzurum, while a separate Ottoman force won a victory over Iranian troops mustering at Kerkuk. Both Erzurum and Baghdad, however, remained in enemy hands.

In 1626, Mehmed Pasha's successor as Grand Vizier, Hafiz Ahmed Pasha, besieged Baghdad for several months. After numerous skirmishes around the city and a major defeat in June, a Janissary rebellion forced him to withdraw. The war in eastern Anatolia and the Caucasus was no more successful. Still nominally an Ottoman governor, Mehmed Pasha the Abkhaz disobeyed an order to march against the Safavid army besieging Ahiska. Instead, he attacked and defeated the Ottoman forces in the region of Erzurum, killing the Janissaries in the fortress. It was not until 1628 that a full army under the command of the Grand Vizier Hüsrev Pasha was able to trap him in Erzurum. Realising that he could not resist a siege, the Abkhaz surrendered and asked for quarter. The Sultan uncharacteristically forgave him and, using a traditional method of pacifying Anatolian rebels, appointed him Governor-General of Bosnia.

The defeat of Mehmed Pasha the Abkhaz, the renewal in 1629 of the Treaty of Zsitvatorok and the engagement of Austria in the Thirty

Years War left the Sultan free to use all his forces against Iran. The
Grand Vizier's expedition was, in its early stages, remarkably successful. Ottoman forces overcame the Iranians in skirmishes near
Baghdad, and then, in 1630, the Grand Vizier defeated a Safavid army
at Mihriban and, as it retreated, took Hamadan and Darguzin, intending to proceed to Ardabil and Qazvin. It was here, however, that he
received a reminder that the Sultan wished, above all, to retake
Baghad, and so he returned and laid siege to the city. After the failure
of the general assault in November 1630, Hüsrev Pasha broke off the
siege and returned to Mosul, allowing Shah Abbas's successor, Shah
Safi, to reverse the Ottoman conquests.

For his failure to capture Baghdad, the Sultan removed Hüsrev
Pasha and replaced him with Hafiz Ahmed. Hüsrev Pasha, it seems,
had been popular with the Janissaries and the Six Divisions of palace
cavalrymen. His removal was the spark which led to a violent rebellion that spread beyond the capital to the cavalrymen in Anatolia.
With the encouragement of the Vizier, Rejeb Pasha, these men came
to the Palace in February 1632 and demanded the heads of the Grand
Vizier, the Chief Mufti and several of Murad's closest associates. To
pacify the rebels, the Sultan released Hafiz Ahmed to his death,
replaced the Chief Mufti and appointed Rejeb Pasha Grand Vizier. At
the same time, he ordered the execution of the former Grand Vizier,
Hüsrev Pasha, in Tokat. His death removed a favourite of the rebels,
but the arrival of his head in Istanbul inflamed the situation. In
March, the insurgents demanded further executions and, more dan-
gerously for the Sultan, the custody of the Princes Bayezid,
Süleyman, Kasim and Ibrahim. On the executions, the Sultan gave
way to the insurgents' demands, while Rejeb Pasha and the new Chief
Mufti agreed to stand surety for the Princes. It was at this point that
the rebels considered dethroning the Sultan. However, some of the
soldiery, including the Agha of the Janissaries, remained loyal to the
Sultan, and it was he who informed Murad of the role of Rejeb Pasha
and Janbuladoghlu Mustafa Pasha in inciting the rebellion. The
Sultan suspected Rejeb Pasha in particular and, in May, summoned
him to the palace and had him strangled. In his place he appointed
Tabani Yassi ('the Flat Footed') Mehmed Pasha .

When, however, the cavalrymen heard that Murad had stopped

part of their pay, the rebellion flared up again. This time the Sultan did not capitulate, but called their leaders in groups to the palace and, from each group, extracted an oath of allegiance. Then he counter-attacked, ordering the immediate execution of captured rebels in Istanbul and the provinces, and the cessation of all payments that did not form part of their regular salaries.

The defeat of the rebellion saved Murad's throne, but it did not end his troubles. It required an expedition under Küchük ('Little') Ahmed Pasha to suppress brigands in Anatolia and end the rebellion of Fakhr al-Din in the Lebanon. Then, in 1633, fire destroyed a large part of Istanbul, the last of a series of calamities which seem to have deeply affected the Sultan and to have made him suspicious of anyone in his entourage. In 1633, he banished his advisor, Kochi Bey, and, in the following year, advised by his mother, executed the Chief Mufti, Ahizade. In 1635, he executed Prince Süleyman and, in 1638, the Princes Kasim and Bayezid, precipitating a crisis of succession in the dynasty, as he had no surviving sons of his own. In addition to frequent and often arbitrary executions, in 1633, with the encouragement of a powerful group of fundamentalist Muslims,[59] he imposed a ban on coffee and tobacco. During this period, the penalty for smoking was death.

Murad's violent measures did, however, restore order in the Empire and allowed him to recover some of the lost military glory of his ancestors. In 1632, Shah Safi invaded Georgia and then laid siege to Van. In the following year, an army under the command of the Grand Vizier, Mehmed Pasha, assembled at Üsküdar and advanced as far as Diyabekir. By September, however, the Iranians had lifted the siege, and the outbreak of hostilities with Poland led to the army's recall. The continuing Tatar raids into Poland and Cossack attacks on Ottoman territory were the cause of tension, and, in 1633, tension led to fighting on the river Dniestr and an Ottoman campaign under Mehmed Pasha the Abkhaz. Mehmed Pasha's assaults on Kamenets and the Cossack fortifications were unsuccessful, and negotiations began. When these led nowhere, Murad appointed Murtaza Pasha to lead a Polish campaign, with full powers to make war or peace. He left Edirne in 1634, and formalised an agreement with Poland. The Ottomans were to remove the Tatar tribes from the Belgorod steppes and the Poles to restrain the Cossacks. The peace freed Murad to undertake a campaign against Iran.

In 1635, at the same time as he sent Uzun Piyale on a naval expedition against the Cossacks, the Sultan left Üsküdar in person at the head of an army. By the end of July, he had reached Erivan and, within a week, the Safavid commander had surrendered and offered his services to the Ottoman Sultan. On the fall of the city, Murad sent Kenan Pasha to take Ahiska, while the main body of the army proceeded to Tabriz. Here, however, the Sultan fell ill and returned to Van, with the Safavid army shadowing but not attacking. At Izmit, on the return to Istanbul, Kenan Pasha joined the Sultan with news of the capture of Ahiska.

The campaign, it appeared, had been successful until, in April 1636, Shah Safi reconquered Erivan and, shortly afterwards, defeated and killed Küchük Ahmed Pasha near Mihriban. Murad did not immediately respond to the losses but, finally, on 8 May 1638, led his army from Istanbul, in the company of the Chief Mufti and the Admiral, to Baghdad. On his progress through Anatolia and the Arab provinces, he ordered the seizure and summary execution of brigands and other miscreants. In mid-October, the army camped outside Baghdad and, on 24 December, the Safavid governor, Bektash Khan, surrendered. In January 1539, Murad entered the city.[60] On the return journey, he fell ill at Diyarbekir and did not reach the capital until June. In the meantime, the Grand Vizier, Tayyar ('the Mercurial') Mehmed Pasha, negotiated the Treaty of Qasr-i Shirin with an envoy of the Shah, bringing to an end a war which had continued intermittently since 1603. The treaty awarded Baghdad to the Ottoman Empire, re-establishing the border between the Safavid and Ottoman Empires that had been fixed at the Treaty of Amasya in 1555.

Murad IV died in 1640, with a reputation as the Sultan who had restored order to the Empire and who, through the Erivan and Baghdad campaigns, had restored Ottoman military glory. His successor Ibrahim, by contrast, was to acquire the epithet 'the Mad'. He was Murad's sole surviving brother and had suffered, it seems, from the terrors of his early life. From his confinement in the palace, he had witnessed the murder of Osman II, the deposition of Mustafa, and the execution of his brothers Süleyman, Bayezid and Kasim. It was only, we are told, with difficulty, and after he had viewed his brother's corpse that his mother, Kösem Sultan, and the Grand Vizier, Kemankesh ('the Bowman') Mustafa Pasha persuaded him to ascend the throne.

Nonetheless, despite his terrors, for the first four years of his reign the Empire, effectively under the control of the Grand Vizier, enjoyed a period of stability. In the 1630s, Murad had attempted to restore its military strength by reassigning to fighting men fiefs that no longer supported military services. In the early 1640s, Ibrahim and his Grand Vizier ordered new fiscal surveys and the issue of new coinage in an attempt to stabilise the Treasury. The same years saw the ratification of the treaty with Iran and, to the relief of the Austrians at a time of crisis in the Thirty Years War, a renewal of the Treaty of Zsitvatorok. In 1644, however, this period of tranquillity came to an end and, with it, the Sultan's mental composure. By this year, the Sultan's personal exorcist, Jinji Hoja and his allies, Sultanzade Mehmed Pasha and Yusuf Pasha, had acquired, apparently with the support of Kösem Sultan, control of appointments to office. In January 1644, they procured the execution of Kemankesh Mustafa and installed themselves respectively as Military Judge of Anatolia, Grand Vizier and Admiral.The coup was the first stage in a crisis.

The first element in this was the outbreak of war with Venice. In July 1644, Maltese pirates had captured a ship carrying the former Chief Black Eunuch of the Harem and many others to Egypt. The Ottoman response was to construct a fleet which, observers believed, was bound for Malta. In fact, when the fleet emerged in 1645, its destination was Crete. The conquest of the island was, it seems, the particular wish of the Sultan and, as it lay on the route to Egypt, it was possible to blame the Maltese attack on the Venetians. With the advantage of surprise, the campaign opened successfully. In August, Chania fell and, in the following year, despite the change in fortunes among the faction in power, there were further victories. Mutual recrimination between the Admiral, Yusuf Pasha, and the Grand Vizier, Sultanzade Mehmed Pasha, led first to Sultanzade's dismissal and then to Yusuf Pasha's execution. Nonetheless, in 1646, troops on Crete under the command of Mad Hüseyn Pasha captured Apokoroni and then, after failing to take Souda, occupied

Rethymnon. At the same time, Mad Hüseyn thwarted Venetian attempts to block the Dardanelles and establish themselves on Tenedos. In the summer of 1647, Herakleion came under siege. Mad Hüseyn's successes contrasted with the problems in the capital. The execution of Kemankesh Mustafa had inaugurated a period of fierce competition for office, which coincided with a deterioration in the Sultan's state of mind. It seems probable that, at the time of his succession, Ibrahim's advisors knew his intelligence to be limited: a treatise on government which the advice writer Kochi Bey wrote for him on his accession is composed in appropriately uncomplicated language. The particular trigger for his insanity, however, seems to have been the dynastic crisis which his brother, Murad IV, had bequeathed. Murad had died with no male heirs at a time when Ibrahim had no children of his own. If Ibrahim were to die childless, the dynasty would be extinct. His first duty, therefore, was to produce male heirs, and this he did with increasing appetite. Duty, however, turned to obsession and, as he withdrew into the private world of the harem, his whims began to undermine the Empire. In 1647, he executed the Grand Vizier, Salih Pasha, accusing him of not enforcing his ban on carriages in the capital. In Salih's place, Ibrahim appointed Musa Pasha, the husband of a favourite companion. However, before Musa could even reach Istanbul, the Deputy Grand Vizier Hezarpare ('Thousand Pieces') Ahmed Pasha persuaded Ibrahim to appoint him in his place. In order to safeguard his own position, Ahmed Pasha pandered to the Sultan's whims, imposing, among other things, taxes to support his obsession with sable and ambergris.

The Sultan's descent into madness coincided with a period of military and political crisis. In 1647, as Ottoman troops laid siege to Herakleion, the Venetians blockaded the Dardanelles, preventing supplies from reaching the army. Once the Ottomans had lost the element of surprise, it had become clear that the Venetians were superior at sea. Having mastered the art of constructing galleons, they enjoyed an advantage, particularly in naval artillery, over the Ottomans, whose war fleet still consisted almost entirely of oared galleys. On land, too, the Venetians made advances. In Dalmatia, the Governor-General of Bosnia failed to capture Zadar and Šebenik, while the Venetians overran a number of fortresses on the Bosnian frontier. In 1647, at a time when the blockade of the Straits was causing food shortages in Istanbul, the Grand Vizier, Ahmed Pasha, refused admission to the palace to the Governor-General of Rumelia, who was bringing news of the Venetian conquest of Klis.

The Sultan's recklessness at a time of crisis led to a revolt. In 1648, on receiving a command to pay a large sum in 'festival tax', the Governor-General of Sivas, Varvar Ali Pasha, rebelled. His additional grievance was the practice of removing governors from office before the completion of their three-year term. The rebellion was not successful. Varvar Ali overcame one government force, but suffered defeat and execution at the hands of Ibshir Pasha. It was, in the end, an uprising within the capital that overthrew the Sultan.

In 1648, a Venetian fleet successfully blockaded the Dardanelles and prevented the Admiral, Ammarzade, from transporting supplies to Crete. He paid for his failure with his life. In June, an earthquake shook Istanbul, which many took as a sign of divine anger. Then in August, the Janissary commanders asked the Chief Mufti, Abdurrahim, for a fatwa justifying the execution of the Grand Vizier. The Mufti did as they wished and then, with this justification, the plotters deposed and executed the first the Grand Vizier and then the Sultan himself.

Ibrahim's successor was his seven-year-old son, Mehmed IV (1648–87).

At the boy Sultan's accession, the most influential figure in the government was his grandmother, Kösem Sultan. Her 'reign' ended with her murder in 1651, probably at the instigation of Mehmed's own mother, Turhan, who assumed the rulership on behalf of her son. In 1656, after a period of political instability, and at a moment of mortal danger following the Venetian annihilation of an Ottoman fleet at the Dardanelles, Turhan surrendered much of her own power to an elderly and almost unknown provincial governor whom she appointed as Grand Vizier. Her perception was remarkable. Köprülü Mehmed Pasha and, after him, his son Fazil Ahmed, revived the fortunes of the Empire, bringing not only political calm, but also military success. It was Fazil Ahmed who brought the Cretan war to a victorious conclusion in 1669. This period was to last until the decision, in 1683, to besiege Vienna. Not only did the siege fail, but it led directly to the formation of the Holy League, a coalition of anti-Ottoman powers. In the sixteen-year war that followed, the Ottoman Empire suffered defeat on land and sea. By the Treaty of Carlowitz in 1699, the Sultan ceded Hungary to the Austrians, and Athens and the Peloponnesos to Venice. Within fifteen years, the Empire had recovered the lost territory in Greece, but Hungary – the most prestigious conquest of Süleyman the Magnificent – was lost for ever.

2 The Dynasty

Reproduction and family structure

The Ottoman Empire was a dynastic state, whose continuing existence was dependent upon the ability of the sultan to produce male heirs and whose political stability was, to a degree, dependent on stability within the imperial family and household. Questions of dynastic reproduction, family structure and succession were therefore matters of major political importance.

It was the rules Islamic or, more precisely, Hanafi law, that determined the structure of the dynasty. These do not, if carried to their logical conclusion, create a family around the persons of husband and wife, but rather a patriarchal household around the person of a father. In law, therefore, the sultan was sole head of the dynastic family, as much as he was sole ruler of the Empire. For this reason, too, the notion of a formally recognised queen – although not of a *de facto* powerful woman – was as alien to the Ottoman Empire as it was to other Islamic polities.

The essential rules of family law are these.[1] A woman may marry only one husband at a time, who must also be the social equal of her family. A man, by contrast, may marry up to four wives simultaneously, and his wife or wives need not be his social equals. A Muslim woman may not, therefore, marry a non-Muslim man, as his religion makes him her social inferior. A Muslim man, on the other hand, may marry a non-Muslim woman, a rule which was to be an important factor in dynastic politics. What was most important, however, for the structure of the dynasty was the rule which allows a man to own and have sexual relations with as many female slaves as his pocket allows. A man may produce legitimate offspring by either a wife or a slave. All his children by a wife are automatically freeborn, and have an automatic right to inherit. So, too, is his child by a slave, so long as he recognises it as his own. When he does so, the child's slave mother acquires a privileged status within the household. Her master may not sell her, and she becomes automatically free on his death. There is no difference in legal status between a man's child by his wife, and a recognised child by a slave, since a person's legal descent is through the father rather than through the mother. These same rules applied to the Ottoman dynasty. Most of the sultans were the offspring of slave mothers, and the sultanate descended in the male line only. Descendants in the female line had no right to the throne, and dynastic custom forbade them to occupy any office superior to that of provincial governor.

The law also permits, or even requires, a man to confine each wife to the house, and obliges him, in return for this, to provide her with adequate maintenance. By custom, rather than by law, other female members of a family tended to suffer similar restrictions, and it was these legal and customary rules that underpinned the institution of the harem, effectively creating a private female world which contrasted with the public world of men. The Ottoman dynasty reproduced this structure. Within the Palace, the Harem was almost inaccessible from the men's quarters, except to the Sultan himself and the eunuchs appointed as its guardians. The Harem may, at times, have been a site of political power, but it was invisible to the outside world. The public sphere of the Palace was exclusively male.

Since females could not inherit the throne, the first duty of an Ottoman sultan or prince was to produce male heirs, which he could by law do either through a wife or through a slave concubine. Before 1450, the sultans usually married, but it seems from an early period to have been the custom of the dynasty to reproduce through slaves, the function of wives being political rather than reproductive.[2]

In Ottoman tradition, the descent of the dynasty begins with the marriage of the first ruler, Osman (d. *c.*1324), with Malhun, the daughter of the dervish Edebali, and mother of the second ruler, Orhan (*c.*1324–62). The story is clearly legendary, but the name Malhun may be a truncated version of a certain 'Malhatun daughter of Ömer Beg' whose name appears as a witness to a trust-deed of Osman's son, Orhan. It is possible that this lady was Osman's wife and Orhan's mother. Her father's title Beg ('lord'), at this epoch, suggests that he was an independent lord who had perhaps married his daughter to Osman for political reasons. This, however, is speculation. The mother of the third Ottoman ruler, Murad I (1362–89) was also, if one is to believe Ottoman tradition, a wife rather than a slave. Her name, as an inscription in Iznik attests,[3] was Nilüfer ('Waterlily'), and the tradition makes her daughter of the Greek ruler of Yarhisar, whom Osman had captured and given as a bride to his son, Orhan. Like most stories of the early Ottomans, however, this tale is quite possibly a fiction: the lady's name suggests that she was a slave.

Whatever Nilüfer's status, the Ottoman preference for reproducing through slaves seems to have become established with Murad I. The mother of his son and successor, Bayezid I (1389–1402) was, as two surviving trust deeds show,[4] a certain Gülchichek ('Rose') and, again, her name suggests that she was not a free woman. Of Bayezid's sons, the chronicler Shükrullah wrote in about 1460: 'He had six sons: Ertughrul, Emir Süleyman [Rumelia, 1402–11], Sultan Mehmed [I, Anatolia, 1402–13; 1413–21], Prince Isa, Prince Musa [Rumelia, 1411–13] and Prince Mustafa. Their mothers were all slaves' He made the same remark of the sons of Mehmed I: 'He had five sons: Prince Murad [II, 1421–51], Prince Mustafa, Prince Ahmed, Prince Yusuf and Prince Mahmud. The mothers of all of them were slaves.' So, too, were Hüma, the mother of Mehmed II (1451–81), and Gülbahar, the mother of Bayezid II (1481–1512). Ayshe, the mother of Bayezid's son and successor, Selim I (1512–20) was an exception. She seems to have been the daughter of Alaeddevle, the ruler of Dulgadir, who had married Bayezid in a political alliance before his accession to the throne, when he was Prince-Governor of Amasya.[5]

Throughout its history, the Ottoman dynasty continued to reproduce through slaves, but between the fourteenth and early sixteenth centuries it was also the custom to restrict each consort's reproductive life to a single son. Once she had borne the sultan a male heir, she never again entered his bed. It was, it seems, the politics of succession that determined this practice. From the moment of his birth, every son of a prince or sultan was eligible for the throne, and so became a political rival to his brothers. Princes did not, therefore, grow up together. Instead, each mother raised her son separately and when, at the age of ten, eleven or twelve, the sultan, as was customary, appointed him governor of a province, his mother accompanied him to his new post and became his moral guardian. In this way, each mother became a senior figure in the household that formed around her son in his provincial posting, and his sponsor in the contest for the throne that would inevitably follow the death of the father.[6]

This at least was the pattern of reproduction and maternal care until the reign of Süleyman I (1520–66). This sultan broke with custom, not apparently for reasons of politics, but for love. In 1521, the Sultan had a single living son, Mustafa, whose mother was a slave concubine called Mahidevran. In the same year he produced another son, Mehmed, by Hurrem, the concubine whom European sources remember as Roxelana. At this point, by dynastic custom he should have had no more sexual contact with her, but instead, between 1522 and 1531, she bore him six more children, including his eventual successor, Selim II (1566–74). Such was his affection for Hurrem that, in 1533, in a break with tradition which seems to have scandalised contemporaries, he set her free and married her. When she died in 1558, she was buried in the grounds of the Süleymaniye mosque, next to the Sultan's own mausoleum, as a lasting token of his affection. Hurrem's position as mother of more than one son altered the political structure of the dynasty. Unlike previous mothers of Princes, she did not accompany her sons to their governorships in the provinces, but remained in Istanbul at the centre of power, with immediate access to the Sultan. In this sense, she prefigured the powerful women of the late sixteenth and seventeenth centuries.[7]

Hurrem set a precedent. Before his accession to the throne, Süleyman's son, Selim II, had produced several daughters and one son by his favourite concubine, Nurbanu, by birth a Venetian of noble, if illegitimate descent. After his accession, he produced six more sons, each, it seems, by different mothers, but he differed from his predecessors in that he recognised his son by Nurbanu, Murad III (1574–95), as his legitimate heir, and followed his father in – apparently – taking Nurbanu as his legal wife, giving her a position of power, similar to the one which her mother-in-law Hurrem had enjoyed. Unlike Hurrem, however, Nurbanu outlived her husband and, between 1574 and her death in 1583, she continued to enjoy a political role as mother of the reigning sultan, although she was apparently not resident in the Palace after Selim II's death. Her successor, Safiye,[8] followed a similar career. She too was a favourite concubine with whom Murad III had apparently enjoyed a monogamous relationship until the death of their second son in 1581. Between this date and his death, Murad produced, apparently at his mother's instigation, nineteen sons by different concubines, but it was still Safiye's surviving son, Mehmed III (1595–1603) who ascended the throne in 1595, with his mother, Safiye, as a dominant figure. The power of the queen mother became particularly pronounced during the seventeenth century, with the long 'reign' of Kösem Mahpeyker, the favourite of Ahmed I (1603–17). She was the mother of four of Ahmed's sons, of whom two, Murad and Ibrahim, were to become Sultan. Her period of power began in 1617, when Ahmed's mentally defective brother, Mustafa I (1617–18, 1622–3), came to the throne. After Mustafa's deposition in the following year, his successor Osman II (1618–22) – Ahmed I's son by a different mother – banished her from the Palace, but she returned after Osman's murder in the Janissary rebellion. Osman's successor was the feeble minded Mustafa, and his accession to the throne brought his own mother temporarily to a position of power. Mustafa, however, lost his throne after less than a year and it was then that Kösem's own son, the twelve-year-old Murad IV (1623–40) became sultan. With his accession, Kösem effectively took over the government on his behalf, and remained his close advisor even after he had reached adulthood. On Murad's death, her last surviving son, Ibrahim (1640–48), succeeded. When his mental instability threatened the safety of the realm, Kösem seems to have played a role in conducting the government, and continued to do so after Ibrahim's deposition in 1648, until her murder in 1651, at the instigation, it is rumoured, of Turhan Sultan, mother of the new Sultan, Mehmed IV (1648–87). For the next five years, Turhan was regent on her son's behalf until, with her consent, Köprülü Mehmed Pasha assumed the post of Grand Vizier in 1656, with virtually sovereign powers. From this date, the political power of the queen mothers faded.

The Ottoman dynasty, therefore, reproduced almost exclusively through slave concubines. Before the reign of Süleyman, the role of these women was each to produce and educate a single son. It was they who were responsible for their sons' upbringing and welfare, but they had no part in the government of the Empire, except perhaps in the provinces to which the sultan had assigned their sons as governors. With the reign of Süleyman I, the pattern changed. From the time of Hurrem, it was quite usual for a concubine to give birth to more than one son and, with the death of her consort, to assume the role of queen mother, with a powerful influence over her son, the ruling sultan. This development reached its height in the careers of Kösem and Turhan, two women whose strong personalities seem to have held the dynasty together during almost forty years of dynastic, political and military crises. The position and power of the queen mother was never formalised, but both foreign and Ottoman observers were aware of its reality and indeed, in a system where proximity to the sultan was a source of power, it seemed quite natural.[9]

Despite the Ottoman dynasty's preference for reproducing through slave concubines, in the first century and a half of Ottoman rule, royal marriages were commonplace.[10] Their purpose, however, was always political and never reproductive. Whether Osman married Malhatun, and whether Orhan's consort, Nilüfer, was a wife or concubine are matters for speculation. The earliest certain reference to the marriage of an Ottoman ruler appears in the Byzantine Chronicle by the Emperor John VI Kantakouzenos, who records, in his version of the story, how Orhan requested his daughter Theodora in marriage,[11] promising Kantakouzenos that he would be 'as a son, and place his entire army under Kantakouzenos's orders'. The marriage took place in 1346 and, following the ceremony, Orhan did in fact supply his father-in-law with troops which were a factor in his seizure of the Byzantine throne in 1346. What the marriage had done was to establish an alliance between the two families. After John Kantakouzenos's abdication in 1354 and the accession of John V Palaiologos, with whom Orhan had no family links, Ottoman attacks on Byzantine territory began again. At the same time, Orhan continued to support the Kantakouzenos family, sending troops to Kantakouzenos's son, Matthew, in his unsuccessful attempt to wrest the Byzantine throne from John V Palaiologos. This Emperor's solution to Ottoman aggression was to try to link his own family to

Orhan's. In 1358, he betrothed his daughter Eirene to Orhan's son Halil, with a request that the elderly Orhan appoint Halil as his successor. Again, he hoped that a family alliance would result in Orhan's sparing his territory and supporting his throne. The plan failed: the marriage never took place and Halil did not succeed Orhan.

The practice of marrying into foreign dynasties was to continue under Orhan's successor, Murad I, but with an important difference. Orhan's marriage to Theodora had made him an equal or, if one is to believe John Kantakouzenos, a junior partner in an alliance. By Murad's time, marriage had become an instrument of subjugation. Some time after 1371, Murad married Thamar, the sister of the Bulgarian Tsar Shishman of Tarnovo. The purpose of the match was, it is clear, to reduce Shishman to the status of vassal, owing Murad allegiance, possibly the payment of tribute, and certainly the provision of troops to Murad's army. It was Shishman's failure to perform this last duty that led to Murad's despatch of an army against the Tsardom in 1388.

Bayezid I's marriages were similarly instruments of political domination. The first of these took place in the late 1370s, when his father married him to the daughter of Yakub, the lord of the neighbouring Anatolian principality of Germiyan. The reason for the arrangement was clearly territorial gain, since the girl brought with her as a marriage portion the capital of Germiyan, Kütahya, and other towns in the principality. In 1394, when he had succeeded to the throne, Bayezid married the daughter of the Countess of Salona, a Frankish principality to the east of Athens. With the bride, he acquired half of her mother's county. Both these marriages were, in legal terms, peculiar, since Islamic law does not require the bride to bring a dowry, as these two ladies clearly did. These acquisitions of land through marriage seem, therefore, to have been cases of the Ottoman sultans adopting, to their own advantage, the customs of their Greek and Latin neighbours. Bayezid's other marriage was more conventional. Probably in 1392, he married Olivera, sister of Stephen Lazarević of Serbia, an arrangement which reduced Stephen to vassalage, with an obligation to provide troops and tribute. In return Bayezid could offer Stephen protection, particularly against the ambitions of the King of Hungary.

Matrimonial arrangements such as these were possible only when the Ottomans were a dominant military and political power. During the civil strife which followed Timur's defeat of Bayezid in 1402, the warring Ottoman Princes no longer contracted marriages in order to dominate their neighbours, but rather to create alliances which were useful in the fight against their brothers. Thus, when Prince Musa landed in Wallachia in 1409, to challenge his brother Süleyman's ascendancy in Rumelia, he secured the alliance of Voyvoda Mircea of Wallachia by marrying this ruler's daughter. Four years later, when he had defeated Süleyman, he married the illegitimate daughter of the Despot Carlo Tocco of Ioannina, in an attempt to secure an alliance against his brother, Mehmed. Mehmed, in the meantime, had married a princess of Dulgadir, forming an alliance in Anatolia that would protect his south-eastern border from a possible Timurid, Mamluk or Karamanid attack, while he fought his brother in Europe. At the same time, his Dulgadirid father-in-law provided him with troops for his final attack on Prince Musa in 1413.

Murad II continued the practice of marrying into foreign dynasties. In 1423, the lord of Kastamonu, Isfendyaroghlu, attacked Murad's lands, provoking the Sultan into a successful counter-attack. Isfendyaroghlu sued for peace and, as a condition for Murad's non-aggression, gave the Sultan his infant daughter in marriage, and agreed each year to provide troops for his army. Murad's second marriage, in 1435, was to Mara, the daughter of the Serbian Despot George Branković, whose allegiance was essential to Murad in securing the frontier with the Kingdom of Hungary along the Danube. The marriage of his son, Mehmed [II] in 1450 to Sitti Hatun of Dulgadir[12] had a similar function of securing his eastern frontier in Anatolia. This too must have been the purpose of the marriage of Mehmed's son, Bayezid [II] to Ayshe Hatun, daughter of Alaeddevle of Dulgadir, whose lands adjoined the province where the Prince was governor.

This was the last marriage of an Ottoman prince or sultan with a foreign princess. What is most striking about these marriages is that they seem, for the most part, to have been sterile. Murad II eventually produced a son by the daughter of Isfendyaroghlu, and Selim I was, exceptionally, the son of a princess but, in general, the function of dynastic wives was not to reproduce, but to secure the loyalty of their fathers as allies or vassals of the Ottoman sultan, and in the latter case to live as hostages at the Ottoman court. Marriage for the Ottoman sultans was a political expedient. When it was no longer useful, they discarded the practice.

The marriages of Ottoman princesses, insofar as records of them survive, seem to have followed a similar pattern. Before the mid-fiftenth century, they married into foreign dynasties. Thereafter, their marriages were domestic. Murad I married one of his daughters to Süleyman Pasha, the lord of Kastamonu, and another to Alaeddin, the lord of Karaman, whom her brother, Bayezid I, was to defeat and kill in 1397. There was another match with the Karamanids in the next century, when Ibrahim of Karaman (d. 1463) married Sultan Hatun, a daughter of Mehmed I, by whom he had six sons. The events following Ibrahim's death, when these disputed the succession with a son of Ibrahim by another mother, indicate that there could be an advantage to the Ottoman sultan in such an arrangement. The succession dispute gave Mehmed II a pretext to interfere in the affairs of Karaman, and to settle the dispute in favour of his own cousin, Pir Ahmed. Presumably too, when Murad II married a daughter to Kasim, the son of Isfendyaroghlu of Sinop, whose daughter he himself had married, his aim was to link the Ottoman and Isfendyarid dynasties to the advantage of the Ottomans. However, since legal descent is in the male line, the offspring of princesses married into foreign dynasties were not, in a legal sense, Ottoman, and these marriages could not therefore serve to establish Ottoman claims to territory. Furthermore, since the law forbids Muslim women to marry non-Muslims, Princesses were available only for marriage into Muslim dynasties and not into the Christian dynasties of the Balkans. For these reasons, the marriage of princesses to foreign rulers seems to have been an unimportant element in Ottoman dynastic policy.

After about 1450, the practice ceased. From the reign, certainly, of Bayezid II, it became a fixed custom to find spouses for the sultan's sisters, daughters and granddaughters among the ruling élite of the Empire. Bayezid's daughter, Hundi Hatun, for example, married Hersekzade Ahmed Pasha, who held the post of Grand Vizier five times during the reign of his father-in-law and under his successor, Selim I. This practice was not, in fact, new since Chandarli Mehmed, the brother of Murad II's Grand Vizier, Chandarli Halil, had married Mehmed I's daughter, Hafsa,[13] and there must have been similar marriages. From the mid-fiftenth century, however, it became the normal, and probably the invariable, practice.

During the second half of the reign of Süleyman I, it became customary for the Grand Vizier to marry into the royal family. Rüstem Pasha, for example, Grand Vizier between 1544 and 1553, and again from 1555 until his death in 1563, married Süleyman's only daughter, Mihrimah (d.1574). Sokollu Mehmed, Grand Vizier to Süleyman's son, Selim II, was similarly the Sultan's son-in-law. This pattern of marriages was to be the norm until the end of the Empire,[14] and clearly benefited the dynasty. By tying statesmen into the royal family, it reduced the risk of their establishing households which were independent of the sultan and, by requiring that the husbands of the royal brides divorce their other wives, it prevented their making marriage alliances with other households that might challenge the sultan's power. These royal wives must also have acted as spies for the sultan, reporting on the activities of his ministers.

The purpose of marriage, therefore, was always political. It was concubines and not wives that assured the reproduction of the dynasty.

Succession

After reproduction, the most essential element in ensuring the continuity of the dynasty, and so of the Empire, was managing the succession.

How exactly the first ruler of the Ottoman dynasty achieved recognition as a sovereign lord is unclear. Ottoman tradition locates the beginning of Ottoman independence in the first performance in Osman's name of the Friday Prayer, the religious ceremony through which, in Islam, a ruler announces his sovereignty. This, the tradition asserts, took place in the town of Karajahisar in the Sakarya valley. The chroniclers have assigned various dates to this event, and often embellished it to accord with their own particular understanding of Ottoman legitimacy. Whether the Karajahisar tradition is accurate or not, the survival of a coin bearing the inscription 'Struck by Osman son of Ertughrul'[15] does confirm that Osman considered himself an independent ruler, since the issue of coinage, like the performance of Friday Prayer in the ruler's name, amounted to a declaration of sovereignty. Succession in the Ottoman dynasty, therefore, begins with succession to Osman.

Osman was followed by his son, Orhan who, according to a fifteenth-century tradition, succeeded to the throne during his father's lifetime. A second traditional story tells how, on Osman's death, Orhan's brother, Ali Pasha, voluntarily renounced all claims to rulership and retired to a life of contemplation. The first of these tales might perhaps be true, but the second is certainly a legend which an early fifteenth-century chronicler concocted in order to provide a model of how the succession should be managed, in contrast to the sanguinary practices of his own day.[16]

In one respect, however, the chronicler's story is correct. Even though Orhan never had a brother called Ali Pasha, he does appear to have succeeded to the throne without the bloodletting which characterised the beginning of subsequent reigns. Orhan's trust deed of 1324 records, among the witnesses to the document, the names of his four brothers. One of these, Pazarlu, the Chronicle of John Kantakouzenos records as a commander at the battle of Pelekanon in 1328, suggesting that during Orhan's time, the ruler's brothers played some part in the government of his realms. So, too, did his sons. Orhan's eldest son, Süleyman Pasha, who predeceased his father in 1357, was Ottoman commander in Thrace in the 1350s, and captured Ankara in 1354. The Byzantine Chronicle of Nikephoros Gregoras, too, notes that Orhan's son, Halil, was the governor of land on the Gulf of Izmit in 1357. Taken together, these fragmentary records suggest that, while Orhan was a sovereign ruler governing an indivisible realm, his brothers and sons continued to play important roles as governors and military commanders.

Why Orhan, rather than any of his brothers, should have succeeded Osman is not clear. What is, however, certain is that, after his reign, the mode of succession was very different. In about 1400, the poet Ahmedi, in his brief verse history of the Ottoman 'kings' wrote of Orhan's successor, Murad I (1362–89): 'His brothers became enemies to him / The affairs of all of them were ended at his hands / They were all destroyed by his sword.' Although Ahmedi is unspecific in detail, the sense of Ahmedi's lines – provided one interprets 'brothers' in its literal meaning[17] – is quite clear. Following his succession, Murad killed all his brothers, perhaps during the course of a civil war, and established a precedent which the dynasty was to follow for over two hundred years after his death. From Murad's time, the succession passed to whichever son of the sultan defeated and killed his brothers or other claimants to the throne.

Murad's son, Bayezid I (1389–1402) succeeded his father after executing his brother Yakub, according to a widespread tradition, on the battlefield of Kosovo in 1389.[18] Thereafter, he ruled as Murad's only surviving son until his defeat and capture at the battle of Ankara in 1402, an event which initiated the longest succession crisis in Ottoman history, the civil war of 1402–13.

The events in this struggle show how deeply rooted two principles of dynastic succession had by then become. The first, which seems to date from the earliest days of Ottoman rule, was that Ottoman territory was indivisible. The sons of Bayezid fought each other to the death rather than split up the lands that remained to them after Timur's victory. The second principle was that none of the sultan's heirs enjoyed primacy in the succession. The sultanate passed to whichever one of them could eliminate the competition. This seems also to have been a principle which the subjects of the dynasty recognised. Of the contestants for the sultanate in the civil war, only Isa, in his brief campaign of 1402–3 in western Anatolia, seems to have suffered rejection by his would-be subjects, and relied entirely for support on foreign dynasties. His brothers, Süleyman, Musa and Mehmed made foreign alliances, but were also to gain acceptance and raise troops in the territories which they controlled. Ottoman subjects were, it seems, prepared to accept as ruler almost any legitimate heir to an Ottoman sultan, without regard to any order of precedence.

Mehmed I (1413–20) emerged as victor in the civil war, after his brother Musa had defeated and killed Süleyman in 1411, and he had himself defeated Musa two years later. These two fratricides did not, however, put an end to civil strife. After 1411, the Byzantine Emperor had assumed the custody of Süleyman's son, Orhan and, on at least two occasions, tried unsuccessfully to use him to foment conflict in the Ottoman lands. More important, however, was the survival of Mustafa, probably the youngest of Bayezid's sons. His fate in the aftermath of the battle of Ankara is unknown but, in 1415, he was in Trabzon, and next year raised an army in Rumelia and led an unsuccessful revolt against his brother. He, too, fled into the custody of the Byzantine Emperor, and was still alive when Mehmed I died in 1421.

It seems, from admittedly inconclusive evidence, that Mehmed I tried to end the practice of fratricide by abandoning the principle of indivisibility and bequeathing his lands in Rumelia to his elder son, Murad, and those in Anatolia to his younger son, Mustafa. Mehmed I's viziers, however, did not accept this scheme. Instead, they concealed the old Sultan's death and summoned his elder son, Murad, whose reign as Murad II (1421–51) began with renewed civil war. His first battle was not, however, against his brother Mustafa, but against his uncle of the same name who, when the Byzantine Emperor released him from captivity, established a short-lived régime in Rumelia, minting his own coins and gaining the allegiance of the Rumelian lords. Mustafa defeated Murad's army under Bayezid Pasha, killing its commander and then, proclaiming himself Sultan at Edirne, crossed the Straits to Anatolia. From Lake Ulubat, more by trickery than by superior force, Murad drove Mustafa back across the Straits to Edirne, where he seized and hanged him as though a common criminal.[19] This was not, however, the end of the civil war since, in the second half of 1422, with the sponsorship of the Byzantine Emperor and some of the dynasts of Anatolia, his brother 'Little' Mustafa had established himself as Sultan in Iznik. In January, 1423, Murad crossed the Straits to Iznik and, having defeated his brother, had him strangled.

At his death in 1451, Murad left two sons, the adult Mehmed II (1451–81) and an infant son by the daughter of Isfendyaroghlu of Sinop. Mehmed's first act on entering the palace at Edirne was therefore to ensure the security of his throne by ordering the execution of the boy. The succession of his son, Bayezid II (1481–1512), was less straightforward.[20]

Immediately on the death of Mehmed II, the viziers sent messages to his sons, Bayezid in Amasya and Jem in Konya. Bayezid was the first to arrive in the capital and, with the support of the Grand Vizier

Gedik Ahmed Pasha and, crucially, with the backing of the Janissaries, occupied the throne. When his brother Jem proclaimed himself Sultan in Bursa, and Bayezid rejected his proposal to divide the Ottoman lands between them, it was Gedik Ahmed who defeated the Prince at Yenişehir. Jem, however, escaped with his life and fled to the protection of the Mamluk Sultan of Egypt. In 1482, he returned to Anatolia, but when his army dispersed, he took refuge with the Knights of St John on Rhodes. At this stage, Bayezid made an agreement with the Grand Master to keep Jem in safe custody against an annual payment. His next move was to execute Gedik Ahmed, whom he seems to have suspected of disloyalty, and Jem's infant son. In a note in his own hand to a slave called Iskender, he wrote: '. . . You should know that I have killed Gedik Ahmed. You too should not spare Jem's son, but have him strangled. This is extremely important, but no one must be aware of it . . .'[21]

Jem's custody with the Knights marked the entrance of the Ottoman sultan into western European politics. The Knights transferred Jem to the safekeeping of their castles in France until 1489 when, contrary to the agreement, they handed him to the Pope. Bayezid had no alternative but to transfer payment from the Knights to the Pope to keep Jem in custody and, especially, to prevent his coming into the hands of the King of Hungary, or of any other potential enemy of the Ottomans. Given the danger that his brother's release might cause, in 1490, Bayezid undertook not to attack Venice, the Papal States or Rhodes. In 1494, the Pope and the King of Naples sought his alliance against Charles VIII of France, but to no avail. When a triumphant Charles entered Rome in 1494, he took possession of Jem, declaring at the same time that he would lead a Crusade against the Ottomans. The prospect of the Ottoman Prince returning as a protégé of the victorious King of France caused a panic in Istanbul.[22] However, in February 1495, Jem died in Naples still in the custody of the King, and the danger passed. Nevertheless, it was not until the return, after much negotiation, of Jem's body in 1499 and his public burial in Bursa, that Bayezid could be certain that his throne was secure.[23]

Ten years later, a new crisis erupted.[24] By 1509, Bayezid II was old and ill. Since his death seemed imminent, the contest to succeed him began when he was still on the throne. What was apparently the first move among his heirs came in 1509, when one of his sons, Korkud, fled from Antalya, where he was governor, to Egypt, most probably to seek the support of the Mamluk Sultan in the impending battle for succession. He returned a year later but again, presumably with an eye to the throne, disobeyed his father in moving from Antalya to Manisa, a princely residence closer to the capital.

Korkud's move to Manisa coincided with the violent rebellion, beginning near Antalya, of the Shiite sectary, Shahkulu, who defeated Korkud's troops and all the provincial forces which the Sultan sent against the insurgents. The revolt had humiliated Korkud, but provided an opportunity for his brother Ahmed, the governor of Amasya. In June 1511, Bayezid sent an army under the effective command of the Grand Vizier Hadim Ali Pasha, a supporter of Ahmed, and the nominal command of Ahmed himself. Ahmed's presence at the head of an army distinguished him as the favourite son to succeed, even though the death of the Grand Vizier in the final battle with Shahkulu removed a powerful supporter. The death, shortly afterwards, of his brother Shehinshah, the governor of Konya, removed another obstacle to Ahmed's succession.

During these events, Bayezid's younger son, Selim, was also preparing for a conflict with his brothers. In 1510, he wrote to his father, complaining of his governorship in the remote Black Sea province of Trabzon, and demanding an alternative in Rumelia. His letters also complained of plots to bring Ahmed to the throne. When Bayezid refused his request, he left Trabzon without authorisation and crossed the Black Sea to the Crimea where, he told Bayezid's envoy, he would 'bring the Khan of the Crimea to his cause, and establish a marriage-relationship with him'. Refusing Bayezid's offer of a governorship in Anatolia, he sailed to Kilia in Moldavia with his own followers and Tatar troops, clearly hoping to seize the throne with the Khan's assistance.

Bayezid, meanwhile, ordered the governors in Rumelia to prepare a force to encounter Selim but, before the armies met, Bayezid's envoys persuaded the Prince to turn back, by offering him the governorship of Silistra on the Danube, with permission to make raids into Hungary. This provided Selim with an opportunity. He retired to

Stara Zagora and collected an army but, instead of attacking Hungary, he marched towards Istanbul, encountering Bayezid's forces not far from the city. On this occasion, Bayezid was victorious, leaving Selim with no choice but to return to the Crimea and ask for his father's forgiveness.

Selim's withdrawal was Ahmed's opportunity. With the encouragement of his father and the new Grand Vizier, Hersekzade Ahmed Pasha, he marched to Istanbul, with the evident hope of succeeding to the throne during his father's lifetime, and thereby justifying Selim's complaint that Ahmed's appointment to command the army in Anatolia was an indication that he was Bayezid's chosen sucessor. An Ottoman sultan, however, needed the support of the Janissary Corps, and this Ahmed could not win. In September 1511, as Ahmed approached the Bosphorus, the Janissaries rebelled on Selim's behalf. Ahmed's failure to defeat and pursue the rebels in Anatolia had lost both him and his father the military support on which the Sultanate depended. A group of Janissaries was later to appear before Bayezid and openly declare: 'You are finished. We need a Sultan and so we have made Lord Selim Sultan . . . The throne and the realm are his.' In these circumstances, Ahmed did not dare to cross the Straits.

Instead, he returned to Anatolia and began to act as an independent ruler, issuing decrees and making appointments as though he were sultan. With this, the balance of politics changed. As a rebel, Bayezid could no longer support Ahmed. Instead, he appointed Selim commander of an army to pacify his son. Seeing an opportunity, Selim advanced towards Istanbul. So, too, did his brother Korkud, arriving there at the end of March 1512, with no troops, but with cash to win the Janissaries to his cause. Korkud's effort to gain the throne failed. Instead, his brother Selim arrived with an army and, with Janissary support, forced his father to abdicate. He ascended the throne in April 1512. Bayezid died shortly afterwards, possibly of poison, while Korkud retired to Manisa.

Ahmed did not recognise Selim's Sultanate and continued to act as an independent ruler. In July, 1512, Selim crossed the Straits to Bursa, forcing Ahmed to withdraw to Amasya, and then to cross the eastern border of the Empire into Iran. From here, he wrote to Selim, suggesting that they should divide the realm. Selim rejected the suggestion and, in February 1513, Ahmed returned to the attack. Selim, meanwhile, had begun systematically to eliminate his rivals. Later in 1512, he executed all Bayezid's grandsons who were resident in Bursa and then, early next year, he sent a force against Korkud in Manisa.

When these troops entered Manisa, Korkud had fled. Selim's agents eventually found him in a cave near Antalya, hiding there, presumably, in the hope of escaping to Egypt or Rhodes, as his uncle Jem had done. They took him prisoner, and Selim's Chief Doorkeeper, Sinan Agha, executed him in March 1513, a few days' journey from Bursa. Ahmed, in the meantime, on his advance westwards, defeated Selim's forces under Biyikli ('the Moustachioed') Mehmed Agha and the Governor-General of Anatolia. At the beginning of April, Selim left Istanbul, leaving his son Süleyman to guard the city from the west. On 15 April 1513, he defeated Ahmed at Yenişehir, and captured the fugitive prince at Izmit, where Sinan Agha put him to death. This was not, however, the end of dynastic blood-letting. Ahmed had left his son, Osman, to guard Amasya in his absence, but when the Governor of Sinop attacked the city, Osman fled. Amasya surrendered, and Osman eventually became the captive of the Governor. In May 1513, on Selim's orders, he was executed, together with Ahmed's grandson, Mustafa, whose father, Prince Murad, was a fugitive in Iran and, by now, the only possible challenger to Selim's throne. However, with the execution of Osman, Selim clearly thought his throne to be secure.

In 1520, Selim died, leaving a single son, Süleyman, who succeeded him without a contest. By 1550, however, Süleyman was visibly an old man and, in 1552, apparently ailing. A few years later, the Habsburg ambassador, Busbecq, was to comment that he took pains to hide his poor complexion with 'a coating of white powder', and that 'it is generally believed that he has an incurable ulcer or gangrene in his leg'. Given their father's apparent infirmity, it was inevitable that his sons would begin plotting the succession, and inevitable too that, given the experience of his grandfather, Süleyman should begin to suspect their intentions.[25] The first victim of his suspicions was Prince Mustafa, his eldest son. In 1553, perhaps in order to squash rumours of his illness, he personally took command of the expedition to Iran. At Eregli, before the army had entered the passes through the Taurus mountains, he summoned Mustafa to his pavilion, and had him executed in his presence.

Why Süleyman should have suspected Mustafa in particular is a matter for speculation. Certainly, an undated leter which the Prince sent to Ayas Pasha contains strong hints that he was aiming for the Sultanate: 'Praise be to God, among the claimants to the inheritance, the capacity and aptitude which is in [me], your sincere friend, is manifest to your noble knowledge.' Furthermore, his popularity with the Janissaries and other sections of the army meant that, if he attempted a coup, he would probably be successful. It was, after all, the Janissaries that had forced Bayezid to retire and brought Selim to power. Ottoman historians, however, have plausibly attributed Mustafa's end to a conspiracy between Süleyman's wife, Hurrem, their daughter, Mihrimah, and Mihrimah's husband, the Grand Vizier Rüstem Pasha. Mustafa was Süleyman's eldest son, by the concubine Mahidevran. His other sons were by Hurrem, who wanted one of them to succeed to the throne and, to this end, wished to remove Mustafa. Her accomplice in the plot was her son-in-law, Rüstem Pasha, whom Ottoman tradition regards as responsible for Mustafa's death. Indeed, an anonymous petition to Süleyman accuses Rüstem Pasha of forging a letter from Mustafa to the Shah of Iran, in order to implicate the Prince in a charge of plotting with the enemy. It is therefore most probable that Hurrem and, through his wife, Mihrimah, the Grand Vizier plotted Mustafa's downfall, but it was also inevitable that, as Süleyman grew older, his other sons should take measures to secure the succession.

Süleyman completed the annihilation of Mustafa's faction by executing first his Standard Bearer, his Master of the Horse, and other office holders in his household, and finally his son. With the death, shortly afterwards of Hurrem's third son, Jihangir, two Princes remained, Selim and Bayezid, both sons of Hurrem.

Süleyman at first appeared to favour Selim, taking him with him on the campaign against Iran in 1553–4. Soon afterwards, however, he appointed Bayezid governor of Kütahya, nearer to the capital than Selim's residence at Manisa, a move which seemed to indicate that he favoured Bayezid. At this stage, it was probably their mother, Hurrem, who maintained the peace between the Princes, and between each of them and their father. After her death in May, 1558, the rivalry became more intense.

Faced with both Princes' attempts to influence factions in Istanbul, and Bayezid's attempts to disrupt essential trade in the area of Selim's governorship, Süleyman threatened to break all law and precedent by fixing the succession in the female line, and giving the throne to his sister's son, Osmanshah. At the same time, he ordered Selim to transfer to Konya, and Bayezid to Amasya. It was this decision that precipitated a civil war.

Since Amasya is further from Istanbul than Konya, Bayezid protested, delaying his departure from Kütahya until the end of October 1558, and then proceeding slowly with constant threats to turn back. At the same time, he taunted his brother with cowardice, and from his father demanded increased revenues for himself and his sons. When Süleyman, after promising, did not meet his demands, Bayezid's tone became even more strident: 'You are the Sultan of the World. When you tell lies like this, which of your words can we believe in future?' Bayezid did not confine his defiance to words. On his journey to Amasya, by seeking money from his father, taxing towns and borrowing, he began to raise cash for an army and also to recruit troops from among discontented fief holders, tribesmen and peasants.

Selim's tactic, which was probably a reflection of his character as much as a deliberate strategy, was the opposite of Bayezid's. He presented himself as an obedient son, submitting to every command of his father's. While forcing Bayezid to go to Amasya, Süleyman allowed Selim to proceed to Bursa and stay in the city until Bayezid had passed Ankara. Since Bursa was close to the capital, Selim's presence there would allow him to block Bayezid's route if, as he threatened to do, he should try to return and march on Istanbul. When Selim finally left for Konya, he asked his father for cannon from the ships at Izmir, as defence should his brother attack. Early in 1559, still receiving his brother's taunts, he reached Konya. By this time, it was clear that he was his father's favourite. When he had ordered the Princes to Amasya and Konya, Süleyman had also sent the Vizier Pertev Pasha to Bayezid and the Vizier Sokollu Mehmed Pasha to Selim, evidently to ensure compliance with his orders. Pertev Pasha

turned back after persuading Bayezid to continue to Amasya, while
Sokollu Mehmed remained with Selim as his advisor throughout the
crisis. He was later to marry Selim's daughter, Ismihan, and to occupy the post of Grand Vizier throughout his reign.

In addition to Sokollu, the Sultan ordered the Governors-General
of Anatolia and Maraş to join Selim with their forces and, when
Selim requested that the Governor-General of Karaman reinforce
him 'with the cavalrymen in his province, for the removal of sedition
and the protection of the honour of the Sultanate', Süleyman com-
plied. He also ordered Selim to enrol troops from among the peasantry. Since Bayezid had refused to disarm unless his brother did
likewise, a battle was inevitable.

By this time, Süleyman's support for Selim was public knowledge. In
addition to the forces which he had already assigned, he mobilised the
troops in Rumelia, eastern Anatolia and Syria, and despatched Rüstem
Pasha to Afyon, to keep a watch on developments. Süleyman's open
partisanship became more evident when he obtained a fatwa from the
Chief Mufti, Ebu's-su'ud, ruling that it was licit for the Sultan to fight
against and kill the forces of his rebellious son. At the same time, the
Mufti's own support for Selim is clear from a letter which he wrote to
the Prince during his struggle with Bayezid, saying that, as commanded, he was praying for a successful outcome.[26]

The declaration that he was a rebel left Bayezid with no choice but
to attack his brother before he had time to assemble his army. Selim,
meanwhile, had received a command not to attack, but to remain at
Konya to encounter Bayezid's forces. The two armies met at the end
of May 1559. After a battle of two days, Selim's army was victorious.

Bayezid, however, escaped with his life and fled to Amasya, once
again seeking his father's forgiveness. This Süleyman would grant
only if he would execute those who had 'led him astray.' Bayezid
largely disregarded the order, beheading only three of his suite. In the
meantime, in June 1559, Süleyman had sent Selim and Sokollu
Mehmed at the head of an army towards Amasya, and ordered the
governors on all his frontiers to intercept Bayezid if he attempted to
flee, while he himself waited at Üsküdar, ready to mobilise against his
son. In July, Bayezid fled from Amasya with his five sons, and an
army of several thousand which increased as he fled eastwards, main-

taining his men through forced loans and the levy of animals and provisions. Refusing to give battle to the pursuing Governors-General of Diyarbekir, Karaman and Erzurum, he continued his flight to Sa'dchukur on the border with Iran. Here he defeated a small force which came in his pursuit, but this did not improve his chances of success against the armies of the three Governors-General, Selim and Sokollu and, behind them, of Süleyman himself. In August, he crossed the border into Iran. In October, 1560, the Safavid Shah Tahmasb gave him a magnificent reception in his capital, Qazvin. Süleyman, in the meantime, disposed his troops along the frontier from Erzurum to Baghdad 'because it would be inappropriate for the army to disperse before definite news [of Bayezid] is known'. He was now in the same situation as his grandfather, Bayezid II, had been, when Jem was a captive of the French King, Charles VIII. Tahmasb could, at any time, invade, with an Ottoman prince in his following. To avert the danger, Süleyman opened negotiations with the Shah, only in December allowing Selim to return to Konya and the army to demobilise.

In Qazvin, Bayezid's position had dramatically changed. When suspicions arose between him and Tahmasb, the Shah, instead of treating him as an honoured guest, imprisoned him with his four sons, and began to disperse his followers, meanwhile continuing to negotiate with Süleyman. By July 1561, Süleyman had offered 900 000 ducats from himself, 300 000 from Selim, and the fortress of Kars, against Bayezid's delivery to Selim. Tahmasb, however, continued to delay until, in March 1562, his envoy reached Selim's court in Kütahya with the suggestion that Selim's good fortune depended on the execution of Bayezid and his sons, and that Tahmasb would grant this in exchange for peace 'until the Day of Resurrection'. Selim and his father accepted the proposal and, in July 1562, their envoys reached Qazvin to take custody of Bayezid. When the Shah delivered the Prince, Selim's man, Ali Agha, killed him, together with his four sons. The Sultan at the same time ordered the execution of his fifth son, an infant who was with his mother in Bursa. With this act Selim remained as the sole claimant to the Ottoman throne. In return for his compliance, Tahmasb gained a peace treaty, 500 000 ducats, and gifts for himself and his children.

The execution of Bayezid and his sons initiated a change in the mode of succession. From the time probably of Osman I, it had been customary for all the sons of the sultan to serve in governorships in Anatolia, and for each son to have an entitlement to the succession. From the time of Bayezid's death, only the eldest son served in the provinces, and it was the eldest who succeeded. The change, however, came about by chance rather than by policy. After 1562, Selim was Süleyman's sole surviving son, and succeeded to the throne unchallenged. At the time of his succession as Selim II (1566–74), he had only one son, the future Murad III (1574–95). His other sons he produced only after he had become Sultan and, by the time of his death in 1574, none of these was yet old enough to serve as governor. Of Murad III's sons, too, only the eldest, the future Mehmed III (1595–1603) became a provincial governor. This, too, happened by chance. Apart from Mehmed, all his other sons had been born after 1581 and the oldest, at the time of his death, was only eleven, and only on the verge of entitlement to a governorship. Nonetheless, precedent became practice and, after Süleyman's time, seniority rather than fratricide after success in a civil war became the normal principle of succession.

The practice of fratricide had never gained popular approval. The story of how Orhan's 'brother', Ali Pasha, voluntarily renounced rulership in favour of Orhan had come into being in the years 1422–3, at the time of the civil war at the beginning of the reign of Murad II. The tale does not reflect a real historical event, but rather the desire of contemporaries for a peaceful succession to the throne and an end to dynastic bloodletting. The redactor of the text even appended a moral to the tale: 'In those days Padishahs and Lords took counsel with their brothers. They honoured and respected each other. They did not kill each other.'²⁷ When official chroniclers tried to justify the practice, they had recourse to hyperbole. Mehmed Pasha of Karaman, a Chancellor and vizier to Mehmed II, added to his story of the execution of Bayezid I's brother, Yakub, the comment: 'As will not be hidden to those of sound intelligence, there was the possibility of great evil in [Yakub's] continuing to live. The Sultan dealt with him as was necessary and "necessity justifies what is forbidden." ' Similarly, in justifying Mehmed II's execution of his father's infant son by the daughter of Isfendyaroghlu, Kemalpashazade in the early sixteenth century wrote: 'Though he was still an immature child, action was taken by counsel of experienced elders . . . and it was seen to be the better course to root up the sapling of mischief, before it put forth leaves and branches.' Most famous, however, is the clause in the so-called 'Law Book of Mehmed II', justifying fratricide: 'To whichever of my sons the Sultanate shall be granted [by God], it is appropriate that he should kill his brothers for the good order of the world. Most of the ulema have declared this permissible.' This clause is, in all probability a sixteenth century addition to the 'Law Book',[28] by either Selim I or Mehmed III, to justify their own manner of accession, and represents an attempt to combat popular revulsion at what had happened.

Neither these literary flourishes nor the lavish distribution of gifts after each fratricide could reconcile popular opinion to the practice. A poem lamenting Prince Mustafa's death in 1553 and attacking his father was still in circulation in the eighteenth century, and in the words of another poet, Tashlijali Yahya (d. 1575–6), the Prince's 'error was not specified, his sin unknown . . .' and the 'souls of men were made level with the dust'.[29] A year after his death, an imposter claiming to be Mustafa could gain a following in his name. Prince Bayezid similarly left many mourners and adherents. In 1565, the authorities arrested a group of men in Beyşehir for a public perfomance which re-enacted his life.

Royal fratricide did not, however, end with the undisputed successions of Selim II, Murad III and Mehmed III. On the day of Murad's accession in 1574, the people of Istanbul witnessed his father's coffin emerging from the palace to the mausoleum by the Hagia Sophia and, following it, the coffins of the five child Princes. Murad III's Jewish physician, Dominic of Jerusalem, reports rumours that even the Sultan himself had hesitated to order their execution. On the night of the accession of Mehmed III in 1595, 'nineteen innocent Princes were', in the words of the contemporary historian Pechevi, 'dragged from their mothers' knees and joined to the Mercy of God'. When the cortège of nineteen coffins left the palace gate, another contemporary chronicler, Selaniki, noted: 'God Most High let the Angels around the Throne hear the crying and weeping of the people of Istanbul.'

It was, it seems, this 'crying and weeping' that brought the practice of fratricide to an end. When Mehmed III died in 1603, he left two sons, the fourteen-year old Ahmed and his younger brother, Mustafa. Both were confined to the palace, and it was a faction in the Inner Palace that fixed the succession on Ahmed, presenting the new Sultan on the Throne, as a *fait accompli*, before a meeting of the Imperial Council.[30] Ahmed died in 1617, when he was less than thirty, leaving a problem of succession for which there was no precedent. With the ending of the practice of fratricide, his brother Mustafa was still alive and, by the new principle of seniority, entitled to inherit the throne. Mustafa, however, was mentally defective, presenting the dilemma of whether to give the throne to a minor, Osman, or to an idiot, Mustafa. This time, the negotiations took place between a representative of the Inner Palace, Mustafa Agha, and two dignitaries from outside, the Deputy Grand Vizier, Sofu Mehmed Pasha and the Chief Mufti, Es'ad. It was, in Pechevi's version of events, Mustafa Agha's word that was decisive. He argued that public disapproval was inevitable if a child came to the throne when an adult candidate was available, and that Mustafa's 'defect in intelligence came from his long confinement . . . and he might come to his senses if he had contact with people for a while'. It was the decision of this group of people that brought Mustafa to the throne.

Mustafa's mental condition did not, however, improve. He was, Pechevi tells us, in the habit of 'scattering the gold and silver coins, with which he filled his pockets, to the birds and to the fish in the sea, and to paupers whom he met in the street', and when 'the Viziers came to present business to him . . . he would push their turbans and uncover their heads'. The same group of people as had planned his accession now plotted his deposition. In February 1618, they called the dignitaries and troops to the Palace, where Mustafa Agha locked the door on Mustafa and, as the Throne was set up, released Ahmed's eldest son, Osman, from the other.

Mustafa, however, survived in his confinement in the Palace and, four years later, came to the throne again, this time through the rebellion of a different faction. During his brief reign, Osman had, it seems, lost the confidence of the ulema who were, in particular, jealous of the influence of his spiritual advisor, Ömer Hoja. Most importantly, however, he had lost the support of the Janissaries through his treatment of them on the Polish campaign of 1621, and because, as the Janissary chronicler, Tughi, recorded, 'when they were guilty of a misdemeanour, such as being found in a tavern, they were flogged with four or five hundred strokes, put in stone-ships for punishment, and their livelihood and salary cut off'. It was clear to them that Osman wished to replace them with arquebusiers levied in Anatolia.

In 1622, the Janissaries rebelled, demanding the execution of the Grand Vizier, Dilaver Pasha, Ömer Hoja and others. When Osman, against the advice of the senior ulema, refused, the Janissaries forced their way to the Palace. They located Mustafa and, in Tughi's account, because the door of his chamber was inside the Harem, climbed onto the roof and, stripping the lead from the dome and the bars from the window, pulled Mustafa up with a rope taken from the curtains of the Council Chamber. He had, Tughi says, been deprived of food and water for two days. They took him out and, despite the ulema's declaration that it was illegal, swore the oath of allegiance, eventually forcing the ulema to do the same. When Osman finally acceded to their wish, and had Dilaver Pasha and Ömer Hoja executed, it was too late. Instead, they took Mustafa and his mother to the Old Palace and then to the Janissaries' Mosque. Inside the Mosque, a Janissary acquaintance of Pechevi, because he was literate, wrote the commands, in Mustafa's name, which made Mustafa's brother-in-law, Davud Pasha, Grand Vizier, and other appointments. When Osman appeared in the Janissary barracks and at the Mosque, no one listened to his appeals. Instead, Davud Pasha put him in a cart and escorted him to the Castle of the Seven Towers, where he ordered his execution. Meanwhile, the Janissaries took Mustafa and his mother back to the Palace.

Mustafa's second reign lasted a little more than a year. He had come to the throne through a Janissary revolt, which temporarily left power in the hands of his mother and her son-in-law, Davud Pasha. The dismissal as Chief Mufti of Osman's father-in-law, Es'ad, was clearly a move to strengthen this faction.The government did not, however, stabilise. Davud Pasha's vizierate lasted only twenty-six days, and he lost his life in January 1623. There followed a succession of grand viziers, whose precarious tenure depended on the support of the Janissaries or of the Cavalry of the Six Divisions, which they bought with donations from the Treasury. There were frequent riots and looting in the capital, and rebellion in the provinces. 'In short,' wrote Pechevi, 'it was spread abroad that the world was going to ruin and that the Sultanate was collapsing.' The solution of the new Grand Vizer Kemankesh ('the Bowman') Ali Pasha, the Chief Mufti Yahya and the other great ulema, was to depose the Sultan, of whom, in Tughi's words, they said: 'Our Sultan has no powers of disposal; he has no part in the loosing and binding of affairs. He is defective in intelligence. What is called the Imperial Rescript is the writing of the slave-girl, Sanevber . . .' The ulema sent word to Mustafa's mother that they would test his intelligence with two questions: 'Whose son are you?' and 'What day of the week is it?' His throne depended on his ability to answer these. His mother, however, prevented even this examination, and agreed to her son's deposition, provided that he escaped with his life.

In September 1623, the Grand Vizier and the Chief Mufti brought the twelve-year-old Murad IV (1623–40) to the throne, the second of Ahmed I's sons to become Sultan. At the same time, they brought his mother, Kösem, back from the Old Palace. When Murad died seventeen years later, only one male member of the dynasty survived. This was Ahmed I's younger son, Ibrahim (1640–8). Since there were no rival candidates to the throne, there could be no faction to oppose his succession.

Since Mehmed III's accession in 1595, fratricide was no longer the means of securing the throne. Nonetheless, the practice of father killing son, or brother killing brother had not stopped altogether. Shortly before his own death in 1603, Mehmed III had ordered the execution of his elder son, Mahmud, fearing that his popularity was a threat to his own throne. Osman II had executed his brother, Mehmed, in 1620, despite the refusal of his father-in-law, the Chief Mufti, Es'ad, to sanction the killing. Murad IV ordered the execution first of his brothers Bayezid and Süleyman when he was on campaign against Erivan in 1635, and then of Kasim in 1638.

It was, in the view of the Ottoman chroniclers, constant fear of execution that had clouded the mind of Murad's younger brother and successor, Ibrahim (1640–8). This Prince, wrote the contemporary Katib Chelebi: 'had spent most of his precious life in prison [in the

Palace], and when his brothers were martyred, fear for his life produced an imbalance in his temperament'. It was this mental instability that was to cause the next dynastic upheaval.

By 1648, Ibrahim's extravagant spending on luxuries during a time of war had emptied the Treasury, and his inappropriate appointments had created a political crisis. The decision to remove first the Grand Vizier and then the Sultan seems to have originated within the Janissary Corps, although as a plot by the officer Murad Agha, rather than among the common soldiers. The Janissary plotters allied themselves with the Chief Mufti, Abdurrahim and 'the great Mollas' and, at an assembly at the Mosque of Mehmed the Conqueror and later at the Janissaries' Mosque, declared the Grand Vizier, Ahmed Pasha, deposed and Koja Mehmed Pasha appointed in his place. The new Grand Vizier's men found Ahmed Pasha in hiding, and then 'a fatwa was issued and, after [Ahmed Pasha] had been strangled, his corpse was thrown out . . . That day in the Square, the people crowded round the corpse and cut it to pieces.'

With the removal of the Grand Vizier, the plotters agreed on the deposition of the Sultan and the accession of his seven-year-old son, Mehmed IV (1648–87). When the Queen Mother, Kösem, refused to send the boy to the Mosque for the ceremony of allegiance, the crowd went to the Palace, where Kösem still resisted, complaining, in Katib Chelebi's words: 'For so long, you have permitted my son to do whatever he pleases. You never once advised him . . .' The argument lasted for two hours. In the end, the Queen Mother capitulated only when they threatened to enter the Inner Palace. Then 'as was customary, the Throne was set up before the Gate of Felicity . . . the Sultan ascended the the Throne and the men of loosing and binding acknowledged allegiance.'

Ibrahim, Katib Chelebi continues, was imprisoned in the Palace. However, when a rumour spread that some of the courtiers of the inner palace were planning to restore him to the throne, the Chief Mufti, Abudurrahim, issued a fatwa permitting 'the deposition and execution of a Sultan who has caused disorder by not giving positions in the ulema and the army to worthy men, but to unworthy ones in exchange for bribes'. Then he, the Grand Vizier and the Agha of the Janissaries entered the Inner Palace with an executioner, Black

Ali. They unlocked the door of Ibrahim's prison, and Black Ali entered and strangled the deposed Sultan. The Sultanate now rested securely with Ibrahim's son, Mehmed IV. Effective power passed to Mehmed's mother, Turhan Sultan.

In the absence of any fixed law of succession, beyond the rule that the Sultan had to be a male member of the House of Osman, and another that prohibited descent in the female line, most of the Sultans between 1362 and 1648 had come to power as the candidate of a successful faction. Before the execution of Prince Bayezid in 1562, the competing factions formed around the princes themselves, when they served as provincial governors during the lifetime of their father. The actual or imminent death of the father was a signal for fratricidal strife between the rival princes and their supporters. From the reign of Selim II, the system changed. Neither Selim's son, Murad III, nor Murad's son, Mehmed III, had brothers who were old enough to serve as provincial governors, with the result that both came to the throne with no rival faction to contest their claim. This set some kind of a precedent since, from the time of Mehmed III, succession was in practice by seniority. Furthermore, public outrage at Mehmed III's execution of his nineteen brothers brought to an end the practice of automatic fratricide on accession to the throne, with the result that the Sultanate no longer passed in unbroken sucession from father to son.

The principle of seniority was a fragile one. Neither Osman II nor Murad IV felt that it gave them security against rival claims by their brothers, some of whom they executed in order to secure their own thrones. Nor did it mean that Sultans could dispense with the support of factions. After 1595, however, these could no longer form around the persons of princes, since the ruler's sons no longer served as governors in the provinces, but remained as prisoners in the palace. Ahmed I came to the throne through a coup by the courtiers of the Inner Palace, who had hidden Mehmed III's death from the world outside. It was a more representative group, made up of senior members of the Inner Palace, the civil government and the ulema that fixed the succession in favour of Mustafa, subsequently deposed him, and made Osman II Sultan. Osman's downfall and murder was the consequence of a Janissary rebellion, which brought Mustafa to the throne for a second time and temporarily placed power in the hands of his mother and brother-in-law. An alliance between the Grand Vizier, the Chief Mufti and the ulema secured Mustafa's removal from the throne, and the accession of his nephew, Murad IV. Ibrahim needed no faction to bring him to the throne, as he was the only surviving candidate; but it was again an alliance, this time between Janissary officers and ulema, that brought about his downfall and the accession of his eldest son, Mehmed IV.

Legitimisation

By 1650, the Ottoman dynasty had ruled for three and a half centuries. The Empire was the inheritance of the ruling Sultan which he, in his turn, would bequeath to his successor. The long continuity of the dynasty and the conception of the Empire as a kind of personal property made it unthinkable that the throne could pass to anyone who was not a member of the Imperial dynasty. These were aspects of dynastic rule which the ceremony of accession served to emphasise.

The first and most essential act in the accession of a new sultan was the actual possession of the throne. This, by itself, made him the ruler. This principle was most obvious in the case of Ahmed I in 1603. The Viziers, the Chief Mufti and the other ulema received notice that the Sultan required their attendance before the throne. None of them knew of Mehmed III's death, and they expected him to appear. Instead, the boy Ahmed I emerged from the Inner Palace and ascended the throne, leaving those present with no choice but to accept that he was Sultan. It was from this moment that his Sultanate began. The principle that physical occupancy of the throne marked the beginning of the new reign presumably dated from the earliest years of the dynasty, as presumably did the second element in the coronation, the oath of allegiance.

The first reference to this ceremony dates from 1481, when the contemporary chronicler, Bihishti, described the accession of Bayezid II: '[Bayezid] took his place at the heart of the heaven-like throne. The commanders of the left and right, and soldiers as numerous as stars made their act of allegiance and obedience, and the humble and the great made their submission.' The ceremony, one may assume, was much older than Bayezid, and clearly originated as a public or semi-public appearance of the new ruler before his troops and powerful subjects.[31] Bihishti gives the impression of a large gathering. From the late fifteenth century, however, the sultans increasingly withdrew from public sight. The act of allegiance became the preserve of a small group of powerful men, which usually included the grand vizier and the chief mufti, and took place before the throne in the Palace. The idea of the act of allegiance also changed over the centuries. In origin, one may speculate, an act of acclaiming the new sultan, from the mid-sixteenth century, it acquired a quasi-judicial significance. From the 1540s, Süleyman I promulgated the notion that the Ottoman Sultan was Caliph, that is the successor to the Prophet Muhammad and the Four Rightly Guided Caliphs as supreme head of the Muslim community. In sunni theology, the Caliph acquires office as the outcome of a contract which he makes with 'the men of loosing and binding' and it seems, therefore, that from the succession of Selim II in 1566, a function of the act of allegiance was to form the contract which confirmed the Ottoman Sultan as 'Caliph of the Muslims'.[32]

From the late sixteenth century, other elements became added to the ceremony of accession, which served primarily to emphasise the continuity of dynastic rule in the eyes of the people of the capital. Firstly, it became customary for the burial of the deceased Sultan to follow immediately the enthronement of his successor, a practice which emphasised continuity by linking the two ceremonies, and one which also prevented public knowledge of an interregnum. When Mehmed II had died in 1481, before his successor was able to ascend the throne, the Janissaries rioted and looted the capital. They stopped only when the viziers placed Mehmed's grandson, Korkud, on the throne until his father, Bayezid, arrived in the capital. The ceremony of delaying the funeral of the old sultan until the accession of the new one, served to conceal the death of a sultan and to prevent such a period of anarchy occurring again. The second new development in the accession ceremony was the pilgimage to Eyüp.[33]

Eyüp is a suburb of Istanbul on the Golden Horn where, according to a tradition which dates from the late fifteenth century, the body of

Abu Ayyub lies buried. Abu Ayyub, Muslim historians assert, was a Companion of the Prophet, who fell during the first Muslim siege of Constantinople. An Ottoman legend, which formed between 1453 and the early sixteenth century,[34] tells how, after the conquest of Constantinople, the Sultan ordered his spiritual guide, the dervish Akshemseddin, to find the tomb of Abu Ayyub, and the spot which Akshemseddin indicated became the site of the shrine. During the course of the sixteenth century, it became the most popular site of Muslim pilgrimage in or near the capital, linking the city with the Prophet and placing its conquest by Mehmed II within Muslim apocalyptic tradition.

From the accession of Selim II in 1566, the royal pilgrimage to Eyüp became an essential element in the ceremony of accession. The contemporary Selaniki describes how, 'according to the ancient law of the Ottomans, [the Sultan] set out to make a pilgrimage to the mausolea. Beginning with Abu Ayyub the Helper [of the Prophet], he went to the mausolea of his mighty ancestors, the Ottoman Sultans, and at each mausoleum bestowed 30 000 akches in alms.' The pilgrimage served to emphasise both the dynasty's link with the Prophet through Abu Ayyub and, through the visit to the ancestral tombs which, with their associated royal mosques, dominated the Istanbul skyline, the continuity of Ottoman rule.

Before 1566, however, the pilgrimage was not a part of the ceremony of accession. The practice had begun, it seems, in 1514. In this year, Selim I camped near to Eyüp at the start of his campaign against the Safavids, awaiting transport to ferry his troops across the Bosphorus. During the few days' delay, he made several pilgrimages to the relatively new shrine of Abu Ayyub and then, in the words of the Chancellor and historian Jelalzade: 'seeking the aid of the purified souls of his ancestors', he visited the tombs of his father and grandfather. His son Süleyman adopted the same procedure before his departure on the Hungarian campaign in 1526. A practice which had begun in 1514 almost by accident thus became a ritual. It was at first a ceremony which preceded a military campaign, and Selim II adopted it at his accession probably because he was to leave immediately to join the Ottoman army at Belgrade, as it was returning from Hungary with the corpse of his father. From the time of Selim II, however, it became part of the ceremony of accession. Henceforth, all newly enthroned Ottoman Sultans left the palace by water, went up the Golden Horn to the shrine at Eyüp, and returned by land, passing through the Edirne Gate in the city walls, and visiting in turn the tombs of the previous sultans. The ceremony, apart from demonstrating the Islamic and dynastic legitimacy of the new sultan, must have had another function. From the late fifteenth century, the sultans had increasingly withdrawn from public view[35] and, in particular, the act of allegiance had ceased to be a public event. The pilgrimage to Eyüp therefore became an occasion for the people of Istanbul to acclaim the new sultan before he withdrew to the Inner Palace.

There was a final element in the accession ceremony. In the seventeenth century, it became customary for the chief mufti or other high religious dignitary to gird the new sultan with a sword at the shrine of Abu Ayyub. The earliest reference to this ceremony appears, it seems, in Pechevi's account of the accession of Mustafa in 1617, suggesting that this was the first occasion on which it happened. It is conceivable that the grand vizier and chief mufti who had brought him to the throne wished to compensate for Mustafa's visible lack of capacity as a ruler by an act which ceremonially invested the Sultan with martial virtue. Whatever its origin, the ceremony of girding was to survive until the accession of the last sultan in 1918.

The ceremonies surrounding the accession of a new sultan reached their final form in 1617. At all times, however, it seems that the moment at which the new reign began was when the sultan took possession of the throne. The ceremonies which followed confirmed him in his dignity, but it was not they that created him ruler. This indicates a belief that rulership was inherent in the House of Osman, and this was a belief which the sultans had to justify.

The primal role of the Ottoman sultan was as a leader in war. The first Ottoman ruler, Osman, emerges from his depiction by the contemporary Byzantine chronicler, Pachymeres, as a war-leader whose successes against Byzantine forces attracted young men 'eager for booty' from far beyond his own realm. He was the first in a line of warrior sultans which lasted until Süleyman I, whose death before the fortress of Szigetvár in 1566 won him the title of 'warrior and martyr'.[36] Up to this time, the warrior image seems to have been an essential prop to sultanic authority. It is clear, for example, that when Bayezid II failed to lead his army in person in the war against the Mamluks between 1485 and 1490, he faced severe criticism. This the chronicler and panegyrist, Tursun Bey, tried to rebut by putting the criticism of Bayezid into the mouth of a callow youth, and having 'an old man [whose wisdom is as] deep as the sea' reply by saying: 'It is forbidden to enquire into the secrets of the Sultanate . . .'. It was to counter these criticisms, too, that Tursun Bey presented Bayezid's conquest of Kilia and Akkerman as greater even than the victories of his father, Mehmed the Conqueror.

By the mid-sixteenth century, however, the notion of the sultan personally leading his armies to victory was an anachronism. The huge extension of the Empire's boundaries between 1517 and 1540 meant that it was no longer possible to add vast territories to the Empire in a single year's campaigning. Warfare instead became prolonged with no spectacular conquests, and requiring the army for years in succession to overwinter near the front.[37] At the same time, the increase in the Empire's size added to the complexity of its administration. In these circumstances, the removal of the sultan from the capital for the whole length of a campaign became impossible and, from the reign of Selim II, the sultans rarely took to the field with their army. This change in circumstances also coincided with a change in the character of the sultans. Before Süleyman I, Bayezid II had been an exception in possessing a pacific temperament. After Süleyman, few Sultans had a taste for warfare.

Nonetheless, the notion of the sultan as a warrior persisted. In 1596, after three years of unsuccessful warfare against the Habsburgs, Mehmed III, at the instigation of the Janissaries, the Grand Vizier and his father's tutor, Sa'deddin, accompanied the army to Hungary. Under the nominal command of the Sultan, the Ottoman troops captured Eger, and, at the battle of Mezö-Keresztes, snatched victory from defeat. Mehmed, however, refused to 'lead' another campaign, and the war continued for another ten years. The last spasm of the tradition of warrior sultans came with the reigns of Osman II, who led an unsuccessful campaign against Poland in 1621, and Murad IV, whose reconquests of Erivan in 1635 and Baghdad in 1638, gave him a place in Ottoman tradition as the last sultan who in person led his troops to victory. Both Osman's and Murad's campaigns came at a time when the Ottoman élite were aware of a need to reform and renew the institutions of the Empire and, within this context, they were an attempt to re-establish the old tradition of the sultan as war leader.

Within a polity that existed to wage war, the sultan's role as a leader in war was in itself enough to legitimise his rule. War, however, also bestowed a religious legitimacy. In Islamic law, Holy War against the infidels is an obligation on the Muslim community, and in their battles against Christian enemies, the sultans could portray themselves as fulfilling God's Law.[38] It became customary in this context to refer to the sultans in particular, and to their troops in general, as *ghazis*, a word which has an everyday sense of 'warrior' or 'raider' but which, when Islamic jurists and historians adopted it as one of the terms for a person engaged in holy war, also acquired the sense of 'holy warrior'.[39] The notion of the sultan as a *ghazi* was particularly effective as a legitimising device, since epic accounts of heroic deeds against the infidels also formed a strand in popular Muslim culture, and 'Books of Holy War' constituted a branch of popular literature. The *ghazi*, therefore, is a figure who appears both in learned works, and in popular entertainments. In consequence, by adopting 'Ghazi' as a title, the sultans could appeal to a wide spectrum of their Muslim followers. It seems likely that the Ottoman rulers adopted this title during the fourteenth century, following the example of earlier Muslim sovereigns, but clear evidence is lacking. The earliest certain reference to this claim is in the work of the poet and moralist, Ahmedi who, in his brief verse 'history' of about 1400, presents the 'Ottoman Kings' and their followers as holy warriors, and prefaces the passage with a description of the qualities of a *ghazi*. In later chronicles, these virtues adhere almost exclusively to the person of the sultan. By the late fifteenth century, in the words of the chronicler, Neshri, the Ottoman sultans had become 'the pre-eminent ghazis ... after the Apostle of God [Muhammad] and the Four Rightly Guided Caliphs'. This was an idea which was to linger until the end of the Empire, even when the sultans had withdrawn from leadership in war. In the last years of the Empire it enjoyed a revival when, following Osman Pasha's heroic defence of Pleven in 1876,

Sultan Abdülhamid II (1876–1909) added the word 'the Ghazi' to his Imperial Cypher, which appeared at the head of documents, on coins and in public places.

The idea of the sultan as a *ghazi* had two functions. Firstly, it justified the Sultans' wars against Christians as the fulfilment of God's Command. Secondly, it justified the Sultans' possession of former Christian territories. Land which Muslims take from infidels passes, in law, into the dominion of the Muslim sovereign. The Sultans were therefore legitimate rulers of land which they had taken from Christians. This presents an obvious problem. The Ottomans fought against Muslims as often as they did against Christians, and conquered as much Muslim as Christian territory.

To justify war against Muslims, Ottoman chroniclers in the fifteenth century presented the Muslim adversaries of the Ottomans – for example, the Karamanids – as hindering the Holy War. In about 1460, the historian Shükrullah depicted Murad I as consulting with the ulema and acquiring a religious sanction to attack his Muslim neighbours, because these were planning to attack him from the East, while he pursued the holy war in the West. An Anonymous Chronicle of 1485, explained how the Sultan's Muslim neighbours incited the infidels against the Ottomans and then, when they were preoccupied, 'seized the opportunity to attack from the other side'.

In the sixteenth century, Ottoman propaganda changed. Throughout this century, and into the seventeenth, the sultans' most powerful Muslim opponents were the Safavids of Iran. The Safavid shahs, unlike the Ottoman sultans, were shi'ites, and, most significantly, claimed quasi-divine status as heads of the Safavid Religious Order. These heterdox claims allowed the Ottomans to present the Safavids as rebels against the legitimate authority of the Ottoman sultans and, more importantly, as apostates and infidels. The Safavids, the Ottoman Chief Mufti, Ebu's-su'ud declared in 1548, were 'rebels and, from many points of view, infidels'. This statement allowed Ebu's-su'ud, like his predecessors and followers, to rule that war against the Safavids was legitimate holy war. So appalling, in fact, was Safavid heresy that 'fighting against these is more important than fighting the infidels'.

These were the justifications for waging war against Muslims. A further justification, not so much for waging war as for acquiring Muslim territory, was to emerge in the late fifteenth century. The most important and the longest lived dynasty in pre-Ottoman Anatolia had been the Seljuks of Rum who had ruled in central Anatolia for much of the twelfth and thirteenth centuries. The dynasty had become extinct shortly after 1300. A series of legends in the earliest Ottoman chronicles tell how a Seljuk sultan called Alaeddin had granted lands in Söğüt on the Byzantine frontier to Osman's father; and how the same sultan had bestowed on Osman a 'horse-tail standard, drum and robe of honour' as symbols of investiture. The purpose of these tales was clearly to give the Ottomans legitimacy by linking them to the Seljuks. The stories reached their definitive form in 1485, in Neshri's 'History of the Ottomans'. In Neshri's version, it was Alaeddin I (d. 1237) who granted land to Osman's father, and Alaeddin III (d. 1303) who sent the standard, drum and robe to Osman and, being childless himself, appointed Osman as his successor. This last development of the story made the Ottomans the legal successors to the Seljuks, and therefore rightful heirs to Seljuk territory in Anatolia. An obvious corollary to this was that the dynasties that had established themselves in the old Seljuk realms were mere usurpers of land which, by right, belonged to the Ottomans. Warfare against them and seizure of their territory was therefore legitimate. Ottoman historiography down to the twentieth century was to enshrine Neshri's story of the Seljuk inheritance.

These elements in Ottoman propaganda and mythology legitimised warfare and the acquisition of territory in east and west. However, the claims of the sultan to rulership as members of a particular family required a further justification. This the Ottoman genealogy provided.[40] The Ottoman 'family tree' seems to have originated early in the reign of Murad II (1421–51), at a time when the Ottomans felt the need to reassert their claims to rulership after the defeat by Timur and the civil war. The key figure in the creation of this genealogy was Yazijioghlu Ali, whom Murad seems to have employed in his chancellery in the 1420s. Yazijioghlu found the materials in the legends of Oghuz Khan, the mythical ancestor of the western Turks. Oghuz Khan, in this tradition, was the grandson of Noah through Japheth and had six sons and twenty-four grandsons, who were ancestors of the legendary twenty-four tribes of the western Turks. Yazijioghlu traced the Ottoman line through the senior son and senior grandson of Oghuz Khan, so giving the Ottoman sultans a hereditary primacy among Turkish monarchs. He reinforced this message with a tale of how, on the collapse of the Seljuk dynasty, the Turkish rulers of Anatolia elected Osman as their overlord on grounds of his descent. Yazijioghlu, in fact, based his genealogy on a version of the Oghuz legends which appears in a Universal History which the chronicler and statesman, Rashid al-Din, composed for the Ilkhanid ruler, Ghazan Khan (1295–1304). This names the grandson from whom the Ottoman House descended as Kayi. Other versions of the genealogy grew up during the course of the fifteenth century, but all make the Ottomans descend from the senior son of the senior son of Oghuz Khan.

The Oghuz genealogy arose at a time when the Islamic monarchs of Anatolia and Azerbaijan, who were the immediate rivals of the Ottomans, were all Turkish, and compiled their genealogies from similar Turkish materials. The Ottoman genealogy served to show that the Ottoman sultans were superior by descent to these neighbouring dynasts. By the mid-sixteenth century, when the political situation of the Empire was quite different, and the culture of the élite was cosmopolitan and Islamic rather than Turkish, the genealogy lost some of its legitimising force. Nonetheless, it remained fossilised within the historiographical tradition until the twentieth century. There was, however, one change. From the early sixteenth century, under the influence of a Prophetic tradition which foretold the conquest of Constantinople by the sons of Isaac, historians began to trace the early genealogy through Shem and Esau rather than through Japheth.[41] This genealogy is at odds with the original version of the dynastic descent, since it disassociates the sultans from the Turks, whom tradition depicts as descendants of Japheth, and links them through Shem to the Arabs ('Semites'). This, however, is in keeping with the increasingly cosmopolitan character of the Ottoman élite in the sixteenth and seventeenth centuries, who would no longer comprehend the significance of the Turkish descent from Oghuz Khan, but for whom a link with the Arabs might indicate a connection with the Prophet.

The Oghuz genealogy, in its various versions, provided the sultans with a physical descent which vindicated their claims to rulership. To claim a religious legitimacy, they also required a spiritual genealogy and evidence of divine approval. They acquired this through a series of popular tales which appeared first in late-fifteenth-century chronicles, and later became embedded in the historiographical tradition. In Islamic belief, God speaks to man in dreams, and a number of stories in the early chronicles tell how God promised Osman and his father in dreams that He would exalt their descendants. The most famous of these episodes, which became canonical in later tradition, occurs in the chronicle of Ashikpashazade of about 1484, and describes Osman's dream when he was a guest of the dervish, Edebali. In it, Osman sees a moon rising from Edebali's breast and entering his own. Then a tree grows from his navel and covers the world. In the shadow of the tree were mountains, with water flowing from their feet, and people drinking the water, cultivating their gardens and making fountains. In the morning, Edebali interpreted the dream as meaning that God had granted rulership to Osman and his descendants. At the same time, he betrothed his daughter to Osman. She became the mother of Orhan, and so the female ancestor of the dynasty.

The function of the story is to show, firstly that God had intended the Ottoman dynasty to be rulers, and secondly to provide it with a spiritual genealogy through Edebali. Edebali, whether he was real or legendary, was a figure who occupied an important position in the spiritual lineage of the Vefaiyye Order of dervishes, to which Ashikpashazade also belonged. In the Vefaiyye, as in all Dervish Orders, each master has his own spiritual master, leading back in an unbroken chain to the founder of the Order. In the case of the Vefaiyye, this was to Abu'l-Wafa of Baghdad (d. 1107). From this point, the Order traces its spiritual lineage back to the Prophet Muhammad and, through the Angel Gabriel, to God. Ashikpashazade's story of Osman's marriage to Edebali's daughter, therefore, links the Ottoman sultans to his own Order, the Vefaiyye, and provides them with a spiritual descent, going back through Abu'l-Wafa to the Prophet. This religious lineage complements the political genealogy going back through Oghuz Khan to Noah.

The genealogies of the dynasty and the dream stories derive their material from popular belief, and in this reflect the relatively modest pretensions of the sultans in the fifteenth century, when the stories emerged. In the sixteenth and seventeenth centuries the claims of the Sultans became more grandiose and, at the same time, more dependent on learned tradition.

In 1453, Mehmed II captured Constantinople and, through its possession, acquired from the defeated Byzantine Emperor claim to the Roman Imperial title. This did not, however, feature prominently in Ottoman titulature until a century later. From 1526 onwards, the sultan's greatest opponents in the west were the Habsburg Emperors, of whom the greatest was Charles V, King of Spain and Holy Roman Emperor: rivalry between Süleyman I and Charles V was a dominant theme of the mid-sixteenth century.[42] In 1547, Süleyman concluded a treaty with Charles and his brother, Ferdinand of Austria, in which he granted peace in exchange for tribute for the lands which the Habsburgs held in Hungary. In the text of the treaty, Charles no longer refers to himself as 'Holy Roman Emperor' but simply as 'King of Spain',[43] and it was from this moment that Süleyman regarded himself as having wrested the title of Roman Emperor from his rival. Henceforth, epithets such as 'Caesar of Caesars' begin to appear in Ottoman titulature.[44] The importance to the sultans of the Roman title became apparent at the time of the negotiation of the Treaty of Zsitva-Torok in 1606. The Habsburg Emperor would not accept the title 'King', but neither would Ahmed I concede the title 'Caesar'. The compromise which the Ottomans found was, in the seventeenth and eighteenth centuries, to keep the title 'Caesar' and to address the Habsburg rulers as 'Emperor'.[45]

The Ottoman claim to the title of Roman Emperor was not the end of the sultans' imperial pretensions. In the mid-sixteenth century, Süleyman added 'Chosroes of Chosroeses' to his sultanic titles, presumably, since 'Chosroes' is a generic name for the ancient rulers of Iran, in celebration of his victories over the Safavid shahs. By the midpoint of his reign Süleyman styled himself 'Sultan of the Arabs, Persians and Romans'. However, the most important title that he bequeathed to his successor was 'Caliph' or 'Imam', words which, in a political context, imply supreme headship of the Islamic world.

The concept of the Caliphate is one that derives from Islamic theology and historiography. The sunni Muslim historians give the title to the four successors of the Prophet – Abu Bakr, Umar, Uthman and Ali – whom they revere as the 'Rightly Guided Caliphs.' Thereafter, the title became attached in particular to the Abbasid rulers between 750 and 1258. These associations gave the term a historical dignity. From the tenth century onwards, the sunni theologians began to develop a theory of the Caliphate, although they prefer the terms 'Imam' and 'Imamate' to 'Caliph' and 'Caliphate'. The Imam, in their view, achieves office as the result of a contract which he makes with one or more 'men of loosing and binding' and, for the contract to be valid, the Imam must fulfil a number of conditions. These vary from writer to writer, but one on which all agree is that the Imam must belong to the Prophet's tribe, the Quraish. In sunni theory, therefore, the Caliphate or Imamate is contractual rather than hereditary.

Caliph, as a title of the Ottoman sultans, appears for the first time in 1424, but its use at this time was rhetorical rather than specific. It was not until the reign of Süleyman I that the Sultan began to claim the title ex officio. His chief propagandist in this was the Chief Mufti, Ebu's-su'ud who, realising that the Ottoman sultans could not claim to be from the Quraish – the genealogy was already fixed –, ignored the classical theory of the Caliphate,[46] and instead asserted that the Ottoman Sultan occupied this position by divine right. He was the one upon whom 'God Most High has bestowed the Caliphate of the Earth'. He asserted, too, that the Ottoman sultans were the 'inheritors of the Great Caliphate' – a reference to the Rightly Guided Caliphs – and that they inherited the office 'from father to son'. This was a view which directly contradicted the classical theory, whose only influence on the Ottomans seems to have been the form of the oath of allegiance. These assertions effectively make the the Ottoman sultans direct heirs to the Rightly Guided Caliphs, who were the immediate successors to the Prophet. It was therefore a claim which implied rulership of the entire Islamic world. It was also one which was to last, with many vicissitudes until the end of the Empire.[47]

There were therefore many strands to Ottoman claims to legitimacy, each of which had emerged at a different time to meet different circumstances. The original justification of the sultan's right to rule was as a leader in war. By 1400 at the latest this role had been sanctified, and he had become a leader of holy war. Warfare against Muslim dynasties was justified, because these distracted him from this sacred task. At the beginning of the fifteenth century, following defeat and civil war, the sultan re-established his claim to rightful rulership by the creation of the Oghuz genealogy. The fabrication, later in the same century, of a spiritual genealogy and of tales which 'proved' that Ottoman rule was divinely ordained, gave a religious sanction to the Sultanate, which paralleled its secular descent from Oghuz Khan. By 1500, the sultan began to legitimise his rule in Anatolia on the foundation of a story that made the Ottomans legal heirs of the Seljuks. From 1453, but especially after 1547, he could claim to have inherited the title of Roman Emperor, while victories over the Mamluks and Safavids made him 'Chosroes' and 'ruler of the Arabs and Persians'. In the sixteenth century, Süleyman laid claim to the title and office of Caliph. Of these legitimising devices, those of Holy Warrior, successor to the Seljuks and Caliph were to survive into the twentieth century.

3 Recruitment

By the sixteenth century, the sultan governed his domains largely through the 'Slaves of the Porte'. These were the men whom he had recruited to serve as ministers, provincial governors or troops, and whom he paid through the Treasury or by the allocation of fiefs. It was, however, a system of government that had taken two centuries to evolve.

An account of how the earliest sultans governed their principality, and who entered their service can only be brief and highly speculative. The fifteenth-century chronicles present the first ruler, Osman (d. *c.*1324), as distributing lands and commanderships to members of his family and to the warriors in his entourage. The names of the warriors seem, in fact, to be inventions, deriving from toponyms in north-western Anatolia[1] rather than from accurate historical memory, but the idea that Osman delegated powers to his family and soldier companions might nonetheless be true. The same practices probably continued into the reign of his son, Orhan (*c.*1324–62). The names of his four brothers and a sister appear as witnesses to his trust deed of 1324; the Byzantine Chronicle of John Kantakouzenos mentions his brother, Pazarlu, as a commander at the battle of Pelekanon in 1328; and his son Süleyman Pasha acted as a semi-independent military commander until his death in 1357.[2] His son Halil seems to have been governor of lands along the Gulf of Izmit in the late 1350s. The impression is of an informal mode of government, with offices shared among members of the ruling family and its entourage.

This system very probably came to an end during the reign of Murad I (1362–89). Murad, it seems, was the first sultan to execute his brothers, with the result that the Ottoman realms were no longer the shared patrimony of all members of the ruling family. Sultans' sons continued to act as provincial governors and army commanders, but strictly under the tutelage of their fathers, and without the freedom of action that Süleyman Pasha had apparently enjoyed.

Another factor bringing a change in the mode of government was the expansion of Ottoman territory and the emergence of the marcher lords. As the Ottoman realms became larger, the conquering lords acquired lands and revenues in the new territories, which established them as local powers, with their own troops and retainers. The foremost of these lords was Evrenos (d. 1417) who, during Murad's reign, acquired vast landholdings in Macedonia, which his decendants were to retain until the twentieth century.[3] Other marcher lords – notably the families of Mihal, Malkoch[4] and Turahan – established themselves in the newly conquered lands in Europe in the late fourteenth and early fifteenth centuries. Quite possibly there was a similar phenomenon in Anatolia, but the sources are too meagre to permit anything more than speculation. As Evrenos and other conquerors established themselves in the new territories, another family, the Chandarlis, emerged as both military leaders and political advisors to the sultans. The first of this line, Hayreddin Halil (d. 1387), combined the roles of army commander and vizier to Murad I. For this reason, Ottoman tradition regards him as the first grand vizier, a post which his descendants were to occupy until 1453.[5] At the same time, the Ottoman conquerors frequently did not remove the dynasties that had ruled in pre-Ottoman times, but instead maintained them as vassals under Ottoman suzerainty.

These developments made Murad I's position different from that of his father and grandfather. In the sense that he no longer had to share authority with his brothers, he was evidently stronger than they. At the same time, however, the appearance of the marcher lords, and the continued rule of semi-independent local dynasties clearly limited his power. He was not an absolute ruler, but rather the most powerful in a confederation of great lords, who were his allies and vassals rather than his servants. To establish their own position, therefore, Murad and his successors had to secure a following who were subordinates rather than confederates, and whose loyalty to the Ottoman dynasty was unquestionable. The source of such a following, in the absence of modern institutions, could only be the sultan's household, and it was largely through members of their households, employed as governors or soldiers, that the Ottoman sultans came to govern the Empire.

Islamic law and tradition combined with the particular circumstances of the Ottoman dynasty to define the nature of the imperial household. The exclusion from government of the female line, the practice of fratricide between 1362 and 1595, and the seclusion of the princes thereafter made the sultan the unchallenged patriarch of the dynasty, severely limiting the role of the imperial family at large. Only the sultan's sons had a share in government after 1362, and then only under surveillance as provincial governors. In the absence of blood relatives on whom to confer office or devolve power, the sultan had to turn to other members of the household. Law and precedent determined who these were to be.

Islamic law permits slavery and, by creating a category of 'licensed slaves', makes it possible for them to carry out transactions on their owners' behalf. Slaves could therefore become trusted and important figures. Furthermore, despite their servile status, they could, through membership of an élite household, occupy an elevated social rank. The 'slave household', therefore, became a feature of Islamic society, and Islamic rulers had, from early Abbasid times in the eighth century, created armies of slave troops, and used slaves in the government of their realms. This was true also of the Seljuks of Rum and probably also of the successor dynasties that had ruled in Anatolia before the Ottoman conquest. The Seljuks in the thirteenth century had employed slaves as troops and as military commanders, in the palace and in the government, and had even established a school in Konya for their education.[6] The Byzantine emperors, too, employed bodies of foreign troops whose origins set them apart from the ordinary subjects of the Empire.[7] With these precedents, it was perhaps inevitable that the Ottoman sultans should form their household on the institution of slavery and the employment of 'foreigners'. Furthermore, with the elimination of the sultan's adult blood relations from the household and government, his dependence on slaves became more pronounced. Recruitment into the imperial service usually, therefore, meant recruitment as a slave.

Islamic law is clear on who may and may not be enslaved. In the first place, it forbids the enslavement of Muslims, although slaves who convert to Islam do not lose their servile status. Secondly, it defines which non-Muslims may legally be enslaved. For this purpose, it divides the world into the Muslim and non-Muslim realms, and affords no protection to the life or property of persons living in the non-Muslim world. This means in practice that it is permissible to kill or enslave non-Muslims living under a non-Muslim sovereignty. The status of a non-Muslim living under a Muslim sovereignty is different. By virtue of paying a capitation tax levied on adult males, they enjoy the status of protected infidels. The law protects their lives and property and they may not be enslaved. Slaves, therefore, originate as captives from the non-Muslim world. Once brought into the Realm of Islam, they become property that their owner may sell, hire out, bequeath or give as a gift. The status is also heritable. The children of slaves have servile status, but if one of the parents is free, the child follows the status of its mother. Owners can also free slaves by a simple verbal declaration or by a number of other devices.[8]

Slaves could therefore enter a household by capture, purchase, inheritance or gift, and the Ottoman sultans acquired slaves by these means presumably from the early decades of the Empire. By the end of the fourteenth century, however, recruitment on a large scale had become systematic, using two methods.

The first of these was to impose a levy on the captives which Ottoman soldiers brought back from raids and wars in Christian territories. The law that gives the Muslim sovereign the right to a one-fifth share of the spoils of war justified the practice, although there is no evidence to suggest that the sultans made the levy at precisely this rate. It seems quite possible that the practice began during time of Osman or Orhan, but Ottoman chronicles locate its origin in the reign of Murad I. They attribute it to Chandarli-Hajreddin and a certain Kara Rüstem of Karaman who, they assert, advised Murad: 'take one-fifth of the prisoners coming from raids, and if someone does not have five prisoners, take twenty-five akches for each prisoner'.[9] It is doubtful whether this tale is in detail true. However, raids into Europe became more intense and widespread during Murad's reign, increasing the number of prisoners available. At the same time, Murad needed to bolster his own political supremacy by increasing the size of his household, and these factors perhaps combined to necessitate the institution of a formal and regular levy during his reign.

The main purpose of the levy was to provide recruits to the Janissaries, the sultan's household Infantry, and the chroniclers in fact tend to associate the establishment of the levy with the foundation of this corps. Other recruits, however, went to serve directly in the Palace or, after their establishment at an uncertain date, in one of the Six Divisions of household cavalry.

For about a century and a half after the time of Murad I, warfare and raiding continued to be a bountiful source of recruits to the sultan's service. With the establishment, probably during the reign of Bayezid I (1389–1402), of a body of raiders who received land and tax exemptions in return for an obligation to conduct razzias into enemy territory, raiding became a formalised activity.[10] This ensured a constant flow of captives, even outside periods of formal warfare. The Burgundian, Bertrandon de la Brocquière, for example, recalls how, in 1432, in the Maritsa valley in Bulgaria, he encountered 'about twenty-five men and ten women, tied together with heavy chains about their necks. They had recently been captured in the Kingdom of Bosnia during a raid by the Turks, and were being taken to Adrianople by two Turks to be sold.' The chronicler Ashikpashazade remembers with relish an incursion over the Danube in 1440, where 'the raiders were so sated that they were selling exquisite slave-girls for the price of a boot'. Every war and every successful raid produced its crop of slaves, and on these the Sultan claimed the right to impose the levy.

It is difficult, in the absence of records, to establish how effective and how systematic the sultans were in extracting their share of prisoners-of-war. The reign of Bayezid II (1481–1512), however, saw an attempt to systematise and codify Ottoman law, and it was no doubt in this context that Bayezid, in 1493, issued a decree to regularise the collection of prisoners for imperial service. The order was in response to a request for guidance from a certain Yusuf, who was the officer responsible for making the levies from the young men captured by the raiders in Rumelia. The decree lays out how

the commander of the raid is to be rewarded with twenty-five of the lads which he brought in by his own efforts, the officers in charge of the levy with five each that they won themselves, the higher ranking officers with one each of those that they won themselves, and the lower ranking officers of the raiders with one between two of those that they won themselves. The rest, from the age of ten to seventeen are to be taken [by Yusuf]. If some of those over the age of seventeen show signs of being suitable, they too are to be taken, the owner being paid three hundred akches from the Treasury for each lad. The lads must not be crippled or sick, or show signs of reaching puberty, or have begun to grow a beard.

To ensure that the captive lads reached the capital, the decree orders both the officer in charge of the levy and the commander of the raid to make a register, which their representatives must bring with the prisoners. This allowed the authorities to check whether any of the lads had gone missing between assembly on the frontier and arrival in the capital. A copy of the same decree exists which substitutes for the formula: 'I [the Sultan] have commanded . . .' the phrase: 'The law is as follows . . .', suggesting that this particular decree to Yusuf acquired the status of a general law regulating the collection of prisoners for the sultan.

Wars and raids into Europe continued to be a source of slaves during the sixteenth century, but probably not on the same scale as before. Before 1526, the line of the Danube and the Sava formed the boundary between the Ottoman Empire and the Kingdom of Hungary, and raids across the rivers ensured a continuous flow of prisoners. However, after the defeat of the Hungarian King at Mohács, and the establishment on the throne of a king loyal to the sultan, Hungary ceased to be a raiding ground. In 1541, central Hungary became an Ottoman province, bordering on the well fortified Habsburg lands to the west. In these circumstances, the regular, large scale incursions of the Ottoman raiders were no longer possible. Furthermore, in 1595, the destruction in battle of many thousands of the raiders put an end to their organisation in its traditional form. These factors limited the supply of slaves. Writing in the 1640s, the historian Ibrahim Pechevi commented on how the supply of slaves had ceased, which had formerly allowed governors on the frontier to maintain large households and retinues. At some time, the practice of levying a proportion of prisoners for the sultan must also have stopped.

Prisoners, however, continued to come into the Empire, especially from Tatar raids into Russia and Poland, from the Caucasus, and from sub-Saharan Africa via Egypt, and the sultan continued to recruit slaves from these sources.

It is clear, nonetheless, that the supply of slaves from outside the Empire's borders was insufficient. The sultans therefore established a second and more reliable source of supply. This was the *devshirme* or 'Collection',[11] whereby the sultans levied the slaves from among their own Christian subjects. In Islamic law, the practice was illegal, since non-Muslims in the Empire had the status of protected infidels, and so could not be enslaved. The question of its legality, however, although a subject of debate in the sixteenth century,[12] never affected practice, and the Collection became the main source of recruitment into imperial service between the fourteenth and late sixteenth centuries, and the practice did not disappear entirely until the eighteenth.

It is impossible to establish exactly when the Collection began. However, a sermon of 1395 by the Metropolitan of Thessaloniki laments: 'What would a man not suffer were he to see a child whom he had begotten and raised . . . carried off by the hands of foreigners, suddenly and by force, and compelled to change over to alien customs and become a vessel of barbaric garb, speech, impiety and other contaminations?'[13] Two years later, an Italian, Caluccio di Salutati, reported that the Turks 'seize boys of ten to twelve years for the army'.[14] Both comments seem to refer to the Collection, indicating that the institution was in existence by the 1390s. It came into being, therefore, sometime during the fourteenth century. This was a period when the Turks of western Anatolia seem to have had a limited understanding of Islamic law and probably, therefore, only a hazy notion of the statutes of slavery in terms of which later generations were to understand the Collection and the status of the sultan's servants. This may explain the easy acceptance of an institution that was, in Islamic terms, illegal.

In 1438, a Brother Bartholomew de Jano again referred to the Collection in his 'Letter on the barbarity of the Turks'. Here he reports how the sultan was taking one in ten Christian boys 'from ten to twenty years, whom he makes his special slaves and shield-bearers and, what is worse, Saracens'. He spoke of the practice as 'something which the Sultan never used to do', as though it were something new. This indicates probably that Brother Bartholomew was simply unaware that the Collection of youths was a regular event, but possibly that it had ceased during the civil war between 1402 and 1413, and was only now beginning again.[15]

In one respect, Brother Bartholomew's account was certainly wrong. It is unlikely that the sultans ever collected youths at the rate of one in ten. The Serb, Constantine Mihailović, who served in the Ottoman army between 1453 and 1463, in fact refers to the lads which the sultan collected in his own realms as *chilik*, a word which clearly derives from Persian *chile-yek* (one in forty), and obviously represents the rate of the levy. This is also the rate which appears in a document from the early sixteenth century, which served as a template for sultanic decrees ordering the collection of lads for imperial service. The text begins: 'I [the sultan] have ordered that, in the judicial district of [. . .], comprising [x] households, and in that of [. . .] comprising [y] households, [a] and [b] lads respectively, a total of [c], be collected, at the rate of one lad per forty households . . .'.

The rate of the Collection, therefore, was one lad in forty households. The document continues by laying out the procedure which the Collection was to follow. The official in charge was to take with him a Janissary officer and

go without delay to these judicial districts, to warn the people by proclamation . . . and, without omitting a single village, to gather all the sons of the infidels and of the notables, together with their fathers, and have them brought before him, and to inspect them personally. If any infidel has several sons, he is to enregister and take and detain a good one for Janissary service, of the age of fourteen or fifteen or, at the most, seventeen or eighteen; but he is not to take the son of a man not having several sons and, after taking one, he is to send the others back to their father, without any injustice.

An early seventeenth-century work entitled *The Laws of the Janissaries*, which offers remedies for current deficiencies in the Janissary Corps by reference to the ideal practices of the past, lays out the principles of selection. The officers in charge should not take the sons of important men, priests, or men of good descent. They should not take only sons, because these help their fathers in farm work, and if they are not there, the father will not be able to cultivate his land and pay taxes. They should not take orphans, because they are 'opportunist and undisciplined'; boys with a squint, because they are 'perverse and obstinate'; tall lads, because they are 'stupid', or short lads, because they are 'trouble makers'. Nor should they take lads who are 'fresh faced and beardless', because they appear 'despicable to the enemy'. It was forbidden, too, to take married men or crafts-men. Men who could earn a living through a craft would not be pre-pared to endure hardship.

There were other categories which the author of *The Laws* exclud-ed. Above all, they should not take Turks. If they were to do so, their relatives would also claim to be slaves of the sultan and demand tax exemptions, or seek to enter the Janissary Corps. At the same time, governors would think them to be genuine imperial slaves, leading to indiscipline. The Turks, too, the author describes as 'merciless, and with very little in the way of piety or religion'. Instead, the author continues, the benefit of taking the offspring of infidels is that 'when they become Muslims, they become zealous for the religion, and enemy to their family and dependents'. This was probably an exag-geration. A document of 1572 shows a Janissary presenting a petition to the sultan on behalf of his family in Albania,[16] indicating that he had neither 'become enemy to them', nor lost contact. Similarly, a case in the Istanbul Court Register for 1612–13 has an entry which records a case where a governor in Anatolia – clearly a product of the Collection – collaborated with his brother, a local priest, in making illegal exactions from the population of his district.[17] These cannot have been isolated cases of continuing contact. Nonetheless, any lad levied through the Collection owed his present livelihood, with its regular salary, and his future career to the sultan and not to his fami-ly or kin and, in this sense, the most vital link with his background was severed.

There was, however, one Muslim group that was liable for the Collection, and these were the Bosnians. The reason, according to the author of *The Laws*, was that at the time of the conquest of Bosnia in 1463, the inhabitants had at once submitted to the sultan and accept-ed Islam. When the sultan offered them a privilege in return for their actions, they requested that they become subject to the Collection, and since then, the sultan had taken lads from that region. Most of these, *The Laws* informs us, were allocated to the palace or to the Palace gardens. *The Laws* dates from the early seventeenth century. Nonetheless, since the cadastral surveys from after 1463 do show that there were many conversions in Bosnia following the Ottoman conquest,[18] its story of how the Collection started in Bosnia does have some credibility.

The areas where the sultans made the Collection were the Balkan Peninsula and Anatolia, with the former providing most recruits, presumably because it was an area with a majority Christian population. In Anatolia, the majority population was Turkish, and so not eligible. Furthermore, some areas of Anatolia seem at certain times to have been exempt. The author of *The Laws* informs us that it was against regulations to collect lads from, for example, the area between Karaman and Erzurum, 'because they are mixed with Turcomans, Kurds and Georgians'. Nor did the sultan extend the Collection to the Arab lands after their conquest in the sixteenth century.[19]

These were the areas and populations that were subject to the levy, and the principles on which the officers in charge made their selection. Once they had chosen and assembled the lads, the next task was to bring them to the capital. The first stage was to organise the boys, according to the sixteenth-century template, into groups of 100–150, or into groups of 200 according to *The Laws*, and then to make a separate register for each group. For every lad, they should, according to the template, show 'his name, the name of his father, the name of his village and of the holder of the fief to which the village belongs, and a description of the boy, so that if he disappears, reference to the register will show who he is and where he comes from, so that he can easily be recovered'. A purpose of the registers was also to prevent roughnecks joining the consignments of boys, and to prevent corruption on the part of those making the levy, for example, by selling their charges privately as slaves. Thus assembled, the lads travelled under guard to Istanbul, staying overnight in villages. The template decree forbids them to stay for more than one night in order to minimise the hardship to the villagers who provided food and shelter.

Once in Istanbul the escorts delivered them to the Agha of the Janissaries.

The Agha had first to check that the boys who arrived in Istanbul tallied with those whose descriptions appeared in the registers, noting those that had fallen ill and any that had not arrived. As a further precaution against fraud, the decree required the officer in charge to make a second register, so that when he later arrived in the capital, the Agha of the Janissaries could compare the two registers, a process which would allow him to detect any falsifications. *The Laws* describes the next stage in the proceedings. The two Janissary officers subordinate to the Agha – the Agha of Rumelia and the Agha of Anatolia – would appear with their clerks and, in the presence of the Agha, a surgeon would examine and circumcise each of the boys in turn. They would next allocate the best looking lads to the Palace. These were the ones who would receive an education in the Palace Schools[20] and sometimes, after serving the person of the sultan, receive appointments to governorships or other offices. The physically strong ones they appointed to work in the Palace gardens. This too could sometimes lead to a privileged position.

The destination of most of the lads, however, was the Janissary Corps, the sultan's personal infantry troops. Admission to the Corps was not, however, immediate. Whereas the good-looking boys received an education in the palace, the future Janissaries received an entirely different form of training. The first step was to sell each boy – traditionally, according to *The Laws*, for one gold piece – to Turkish farmers in Anatolia. The payment was a token: it was to prevent these boys refusing to work, on the grounds that they were the slaves of the sultan. They remained 'with the Turks' for about seven or eight years. The reason for this practice was, in the first place, to accustom the lads, through regular farm work, to hard physical labour. For this reason, *The Laws* insists, it was forbidden to sell them to 'judges or the learned', because these have no landholdings where the future Janissary 'would become accustomed to hardship.' Equally, it was forbidden to sell them to tradesmen because, instead of going to war, they would earn a living through craft; or to the people of Istanbul, 'because their eyes would be opened wide by being in the city, and they would not suffer hardship'. The second reason for the practice was to teach them the rudiments of Islam, through living in an Islamic environment, and finally to teach them Turkish. Before the large-scale admission of Turks into the Janissaries from the late sixteenth and early seventeenth centuries, very few members of the Corps would have spoken Turkish as a native language. It was, however, the lingua franca of this polyglot body of soldiers, and indeed of the ruling élite of the Empire, and its acquisition was essential.

The supervision of the lads who were 'with the Turks' was the responsibility of the Aghas of Rumelia and Anatolia. Each of these had a staff of ten to fifteen men, who were responsible for the capture and sale of any who tried to escape. At the end of the period, they recalled the boys, who were by now adult, and allocated them a wage of an akche per day. *The Laws* gives seven or eight years as the period which the boys spent with Turkish farmers, but this was probably an average and not a precise figure. Rather, the Aghas recalled the youths as vacancies arose in Istanbul.

The next stage was not, however, to enrol the recruits into the Janissaries. Instead, the officer known as the Agha of Istanbul allocated each youth to one of the thirty-one dormitories in the barracks of the novices near the entrance to the Palace. These, *The Laws* informs us, performed duties for the sultan. It mentions in particular the transport of firewood to the Palace, manning the vessel which brought snow from the mountains near Bursa to the sultan's ice-house, and manning the vessels which carried troops over the Bosphorus to and from Üsküdar. In describing the duties of the Novices, the author of *The Laws* unfavourably compares the situation in his own time, when there were 12 000 novices, but only twelve ships, with the age of Süleyman I (1520–66), when there were 4000 novices and 72 ships. He complains, too, of the frequent loss of boats in his own day, as a result of unskilled seamanship.

These were not the only tasks that the novices performed, and not all novices lived in the barracks outside the Palace. Others served in the various imperial gardens or, for example, as palace laundrymen or cooks. A more significant number became apprentices in the naval dockyards in Istanbul or Gallipoli, where documents from the first half of the sixteenth century show them working as caulkers, carpenters, oarmakers, bombardiers, blacksmiths, pulley-makers and oakum workers.[21] The practice of employing them in the dockyards continued into the seventeenth century.[22] Records from later in the sixteenth century also record them working as blacksmiths and builders in royal construction projects, such as the Selimiye Mosque in Edirne in the early 1570s.[23] Others, on completing their service 'with the Turks', became apprentices in technical units of the army, such as the Imperial Gunners or the Imperial Armourers. These apprenticeships in dockyards, building sites and military units may, strictly speaking, have contravened the prohibition on the Janissaries learning a trade, but the crafts which they learned were those which were essential to the prosecution of war, and so for the efficiency of the Janissaries as a military unit. It was after their service as novices that the sultan finally drafted them into the Janissary Corps. This event took place not on fixed occasions, but as and when vacancies occurred.

Towards the end of the sixteenth century, the Collection as a source of recruitment to the Palace and to the Janissary Corps began to break down and, during the course of the seventeenth century, Collections became increasingly rare. After the early eighteenth century, they ceased altogether. The author of *The Laws*, who composed his work in order to lay out for Ahmed I (1603–17) past practice as a basis for present reform, saw changes in the method of recruitment to the Janissaries as the source of anarchy. Later reform tracts, from the reigns of Osman II (1618–22) and Murad IV (1623–40) support him in this view.

Exactly what replaced the Collection as the source of recruitment to the palace is not clear, although some new entrants appear to have come from the households of great men. In the case of the Janissaries, the pattern of admission to the Corps is a little clearer. From the fourteenth century until the late sixteenth, recruitment was through the levy on prisoners-of-war or the Collection. It was apparently only in the reign of Selim I (1512–20) that the Janissaries received permission to marry, and this permission applied only to retired men and some of the officers. Nor could the Janissaries, as slaves themselves, legally acquire concubines. This limited the number of legitimate offspring and so prevented the Janissaries forming a hereditary caste. In time, as the ban on marriage became less stringent, it became customary to admit as novices the sons of Janissaries 'who were capable of service on the ships'. These, however, formed a small minority. Lists of Janissaries and novices from the sixteenth century[24] show very few of them with a Muslim father.

It was from about 1570 that the old pattern of recruitment began to collapse. From the reign of Selim II (1566–74), if the author of *The Laws* is to be believed, it became quite usual to accept into the Janissaries the sons of members of the Six Divisions of household cavalry, or of other officers of the imperial household. This he saw as a source of corruption. Far worse, however, was the admission of native-born Muslims. They used various means to achieve this. Some, *The Laws* tells us, bribed the clerks to inscribe them as being sons of household cavalrymen. If they claimed to be the sons of Janissaries, it should have been possible to check this assertion, but they avoided this difficulty by claiming that their fathers belonged to a different division in the Corps. *The Laws* also describes how, in the time of Murad III (1574–95), Turks presented themselves alongside the consignments from the Collection, bribing the surgeons who carried out the circumcisions and persuading the clerks, who registered them, to enter their parents' names as 'senseless names in infidel languages'. Far more, however, entered the Janissaries as protégés of the commanders and officers. This practice *The Laws* describes as an 'illness', which had altogether removed the need for the Collection.

This change in the method of recruitment, which allowed Turks and other Muslims into the Janissaries was, for the author of *The Laws*, a disaster which had led to a loss of military prowess and defeat in wars. In the 1630s, the reform writer, Kochi Bey, agreed with him, noting that, in his own time and especially since the 1620s, the Corps had admitted 'city boys of unknown religion, Turks, Gypsies, Tats, Kurds, outsiders, Lazes, Turcomans, muleteers and camel-drivers, porters and confectioners, highwaymen and pickpockets, and other people of various sorts'. He, too, saw a return to the old ways as essential if the Janissaries were to regain their former glory.

These authors were undoubtedly acccurate in their observation of how recruitment to the Janissaries had changed. The transformation was not, however, as they believed, simply the result of corruption.

Enrolment in the Janissaries did bring benefits, notably a regular salary from the Treasury, and this no doubt encouraged the ineligible to seek to join the Corps illegally. The main factor, however, was the increase in the number of Janissaries between the mid-sixteenth and seventeenth centuries. Ottoman Treasury documents record 7886 Janissaries in 1527. By 1567, there were 12 798 and, by 1609, 39 282.[25] This growth was in response to military need. As the use of firearms increased during the course of the sixteenth century, and especially during the Austrian war of 1593–1606, infantry began to play a more important role on the battlefield, with the result that the number of footmen increased in relation to the number of cavalrymen.[26] One way in which the Ottomans met this demand was to increase the number of Janissaries. As a result the old methods of recruitment no longer met the demand for new entrants, and the only way to raise numbers was to admit Turks and other groups that regulations had previously excluded. Furthermore, with this expansion in numbers, the role of the Janissaries changed. They no longer formed a small corps of élite household troops, but became instead one of the largest contingents in the Ottoman army. This put them, in practice if not in theory, outside the imperial household, and in so doing changed their status from household slaves to free men. In these circumstances, their recruitment as slaves was no longer relevant.

The seventeenth-century reform writers placed great emphasis on the heritability of status and the exclusion of ineligible groups from holding office, and saw failure to observe these principles as a symptom of decline. In response to this worry, Ahmed I (1603–17) did in fact abolish the practice of allowing the sons of office holders other than Janissaries into the Corps, but the prohibition clearly made no difference. The expansion of the Corps in response to new methods of warfare made changes in Janissary recruitment inevitable.

4 The Palace

Palaces

Since the sultan himself was the ruler of the Ottoman Empire, the centre of government was wherever he happened to be. This meant *par excellence* the Palace, but when he left his residence, the government followed. Before the accession of Selim II (1566–74), such absences were frequent, since sultans often led military expeditions in person, and were often absent from the capital during the campaigning season. When this happened, some at least of the sultan's ministers would accompany the campaign, as would the treasury to pay wages and make purchases, and clerks with financial and other registers to record, for example, deaths in battle and new appointments to replace the fallen.

The early sultans were clearly very mobile. Ibn Battuta in 1333, described Orhan (c.1324–62) as possessing 'nearly a hundred fortresses, which he is continually visiting and putting to rights'. In the following century, the sultans became more sedentary than Orhan had been, but an annalist who compiled a chronology of the reign of Murad II (1421–51) still noted whether the Sultan during the summer went on campaign, remained in his capital, Edirne, or went to a summer resort. Mehmed II (1451–81), it seems, continued the practice of spending time in upland pastures, at least as a means of escaping the plague epidemics which visited Istanbul, but after his time, it seems that the sultans normally left the Palace only for military campaigns, hunting expeditions or pleasure trips. After 1566, with the exceptions of Mehmed III (1595–1603) who accompanied the army to Hungary in 1596, Osman II (1618–22) who led the Polish campaign of 1621, and Murad IV (1623–40) who recaptured Erivan in 1635 and Baghdad in 1638, the sultans no longer went to war in person. The Palace – or rather, Palaces – had become their permanent place of residence which they rarely left. Thus, over three and a half centuries, they gradually withdrew from daily contact with their subjects and, except on ceremonial occasions, from public view.

It is not clear whether Osman, the first of the Ottoman line, established a permanent residence. Ottoman tradition, however, presents him as declaring his sovereignty at a town called Karajahisar, which may correspond to the Greek town of Malagina in the Sakarya valley. This was the site of a Byzantine bishopric,[1] and it is possible that Osman took up residence there in the old Bishop's Palace. It was also at Malagina that the captive Greek cleric, Gregory Palamas, met Orhan in 1354, describing it as 'a village built on a hill, surrounded by mountains . . . enjoying a cool climate even in summer', two days' journey from Bursa. Orhan's successor, Murad I (1362–89) seems also to have spent time in the same place. The Genoese in 1387 did not conclude their treaty with him in the royal capital of Bursa, but at Malagina. The text records that it was 'enacted in Turkey in a certain small settlement called Mallaine, inhabited by the aforesaid lord'.[2]

By the time of Orhan, however, Bursa was the royal capital and site of the Ottoman Palace, although details of this building are elusive. Orhan must have taken over or constructed a royal residence at Bursa after he had captured it in 1326, and his successors continued to reside there at times until 1402, when a detachment of Timur's army pillaged the city. It did not survive the sack as a main residence, but it seems that, until the sixteenth century, members of the sultan's family, such as his grandchildren, might live there.

Orhan's successor, Murad I, built the first Palace of which there is a description, and which was to become a far more important residence than whatever survived or was rebuilt at Bursa after 1402. This is the Old Palace at Edirne, which the Ottoman traveller Evliya Chelebi was to describe when it was still standing in the second half of the seventeenth century. Murad must have started building immediately after the conquest of the city, probably therefore in the early 1370s. According to Evliya, Prince Musa (Rumelia, 1411–13) extended and fortified the building. Its massive outer wall, Evliya tells us, formed a square with a single iron gate in the north side. This is probably much as Bertrandon de la Brocquière had seen it in 1433, when he had entered the Palace by this gate, and seen Sultan Murad II emerge from his chamber into 'a very large courtyard', and take his seat in a gallery along its end. These accounts suggest that the buildings within the Palace were ranged within a square outer wall, around a single courtyard.

In 1451, the last year of his life, Murad II began the construction of a second palace in Edirne, which was to replace the Old Palace as a royal residence.[3] Although, by the time of its completion in 1454, work had already begun on a palace in the newly conquered Istanbul, the Edirne Palace continued in use. Murad began the construction outside the city, on the west bank of the river Tunca. His son, Mehmed II continued the work, again on a plan of buildings ranged around an inner and an outer courtyard. He also constructed a bridge from the Palace to the island in the river, which was to serve as a pleasure garden and a hunting ground. Successive sultans added to the palace. Süleyman I (1520–66), Evliya Chelebi remarks, spent his winters here when he returned from his Hungarian campaigns. He added a bridge from the eastern bank of the river to the island, water depots, and an Imperial Chamber in the Harem. His successors added kiosks, but the Palace was to reach its greatest size during the reign of Mehmed IV (1648–87) who, as his contemporary, Evliya Chelebi notes, 'because he is fond of hunting, spends most of his time in the city of Edirne'.

The conquest of Istanbul meant that the Edirne Palace did not become the chief royal residence except during the reign of Mehmed IV. In 1454, Mehmed II ordered the construction of a new palace in the centre of the city, on the site of the Byzantine Forum of the Bull. By 1458, it was complete. The contemporary historian, Tursun Bey, informs us that, within the square formed by the outer walls, he constructed the imperial harem 'to whose courtyard the sun could not find a path, . . . delightful palaces and pavilions for his enjoyment, and for the comfort of his intimates and pages . . . , protected by trustworthy and pious eunuchs'. Between the palace buildings and the outer walls, he created a private hunting ground, 'filling it with wild beasts'. This Palace did not long remain in use as the Sultan's principal residence and as the seat of his government. When building work was finished, Mehmed II immediately ordered the construction of a new Palace. On its completion, the Old Palace became exclusively a residence for the women of the Imperial Harem.

The site which the New Palace[4] was to occupy seems to have appealed to Mehmed's imperial ambition. Its outer gate led to the Hagia Sophia – to the Ottoman imperial mind, a symbol of Roman sovereignty – and it occupied a hill on a promontory, commanding views from Europe over to Asia, and across the Bosphorus which links the Black Sea to the Mediterranean. The building work took place during the 1460s and 1470s, according to a basic plan which has survived the numerous additions and alterations of later centuries.

An outer wall divided the new palace and its extensive gardens from the city, with the old city walls along the Golden Horn and the Sea of Marmara protecting it from the seaward side. The palace itself occupied the highest position within this enclosure. Entrance was by the Imperial Gate, close to the apse of the Hagia Sophia, and leading into the First Courtyard. Once through the gate, the visitor saw on the left the Byzantine church of St Irene, which served as an armoury for the Palace, and ranged around the courtyard were the dormitories of the novices, storehouses and other domestic and service areas. One may imagine the court as an area of activity and noise. At the far end, opposite the Imperial Gate was the Middle Gate, crenellated and flanked with two 'Frankish towers.' Through this gate was the Second Court. Entry was permissible only to members of the court and government, and to members of the public who were presenting petitions to the sultan's Imperial Council. No one, apart from the sultan, could enter the court on horseback, and strict silence was the rule. Commentators in the seventeenth century remarked on the use of sign language in the palace and this, no doubt, enabled courtiers to communicate. In the far left corner, the visitor saw the Council Chamber, which Süleyman I (1520–66) was to replace in the 1520s with a more imposing building. It was here that the imperial council, the central organ of the sultan's government, held its sessions. Ahead lay the Gate of Felicity, with a colonnade on either flank. On the right were the vast kitchens, which the architect Sinan (d. 1588) was to renovate after a fire in 1574 and, behind the wall on the left, the Imperial Stables. These simple structures formed a backdrop for the elaborate ceremonials of the court.

The Third Court, beyond the Gate of Felicity, was the private residence of the sultan and inaccessible not only to the public but even, except on formal occasions, to the Empire's statesmen. Immediately behind the gate stood the Chamber of Petitions, which Süleyman I was to reconstruct at the same time as he built the new Council Chamber. It was here that the sultan gave audiences and received foreign embassies. When imperial decrees refer to petitioners submitting their letters 'to my Threshold of Felicity' or 'to my Exalted Threshold' they refer, metaphorically, to the sultan seated in the Chamber of Petitions on the threshold of Gate of Felicity. In the far right corner of the Third Court itself stood the sultan's Inner Treasury and the bathhouse. In the far left was the sultan's Privy Chamber. Behind the court, where the land slopes steeply to the sea, was a garden. Later sultans were to add new structures to the Third Court, most notably perhaps the Erivan Pavilion and the Baghdad Pavilion, which Murad IV (1623–40) added to celebrate the reconquests of the these cities.

The Third Court, as the sultan's private residence, gave entrance to the Harem. In Mehmed II's original plan, this seems to have been small, but it appears that more women came to live in the Palace during the course of the sixteenth century. This tendency began probably in the reign of Süleyman I, during the ascendancy of his wife, Hurrem, before her death in 1558, and became particularly pronounced during the reign of Murad III (1574–95), who moved his Privy Chamber into the Harem. It was during the reign of Mehmed III (1595–1603) that the Queen Mother and her entourage took up residence in the Palace. It grew still further in the early seventeenth century, when the practice of sending the princes to governorships in Anatolia ceased, and the practice of royal fratricide was no longer normal. On the death of a sultan, however, the ladies of his harem left for the Old Palace, which remained, apart from the eunuchs, an exclusively female residence.

The two buildings in the Third Court, to either side of the main gate, were the Great Chamber and the Small Chamber. It was here that the sultan's pages lived and received their education. Since many of these were to graduate from service as courtiers in the Inner Palace, to service in governing the Empire, the Chambers in some ways were the foundations of the sultan's power.

The household

As far as was politically feasible, the sultans ruled the Empire through members of their own household, whom they had appointed to government office. This was a tendency which began probably in the late fourteenth century, and had become very pronounced by the late fifteenth. In its structure, the sultan's court was typical of any large household in the Ottoman Empire, or in the Islamic world. It was larger, richer and more magnificent than the households of viziers, provincial governors or other wealthy Muslims, but not, in its essentials, different.

Relatively few members of the imperial household were legally free: the sultan himself, his children and other family members, teachers and religious instructors, prayer leaders, doctors, the mutes, dwarves and wrestlers who served for his entertainment, and a few others. The rest were slaves. In a great Muslim household, however, to be a slave was not necessarily to occupy a menial position, and the affection in which owners often held their slaves or manumitted slaves is evident from the many deeds of trust which name them as beneficiaries. Furthermore, servile status did not necessarily imply a low social position. A person's rank in society depended less on their status as slave or free person, than on the status of the family or household to which they belonged. A slave in a wealthy and powerful household could enjoy greater prestige than a person who was free but poor. It was proximity to the great that bestowed repute. The most honoured position below that of sultan himself, was to be his slave, and it was, as far as possible, through their slaves that the sultans ruled the Empire.

The sultan acquired some of his slaves as gifts. Bayezid II (1481–1512), for example, received the Genoese lad, Menavino, who served as a page from 1505 until his escape in 1514, from a pirate. Others he purchased. Murad IV bought the Pole, Bobovi, who served as a palace musician until his dismissal in 1657, from the Tatars who had captured him in a raid. Others came as prisoners-of-war. The most bounteous source, however was the Collection, the levy made on the sultan's own non-Muslim subjects. A few, such as the Abkhazian Grand Vizier, Melek ('the Angel') Ahmed Pasha,[5] were not slaves, but had received an education in the Palace after presentation to the sultan.

From the time of its completion in the 1470s, the most favoured of the sultan's slaves received their education at the New Palace, in the Great and Small Chambers in the Third Court. This was not, however, the only site of a Palace School. Some such institution had presumably existed in the Old Palace at Edirne in the fourteenth century and the first half of the fifteenth, and a school continued to function in the New Palace in that city even after Istanbul had become the main residence of the sultan. Within Istanbul, there were schools outside the Palace itself. The first of these was the Galata Palace, a foundation of Bayezid II (1481–1512); the other, after 1536, was the Palace of Ibrahim Pasha on the Square of the Hippodrome. Nonetheless, the school in the Third Court remained the most prestigious. In Bobovi's day in the mid-seventeenth century, a page had to serve an apprenticeship in one of the Outer Palaces before admission to the Greater or Lesser Chamber.

The pages, the Genoese Menavino tells us, entered the Palace School 80–100 at a time. They first learned to speak 'vulgar Turkish', the lingua franca of the palace and of the Empire's cosmopolitan élite. After five or six days, they began to work on the alphabet. The boys spent the entire day under the supervision and fierce discipline of the eunuchs and the masters of the school. These taught them the alphabet, to read and recite the Quran, and the articles of the Islamic faith. They could then proceed to study Arabic and Persian 'both vulgar and learned', two languages that were essential for writing and understanding literary and official Turkish, and which were both in use for keeping legal and financial records.

Menavino entered the Palace School in 1504. When Bobovi came there a century and a half later, the curriculum seems hardly to have changed. The purpose of the education, Bobovi emphasises, was 'not to make great scholars of them, and not to demand more than a great respect for books, especially for the Quran'. Their progress, he says, depended on their own interests. Those who studied Islamic law could hope eventually to acquire a lucrative position as Imam at one of the Royal Mosques. Those who mastered Persian and calligraphy could hope to become clerks to the Ttreasury, the Imperial Council, or in the household of a great man. Those who studied 'law and the ordinances of justice' might acquire a governorship. Since the pages were ultimately to form a military class, they also received instruction in the military arts, Bobovi describing their training and skills in archery, horsemanship, wrestling and javelin throwing. A graduate of the palace schools had therefore received both a martial and a literary training. In both aspects, however, their education remained mediaeval. Their military prowess belonged, by the seventeenth century, to the sportsfield rather than to the battlefield, and it was still the mediaeval Persian classics that formed their literary tastes.

During their period of education, Menavino and Bobovi tell us, the lads could not leave the Palace, their only contact with the outside world being through the eunuchs called the 'gate-boys'. Their formal education ended, Menavino tells us somewhat inconsistently, at the age of twenty-five. Bobovi says 'after seven or eight years'. Those who were to leave appeared before the sultan who, in Menavino's time, 'gave each one a cloak of brocade and one of his best horses, and admonished them: If anyone has seen a wrongdoing in the Palace, they should not make it known, but keep it to themselves.' Those who left the Palace at this time normally, it seems, joined one of the Six Divisions of cavalry attached to the Palace. This was not an exclusively military or ceremonial position, although these cavalrymen fought in battle and rode on either side of the sultan on campaign and in processions. Members of these Divisions, as educated men, often had other functions, notably as tax collectors. Attachment to the palace cavalry was, the Venetian Ramberti observed in the mid-sixteenth century, 'like a ladder to mount to higher positions'. A cavalryman might also receive as wife a girl from the Imperial Harem who, like him, would be a slave of the sultan.

Not all the lads did leave the palace on completing their education. Those who remained became pages of the Chambers of the Inner Palace, directly serving the person of the sultan. The organisation of the chambers, as Menavino describes it, remained largely intact at the time of Bobovi. The Chamber with the lowest status was, it seems, the Larder where, Menavino says, 25 pages of 20–22 years, serving under a eunuch, 'are charged with the care of this room where there are juleps, sweets and all sorts of spices and everything necessary for the private cuisine of the Sultan'. Above the pages of the Larder, and again under the eye of a eunuch, came the pages of the Treasury, responsible for the sultan's personal treasure in the Third Court, where 'there are various sorts of garments of brocade, gold and silver vessels of many kinds, jewels and money . . .'. To these Ahmed I (1603–17) and Murad IV respectively added and enlarged the Campaign Chamber, which Bobovi describes as 'the Chamber of the Pages who serve the Sultan when he goes on journeys'. The most prestigious, however, was the Privy Chamber.

It was the pages of this Chamber who served the sultan directly, and from whom he selected those that were in constant attendance. Already in 1433, Bertrandon de la Brocquière had observed Murad II leave his room in the Old Palace at Edirne with 'only those boys who accompany him to the door of the Chamber', suggesting that by this date the sultan already chose a retinue from the lads of the Privy Chamber. Menavino, in the early sixteenth century, stated that 'the Sultan's principal and favourite [pages of the Chamber] are only three', defining them as the Cloth Bearer, 'who continually gives him to drink and brings his clothes which he needs in the rain'; the Water Bearer, 'who brings his water wherever he goes, and shirts to change into'; and the Weapons Bearer, 'who carries his bows, arrows and sword'. In the second grade were fifteen boys who 'make the bed, sweep, make the fire and similar things'. In the next century and a half, the organisation of the Privy Chamber seems not, in its essentials, to have changed. The number of pages in attendance seems to have increased slightly – Ramberti in 1548 mentions six, and Bobovi in 1658 mentions four, the Weapons Bearer, the Cloth Bearer, the Stirrup Bearer and the Turban Lord – and the total number of boys in the Chamber had increased by the mid-seventeenth century to 40.

A page who had graduated from the Larder to the Privy Chamber had before him the prospect of a career in the highest offices of the Empire, the Privy Chamber itself in some respects symbolising the ideals of sultanic government. A page could serve there only if he had caught the eye of the sultan, and preferment within it depended entirely on royal patronage. The pages themselves were slaves, who performed the most menial tasks for their master, whether practical or ceremonial. At the same time, they occupied a position of immense privilege, since proximity to the sultan meant proximity to the greatest source of power and patronage. Equally, the pages who attended most directly on the sultan could converse with him and, to some degree, control the information which he received. In this way, they could begin to exercise political power. Bobovi noted in particular the special position of the Chief Barber who shaved the sultan daily, and therefore, unlike the grand vizier, had the opportunity to speak to him every day. The Privy Chamber was, in fact, a microcosm of how the sultans governed. A page might graduate from the Palace to become a governor or vizier and use his links to the Palace to his political advantage. But he could never forget that he was also a slave who was dependent on the sultan's patronage for advancement, and was equally liable, at the sultan's behest, to abasement and execution.

The pages of the Chamber were not the only residents of the palace, although they were the ones who came regularly into close contact with the sultan and were, for this reason, the most likely to receive preferment in the world outside. They could also graduate to offices within the Palace, which again brought them face to face with the sultan: for example, as Master of the Standard, who kept the flags and banners of the sultan's army; as Master of the Stable who, already in Menavino's day, had under him 900 men, and who assisted the sultan to mount his horse; or as Head Gatekeeper, in command of – in Menavino's day, 500 and, in 1600, over 2000 – Gatekeepers, who formed a military corps, guarding the Palace gates and carrying out executions. There were other officers of the Palace with privileged access to the sultan: the Head Falconer and Master of the Hounds, who would accompany him on the hunt, and especially the Head Gardener. The gardeners of the Palace, as their name implies, worked in the Palace gardens, producing flowers, fruit and vegetables for consumption in the Palace and for sale. They were also soldiers, and acted as royal bodyguards. Indeed, during the Janissary revolt of 1622, which ended with the murder of Osman II (1618–22), the Janissaries hesitated before entering the Palace for fear of ecountering the armed gardeners. The Head Gardener also had, from before Menavino's day until the late eighteenth century, jurisdiction of the shores of the Bosphorus up to the Black Sea. He was also helmsman of the sultan's barge, and it was in this capacity, Bobovi emphasises, that he was in the privileged position of speaking to the sultan during royal excursions by boat.

There were numerous other hierarchies of slaves in the Palace: cooks, pastry-cooks, stewards who carried food from the kitchens to the sultan's apartment or to other parts of the Palace, water carriers, woodcutters who chopped and carried wood, Novice Janissaries, *chavushes* who conveyed people to the sultan, acted as marshals during ceremonies and carried Imperial Decrees to addresses outside the capital and so on. For all their order and decorum, the three Courts of the Palace and the secluded world of the Harem were as as crowded and prone to epidemics as the cramped quarters of the city outside the walls.

Of the permanent residents in the palace, the most powerful, until the last decade of the sixteenth century, was probably the chief white eunuch. This was the Agha of the Gate, whom the sultan promoted from among the eunuchs of the Inner Palace. The Law Book attributed to Mehmed II names him as the preferred channel for petitions to the throne, giving him the opportunity to influence both the petitioners and the sultan. From the late sixteenth century, however, he seems to have lost some of his influence to the chief black eunuch, who bore the title of Agha of the Abode of Felicity or, more colloquially, Agha of the Girls. The eunuchs of the Third Court were white, while those of the Harem were black, and the political influence of the chief black eunuch began to rise in the late sixteenth century, when the size of the Harem grew and the powerful queen mothers took up residence there. As the only senior officer of the court with access to both the male and female worlds of the Palace, the Agha of the Girls became an important political figure. Bobovi comments

This [black] officer,' 'is more important than the [white] Agha of the Gate because, in addition to greater revenues, he has easier access to the Prince, and more occasions to approach him at any hour, even when he has retired with his mistress. These are the men who direct the best part of the affairs of the Empire and, while they have perhaps never left the Palace, which they entered when very young, they give advice on state interests and use the favourable ear of the master at will to their own liking.

The Imperial Council

The sultans ruled the Empire through their court as much as through
formal organs of government, and for this reason it is usually impossible to follow to their source important political decisions, such as
whether to go to war or whether to seek peace. Such resolutions, it
seems, were the product of discussions which rarely left a written
record. In a somewhat dubious story, the Serbian Janissary,
Mihailović, claims that the decision to invade Bosnia in 1463 was the
result of a private conversation between two viziers, Mahmud Pasha
and Ishak Pasha, which he and his brother, the Court Treasurer, over-
heard in the vault of the Treasury. The sultan could, if he wished,
bypass the formal structures of government altogether, as Bayezid II
did in his negotiations with the Knights of St John over the custody
of his brother Jem.[6] The declaration of war in 1593 was, Pechevi
informs us, the outcome of a discussion in the presence of Murad III
between the Grand Vizier, Koja ('the Elder') Sinan Pasha, the commander of the recent Iranian campaign, Ferhad Pasha, the sultan's
tutor and Historian, Sa'deddin and Dervish Hasan, a falconer and
'Steward of the Gate' from the Palace. Of this group, Ferhad Pasha
and Sa'deddin opposed the war, but could not overcome the insistence of the grand vizier. When the question of whether to introduce
galleons into the Ottoman fleet arose early in the Cretan War of the
mid-seventeenth century, it was the Chief Mufti – who had no formal
role in the government – who sought advice on the matter from
Katib Chelebi.[7] There never, it seems, was a formal mechanism for
policy making. All decisions in theory were the sultan's own. What
mattered, therefore, was the character of the sultan, and the individuals or factions who had his ear.

There were, however, institutions which made the administrative
and less crucial policy decisions. Of these, the most important was the
Imperial Council,[8] the *divan*, which, under the presidency of the grand
vizier, acted on the sultan's behalf and issued decrees in his name. Its
meeting place before the 1470s is uncertain. From the late fourteenth
century, it presumably met in the Old Palace in Edirne or wherever
else the sultan was in residence and, after the conquest of Istanbul, initially in the Old Palace. From the 1470s, the Council normally met in

the Council Chamber in the Second Courtyard of the New Palace. On campaign, however, it assembled in the tent of its president, the grand vizier, which he always pitched near to the sultan's own pavilion.[9] From the second half of the sixteenth century, when the grand vizier either did not go on campaign or else appointed a deputy during his absence, the Council Chamber was the scene of meetings throughout the year.

In its origins, the council was presumably an informal group of lords which had the function of advising the sultan on political and military matters, and acting as a court to which the sultan's subjects could bring lawsuits and complaints. These were functions which it was to retain throughout its history. It is probable that during the fourteenth century, the sultan himself would preside at meetings. The Egyptian chronicler, Ibn Hajar, transmits a report from a doctor who had attended Bayezid I (1389–1402), noting how the sultan 'would sit early in the morning on a broad eminence, with the people standing away from him at a distance where he could see them. If anyone had suffered an injustice, he would submit it to him, and he would remove it.' The report does not mention anyone with Bayezid, but it is unlikely that he would have been alone. Ibn Hajar's doctor was perhaps reporting on a public appearance of the sultan and his advisors, the informal predecessors of the Imperial Council.

This vignette of the sultan personally dispensing justice, apparently in the open, is probably typical of the informality of Ottoman government in the fourteenth century. A story which Ashikpashazade tells of the death of Mehmed I (1413–21) indicates that, at that time too, there was an expectation that the sultan would appear before his subjects and preside over semi-public meetings of his council. When Mehmed died, the Viziers sought to conceal the fact until the arrival of his elder son, Murad, to take the throne. They continued to hold a council every day at the Sultan's 'Gate' – presumably in the Palace at Edirne – 'giving out governorships and fiefs and seeing to affairs'. However, when a group of soldiers threatened rebellion because they had not seen the sultan, the viziers brought the corpse to the gate, with a lad behind to move its arms, so that it would appear as if the sultan were alive and stroking his beard. A brief description of the sultan and his Council also appears in the 'Holy Wars of Sultan

Murad [II] son of Mehmed Khan'. Here the anonymous author presents Murad II as presiding – obviously not in public – over the council meeting in 1444, which considered the proposals for peace that the King of Hungary's envoys had brought.

These scattered references suggest that probably during the fourteenth and certainly during the fifteenth century, a small group of viziers advised the sultan on political and administrative affairs, and had the power to make appointments in his name. In some of its functions, it worked in semi-public view and, in its judicial role, fully in public. It seems too that the sultan often presided over the council in person, suggesting that relations between sultan and viziers were still informal, with the sultan's advisors in the role of allies as much as subordinates.

Ottoman tradition credits Mehmed II with abandoning the practice of attending meetings in person. Henceforth, the council met under the presidency of the grand vizier: indeed, it may be the assumption of this role that led to the definition of the Grand Vizierate as a formal office of state. Menavino, however, indicates that in his day, the sultan – presumably Bayezid II – continued to summon the council to audiences, where 'he would begin to speak and each one to reply to what was proposed according to their judgement, and thus they would provide for war and all matters of the state'. Menavino's description of the elaborate ceremonies that accompanied the audiences makes it clear that they were very different from the apparently informal meetings of the sultan with his council before the days of Mehmed II. It was on these occasions, too, that the sultan, by the award of a black cloak, indicated which of his counsellors or courtiers had merited the death penalty. The executioner would kill men of high rank by strangling and, before a horse with a black covering could carry the dead man to his house, a courier went ahead to place a black staff over the portal. Men of lower rank the executioner decapitated, placing the heads on a carpet outside the palace. These rituals of death, coupled with the ceremony of audience symbolised the absolute power of the sultan within his own household, and the abject status of even his most powerful counsellors. At the same time, the sultan's absence from the day-to-day meetings of the council served to emphasise his remoteness.

Nonetheless, despite their increasing distance from the council, the sultans devised a means of keeping a check on its deliberations. Guillaume Postel, who had accompanied the French ambassador to Istanbul between 1536 and 1538, and had again travelled in the Ottoman Empire between 1549 and 1551, describes how, after council meetings, the Grand Vizier would go 'to report to the Sultan all the truth: what had been discussed and matters of importance. At this time, lying is mortal, because often the Sultan is listening at a window overlooking the said Chamber without being seen or noticed. And even if he were never there, one always thinks that he is.' The window which Postel describes was, if a statement by the Chancellor Jelalzade Mustafa is correct, the creation of Süleyman I, presumably in the first years of his reign, since it was from here in 1527 that he watched the trial of the heretic Molla Kabiz, who had preached the superiority of Jesus over Muhammad.[10] Another tradition, however, attributes the construction of the window to Mehmed II. Sultans after Süleyman evidently continued to watch proceedings in the council chamber, since Bobovi in 1658 still refers to 'the window through the blinds of which the Sultan watches the assembly of the Imperial Council'. However, he also suggests that during his time in the Palace the sultan – in a reference possibly to Murad IV – had again started to attend at least some of the council meetings. He describes these occasions as far more informal than had been usual in the previous century: '[The Sultan] often participates in this assembly in person, where he proposes the subjects which they deliberate upon and receives advice from each.'

Although membership of the Imperial Council became larger over the years, the titles and functions of its officers had become fixed by the reign of Mehmed II at the latest. The viziers were responsible especially for political and military matters. They not only dealt with questions of war in the council, but also served on the battlefield, either independently, or under the command of the sultan or of a vizier of superior rank. Beside the viziers sat the military judges (*kadi'asker*), the chief judges of the Empire, who were responsible for judicial matters that came before the council. Below them sat the treasurers (*defterdar*) who issued financial decrees in the sultan's name, and the chancellor. The Turkish title of the chancellor – *nishanji* – or,

in its Arabic form, *tevki'i*, means literally 'the one who affixes the
Sultan's cypher to documents'. This was, in essence, his function,
since the appearance of the imperial cypher on a document was a
guarantee of its authenticity, and it was the chancellor who oversaw
the clerks who drew up decrees and other documents, ensuring that
their contents were correct and that they conformed to the rigid con-
ventions of the Ottoman chancellery. These were the members of the
council who participated in its discussion.

The number of viziers in the Imperial Council grew over the centuries. It is impossible to determine how many there were during the
first century of the Empire's existence but, by 1421, three was probably the usual number. Ashikpashazade names Hajji Ivaz Pasha,
Bayezid Pasha and Chandarli Ibrahim as the viziers at the time of
Mehmed I's death in this year. The same was true a century later.
Menavino, in the early sixteenth, refers to 'the three Pashas', but by
the mid-century there were usually four. However, the number was
not steady. The Hospitaller, Antoine Geuffroy, notes in his *Short
Description of the Grand Turk's Court* of 1546, that there were four viziers,
'but often there were only three, as was once the case'. The starting
point for this increase in numbers may have been Süleyman I's
appointment to the council of the Admiral Hayreddin Barbarossa in
the early 1540s. From that time until 1566, there were generally four
viziers. From 1566, there were five and, from 1570–1, seven. For a
while in 1642 there were eleven,[11] but since, by this time, men with
vizieral rank often served in the provinces, they cannot all have been
full-time members of the imperial council. The only provincial governor who acquired an *ex officio* right to attend meetings of the council was the Governor-General of Rumelia. A campaign diary of
Süleyman's expedition against the Safavids of 1533–6 records:

It was commanded that when there is a Council, the Governor-General of
Rumelia should come to the Council and sit with the Pashas. The Governor-
General of Anatolia should not come. If it happens that there is a matter
which has to be submitted, then he should sit with the Pashas.

His attendance, therefore, was not regular, but only when there was a
matter that fell within his sphere.

Ottoman tradition dates the creation of the post of military judge to the reign of Murad I, and since, from the early days of the Empire, the sultan must have needed a legal advisor on his council, this tradition is quite possibly correct.There was it seems, only one military judge on the council until the last years of Mehmed II. The creation of a second was, according to the sixteenth-century biographer Tashköprüzade, the work of the Grand Vizier, Mehmed Pasha of Karaman. At the time, Tashköprüzade tells us, the sole military judge was Molla Kastellani, and Mehmed Pasha, fearing the effect on the Sultan of his outspoken love of the truth and seeing the need to counteract his influence, proposed that henceforth there should be two. It was Mehmed Pasha who appointed Kastellani as Military Judge of Rumelia, while he promoted the Judge of Istanbul to become Military Judge of Anatolia. From that time onwards, these two office holders became regular members of the Imperial Council. In the early seventeenth century, Tashköprüzade's continuator reported that, after his conquest of Syria and Egypt, Selim I (1512–20) created a third military judge to represent the legal affairs of these provinces. However, the enmity between the appointee and the Grand Vizier, Piri Pasha, soon led to the abolition of the post. Henceforth, there were usually two military judges, although in 1545, the Italian, Luigi Bassano, reported three.

The number of treasurers on the Imperial Council also increased over the years. In the fifteenth century, there was perhaps one. By 1526, there were two.These, it seems, were responsible for the imperial estates and revenues in, respectively, Rumelia and Anatolia. By 1539, there were three treasurers and, from 1587, four, overseeing the revenues of Rumelia, Anatolia, Istanbul and 'the Danube'; that is, the west and north coast of the Black Sea. These were the treasurers on the Imperial Council. There were others in the provinces, notably at Aleppo, a post which dates probably from the conquest of Syria in 1516. The increase in numbers clearly reflects the growing importance of the treasury, especially from the end of the sixteenth century. This was a time when inflation and increasingly expensive but unprofitable wars led to shortfalls in revenue and the occasional inability to pay the troops. In 1572, the government debased the silver akche. Another debasement of 50 per cent in 1584 led to Janissary riots. Further debasements and late payment followed in 1589, 1593 and 1606. There were further crises as the seventeenth century advanced. In these circumstances, raising cash became a primary duty of the council, bringing with it a rise in the numbers and status of the treasurers.[12]

The post of chancellor must date from the earliest days of the Empire. Ottoman documents from the fourteenth century are extremely rare, but the few which survive suggest that the sultans already possessed a chancellery. In fact, the earliest surviving sultanic cypher, which it was, nominally at least, the chancellor's function to draw,[13] appears on Orhan's trust deed of 1324.[14] The office may, therefore, date back to this time. There seems, however, never to have been more than one chancellor in the council, despite the growing number of clerks in his department, as council business increased during the sixteenth and seventeenth centuries. Until the early sixteenth century, there may also have been – unless the reference is simply to the treasurer – another member of the council, the assayer, since Spandounes talks of 'an office which is concerned with the weight of money, which also occupies a seat in the Council of Pashas'. The reference, however, seems to be unique.

The members of the Imperial Council – viziers, military judges, treasurers and chancellor – represented the different branches of the sultan's government and, from the sixteenth century, their posts became, more or less, mutually exclusive. Military judges or chancellors, for example, did not as a rule become viziers. Each position tended to represent the pinnacle of a specialised career, whether as governor or military commander in the case of viziers, in the learned and legal professions in the case of military judges, in the financial service in the case of treasurers, or in the scribal service in the case of chancellors. This, however, had not always been the case. There seems to have been a greater fluidity in the functions of council members before the end of the fifteenth century. Chandarli Ibrahim, for example, became Vizier in 1420, after serving since 1415 as a Military Judge. Mehmed Pasha of Karaman came to the Grand Vizierate in 1476, after occupying the Chancellorship for twelve years. Such functional changes seem to have become rarer in the sixteenth century.

There was also change, from the mid-fifteenth century, in the backgrounds of members of the council, at least of the viziers. What is most striking about the century before the conquest of Constantinople is the hereditary right to the vizierate of a single family.[15] The first of these was Chandarli Hayreddin Pasha who, according to Ottoman tradition, began his career as a judge in Bilecik, Iznik and Bursa. The same tradition makes Murad I appoint him as Military Judge and finally, in 1380, as Vizier. In this position, he acted both as governor and military commander, roles which the viziers were to preserve. He died at Serrai in 1387. His son, Chandarli Ali, succeeded him as vizier to Murad I, Bayezid I and Bayezid's son Süleyman (Rumelia, 1402–11), on whose behalf he was one of the negotiators of the Gallipoli Treaty of 1403. He died in 1406. In this year, his brother, Ibrahim, was judge in Bursa. By 1415, Mehmed I had appointed him Military Judge. In 1420, he became Second Vizier to Bayezid Pasha and, after the latter's death at the hands of Murad II's uncle, Mustafa, succeeded him as First Vizier. He died in 1429.

The Chandarli line of viziers continued with Ibrahim's eldest son, Halil, who was First Vizier by 1443. By 1447, Chandarli Halil's son, Süleyman, who predeceased his father, was Military Judge. Halil's downfall came with the accession of Mehmed II. The Sultan evidently disliked him, as he was responsible for deposing him from the throne in 1446, and reinstating his father after the latter's abdication.[16] More importantly, however, Halil had opposed the siege of Constantinople in 1453 and indeed, according to the report of Leonard of Chios who was in the besieged city, actually collaborated with the defenders. Not long afterwards, the Sultan had Chandarli Halil executed.

This was not, however, quite the end of the Chandarli era. In 1453, Chandarli Halil's son, Ibrahim, was judge in Edirne. In 1465, Mehmed II appointed him Military Judge and, eight years later, tutor to his son Bayezid in Amasya. On his accession to the throne in 1481, Bayezid brought with him his own entourage from Amasya to the capital, appointing Chandarli Halil Military Judge of Rumelia. In 1486, he became a Vizier and finally, in 1498, Grand Vizier. Two years later, he died in the campaign against Navpaktos (Lepanto). Ibrahim was the last of the Chandarlis to occupy the vizierate.

Mehmed II's execution of Chandarli Halil was clearly an act of personal pique rather than of policy. Nonetheless, it represents a moment of change in the institution of the vizierate. Before 1453, most – although not all – of the viziers seem to have been freeborn men of Muslim and Turkish descent. After 1453, Turkish Muslim viziers were the exception. Instead, the sultans came to rely on men who had grown up in the royal household, rather than on men from Muslim households that enjoyed independent power and influence. In the provinces, members of the great Muslim families, especially those of the Rumelian marcher lords, continued to flourish and to receive office from the sultan, but as provincial governors rather than as viziers in the capital.

Nonetheless, the vizieral appointments of Mehmed II and Bayezid II indicate that these sultans were still careful to harness local dynastic interests to Ottoman service. A number of the viziers whom they appointed were not 'raised from the dust' as was, typically, to become the case in the sixteenth century, but were rather the scions of former Christian dynasties. The longest serving of Mehmed II's grand viziers was Mahmud Pasha, who occupied the post for most of the period from about 1455 until his execution in 1474. Mahmud's origins are not certain. However, a Ragusan document of 1458 gives him the Slavonic family name of Andjelović,[17] suggesting that the story that he was a descendant of the Angelos lords of Thessaly is correct. It seems, too, that during his vizierate, members of his family continued to exercise power in Serbia since, in his account of the capture of the Serbian fortress of Smederovo in 1458, the chronicler Neshri claims that Mahmud's brother was in the fortress at the time of the siege, and that it was he who negotiated its surrender. It was perhaps also because of Mahmud's Serbian connections that the Sultan put him in command of the expeditions that finally overran the Despotate of Serbia in 1458–9, and the Kingdom of Bosnia in 1463.

Mahmud Pasha was not the only member of a Christian 'noble' family to serve the sultan at this period. The origin of his rival, Mehmed Pasha 'the Greek', was so well known as to become his soubriquet. It is very possible that he was from a 'noble' Byzantine family. This was certainly the case with Hass Murad Pasha,[18] who served not as a vizier on the Imperial Council, but as Governor-General of Rumelia until his death in 1473 in the war against Uzun

Hasan. He was a Palaiologos, a member of the Byzantine imperial family, as was Mesih Pasha[19] who, as Vizier, commanded the unsuccessful siege of Rhodes in 1480. Bayezid II was to appoint him Grand Vizier on three ocasions between 1485 and his death in 1501. Like Hass Murad and Mesih Pasha, Hersekzade ('the Duke's son') Ahmed Pasha,[20] five times Grand Vizier between 1497 and 1516, was also the offspring of a ruling family. His father, Stephen Vukčić-Kosača, the Duke of St Sava, was ruler of a territory in south-eastern Bosnia. It is from his title 'Herceg' ('Duke') that Hercegovina takes its name. His son seems to have converted to Islam and entered Mehmed II's court in 1473–4. The last vizier of such descent was Dukaginzade Ahmed, a member of the Albanian Dukagjin family, descended from Duke John of Shkodër.[21] Like Hersekzade, he too seems to have converted and received an education at the court of Mehmed II. Bayezid II promoted him to become Governor-General of Anatolia. Under Bayezid's successor, Selim I, he became Second and, finally, Grand Vizier until his execution in 1515.

Not all Mehmed II's and Bayezid II's appointments followed this pattern. Other viziers of non-Muslim origin, such as the Albanian Daud Pasha, Grand Vizier between 1485 and 1497, probably came into the sultan's service through the Collection rather than through voluntary conversion. Iskender Pasha, who was Vizier between 1489 and 1496, was the son of a Genoese father and a Greek mother from Trabzon.[22] A few viziers of this era were still of Muslim Turkish descent. Chandarli Ibrahim is the most obvious example, but Mehmed Pasha, who was Vizier late in Mehmed II's reign and again between 1483 and 1485 was also a member of a powerful Turkish family. His grandfather, Yörgüch, and his father, Hizir, had been Tutors in Amasya to the future Sultans Murad II and Bayezid II respectively. Piri Mehmed Pasha,[23] Grand Vizier between 1518 and 1523 was also a Muslim Turk. Nonetheless, a striking feature of the era between the accession of Mehmed II and the accession of Süleyman I is the number of viziers of 'noble' Christian descent. By appointing these men to the highest positions in the government, the sultans were assimilating members of the former ruling families of the Balkan peninsula into the Ottoman élite. This system of assimilation also allowed the sultans to exploit their family connections for political ends and, as the unhappy fates of Mahmud Pasha and Dukaginzade Ahmed exemplify, to bring the pre-Ottoman ruling caste firmly under the sultan's control.

By the accession of Süleyman I in 1521, this process was complete, and no more viziers emerged from this background. It seems that most of the viziers after 1521 were from the western part of the Balkan Peninsula, although there were exceptions. Özdemiroghu Osman Pasha,[24] Grand Vizier in 1584–5, was a Turk, and Jigalazade Sinan, briefly Grand Vizier in 1596, was a Genoese, Scipione Cicala, whom the Admiral, Piyale Pasha, had taken captive in 1560 and presented to the Sultan.

The sixteenth-century viziers were not, however, descendants of ruling dynasties, but rather the offspring of peasants. Typically, they had come to the Palace as lads whom the sultan had levied from his own Christian subjects, through the Collection. In the Palace, they had studied in the Great and Small Chambers in the Third Court and then, after progressing through the ranks of the pages and holding an office within the Palace, the sultan appointed them to a provincial governorship. From the provinces, if they had the ruler's favour, they could return to the Second Court as viziers of the Imperial Council. Lutfi Pasha, Grand Vizier between 1539 and 1541, gave an account of his own career. He was, by origin, an Albanian, and came to the Palace, one may presume, through the Collection. These details he omits, beginning his 'autobiography' in the Palace:

From the time of the late Sultan Bayezid Khan, whose Abode is in Paradise, [I] this humble being, was brought up in the Sultan's Private Apartments through the bounty of the Sultan, as a well-wisher of the Ottoman Porte. When I was in the Private Apartments, I studied many kinds of science. At the accession of His Excellency Selim Khan, I graduated from the post of Cloth-Bearer, to become a Müteferrika with fifty akches [per day]. Then I was Head Taster, then Head Gatekeeper and then Master of the Standard. Afterwards [I became] Governor of Kastamonu and Governor-General of Karaman. Then the vizierate was bestowed on me.

The career of one of Lutfi Pasha's immediate successors, Rüstem Pasha,[25] was similar. He seems to have been a Bosnian by birth, who entered the palace through the Collection. Within the palace, he became the sultan's Weapons-Bearer in the Privy Chamber, and then Master of the Stables. When he left the Palace, he became first Governor-General of Diyarbekir and then of Anatolia. He next joined the Imperial Council as Third Vizier. By 1541, he was Second Vizier and Grand Vizier by 1544. Like Lutfi Pasha, he also married into the imperial family.

What most struck foreigners about this succession of viziers who had originally come to the Palace as lads from the Collection, was the contrast between their wealth and exalted position and the humble estate of their original families. It is to emphasise this difference that Antoine Geuffroy gives a description, perhaps apocryphal, of the father of Ibrahim Pasha, Grand Vizier from 1523 to 1536. He begins with a depiction of Ibrahim, 'from Parga in Albania . . .', who 'because he had grown up young in the Palace with the said Grand Turk, achieved such credit and authority that he commanded absolutely and disposed of everything, without the Grand Turk interfering'. This contrasts with Ibrahim's father: 'a man of nothing, useless, a frequenter of taverns, a drunkard sleeping in the streets like the beasts'.

This systematic use of the Collection to promote men of humble origin to the vizierate, a practice which this story symbolises, is a measure of the increasing power of the sultan. Although members of local dynasties continued to receive appointments in the provinces, sultans no longer felt constrained to appoint them to membership of the Imperial Council. Instead they preferred men who were members of the imperial household and had no links to patronage and authority outside the palace. Ibrahim Pasha is again a good example of the powers which the sultan could exercise. Süleyman I, against all precedent, appointed Ibrahim from the Privy Chamber directly to the grand vizierate, with no previous experience of government. Having thus raised him from nothing to the highest office, thirteen years later, during the Baghdad campaign, he executed him. By choosing them from among the slaves raised in his own household, the sultan was able, if he wished, to exercise absolute power over his viziers.

In the troubled years from the end of the sixteenth century, however, it seems to have been as much the influence of rival factions, both within the Palace and outside, that created or broke viziers. The office of grand vizier became especially precarious, one factor in this being the prolonged wars of the period. If the grand vizier was not also the commander of a campaign, he had to surrender many of his powers of appointment and revenue raising to the commander of the army. On the other hand, if he himself became commander, his absence from Istanbul and the relinquishing of his place on the imperial council to a deputy exposed him to the plots of political rivals.[26] This dilemma, which arose from the lack of distinction between political and military authority, undoubtedly played a part in the rapid succession of grand viziers between 1590 and 1656. Nonetheless, it remained the rule that viziers should, in their origins, be non-Muslim or, at least non-Turkish. In the late sixteenth and early seventeenth centuries, most grand viziers – for example, Koja ('the Elder') Sinan Pasha or Yemishchi ('the Fruiterer') Hasan Pasha – were Albanian. Towards the mid-century, however, Caucasians – Circassians, Abkhazians and Georgians – began to compete with them for office. The first Caucasian grand vizier was Mehmed Pasha the Georgian in 1622–3. The appointment of Mehmed Pasha the Circassian followed in 1624. Melek Ahmed Pasha, who first assumed the grand vizierate in 1650, was Abkhazian, as were his successors Siyavush Pasha in 1651, and Ibshir Mustafa in 1654–5[27]. The same troubled period also saw the appointment of a Georgian in 1651 and a Circassian in 1653. In the end, it could be said that the Albanian faction won in the struggle for office. In 1656, Mehmed IV's mother, Turhan Sultan, appointed the Albanian Köprülü Mehmed as Grand Vizier. His son, Fazil Ahmed Pasha inherited the office and held it until his death in 1676.

If, from the mid-fifteenth century, it was very rare for a Turkish Muslim to become a vizier, this was not the case for the other offices of the imperial council. Before the sixteenth century, the posts of vizier and military judge were not, as the careers of the two Chandarli Ibrahims show, mutually exclusive: a military judge could become a vizier, if not vice versa. In the sixteenth century, however, a new pattern emerged. From this time, military judgeships, and indeed all senior judicial appointments became the preserve of a few fiercely competing learned families. When a member of one of these clans achieved high office, he would use his influence and powers of patronage to advance his kinsmen. An example in the sixteenth cen-

tury is the Chivizade family, the descendants of a professor, a certain
Chivizade Ilyas. Ilyas's son, Muhiyeddin rose to become Military
Judge of Anatolia in 1537. His son, Mehmed, achieved the same position in 1575. Two years later, he was Military Judge of Rumelia. In
1598, Mehmed III made his and his father's teacher, Sa'deddin, Chief
Mufti. In 1601, Sa'deddin's son, Mehmed Es'ad, was Military Judge of
Anatolia, while his brother had succeeded their father in the muftiship.[28] The post of military judge was therefore, unlike the vizierate,
open to Muslim Turks but only to those from a very restricted circle.
It was not open to the mass of judges who held posts in the small
towns of the Empire.

The chancellors and treasurers on the Imperial Council, again
from the early sixteenth century, also came to form a group whose
background was different from that of the viziers. Before 1520, the
council was perhaps more fluid. Mehmed II's last grand vizier,
Nishanji ('the chancellor') Mehmed Pasha had risen to the post from
the Chancellorship. Selim I was to elevate the Treasurer of Rumelia,
Piri Mehmed Pasha, to the post of Third and finally, in 1518, Grand
Vizier. After this date, there seem to have been no promotions from
chancellor or treasurer directly to the vizierate, although from the
1570s, appointments of treasurers to provincial governorships were
not uncommon.[29] The father of the Chancellor, Okchuzade, moved
from the post of Chief Treasurer to become Governor-General of
Cyprus in 1581.[30]

Like the military judges, the chancellors and treasurers seem, as a
rule, to have been Muslim Turks and graduates of the religious colleges. However, the training which followed was scribal rather than
legal, beginning, with appropriate patronage, as an apprentice in a
great household, in the service of a provincial governor or treasurer,
or in the imperial council or treasury itself. The famous Feridun Bey,[31]
for example, began his career as a protégé of the Chief Treasurer,
Chivizade Abdi Chelebi, brother of the Military Judge, Muhiyeddin. It
was probably in Abdi's house that he learned his craft. On Abdi's
death in 1553, he entered the household of the future grand vizier,
Sokollu Mehmed Pasha and, through Sokollu, became Chief Clerk to
the Imperial Council in 1570. Three years later, he was Chancellor. In
1576, however, presumably as a result of Murad III's dislike of

Sokollu, he suffered dismissal and exile. The Sultan, however, recalled him to his post in 1581, after Sokollu's assassination.

Office on the Imperial Council, while itself dependent on the favour of the sultan, gave its holders not only political power and opportunity for independent patronage, but also wealth. Spandounes, for example, reports that, at the time of his death in 1497, the long-serving grand vizier, Daud Pasha, left 'a million gold ducats and this not including his land, mills, villages, horses and other moveables'. Office carried with it not only a valuable fief, but also perquisites. Writing after his dismissal in 1541, Lutfi Pasha spoke of a grand vizier as having 'a fief of 1 200 000 akches. If he realises one and a half times its book value, it amounts to almost 2 000 000 akches. If he receives a sum of 200 000 or 300 000 akches from the Kurdish lords, and [valuable] clothes and horses from the powerful lords, this makes 2 400 000 akches a year.' Lutfi's estimate is undoubtedly an understatement, excluding as it does, gifts from ambassadors and other petitioners, and other profits of office. The grand viziers undoubtedly enjoyed the largest income, but other council members also became wealthy. Antoine Geuffroy in 1546, for example, refers to the two military judges as having 'each a fief of seven thousand ducats'. Spandounes in 1513 had mentioned the same sum, but added that this excluded 'what they earn in extraordinary payments'. The emoluments of the chancellors seem to have been the same, or slightly higher, than those of the military judges.

Enormous though the wealth of high office holders may have been, so too was their expenditure. The sign of a man's status in Ottoman society was the size of his household and the size of his ret-inue when he appeared in public. This involved continuous expense, whether in or out of office. It was normal, according to Kochi Bey in 1631–2, for a grand vizier up to 1574 to own about 1000 slaves, and for other viziers to own about 5–600. In the second half of the seven-teenth century, Evliya Chelebi gives numerous indications of the vast size of the household belonging to his patron, Melek Ahmed Pasha (Grand Vizier, 1650–1).[32] It was, however, not only the viziers who had large followings, but also the other members of the Imperial Council. Of the military judges, Spandounes comments that 'they keep many eunuchs and women' and of chancellors that 'they ride out in great triumph', with Geuffroy adding that they go 'accompanied by a great number of horses and servants'. Ramberti in the mid-sixteenth century reported that the military judges kept 2–300 slaves, the chancellor 300, the Chief Treasurer 1000, and the second Treasurer, 500.

The viziers, military judges, chancellor and treasurers were the executive officers of the Imperial Council. Beside these, there was a scribal service, which prepared material for discussion, kept records and drew up documents for discussion. Such a service must have existed from the early days of the Empire, but the exiguous records from the late fifteenth century suggest that, up until that time, it was a small and more or less undifferentiated body. During the early years of the reign of Süleyman I, however, there seems to have been an increase in the numbers of clerks and a clearer definition of their functions. A register of 1527–35 lists seven clerks 'in the suite of the Treasurers', and 'eleven in the suite of the Chancellor'. By 1531, their numbers had risen to eight and 15 respectively, and by 1561, to nine and 25. Numbers continued to increase in the following decades. By 1605, there was probably a minimum of 50 clerks, by 1609, a minimum of 64 and by 1627–8, 115. These figures clearly do not include all the clerks in the employment of the central government. In 1531, for example, there were also 33 clerks and 17 apprentices attached to the treasury, and seven attached to the Controller of Registers, who headed the land registry.[33] Added to the clerks of the Imperial Council, these and others give a total of 110, a small number in view of the Empire's vast and, at that time, increasing size. Some of these clerks, like members of the Imperial Council, would accompany the sultan on campaigns or, when the sultans no longer campaigned in person, receive attachments to the army commander.[34]

In charge of the clerks was the Head Clerk (*reisü'l-küttab*).[35] His office, according to an uncorroborated eighteenth century source, dated from the reign of Süleyman I. If this tradition is correct, it must have been a creation of Süleyman's early years, since there is evidence of its existence from the early 1520s. The most famous and long-serving of Süleyman's chancellors, Jelalzade Mustafas, received the post of Head Clerk in 1525 and held it until his promotion to Chancellor in 1534. Serving beneath the Head Clerk was, at least in the sixteenth century, a memorandum writer (*tezkereji*), whose tasks documents do not define, but who probably summarised the incoming correspondence and petitions for presentation to the council by the head clerk. He also, it seems, read out the petitions which the grand vizier heard in the council which he held at his own residence, following meetings of the Imperial Council in the Palace. The documents do not, as a rule, define the other clerks of the council by function, and one may assume that they all did similar tasks: recording the decisions and appointments of the council in its day-books, entering the drafts of decrees in the 'Registers of Important Affairs', making the fair copies of these, and drawing up the finalised decrees in their often elaborately gilded versions. The head clerk and, ultimately, the chancellor supervised this work. The second group of clerks, serving the chief treasurer, formed a separate group, presumably because the maintenance of financial records required very specific skills. Persian rather than Turkish was the usual language of treasury documents, and the treasury used a form of script and way of writing numbers that were incomprehensible to the uninitiated. To draw up these documents needed an apprenticeship in the Treasury itself.

Unless, like Jelalzade, chancellor from 1534 to 1557 or Okchuzade, chancellor from 1599 to 1601 and again from 1622 to 1623, they rose to become chancellor or occupy other high office, the clerks of the Imperial Council remain shadowy figures, and it is rarely possible to know anything of their background. Before about 1500, their origins were probably diverse since, up to this time, Greek was the lingua franca of diplomacy, and the sultan evidently corresponded with foreign powers, not only in Greek, but also in their own languages. An anonymous Ragusan in the last quarter of the fifteenth century reported that the sultan had a Chancellery for each language, all under a single chancellor and 'to the Greeks and Italians they write in Greek, to the Hungarians, Moldavians, Vlachs, Slavs and Ragusans, in Serbian, to the Turks, Arabs, Armenians and other nations in [eastern] Turkish, Arabic or Persian'. This diversity of languages suggests a diversity of scribes in the chancellery.[36]

After about 1500, this was no longer the case. Documents in Greek declined both in quantity and quality, and eventually disappeared, as did all documents in languages other than Turkish, Arabic and

Persian. One may assume, therefore, that from about 1520, all clerks of the council were Muslim. It would seem, too, from what little evidence is available that typically they would be graduates of religious colleges, for whom a job as a clerk could be as attractive as the alternatives of College professor, or judge in a small town. It was, in fact, distaste at the prospect of a teaching career that persuaded Okchuzade to follow the scribal path, which led eventually to his chancellorship.[37] Nonetheless, literacy and education were not enough to secure a position. An aspirant clerk needed a patron, who would take him into his own household and procure for him a position in imperial service. The office of clerk of the council in particular required the patronage of the chancellor, one of the treasurers, or of another member of the council. It cannot be accidental that two of the chief clerks in the Imperial Council of Süleyman I were natives of Tosya in Anatolia, since this was the home town of the chancellor Jelalzade Mustafa. It seems rather to be a typical case of an office holder providing employment for his fellow townsmen.[38]

Payment to the clerks could be a wage or come in the form of a fief, with fief holders clearly predominating by 1600 or later. These were not, however, the only opportunities for enrichment, since clerks could also use their connections to acquire interests in tax farms or other enterprises, which could be vital to their support in periods out of office.[39] They existed, in effect, at the lower level of the Ottoman élite.

The full Imperial Council met on four days a week – Saturday, Sunday, Monday and Tuesday – with all the executive members attending. The clerks, however, at least from the late sixteenth century, seem to have attended according to a rota. A register entry of 1585-6 shows 19 to 25 attending on Saturday and Sunday, and 17 to 20 on Monday and Tuesday.[40]

It is clear that many of the most important decisions of state, even if they did involve council members, took place outside the Imperial Council itself. The council was, nonetheless, an executive body, conducting all kinds of government business, as well as acting as a court of law. It conducted foreign affairs, granting audiences to ambassadors and corresponding with foreign monarchs; it oversaw preparations for war, issuing detailed commands for the levy of men, munitions and provisions; it occupied itself with building works, notably with fortresses and aqueducts in Istanbul and the provinces; it dealt with innumerable problems, some important and some apparently trivial, that were the subject of reports and petitions from governors and judges; it made promotions and appointments. As a court, it could hear cases, usually those which involved the military class. It is not, for example, rare to find orders to governors or judges to send fief holders 'bound and fettered' to Istanbul, to appear before the council. It also dealt with complaints of individuals, which judges and others had forwarded, or which the complainant had brought in person. Of these personal petitions, Luigi Bassano wrote in 1545: 'The Pashas hear first the most important causes, and then all the others, of the poor as well as of the rich, so that no one departs without being heard or having his cause settled. Here they employ neither attorneys nor advocates, but each speaks to his affairs for himself as best he can, and anyone who lacks the language makes use of the dragomans, that is, the interpreter . . .'

The length of a council meeting was, according to Guillaume Postel, seven or eight hours, and this seems to correspond with Bassano's account. The council members, he said, ate three times. First, at dawn, immediately after their arrival, then 'at the sixth hour', after the main business, and then after hearing petitions. Meetings ended at midday in the summer, when daybreak was early, and mid-afternoon in winter. The grand vizier, however, after the dispersal of the Council 'goes', in the words of Postel, 'to his house where, in a great hall, he listens to all, down to the meanest man who may present himself, leaving no man to whom he has not given a definitive judgement, or given a *tezkere,*that is, a letter addressed to his judge . . .' This function of the grand vizier recalls the personal audiences with the sultan which the Egyptian doctor had witnessed in the days of Bayezid I.

Since the clerks did not take minutes of the discussions, it is impossible to know how the council arrived at its decisions. Sometimes, however, it is clear how a particular item came onto the agenda, since the opening section in each decree of the Imperial Council lays out the reason for its issue. This was often the receipt of a letter or the arrival of a messenger from a provincial or other authority, whose message the decree repeats in summary. For example, a command of 1564, ordering the Governor-General of Anatolia to provide troops to serve in the Governor of Menteshe's galleys begins: 'The Governor of Menteshe, Ahmed – may his glory endure – has sent a man to make it known that soldiers are necessary for the galleys, which were given to the aforenamed for the defence of the sea-shore.' The decree answers Ahmed's request.[41] Other decrees state simply that the problem which the command addresses 'had been heard about'. Many, however, give no indication at all as to why that particular issue had come to the council. Nor do they give any hint as to the background of a major decision of policy, such as the declaration of war.

All decrees have a standard format, which remained in use to the nineteenth century. After naming the addressee, the first section lays out the reason for issuing the order. This often gives the summary of an incoming message or petition, probably in the form in which the memorandum writer had drawn it up for presentation to the Council. The order itself follows, beginning always with the formula: 'I have commanded that . . .' The first person format is a reminder that the decree, even if in practice it represents a decision of the council, comes from the sultan, on whose behalf the imperial council was acting. At the head of the document stands the sultan's cypher, guaranteeing its authenticity and emphasising its gravity. At its foot are the date and place of emission.[42]

The fact that the Imperial Council had no independent power and that all the documents that it issued, whether letters, decrees or patents of appointments, were in the sultan's name, raises the question of the role which the sultan played in its deliberations and discussions, when he did not attend its sessions in person. He obviously could, if he wished, ignore the council altogether. He could also send formal messages to the council. The so-called 'Law Book of Mehmed II', of which this section probably dates from the late sixteenth century, lays down a procedure for communication: 'For some matters, the Agha of the Gate should give news from me to the outside via the Steward of the Gatekeepers, who should inform my Viziers, my Military Judges and my Treasurers.' In this way, the sultan could, from the seclusion of the Inner Palace determine the Imperial Council's agenda and try to enforce his own will.

Most important, however, were the sultan's interviews with the grand vizier. Lutfi Pasha stresses that no one, not even other viziers, should know the secrets between the sultan and his chief minister, and appends a story of how Selim I had dismissed the Vizier Mesih Pasha after he had dared to ask the Grand Vizier, Piri Pasha, the contents of a recent discussion with the sultan. A memorandum from the Grand Vizier Mehmed Pasha requests an audience with Ahmed I (1603–17) in order to present to him some unspecified military matter,[43] and presumably all grand viziers sought private audiences with the sultan. In Postel's account of the Imperial Council, it was also the grand vizier who presented the results of its deliberations to the sultan. Luigi Bassano, however, also writing in the mid-sixteenth century gives a different account. In his version, after its deliberations, the entire council appeared before the sultan in the Hall of Petitions behind the Gate of Felicity leading into the Third Court. Here, the Military Judge of Rumelia spoke first and, after him, the Grand Vizier, presenting all the business of the council 'which needed to be referred to the Grand Turk'. The Venetian Ottaviano Bon, writing in 1600, follows Bassano's version.

The standardised format of decrees makes it difficult to assess whether or not the sultan was in fact involved in making the decisions which they embody. Most routine promotions and appointments probably remained effectively within the gift of members of the council, even though they required the formal ratification of the Sultan. It is unlikely, too, that the sultan took an interest in every decree which the council issued in his name. It is, however, possible to identify some of the orders which came from the sultan in person. In the 'Registers of Important Affairs', which contain the rough drafts of decrees,[44] the clerks have added the note: 'with the Imperial Rescript' against some of the entries. This indicates that the texts incorporate the Sultan's written command, which he presumably made on a submission which he received from the council. These imperial rescripts might refer to great matters of state, such as the measures to be taken against Süleyman's rebel son, Bayezid, in 1559–60, or matters which, to the modern mind, seem fairly trivial, such as a command in the same year to block up the windows in Cairo which enabled men to see into the women's sections of public bathhouses. These imperial rescripts make it possible to identify at least some of the items of council business which drew the sultan's attention.

In the end, however, it is impossible to estimate with any certainty the degree of the sultan's control over the decisions of his council and his role in the day-to-day government of the Empire. When he attended the council in person, frequently before the mid-fifteenth century, rarely thereafter, he could exercise his authority in person. From the second half of the fifteenth century, when he did not attend meetings, he made his will known in discussions with the grand vizier, by sending messages through the Agha of the Gate, or when the council members presented him with the results of their deliberations. A series of written memoranda from the grand vizier to the sultan also survive from the time of Murad III onwards.[45] The absence of such documents from earlier reigns may mean simply that they have not survived. It is likely, on the other hand, that they indicate the withdrawal of the sultan from direct contact with the grand vizier and the Imperial Council. In one of these, where the Grand Vizier requests an audience with Ahmed I, the Sultan refuses, with the handwritten note: 'You should inform me on paper',[46] suggesting that face-to-face meetings between Sultan and Grand Vizier had become rare.

It is, however, likely that different sultans adopted different styles of rulership, and that practices changed even within a reign. Murad III, for example, is reported to have attended council meetings in person during the early part of his reign, while in the latter part, he became increasingly withdrawn. Furthermore, although law books of the sixteenth and seventeenth centuries define the grand vizier as the sultan's 'absolute deputy' and envisage the monarch as conducting the government solely through the grand vizier – and so through the Imperial Council –, this was probably never the case. The sultan had closer contact with the pages of the Privy Chamber, the Agha of the Gate, the Agha of the Girls or with other courtiers than he did with the grand vizier, and these too could petition the sultan on their own or somebody else's behalf. He might, too, be more inclined to take the advice of his mother, a concubine or the head gardener at the helm of the royal barge than of the grand vizier. The advice writer

Kochi Bey, who presented a treatise to Murad IV in 1631–2, regarded the interference of courtiers in the government as a recent evil, commenting that the grand viziers after Dervish Mehmed Pasha and Nasuh Pasha 'of necessity obeyed and agreed with the inner courtiers, and did not spare their efforts [to do] whatever they wanted'. This, however, seems unlikely. There can have been no time when those in attendance on the sultan's person did not influence his decisions.

5 The Provinces

Provinces

Provinces, in the sense of fixed territorial units with governors which the sultan had appointed, probably did not exist in the Ottoman Empire before the last two decades of the fourteenth century. It is, however, probable, that in the early years of the Empire, Osman (d. *c.*1324) and Orhan (*c.*1324–62) divided their territory into appanages for their sons, other family members, and their most important followers. The only reference to Osman's division of territory appears in the unreliable Ottoman chronicles of the late fifteenth century, which remark that: 'He gave the banner (*Sanjak*) of Karahisar, known as Inönü, to his son, Orhan; and he gave its army command (*subashilik*) to his brother's son, Alp Gündüz . . .'[1] This tale of how Osman shared out land and military command may not be true in detail, but perhaps reflects a reality. The practice of granting appanages and army commands to the ruler's sons acquires a slightly sharper focus in Byzantine chronicles. John Kantakouzenos names Orhan's brother, Pazarlu, as a commander at the battle of Pelekanon in 1328. More notably, it was Orhan's eldest son, Süleyman, who led the Turks across the Dardanelles in 1352 to occupy the Byzantine fortress of Tzympe, and it was with Süleyman that Orhan instructed the Emperor to negotiate in his attempt to regain the fortress. It would seem therefore that, until his death in 1357, Süleyman was governor and army commander in the newly accquired Ottoman territory in Thrace. The Greek chronicler and theologian, Gregoras, also notes that, in 1357, Orhan's third son, Halil, had received lands along the Gulf of Izmit from his father, presumably as an appanage. The later name for the district of Bursa, Hüdavendgar – meaning 'ruler' – suggests that this was the territory belonging to Orhan himself.

177

On this very slender basis, one may perhaps speculate that, by the time of Orhan's death in 1362, it had become customary to allocate land as appanages to Ottoman princes, together perhaps with the leadership of such troops as the land could sustain and other military duties. This was not yet a system of provincial government, and indeed, at this time, the Ottoman principality itself was in size not much more than a province. Nonetheless, some of the elements of the later system seem already to be in place. The vignette of Orhan in the early 1330s, which Ibn Battuta offers, suggests that he was at that time a ruler who intervened personally throughout his realm, rather than one who freely delegated authority to local commanders. However, with increasing age and with the increasing size of his principality, he was happy in the 1350s to delegate the conquest and settlement of Thrace to his son Süleyman, who became, in effect, the governor of a western 'Province'. Thus, by the end of Orhan's reign, two elements of government seem to have emerged. One was the delegation of military command, still at this era to the ruler's family; the other was the grant of appanages, which presumably carried with them an obligation to perform military service.

These were elements which remained in place in the later system of provincial government. Governors received from the sultans appanages, or confirmation of appanages already held, in return for which they provided military service, commanding the troops of their province on the battlefield. Furthermore, until 1595, sultans continued to send out their sons as provincial governors, although their significance in this role diminished as the Empire expanded and they came under closer surveillance.

By the late fourteenth century, there was clearly a need for the formal organisation of Ottoman territory, following the conquests between 1362 and 1400 of Murad I (1362–89) and his son, Bayezid I (1389–1402). It was probably during the first years of Bayezid's reign that the first two administrative provinces of the Ottoman Empire came into being. To the west of the Dardanelles lay Rumelia (*Rumeli*), comprising all the lands conquered in Europe. To the east lay Anatolia (*Anadolu*), comprising all the conquests in Asia Minor. With the eastward expansion of Bayezid's realms in the 1390s, a third province – the Province of Rum – came into existence, with Amasya as its chief town This became the seat of government of Bayezid's youngest son, Mehmed [I (1413–21)], and was to remain a residence of princely governors until the sixteenth century.[2] By 1468, with the annexation of the formerly independent principality of Karaman, there were four. Mehmed II (1451–81) appointed a son, Mustafa, as governor of the new province, with his seat at Konya. But the sixteenth century saw the greatest increase in the number of provinces. This came about largely through the conquests of Selim I (1512–20) and Süleyman I (1520–66), which created the need to incorporate the new territory into the structure of the Empire, and partly through the reorganisation of existing territory.

A list dated 1527 shows eight provinces, with Egypt, Syria, Diyarbekir and Kurdistan added to the original four. These comprised the conquests of Selim I or, in the case of Kurdistan, the outcome of successful negotiations. This province, however, did not survive as an administrative entity. Süleyman's conquests in eastern Turkey, Iraq and Hungary also resulted in the creation of new provinces. The former principality of Dulgadir, for example, became an Ottoman province at some time after its annexation in 1522. After the Iranian campaign of 1533–6, the new provinces of Erzurum, Van, Shehrizor and Baghdad guarded the frontier with Iran. In 1541 came the creation of the province of Buda from part of the old Kingdom of Hungary.[3]

By 1609, according to the list of Ayn Ali, there were thirty-two provinces. Some of these, such as Tripoli, Cyprus or Tunis, were the spoils of conquest. Others, however, were the products of administrative division. When Süleyman I appointed Hayreddin Barbarossa Admiral in 1533, he received the post with the rank of Governor-General of the Islands, a province which the Sultan had created specially for Hayreddin, by detaching districts from the shores and islands of the Aegean which had previously been part of the provinces of Rumelia and Anatolia, and uniting them as an independent province.[4] There were later to be similar changes in Rumelia. In 1580, for example, Bosnia, previously a district of Rumelia, became a province in its own right, presumably in view of its strategically important position on the border with the Habsburgs. Similar considerations led to the creation of the province of Kanizsa from the districts adjoining this border fortress, which had fallen to the Ottomans in 1600.[5] In the same period, the annexation of the Rumelian districts on the lower Danube and the Black Sea coast, and their addition to territories between the Danube and the Dniepr along the Black Sea, created the Province of Ochakov (Özi). At the same time, on the south-eastern shore of the Black Sea, the province of Trabzon came into being. In the words of Ayn Ali: 'By joining the districts of Trabzon and Batum, and annexing them to Gümüşhane and Maçka, a Province has been created.' The purpose of this reorganisation, and especially the creation of the Province of Özi was presumably to improve the defences of the Black Sea ports against the Cossacks.

Provinces, therefore, came into being initially through conquest, and subsequently through the reorganisation of existing Ottoman territory. In the first century of Ottoman expansion, however, conquest did not always entail the annexation of territory. Rather, there was a tendency to keep in place the ruling dynasties of conquered lands and to demand from them an annual tribute and the provision of troops to the sultan's armies. The position of the Shishmanid Tsars of Bulgaria after about 1370, or of Stephen Lazarević of Serbia after his acceptance of Ottoman overlordship in the early 1390s, are examples of this kind of arrangement. It was Tsar Shishman's refusal to provide troops for Murad I in 1387 that led to the Sultan's punitive campaign against Bulgaria in the following year; and Stephen Lazarević's Serbian troops fought in Bayezid's armies at the battle of Nicopolis in 1396 and the battle of Ankara in 1402. For the sultans, the vassal principalities served much the same function as directly ruled provinces: they provided treasure and troops. However, despite sometimes linking the dynasties through marriage, or keeping a son of the vassal ruler as a hostage at the Ottoman court, the control of a dynastic principality was less secure than the control of a directly ruled province.

From the end of Bayezid I's reign, but more especially from the accession of Mehmed II, it became more usual to appoint Ottoman governors than to rely on vassals. In 1395, for example, Bayezid I executed the last Shishmanid Tsar of Bulgaria, and annexed his realm to the province of Rumelia. The native dynasties did not, however, simply disappear. There was a tendency rather for the sultans to appoint members of deposed dynasties, or at least those who survived the conquest and did not flee, to provincial governorships within the Empire, away from their hereditary lands. Thus, for example, the Bavarian captive, Schiltberger, records a certain 'Schuffmanes' – obviously a Shishmanid – as the governor of a district of Anatolia near the Black Sea in 1398. In recording events in western Anatolia nearly twenty years later, the Greek chronicler, Doukas, noted a governor called 'Sousmanes', evidently from the same family. Similarly, there are records in the fifteenth century of members of the Zenevis family, whom Mehmed I (1413–21) had expelled from Gjirokastër in Albania,[6] serving as Ottoman provinical governors.[7] In 1461, Mehmed II expelled the last of the Isfendyarid dynasty from Sinop, awarding him lands near Bursa in exchange for his hereditary territory.[8] The Isfendyarid principality meanwhile became a district of the province of Anatolia. As these examples show, the old dynasties often acquired a new status as members of the Ottoman provincial élite. It was a position, however, which required them to acknowledge the loss of dynastic lands, and to accept that their appointment to office and the assignment to them of revenues was now dependent on the will of the Ottoman sultan.

By 1500, the four central provinces of the Empire – Rumelia, Anatolia, Rum and Karaman – were under direct rule. The sultan, however, continued to maintain a system of tributary principalities north of the Danube. Wallachia, Moldavia and the Khanate of the Crimea, territories which Mehmed II had brought under his suzerainty, remained in the control of native dynasties tributary to the Sultan. So, too, did the Kingdom of Hungary after the battle of Mohács in 1526. It was only, it seems, the need to counter Habsburg claims to the Kingdom and to organise a military frontier against Austria that persuaded Süleyman I to annex part of Hungary as a directly ruled province after the death of the King in 1540. Transylvania, however, remained as a kingdom owing allegiance to the sultan.

By 1550, therefore, Transylvania, Wallachia, Moldavia and the Crimean Khanate remined under the rule of native dynasties who paid tribute to the sultan. Similarly, a few enclaves under the rule of local lords survived in Turkey and the Arab lands, but these now formed districts within larger provinces. By the mid-sixteenth century, apart from the principalities north of the Danube, all provinces came under the direct rule of the sultan.⁹ The governors-general were all his appointees, and he could remove or transfer them at will. Their term of office was limited: governorships were not hereditary, and no one could serve for life. A governor-general's income was also dependent on the sultan. On appointment, he received a prebend consisting of a defined parcel of revenues, raised within the boundaries of his province. This grant, which could in some cases rise to more than a million akches a year, put the governors-general among the wealthiest men in the Empire.¹⁰ The prebend, however, was dependent on the appointment and, unless he was wealthy in his own right, a governor would have no income when he was out of office. He would also receive other perquisites, but these too were by virtue of the office which, in turn, was dependent on the sultan. A governor-general, therefore, had no permanency and no territorial base in a province, and no income from it that outlived his tenure.

The Turkish word for governor-general is *beylerbeyi*, meaning simply 'lord of lords'. There is no early Ottoman source that records this term, but the late-fifteenth-century chronicle of Ashikpashazade implies that, in the fourteenth century, it had the sense of 'army commander'. Specifically, he attaches it to Murad I's commander in Europe, Lala Shahin, and to his successor, Kara Timurtash. Probably by 1400, it had acquired the sense of 'Governor-General of a Province.' This was not, however, so much a change in meaning as an extension, since a major role of a governor-general was to command the troops who held fiefs in his province. In times of war, they would assemble under his standard and fight as a unit in the sultan's army. However, as a territorial governor, the *beylerbeyi* now had wider repsonsibilities. He played the major role in allocating fiefs in his province, and had a responsibility for maintaining order and dispensing justice. His household, like the sultan's in the capital, was the political centre of the province.

The Genoese merchant at the Court of Mehmed II, Iacopo de Promontorio, has left a description of the governor-general of Rumelia, dating from 1475, which gives a good account of the functions of an Ottoman Governor-General between about 1400 and 1600:

The *beylerbeyi* of Rumelia has under him 17 captains, each with a following for himself . . . ; and beyond this, he has particularly under himself 1500 fighting men with their own pay, whom he pays from his own funds. He has an income in Rumelia of 32 000 ducats, through various benefits and, furthermore, very profitable perquisites, principally 4000 ducats from the said captains, and similarly from the abundance of other less important offices, which he grants to whomsoever he wishes. Yet he is obliged, in times of war, to bring with him, at his own expense, the said fighting men, all mounted, one third of them with bow, arrows, cuirass, coat of mail, shield, sword, lance and iron mace, with 150 horses in horse-armour, all in good order; the rest with bows, arrows, sword, shield, mace and lance, apart from those to whom the Signior sometimes grants cuirasses, helmets, bows and coats of mail. He holds Court and Palace in style, like the Grand Turk, according to his own rank. He imposes sentence of death and of all other matters to all the inhabitants of Rumelia and its Provinces *de jure* and *de facto*, and everything that he does is approved by the Signior without any protest. He maintains by him two officers . . . and two Judges as deputies to administer justice; they have 4000 ducats of maintenance among the four of them, together with profitable perquisites . . .

The office of governor-general was the most prestigious and the most profitable in the provinicial government, and it was from among the governors-general that the sultan almost always chose his viziers. There was also, it appears, a hierarchy among the governors themselves. The senior was the governor-general of Rumelia who, from 1536, had the right to sit on the Imperial Council. Precedence among the remainder, according to Ayn Ali in 1609, followed the order in which the provinces were conquered, although he does not make it clear whether this ranking had anything other than a ceremonial significance. However, before 1650, there was another development. During this period, the practice began of appointing some governors-general with the rank of vizier. A vizieral governor, according to the chancellor Abdurrahman Pasha in 1676, had command over the governors of adjoining provinces who 'should have recourse to him and obey his command'. Furthermore, 'when Governors-General with Vizierates are dismissed from their province, they listen to lawsuits and continue to exercise Vizieral command until they reach Istanbul'.

Sanjaks

The districts which made up a province were known as *sanjaks*, each under the command of a district governor or *sanjak beyi* ('lord of a Sanjak'). The number of sanjaks in each province varied considerably. In 1609, Ayn Ali noted that Rumelia had twenty-four sanjaks, but that six of these in the Peloponnesos had been detached to form a separate province of the Morea. Anatolia had fourteen and the province of Damascus eleven. There were, in addition, several provinces where there was no formal division into sanjaks. These, in Ayn Ali's list were Basra and part of the province of Baghdad in Iraq, Al-Hasa in north-eastern Arabia, and Egypt, Tripoli, Tunis and Algiers in North Africa. He adds to the list Yemen, with the note that 'at the moment the Imams have usurped control'.

These provinces were, however, exceptional: the typical pattern was the Province subdivided into sanjaks. By the sixteenth century, these presented a rational administrative pattern of territories, based usually around the town or settlement from which the Sanjak took its name, and with a population of perhaps 100 000.[11] However, this had not always been the case.

It seems more likely that before the mid-fifteenth century, the most important factor in determining the pattern of sanjaks was the existence of former lordships and principalities, and of areas where marcher lords had acquired territories for themselves and their followers. Some sanjaks in fact preserved the names of the dynasties that had ruled there before the Ottoman conquest. The most striking cluster of such names appears in western Anatolia, between the Aegean and Mediterranean coasts and the high plateau. Here the sanjaks of Karesi, Saruhan, Aydın, Menteshe, Germiyan, Hamid and Teke preserve the names of the pre-conquest dynasties. In Rumelia, Kyustendil in Bulgaria is a contraction of 'Konstantin-eli' ('Constantine's land'), named after its lord Constantine Dejanović, killed in battle in 1395. Karlieli ('Carlo's land') in Epiros preserves the memory of its former lord, Carlo Tocco, who died in 1429. The name of the sanjak of Dukakin in northern Albania is a reminder of the rule there of the Dukagjin ('Duke John') clan.

Iacopo de Promontorio's list of the – in his time – seventeen sanjaks of Rumelia also gives a sense of how the Ottoman administration preserved the boundaries of pre-Ottoman lordships. Albania he divides into two: 'Araniti's Albania', comprising the lands to the south, belonging until the early fifteenth century to the Araniti clan, and 'Scanderbeg's Albania', comprising land further north which had belonged to the Kastriote family, and especially to its most famous member, Scanderbeg, who had resisted Ottoman rule between 1444 and 1466. Bosnia, in the same list, appears as two sanjaks, the self-explanatory 'Kingdom of Bosnia' and the 'Other Bosnia', presumably Hercegovina. Serbia, too, Iacopo divides into 'Lazar's Serbia', referring to the territory of Prince Lazar, who had lost his life at the battle of Kosovo in 1389, and the 'Despot's Serbia', presumably the lands of George Branković along the Danube.

In the immediate aftermath of the conquest, Ottoman sanjaks preserved more than the names of their former rulers. Where early cadastral registers of the conquered lands survive, they often reveal the names of fief holders who had evidently occupied the same position before the conquest. For example, the cadastral survey of southern Albania, dated 1431, shows a number of Christian fief holders, who were clearly survivors from the previous régimes. On the eastern border of the Empire, the first Ottoman survey of the sanjak of Amid, made in 1518,[12] designates a group of fief holders as 'Akkoyunlu', evidently clansmen or appointees of the Akkoyunlu dynasty that had ruled the area until 1503. These survivors provided continuity between the old order and the new. Nonetheless, it is equally clear that the new Ottoman rulers sought to counterbalance the influence of these representatives of the old régime by also awarding fiefs in the newly conquered districts to men from distant areas of the Empire. The 1431 survey of Albania shows a group of fief holders as being 'from Saruhan'. This was the old principality in western Anatolia, which Mehmed I had finally annexed in 1417, at about the same time as his forces had occupied southern Albania. What Mehmed clearly did was to remove the fief holders from Saruhan, where they had local connections, and transferred them to Albania, where they had none. Their only source of patronage and protection was the Ottoman Sultan, whose interests they would therefore defend from local challenges. The 1518 survey of Amid shows the same principle at work. The Akkoyunlus in the sanjak held fiefs of a modest value: the highest valued fief went to a man registered as being 'from Rumelia'.

The practice of counterbalancing local with alien fief holders in newly conquered lands probably dates from the early fifteenth century. At the battle of Ankara in 1402, a major cause of Bayezid I's defeat was the desertion to Timur of troops from the old principalities of western Anatolia, which Bayezid had annexed in 1390. These men deserted when they saw their former lords in Timur's army. It was perhaps this experience that convinced the sultans of the need to draft foreign elements into newly conquered districts as a counterweight to the local power holders that had survived the change of régime, and to deport some of the local men to distant provinces where they had no connections.

Immediately after the conquest, therefore, an Ottoman sanjak would often retain the boundaries of a pre-Ottoman lordship, and usually have a fief-holding élite composed of survivors from the old régime and new settlers and deportees. Within a generation, the survivors and their descendants would often have lost their non-Ottoman identity, notably through the conversion of Christians to Islam. With their assimilation, an area which had been an independent principality, or part of one, would become a standard Ottoman sanjak.[13] The passage of time could also bring changes in sanjak boundaries. For example, the Venetian Lauro Quirini's list of sanjaks, which seems to reflect the position in the 1430s, lists Bergama and Manisa as independent units.[14] By the time of Iacopo de Promontorio in 1475, they had become part of the sanjaks of Karesi and Saruhan respectively.

Not all provinces and sanjaks, however, completely lost their special identity. The difficulties that Mehmed II and Bayezid II (1481–1512) had in suppressing the dynasty of Karaman indicate how strong local particularism could be. Furthermore, a few notables retained hereditary rights to governorships. Prominent among these were the marcher lords,[15] who already in the fourteenth century had emerged as a political force in Rumelia. Their origins are unclear, but some had clearly converted to Islam and joined the invading Turks. The name of one of these families, Mihaloghlu – 'Michaelson' – was so clearly Christian that during the fifteenth century a legend emerged describing the conversion of the first 'Michael' and his association with Osman, the first of the Ottoman line.[16] The name of another marcher family, Malkochoghlu, also appears to be a Turkish form of the Slavonic Marković, suggesting that these were descendants of Marko, a Macedonian lord, whose father, Vlkashin, had lost his life at the battle of the Maritsa in 1371. However, the greatest of the marcher lords to emerge in the fourteenth century was Evrenos, whose tombstone records his father's name as Isa, indicating a Muslim Turkish descent.[17] The names of the other marcher lords, such as Turahan, that emerge in the first half of the fifteenth century also suggest Turkish origins.

These lords not only commanded the Ottoman armies in Rumelia, but also exercised political power. Evrenos, for example, was a negotiator at the discussions leading to the Treaty of Gallipoli in 1403. His son, Barak, conducted negotiations with Venice in 1409. Mihaloghlu Mehmed served both Prince Süleyman and Prince Musa during the civil war of 1402–13. His desertion to Prince Mehmed in 1411 was a major factor in Musa's defeat. Most importantly, however, the marcher lords emerged as territorial magnates. The nucleus of Evrenos's vast holdings was around Yiannitsa in the Vardar valley to the west of Thessaloniki, while the Mihaloghlus were lords of Vidin, on the Danube in north-western Bulgaria. As territorial lords, they and their descendants retained hereditary rights to governorships in Rumelia. Lauro Quirini, for example, records a sanjak in central Greece under the name of its lord, Turahan.[18] This sanjak had disappeared by the time Iacopo made his list in 1475, but the family of Turahan continued to occupy positions as sanjak governors. 'Evrenos', on the other hand, appears in the lists of both Lauro and Iacopo as the designation of the sanjak comprising this family's lands in Macedonia. Iacopo adds the note: 'a great lord, formerly Ali Bey son of Evrenos . . . [of the 1500 warriors in the sanjak] the majority are his slaves'. By the sixteenth century, the name 'Evrenos' as the designation of a sanjak had disappeared, although the family's lands remained intact, and family members retained a hereditary right to governorships. The 1527 list of sanjaks, records a member of the Evrenos family as governor of Kruševac in Serbia, and members of the Mihaloghlu family as sanjak governors of Vidin and Nikopol on the Danube in Bulgaria. It was to members of the Malkoch family that the sultan assigned the hereditary governorship of Bosnia after its conquest in 1463.

The local power and claims to office of the great marcher lords and their descendants limited the sultan's discretion in organising territory and in making appointments to governorships in Rumelia. Nonetheless, it appears that at least from the mid-fifteenth century, the Ottoman rulers attempted to restrict their influence. They no longer, it appears, had a part in the central councils of government, as they had done in the fourteenth and early fifteenth centuries, and it would seem none of them rose beyond the rank of sanjak governor. The families, however, survived – in the case of the Evrenosoghlu and Mihaloghlu families, until today – and their local influence continued.

Semi-independent dynasties also survived in some areas of the Anatolian and Arab Provinces. These were not, however, descendants of the Ottoman marcher lords, but rather lords who were locally too powerful for the sultan to remove. For example, in the marshlands of southern Iraq and the desert fringes of Arabia, the sultans tried to gain the allegiance of effectively independent tribal chiefs by giving them the title of Sanjak Governor. It was, for example, by these means that Selim II (1566–74) in 1567 attempted to bring to an end the rebellion of the marsh Arab, Ibn Ulayyan, in the delta of the Tigris and the Euphrates.[19] In south-eastern Turkey, the territories of the Kurdish lords were also semi-independent. These had become part of the Empire after the battle of Chaldiran in 1514, as a result of negotiations with the agent of Selim I (1512–20), Idris of Bitlis. In 1609, Ayn Ali made a note on their formal status. In listing the sanjaks in the province of Diyarbekir, he notes that it had ten 'Ottoman districts' and, in addition, eight 'districts of the Kurdish lords'. In these cases, when a lord died, the governorship did not go to an outsider, but to his son. In other respects, however, they resembled normal Ottoman sanjaks, in that the revenues were registered and allocated to fief holders who went to war under their lord. In addition, however, Ayn Ali noted that there were five 'sovereign sanjaks', which their lords disposed of 'as private property', and which were outside the system of provincial government. Ayn Ali records similar independent or semi-independent districts in the Province of Çıldır in north-eastern Turkey and, most famously, in the province of Van where the Khans of Bitlis ruled independently until the nineteenth century.[20] There were other areas, too, which enjoyed autonomy or semi-autonomy. In the second half of the sixteenth century, Kilis came under the hereditary governorship of the Janbulad family, while Adana remained under the rule of the pre-Ottoman dynasty of Ramazanoghlu. In the Lebanon, Ayn Ali refers to the Druze chieftains with the note: 'There are non-Muslim lords in the mountains.'

There were other autonomous enclaves in the Empire, whether or not they received formal recognition as sanjaks but, by the sixteenth century, these were exceptional. Most of the sanjaks throughout the Empire were under the rule of non-hereditary appointees, who had no permanent family of territorial connections with the area.

The office of sanjak governor resembled that of governor-general on a more modest scale. Like the governor-general, the sanjak governor drew his income from a prebend, which consisted usually of revenues from the towns, quays and ports within the boundary of his sanjak. In areas, however, where there was no town, or where revenues which typically went to the sanjak governor had been assigned to the governor-general or the sultan, then he would also draw his income from agricultural taxes. The first Ottoman cadastral survey of Shkodër in northern Albania, for example, shows that, in 1485, the revenues from the customs, the quay and the fisheries of Lake Boyana had been assigned to the Sultan, while the sanjak governor drew his revenue from the town of Peje and its surrounding villages. A sanjak governor on his first appointment might receive 150 000 to 200 000 akches per year. By the mid-sixteenth century, 200 000 seems to have been normal. He could, however, receive an increase in his living, either as a reward for effectiveness in battle or for some other reason, or by receiving a new and more lucrative appointment in the area. A senior sanjak governor could expect receive 500 000 to 600 000 akches, perhaps while serving in a high yielding district.[21]

Like the governor-general, the sanjak governor was also a military commander. The term *sanjak* means 'flag' or 'standard' and, in times of war, the cavalrymen holding fiefs in his sanjak, gathered under his banner. The troops of each sanjak, under the command of their governor, would then assemble as an army and fight under the banner of the governor-general of the province. In this way, the structure of command on the battlefield resembled the hierarchy of provincial government.

Within his own sanjak, a governor was responsible above all for maintaining order and, with the cooperation of the fief holders, arresting and punishing wrongdoers. For this, he usually received half of the fines imposed on miscreants, with the fief holder on whose lands the misdeed took place, receiving the other half. Sanjak governors also had other duties – for example, the pursuit of bandits, the investigation of heretics, the provision of supplies for the army, or the despatch of materials for shipbuilding – as the sultan commanded. Those on the frontiers might also have special military functions. In the late fifteenth century, for example, the sanjak governors of Bosnia had the duty of making annual raids, usually into Hungary. Similarly, the Mihaloghlu family held not only the hereditary governorship of Vidin, but also the leadership of the raiders (*akinjis*), the troops who in the fifteenth and sixteenth centuries held tax free lands in Rumelia in exchange for making annual raids across the Danube, or acting as the vanguard and as shock troops for the Ottoman army. Sanjak governors in border regions might equally engage in cross-border negotiations over, for example, the return of escaped slaves or the return of prisoners, in accordance with treaty arrangements.

A sanjak governor did not, however, have authority over all the sultan's subjects in his district. What defined authority was, above all, the right to collect taxes, and specifically the right to pocket fines. Sanjak governors collected taxes from lands and properties which they held as prebends, and clearly had full authority in these areas, as they also did in the lands assigned to fief holders, where they usually had the right to half the fines. However, some areas or properties would form a prebend of the sultan or of the governor-general, and a few fiefs were 'free', meaning that the fief holder kept all fines. In these areas, the sanjak governor's men had no right of entry. In addition, privately owned lands and properties, and those belonging to trusts did not come under the authority of the sanjak governor. In this respect, the government within a sanjak was not uniform. Provinces and sanjaks were not, however, the only administrative divisions of the Empire. Each town and city throughout the sultan's realms had a Judge, who acted as judge and notary within his own judicial district, and also as a royal official implementing the sultan's commands. The judge, unlike the sanjak governor, had authority throughout his area, with judgeships forming what has been called 'a parallel system' of administration.[22]

Before about 1600, the sanjak governor, beside the judge, was perhaps the most important figure in Ottoman provincial administration. Nonetheless, the lack of records from before the mid-sixteenth century makes it impossible to know who the sanjak governors were, or how their careers progressed. Before the sixteenth century, many would presumably have held hereditary rights as descendants of formerly independent dynasties or lords. Besides these, the sultans must have appointed some men raised in their own household. By the sixteenth century, a clearer pattern had emerged.

As had been the case since the fourteenth century, sons of the reigning sultan received sanjak governorships on reaching the age of puberty. According to the so-called 'Law-Book of Mehmed the Conqueror', male members of the royal family descended in the female line also had the right to receive a sanjak governorship, but no higher appointment than this. The families of the marcher lords of Rumelia also had an automatic right, either to a governorship in general or to a specific district. In eastern Turkey and northern Iraq, the Kurdish lords and governors of 'sovereign sanjaks' ruled by dynastic right. Far more sanjak governors, however, were graduates of the Palace and, in this sense, members of the sultan's own household. A Law Book from the reign of Selim II in fact lists the fifteen 'Aghas of the Stirrup' who were qualified for governorships. These were the Agha of the Janissaries and his second-in-command, the commanders of the Six Divisions of the Palace Cavalry, the Chancellor, the Master of the Standard, the Head Gatekeeper, the Master of the Stable, the Head Taster and the Head Falconer.[23] In 1609, Ayn Ali was to repeat this list, with a few omissions. It is not clear whether promotion to sanjak governor was ever quite so clear cut as the Law Book implies, but some careers certainly followed this pattern. Lutfi

Pasha, for example, who was to become grand vizier in 1539, served as master of the standard and head gatekeeper in the Palace before 'going out' to become sanjak governor of Kastamonu. Sokollu Mehmed, who was to become grand vizier in 1566, served as head gatekeeper before 'going out' in 1546 as sanjak governor of Gallipoli and Admiral.[24]

However, sanjak governors who had graduated directly from these senior positions in the Palace formed a minority. There were many more who had moved from the Palace or service of the central government, to a lesser post in the provincial government, such as Intendant of the Registers of Fiefs, and from there advanced to become a sanjak governor. In the 1570s, over a third of provincial governors had reached their position through this route. A smaller group – a little over ten per cent at this time – owed their rise to being a blood relative or member of the household of a governor. This pattern of recruitment to governorships was probably typical of the sixteenth century up until the 1580s.[25]

The tenure of a sanjak governor was usually less than three years. As a rule, he could expect reappointment in a different sanjak, often in the same province or region, and often with the possibility of an increase in the value of his prebend. The procedure for reappointment is not, in all details, clear. Records indicate that it was the governor-general who made the recommendation on behalf of the candidate, who would then perhaps present it to the grand vizier, for recommendation to the sultan. When the sultan had approved, the Imperial Council would send a decree to the governor-general, informing him of the appointment, and ordering him to assemble the prebends from which the new sanjak governor was to draw his income. The governor-general would then give the candidate a memorandum of appointment to take to the Palace, where he would receive letters patent conferring on him his new position. It was at this stage that he officially assumed office.[26]

Sanjak governors did not, therefore, make their career in a single sanjak. Each posting was, as a rule, of short duration, although the moves from district to district did allow for increases in income with each new posting. Furthermore, during the fifteenth and sixteenth centuries, to hold office as a sanjak governor was, as a rule, a neces-

sary step in seeking promotion to governor-general. Outside the
hereditary sanjaks, however, each appointment was in the gift of the
sultan, and frequent moves prevented any governor from gaining a
powerful local following and establishing himself as an autonomous
lord.

Fiefs

Lands within a sanjak fell usually into three categories. First, there
was land that was privately owned. Second, there was land that
formed part of a trust and, third, there was land that was at the disposal of the sultan. Private lands were relatively few, since the sultans
aimed to keep as much land as possible under their own control, but
also because Muslim inheritance laws would insist on the division of
the property among the heirs on the death of the owner. Families
preferred, therefore, not to keep landed property in this form. Trust
land, on the other hand, was extensive throughout the Empire. This
was land or property whose revenues went to support the cause
which the founder had nominated in the trust deed, typically a
mosque, hospice, bridge or fountain. The revenues could also, however, go to support the founder, his or her family and descendants
and, since trusts were made in perpetuity and their properties were
indivisible, this was the legal form in which families often preferred
to hold their lands.[27] The most extensive category of land within
most Ottoman sanjaks was, however, *beglik* or *miri*. Both these words
have the sense simply of 'pertaining to', or 'at the disposal of the
ruler', and it was these lands the sultan allocated as fiefs.

The sanjak governors did not, it seems, have rights of entry into
lands which were private property, or which belonged to trusts, but
only into *miri* lands. In this sense, an Ottoman sanjak consisted of a
conglomeration of fiefs in a particular area, whose holders served in
war under the standard of the sanjak governor, and having within it
certain areas where the governor had no authority.

By 1500, the terminology of Ottoman fief holding had stabilised.
The term for the smallest fiefs, with a value of up to 20 000 akches
per year, was *timar*. A larger fief, with a value of up to 100 000 akches, was a *subashilik*, known more commonly after about 1500 as a

zeamet. The largest holding, with an annual value of 100 000 akches or more, was a *hass*.

A typical *timar* consisted of a village or group of villages, and the fields around them, which the sultan had allocated to a cavalryman, who had the right to collect the taxes from his peasants and, in return, provided the sultan with military service. In addition, he was responsible for maintaining order on his land, with the right usually to pocket half the fines for misdemeanours. This duty clearly required him to reside at least within his sanjak, and usually on the *timar* itself, where he would also enjoy a plot of land for his own use. The *timar* holder did not, however, own the land from which he drew his revenues. Rather he held it as a grant which the sultan could revoke, and would do so, especially if the cavalryman failed to appear for military service.

The allocation of land as *timars* was thus a way of maintaining a large and permanent force of cavalrymen, whom the sultan could call upon to serve in the army during each campaigning season. It was these *timar* holders who made up the bulk of the Ottoman armies from the late fourteenth century to the late sixteenth.

The origins of the system clearly lie in the pre-Ottoman period. Most notably, perhaps, the Byzantine emperors began, from the late eleventh century, to allocate land as fiefs to support soldiers. They did not, however, give the soldiers ownership of the land, and the grants were revocable. The Greek word for such a fief was *pronoia*, and the appearance of this term in the fourteenth and fifteenth centuries in Serbia and in Venetian held territory in Albania suggests that fief holding on the Byzantine model had become widespread in the Balkan peninsula.[28] It seems probable, therefore, that when Osman and Orhan made their conquests in Byzantine Bithynia and Thrace, they would have found the system of *pronoias* intact, and that as Ottoman territory spread westwards beyond the former Byzantine realms, their successors would have encountered similar patterns of fief holding. In origin, therefore, the Ottoman *timar* seems to have been an adaptation of the Byzantine *pronoia*.[29] Both *pronoias* and *timars* were grants of land made by the sovereign to a soldier; both were revocable; and in neither case did the soldier become the owner of the land. There are also striking similarities between vocabularies of Byzantine and Ottoman fief-holding. The Greek word *pronoia* means literally 'care, attention'; the Turkish term *timar* means exactly the same thing. The Greek word for a peasant-holding on a *pronoia* is *zeugarion*, meaning literally 'yoke, pair (of oxen)'; the Turkish terms for a similar holding, *chift* or *boyunduruk*, mean the same. The Byzantine unit of land measurement, of forty paces is *stremma*. The word means literally 'twisting' with reference to the measuring rope. The Ottoman equivalent for a plot forty paces square is *dönüm*, a word which means, literally, 'turning'. The Ottoman term for 'incidental taxes due to a *timar* holder' is *bad-i hava* or 'wind of the air', a phrase which would be puzzling were the Byzantine terms for a similar group of taxes not *aër* or *aërikon*. These terms which are fundamental to Ottoman fief-holding, suggest a Byzantine model for the system.

There is other evidence that the Ottoman system of fief-holding was an adaptation of pre-Ottoman practice. In much of central and south-eastern Anatolia, fief-holding did not conform to the pattern found in Rumelia, western Anatolia and elsewhere in the Empire, where all the revenues of a *timar* went to support a cavalryman. Instead, the revenues were divided. One portion, including usually the imposts on the land itself, went to a cavalryman who, like a normal timar holder, had the obligation to perform military service. This portion was at the disposal of the sultan to allocate and revoke at will. The other portion, which usually included the tithe on crops, belonged to the private owner who could dispose of it as he or she wished. The origins of this system of divided revenues clearly lie in the pre-Ottoman period and, since the area in which it was in operation corresponds more or less to the extent of the realms of the Anatolian Seljuks, it is reasonable to assume that it was an inheritance from the Seljuks and their successor principalities. Ottoman cadastral registers also offer scraps of evidence that point to this origin. A register from the time of Mehmed II, for example, records that two private portions of revenue had been bought from the seljuk treasury and sultan in 1284 and 1285. Another register of 1520 notes that the Seljuk Sultan Alaeddin II had granted the private portion in 1255. Ottoman registers record similar transactions as having occurred under the Karamanids and the Akkoyunlus, successors to the Seljuks in south-central and south-eastern Anatolia. The Ottomans seem, in fact, to have maintained more or less intact the system that they found.[30]

There were therefore two types of *timar*, the one where all the taxes went to support a cavalryman, the other where a portion went to support a private owner. The first type is a descendant of the Byzantine *pronoia*, the second continues the practices of the Anatolian Seljuks. Not surprisingly, when the sultans introduced fief-holding to newly conquered lands, where it had not existed previously, as in Hungary after 1541, it was the first type of *timar*, with no private owners, that they introduced.

The allocation of land as *timars* provided the sultan with a standing cavalry army, and also, since the cavalrymen themselves collected the taxes from their *timars*, relieved the treasury of the task of raising revenues and paying salaries. Nonetheless, the system presented its own problems. First, there was the question of mobilisation. When the sultan ordered a campaign, he needed to know the number of troops available, and the obligations of each man in providing horses, weapons, tents and armed retainers; he needed also to be certain that the men would assemble and join the main army at the appointed place. All these things were difficult when the cavalrymen were scattered throughout the Empire. Second, there was the danger that the cavalrymen, particularly in remote areas, would convert their *timars* to private property, which would then slip from the sultan's control.

The government was careful to prevent this happening. It did so in the first place through bureaucratic surveillance. Immediately upon the conquest of a district, a surveyor made an inventory of its taxable resources, showing how these had been distributed, as *timars* to cavalrymen, as *zeamets* to their officers, or as *hass* assigned to the sultan, governors-general or sanjak governors. Any problems which the surveyor could not solve, he submitted to the Imperial Council. The completed survey he would submit to the sultan for scrutiny. Once approved, the Land Registry Office in the capital would codify the results in a 'detailed register'.[31] This typically showed all the towns, villages, hamlets, tribes and cultivated lands in a sanjak. For each settlement or tribe, they would give the names of male heads of household, bachelors and, in some Christian areas, widows, together with the lands which they cultivated. These it would note as a 'yoke', 'half a yoke', or 'less than half a yoke'. It also recorded the landless. In addition, the register would show the estimated yield from each tax levied on every community. It would show how these revenues were divided up between fief holders, and the total annual yield of each fief, whether *timar*, *zeamet* or *hass*. A typical entry in a detailed register would therefore have the heading: 'Timar of A son of B'. Underneath would be a heading 'Village of X' with, beneath it, the name of each male head of household, with an indication of the size of their plot of land. Beneath this, it would list the taxes which the villagers paid, together with their estimated yield, and finally an estimate of the total sum. From the information in these detailed volumes, the land registry office made summary registers, which showed the *timar* holders and other beneficiaries of a sanjak's revenues, and the value of their fiefs. These, in turn, provided the information for the muster registers, which listed the names of all the cavalrymen in a sanjak. It was these that allowed the army commander in times of war to check the list against the men who had appeared for service, and to note any absentees.[32]

The problem with the detailed registers was that they went out of date almost immediately. The registry dealt with this difficulty, in the first place, by noting changes in the margins. Frequently, for example, there were new appointees to *timars* and, in this case, a marginal note would record the name of the new man, together with the date and place of the appointment. In a detailed register of Thessaloniki from about 1445, for example, a marginal note appears against 'The *timar* of Lagato Rayko': 'Died. Hanged when he was proved to be a brigand. Transferred to his son Kraso. July, 1451. Sofia.' Another example from a 1455 register for Skopje notes against the 'Timar of Musa, retainer of [the marcher lord] Isa Bey': 'Given to the Janissary, Yusuf of Stanimaka: he renders service to the fortress. 16 July, 1463. Camp at Kachanik.' To this is added: 'Since this Yusuf of Stanimaka committed homicide, this *timar* has been taken away and given to the Gatekeeper, Kirik Musa, slave of the Sultan . . . August, 1466. Camp at Prilep.'[33] These marginalia were adequate for a few years, but the passing of a generation required the creation of a new register. It became the custom, therefore, every twenty years or so, to make a new register, recording anew all the necessary data. One copy of the register for each sanjak remained in the Registry Office in Istanbul; the sanjak governor held the other.

This system of keeping registers enabled the sultan's government to keep track of the names and the number of *timar* holders throughout the Empire, and thus also to know the total number of cavalrymen available for war. It also made it possible to check the extent of each cavalryman's obligations. A cavalryman had to bring with him on campaign not only a horse, but also his own arms and armour, tents and one or two armed retainers, the level of his obligations being dependent on the value of the income from his *timar*. Many of the registers which survive from the fifteenth century record these obligations together with the other details of the *timar*. For example, a *timar* which appears in the Albanian register of 1431–2 notes that a certain 'Abdullah, [formerly] Page of the Slipper [to the sultan]' held a timar worth 5 310 akches. For this, he had to present himself on campaign 'in person', with 'body armour, 1 man-at-arms, 1 attendant and 1 tent'. The practice of making such 'men and tent notes' in the registers disappeared in the sixteenth century, but by then the existence of a general code laying down the obligations of fief holders had rendered them unnecessary. The value of a cavalryman's income, checked against the code, would determine the level of his obligations.[34]

The registers were the most important means by which the Sultan surveyed and controlled his *timar*-holding cavalrymen. The practice itself of allocating land as timars, on the pattern of Byzantine *pronoias*, must date from the early decades of the Empire, and possibly even from the time of Osman. The practice, however, of making registers developed later. The earliest full and fragmentary registers date from 1431-2, but these demonstrate an already developed system of bookkeeping, suggesting that surveyors and clerks had been compiling such registers for several decades at least. In the absence of firm evidence, it is impossible to be certain, but it is likely that the practice began in the reign of Bayezid I (1389–1402). This emerges from a diatribe against the centralisation of government under Bayezid, which appears in the popular Ottoman chronicles of the late fifteenth century. These make the comment that when Hayreddin Chandarli and

Kara Rüstem 'came to the Ottoman court, they filled the world with deceit: they invented registers of accounts and began piling up money. When [Chandarli]Ali became Vizier, immorality increased.'[35]

The Ottomans evidently inherited the system of keeping registers from the Ilkhans, the overlords of Seljuk Anatolia from 1243. This is evident from the fact that the language of the registers, and of treasury documents in general, is Persian, and from the adoption of the same cypher script for writing numerals as appears in Ilkhanid accounts. The Ottoman registers also show some of the features of Ilkhanid fiscal practices that followed the reforms of Ghazan Khan (1295–1304),[36] notably the concept of the fiscal year, and the use of a single unit of account, in the Ottoman case, the silver *akche*. The *timar* registers, in particular, assign to each *timar* a notional annual value in akches, and it was this figure that determined the cavalryman's obligations. These residues of apparently Ilkhanid practice in the registers also suggest that it was Bayezid I who introduced them, since it was he who annexed the former Seljuk and Ilkhanid territories in central and northern Anatolia and, briefly, Karaman. It is possible that it was from the chancelleries that he found in these areas that the Ottomans derived their system.

Until the late sixteenth century, the registers were the primary means of keeping a check on *timar* holders. In the late fifteenth century, however, the sultan acquired a new means of control. In 1487, during the reign of Bayezid II, a new land and tax survey of the sanjak of Bursa resulted in the issue of a new register which contained, as an introduction, a Law Book which laid out in detail the taxes and fines due from the tax-paying subjects of the district to the fief holders.[37] In future, all new registers opened with a similar Law Book,[38] which could act as a source of reference in establishing the extent of *timar* and other fief holders' rights, especially to taxes. In the sixteenth century, each district came to have its own Law Book, which underwent a revision with each new survey of the sanjak and the creation of a new register. The reign of Bayezid II also saw the compilation of a general Law Book, that aimed to summarise the rules which define membership of the military – that is, the non-tax-paying – class, most of whom were *timar* holders, services owed by fief holders, the obligations of tax-paying subjects, tax regulations, and other matters, including criminal statutes. This general Law Book represents a wish to harmonise, as far as possible, the practice of *timar*-holding throughout the Empire. It appeared in its earliest version in the late 1490s. Further recensions followed, until the appearance of the final version in about 1540.[39] The function of the Law Books was presumably to give the practice of *timar*-holding a statutory framework, and to provide an authoritative source of reference in case of disputes. It is unlikely, however, that this project was wholly successful since, in many places it is evident that the statutes in the Law Books are at variance with what appears in the registers.

The registers and the Law Books allowed the sultan to keep a check on the numbers and identities of fief holders, the value of their fiefs and the services owed, and the laws governing fief-holding, in the Empire at large and in each sanjak. In addition, he came to control, as far as he was able, the manner of appointment.

In the fourteenth and early fifteenth centuries, the manner of distributing *timars* was probably informal and, at least in the border areas, not wholly under the control of the sultan. Some of the earliest *timar* holders would have been survivors from the pre-Ottoman régime who had maintained their status after the Ottoman conquest. Such groups emerged from each phase of Ottoman expansion.[40] The earliest surviving registers from Rumelia show Christian *timar* holders. Similarly, the Anatolian registers show large numbers of hereditary fiefs in the possession of families or tribes, sometimes indicating specifically that these had come down from pre-Ottoman times. A register of the Province of Karaman, for example, records a 'group of cavalrymen in the said village, descendants of Yavash Bey, [who held the village by virtue of] a deed of Mehmed Bey of Karaman.'[41] After the annexation of Kurdistan in the early sixteenth century, the Kurdish lords continued to hold lands as hereditary fiefs in return for military service. However, many *timar* holders in the early Empire were probably relatives, slaves and followers of the sultan and his lords: certainly the Rumelian registers of the fifteenth century record *timars* in the possession of the men of the great marcher lords. The registers of the second half of the fifteenth century, however, suggest an increasing regularity in the system of appointment and a growing central control, a process which culminated in a series of sultanic decrees between 1531 and 1536, which aimed to regularise the allocation of *timars* and to bring it fully under surveillance.

In order to do so, it was necessary first to establish who had an entitlement to a *timar*. In the first place, there were salary holders at court, in the Janissaries or the six divisions, or in the households of pashas. As the earliest surviving records show, there had always been *timar* holders from these categories. However, two decrees from the 1530s, themselves probably revising laws from the time of Bayezid II, try to regularise such appointments by specifying the value of *timars* which they should receive. A gatekeeper of the palace, for example, had an entitlement to a *timar* of 15 000 *akches* per year, as did certain categories of Janissary officer. On the death of a Pasha, his steward was to receive a *timar*, worth 14 000 *akches*, his head gatekeeper, one worth 13 000, while his master of the stables and treasurer both received fiefs of 8000 *akches*. For those who were on the sultan's payroll, transfer from a salaried post to a *timar* probably represented a demotion, as it entailed giving up a salary and leaving the Palace, which was the most prolific source of patronage.

Courtiers and soldiers, who had previously enjoyed a salary, formed a minority of *timar* holders, as did the occupiers of hereditary fiefs. The majority were those who had inherited from their fathers. What a son inherited, however, was a right to a *timar* in general, rather than to his father's *timar* in particular. This right, too, was subject to restrictions, which a decree of 1531 to the Governor-General of Rumelia set out to codify. According to this document, if the holder of a *zeamet* worth 20 000 to 50 000 *akches* per year died in battle and had three 'valiant' sons, these should receive *timars* of 6000, 5000 and 4000 *akches* respectively. If the same *zeamet* holder were to die at home, then two of his sons would receive entitlements to fiefs worth 5000 and 4000 *akches*. The document continues in this way, showing entitlements of heirs to *timars* of different values, ending with those whose *timar* is worth less than 10 000 *akches*. In this case, if the *timar* holder dies in battle, two 'valiant' sons receive *timars* of 3000 and 2000 *akches*; if he dies at home both sons receive *timars* of 2000. It is clear from these regulations that not every son had a right to a *timar*. If a fief was worth more than 20 000 *akches* per year, three sons, and if it was worth less than 20 000, two sons inherited the right. A decree of 1536 reiterates this last point: 'However many sons survive him, [timars] should be given to two of his sons, in accordance with my previous command.'

A son with a hereditary right could occupy a timar at any age. However, if a *timar* holder was still a child, he had to send an armed man to war in his place, and to serve in person on reaching maturity. This the decree of 1536 defines, with the remark that, until that time, any *timar* holder over ten years of age had to go on campaign, but that 'now that campaigns are distant', the age of service was sixteen.

The decrees of the 1530s suggest that, by that time, holders of *timars* and *zeamets* had, to some extent, come to form a hereditary caste, with restricted entry. This was a tendency which the decrees aimed to reinforce. The command of 1531, to the Governor-General of Rumelia, reported that sons of ordinary subjects had unlawfully received fiefs and were using their position to extract money and to 'transgress and interfere'. The Imperial Council had confiscated the fiefs of some of these 'outsiders'. However, the decree continues, from 8 March 1531, no one whose *timar* was recorded in a register should be referred to as an 'outsider' or have his *timar* removed. This established who, from that date onwards, was a member of the military caste. Second, the decree stated clearly which of a fief holder's sons had a right to a timar, and of what value. Third, the decree tried to stop fraudulent claims. A command of 1536 to Lutfi Pasha, when he was Governor-General of Rumelia, states that 'tricksters claiming to be sons of cavalrymen' may appear to demand *timars*. In such a case, the order continues, ten *timar* holders should verify the claimant's identity.

These rules aimed to restrict entry to the class of *timar* holders. Nonetheless, outsiders undoubtedly did acquire *timars*, and there was a limited official recognition of their right to do so. Not all sons automatically qualified for a *timar* on the death of their father. Those excluded could, however, acquire the right to a *timar* before his death through voluntary service in the army. Ordinary tax-paying subjects had no right at all to acquire *timars*, but Lutfi Pasha provides evidence that, in fact, they did, when he lays down the guidelines for such awards: 'If an ordinary subject performs oustanding service and, by

the increase in [royal] favour, receives a *timar* and becomes a cavalryman, you should not offer protection to his relatives, father or mother.' In principle, however, after the 1530s, accession to a fief followed
strict rules.[42]

Rules of succession required enforcement. This the Ottoman government sought to achieve by establishing procedures for recording
and controlling appointments to *timars* and *zeamets*. Some such system must have existed from the late fourteenth century, when the
practice of drawing up registers evidently began, but it is only from
the early sixteenth century onwards that records survive.

It might take years for a person who qualified for a *timar* actually to
receive one: the conquest of new territory which made new lands
available, or a war where large numbers of cavalrymen died, provided the best opportunities. The first stage in the process was for the
governor-general or sanjak governor to draw up a list of candidates
and forward them in a sealed register to the grand vizier in Istanbul,
or elswhere if he was on campaign. The Imperial Council would then
draw up a decree in the sultan's name, ordering the governor-general to award a *timar*, and forward it to the candidate. The next stage
was for the candidate to take the decree with his father's diploma of
appointment to the governor-general, who would then check the
validity of the diploma or, if it was missing, look up his father's timar
in the register. The candidate had also to produce a witness or witnesses from the military class who could testify that he was the son
of a cavalryman. The governor-general would then, when one
became available, confer a vacant timar. This was not, however, the
end of the process. If the *timar* was in Rumelia and worth less than
6000 *akches* per year, in Anatolia and worth less than 5000, or in the
provinces of Karaman, Rum or Maraş, and worth less than 3000,
then the governor-general of the province could himself award the
diploma of appointment. These were '*timars* without memorandum'.
If, however, the *timar* was worth more, the candidate had to acquire a
sultanic diploma from Istanbul. The decree of 1531 to the Governor-
General of Rumelia tightens the rules still further: from that date, all
candidates receiving a fief for the first time required a diploma from
the sultan. It is doubtful, however, whether this rule was universally
observed.

For a candidate to acquire a sultanic diploma, the governor-general had to write a memorandum naming the candidate, the witnesses and designating the *timar*, together with its value. If the diploma of the candidate's father was missing, he would write on the reverse: 'The father's diploma, issued in [such-and-such a year], is lost.' The candidate had then, within six months, to exchange the Governor-General's memorandum for a sultanic diploma.

This required him or his agent to travel to Istanbul, and to go to the office of the controller of the land registry, where a clerk would copy the memorandum into the day book of *timar* allocations in the appropriate sanjak. The office would also establish whether the value of the *timar*, as it appeared in the memorandum, tallied with its value as recorded in the summary register of *timars*. If there was a discrepancy, the clerk would alter the memorandum to accord with the register. The office would also check to see whether the allocation would result in the division of the core of a fief. If it did so, the appointment was invalid. Once the checks were complete and the memorandum registered, it went to the chief clerk, who would authorise the issue of a diploma in the sultan's name. The applicant could then take this and return to his *timar* as a properly appointed cavalryman.[43]

Once in possession of a *timar*, a cavalryman had the opportunity to increase his income. Each *timar* had an indivisible core of land and revenue. However, it was possible to add to this nucleus. To do so a *timar* holder would have to petition the governor-general, sanjak governor, or *zeamet* holding officer, who could present a petition on his behalf. After checking the records, the controller of the land registry could then grant the increase. The greatest opportunity for acquiring supplements to a *timar* was after a battle, when the *timars* of the war dead became available. Indeed, clerks and registers accompanied the army on campaign, making it possible to redistribute *timars* after an encounter with the enemy. The following, for example, is an entry granting a supplement to a *timar* in a register made near the scene of action, immediately after the sea battle of Lepanto in 1571: 'Yalakabad [in the sanjak of Kocaeli]: the *timar* of Ivaz [comprising] the village of Harmanlı and others, [worth] 5000 *akches* per year. Daud, who holds a *timar* worth 3000 *akches* in the said district and is entitled to a *timar* worth 7000 akches, has petitioned that the above-named is dead and his *timar* vacant, and has requested [that it be allotted to himself]. This has been decreed, with the 1000 *akches* surplus.'[44]

Not only could *timar* holders achieve an increase in the value of their *timar*, they could also lose it altogether. Before 1531, it appears that governors-general on their own had the right to remove *timar* holders. The decree of 1531, however, forbids them to attribute crimes to cavalrymen and to remove their *timars* as punishment, stipulating that, in future, if a cavalryman committed an offence, the governor-general should submit the facts to the Imperial Council, which would then take the decision on whether or not to confiscate. Documents from later in the sixteenth century, indicating that the Imperial Council reinstated cavalrymen whom governor-generals had removed without an order to do so, indicate that this is what happened in reality. Once deprived of his *timar*, a cavalryman could 'join the ranks of tradesmen' or, by attaching himself to the retinue of a governor-general, hope to acquire a new *timar*. The process of reinstatement is another matter which the decree of 1531 attempts to regulate.

By the mid-sixteenth century, therefore, the sultan's government had devised procedures for controlling the allocation and tenure of *timars*, and for determining the level of service which a cavalryman had to provide. The basis of the system was taxation of the peasantry, which the government sought to control, firstly by ensuring that the land remained under cultivation, and secondly by determining the rate of taxation.

The status of the peasants on lands allocated as *timars* must have varied from area to area, according to local practice and conditions. Nonetheless, certain rules which aimed to ensure that the land was under continuous cultivation seem to have applied to peasants on *timars* throughout the Empire. Peasants were not, strictly speaking, bound to the soil, but in principle the law forbade them to leave the land uncultivated without paying compensation to the *timar* holder. A Law Book of 1583 for a subdistrict of Sivas expresses this general concept: 'Since it is an accepted custom for farm-breaker's tax to be taken from those who abandon the land and follow another livelihood, this law is considered valid in the said subdistrict.'[45] Law Books for other sanjaks provide more detail. A regulation dated 1539 for the sanjak of Vize seems to be typical: 'If a peasant goes to another place and it is more than ten years since he left, and his land-holding remains uncultivated, according to the law, his cavalryman should take farm-breaker's tax from him. If it is less than ten years, the cavalryman, with the cognizance of the Judge of the time, should remove him and bring him [back] to his place.'[46] In short, if a peasant let a plot lie fallow, he had either to return and cultivate it or, after a certain period, pay compensation. If, however, another cultivator took his place, he paid only the yoke tax on his plot for the year of his departure. The aim of the law was not so much to tie the peasant to the land, as to keep the land under cultivation.

Other rules regulated the peasant's access to the land. A new entrant to a plot had to pay an entry fine to the *timar* holder, and enjoyed security of tenure so long as he continued to cultivate his holding. If, however, he left it fallow for three years, the *timar* holder had the right to expel him. The same rule could also apply if he converted arable to pasture, since pastureland is less productive of taxes, and conversion would result in loss of income for the *timar*. Finally, peasant holdings were hereditary, but only from father to son. Daughters and other relatives could succeed, but only if the *timar* holder considered them capable of cultivation and only if they paid an entry fine.[47]

The purpose of these rules was to maximise the revenue coming from the land to the *timar* holders, who were for the most part cavalrymen, and so to ensure the strength of the sultan's army.

The provinces transformed

Ottoman provincial government, as it had developed between the fourteenth and mid-sixteenth centuries was a rational system. It divided the Empire into provinces, provinces into sanjaks and sanjaks into fiefs; that is, into *hass*, *zeamets* and *timars*. The governors-general, sanjak governors and fief holders drew their income directly from the revenue sources which the sultan had assigned to them and, in return, they served the sultan in provincial government, and also as a cavalry army. The hierarchy of provincial government was equally a military hierarchy. On campaigns, governors-general were commanders-in-chief of all the troops in their province; the sanjak governors commanded all the cavalrymen who held *timars* and *zeamets* in their sanjak. Among the fief holders, too, there was a hierarchy of command, with some of *zeamet* holders acting as officers in command of contingents of *timar* holders. The *timar* holders, too, went to war at the head of a retinue of one or more armed retainers.

The system was clearly effective in both its functions. For much of the sixteenth century – a period for which records and some modern studies are available – there seems to have been an increase in the population of the Empire and in the size and numbers of settlements,[48] suggesting that this was, by and large, a period of prosperity and stability in the Ottoman provinces. The relative orderliness of provincial government may have played a part in this. More obviously, however, the system fulfilled its military function. Year after year, the sultan raised a cavalry army from the provinces, which could measure its effectiveness in victories.

By the late sixteenth century, there had been a drastic change.[49] Ottoman armies no longer enjoyed the victories of earlier times. The Austrian War of 1593–1606 brought disasters and ended in stalemate. More humiliatingly, the wars with Iran after 1603 brought defeat and loss of territory. Contemporary observers who commented on this decline from glory found the reason for it largely in the breakdown of provincial government and, since it was the provinces that supplied the bulk of the army, there clearly was a link.

In Anatolia in particular, the commentators noticed the impoverishment and flight from the land that accompanied the Jelali rebellions. An anonymous author who presented to Osman II (1618–22) a treatise on the problems of the Empire and how to cure them remarked: 'For example, in the Province of Sivas there was such scarcity and famine that it became well known how the peasants ate not only cats and dogs, but also human flesh.' Such conditions, he continues, had led to a drastic fall in revenue. Previously, the Treasury of Sivas had not only covered the expenses of the province, but had also remitted eight million akches annually to the Imperial Treasury. Now, he says, it never remits more than a quarter of a million. The author also noted how viziers and provincial governors no longer possessed retinues of 'valiant slaves' and armouries to match, ready to go on campaign the moment the sultan commanded. In contrast to this old order, he describes Ahmed I's farcical campaign against the Jelalis in 1605, which office holders treated as 'a wedding or a pleasure trip', with many arriving late.

What, however, struck observers most forcefully was the collapse of the *timar* system, which had both provided a cavalry army and helped to maintain order. In the old days, the anonymous author comments, fiefs in Rumelia, Anatolia and the Arab Provinces had produced 200 000 fighting men, and it was with these that the sultan had conquered lands. Now, he continues, most of these had disappeared. The old system of allocating *timars* through governors-general had collapsed and, instead of going to fighting men, *timars* went to the unqualified or into the 'baskets' of great men. By 'baskets' the author was referring to the practice, which became common in the early seventeenth century, whereby great men placed their own nominees in *timars*, while themselves pocketing the revenues. In a question to the author, the Sultan himself noted how 'Viziers, Governors-General, and other office holders', had bestowed *timars* on members of their own household 'down to the cats and dogs'. The result was a loss in the number of *timars* that still produced warriors. Instead, the author claims, those who went on campaign were 'mostly Turks, Gypsies, former brigands and people who have purchased timars'. The breakdown in the old system of allocating and recording *timars* had also led to disputes over possession. The reform writer, Kochi Bey, in the treatise which he wrote for Murad IV (1623–40) in 1631–2, comments that, because fiefs were allocated from Istanbul, only one in ten was undisputed. Ayn Ali, in his treatise of 1609, had noticed the same thing. 'When it is a question of service on campaigns,' he comments pithily, 'not one man appears from ten *timars*, but at the time of tax-gathering, ten men dispute one *timar*.'

The reform writers located the reason for the decline in the corruption of the body politic. 'Because', the author of the anonymous treatise writes, 'the gate of bribery is open, the Provinces face ruin.' The process, they claim, began in the reign of Murad III (1574–95).

The reform writers were accurate in their account both of the 'decline' and of the period when it began. By the seventeenth century, appointment to high office did involve spending money.

Furthermore, surviving documents support their view of depopulation in the provinces, at least in Anatolia, and a drop in the number of *timars*. In 1573, for example, there were 592 *timars* and 51 *zeamets* in the western Anatolian Sanjak of Aydın. In 1632–3, the figures were 261 and 31 respectively, a decline of nearly 40 per cent. Records of appointment also show that, in 1563–4, about 70 per cent of *timars* initially bestowed in the sanjak of Aydın went to the sons of *timar* holders. In 1588–9, during the time of Murad III, this figure had fallen to 19 per cent, in 1610, to less than 10 per cent.[50] This loss of *timar* holders as a hereditary caste was something that the reform writers lamented as a cause of present catastrophe.

However accurate their description of the symptoms of 'decline', the reform writers were undoubtedly oversimplifying in their analysis of its causes.[51] Although the symptoms of this transformation became acute, as the reform writers noted, during the reign of Murad III, there are signs of change from earlier in the century. Kochi Bey and others looked back on the *timar* holders of Süleyman I's day as a closed and valiant military caste, but this picture seems overoptimistic. In the 1530s, the sultan certainly took measures to restrict entry to the ranks of *timar* holders, but this was probably because the lack of new land for distribution was already apparent rather than a deliberate attempt to form a military caste. Furthermore, *timar* holding, at the lowest level, imposed heavy burdens of service in return for a very modest income, and signs of discontent are already apparent before and during the reign of Süleyman I. In 1511, for example, *timar* holders joined Shah Kulu's rebellion. Later in the century, the fact that the rebel Prince Bayezid was able in 1558–9 to attract *timar* holders to his cause is an indication that these were not happy with their position. The long wars with Iran and Austria imposed further burdens, requiring them, during campaigns which lasted for over a decade, to overwinter in the field.[52] During these decades, too, the *timar* holders of Anatolia, who did not serve on campaign, faced the task of maintaining the peace in an increasingly rebellious region.

A symptom of discontent during this period was, increasingly, refusal to fight and desertion. During the Iranian war of 1578–90, *timar* holders frequently sought to avoid service. In this respect, a command of 1583 to the sanjak governor of Bozok is typical. The preamble to the

decree notes that cavalrymen with *timars* worth less than 3000 akches per year were not to go on campaign, but instead to remain behind
to maintain security in the Sanjak. 'However,' the preamble continues, 'it has been heard that most of the cavalrymen, great and small,
in the Province of Rum, have stayed where they are, each one having
acquired, with some excuse [for remaining behind], a Noble
Command of the Sultan . . . They remain behind and receive decrees
[exempting them from service] on the slightest excuse.'[53] The discontent among the cavalrymen, which was already plain during the
war with Iran, turned, during the Austrian war, to desertion and dismissal, the most notorious instance occurring after the battle of
Mezö-Keresztes in 1596. The result, Ottoman historians insist, was to
turn deserters into brigands.

The burdens of service, whether as soldiers on campaign or as
militiamen fighting rebels, made *timar* holding unattractive, at least
for those with low value fiefs. This became especially true in the late
sixteenth century, a period when inflation diminished income, wars
were prolonged, there was little hope of taking booty, and new revenues following the conquest of new territory were no longer available. The resulting discontent among *timar* holders, and consequent
desertion and rebellion, was undoubtedly a factor in the collapse of
the *timar* system which seventeenth-century writers observed in their
own time. There were, however, other causes, military and administrative.

The military development which undermined the timar-holding
cavalry was the increasing use in war of handheld firearms, and with
this, the practice of fighting from entrenched positions. This required
increasing infantry numbers at the expense of cavalry. Until the late
sixteenth century, horsemen had greatly outnumbered footmen in
Ottoman armies. In the mid-sixteenth century, the Janissaries – the
Sultan's standing infantry corps – had numbered about 10–12 000
altogether, while there would normally be about 40 000 cavalrymen
in a single army. However, during the war of 1593–1606, the Ottoman
cavalry proved to be greatly inferior on the battlefield to the Austrian
infantry. The response of the Ottoman government was therefore to
expand its own infantry numbers, which it did by increasing the
number of Janissaries, and by recruiting infantrymen in the

provinces from among the young men who knew how to use firearms.

This solution brought with it a major problem. Payment of the Janissaries and the infantry levies was through the central Treasury, which found itself unable to meet the demand for cash, a problem that the late sixteenth-century inflation exacerbated. One solution was to debase the coinage. In 1585, in order to pay the Janissaries and other troops of the imperial household, the government reduced the silver content in the *akche* by almost 50 per cent. A result of this was a Janissary rebellion in 1589, in protest against receiving payment in debased coinage. Late payment and a further debasement in 1600 of slightly less than 30 per cent, led to further Janissary riots in 1593 and 1606. This solution, therefore, merely caused further problems. Another way was to borrow. In 1591, the government borrowed 70 000 gold pieces to pay the wages of the Janissaries and, after this, there were few years when the Treasury did not call on credit to meet its obligations.[54]

There was, however, another solution, and this was to increase the revenue sources available to the Treasury. Until the late sixteenth century, the government had assigned most taxes in Rumelia, Anatolia and Syria to *timar* holders, who drew on them directly as a source of income. These taxes did not, therefore, come directly to the Treasury. A way to overcome the Treasury deficit was therefore to convert *timars* and *zeamets* to tax farms, whose income the farmers transferred directly to Istanbul. It seems probable that the first large scale transfer came in 1597, following the confiscation of the *timars* belonging to the deserters of Mezö-Keresztes. Thereafter, the number of tax farms increased at the expense of *timars*, a development which mirrored the changes in the composition of the army. Fewer cavalrymen needed fewer *timars* to support them, while the growing number of infantrymen required more tax farms as a source of cash for their wages. This was an important factor in the collapse of the *timar* system that so disturbed the reform writers of the seventeenth century.

Another factor was a gradual change in the way of allocating *timars*. The decrees of the 1530s had formalised entitlement to fiefs and, at the same time, there was a regular procedure for allocation. *Timar*-holding became, by and large, hereditary within the military class, and allocation was by recommendation to the governors-general, and subject to ratification by the sultan. In the late sixteenth century, exceptions to this pattern became common.

During the long wars of 1579–90 and 1593–1606, it became usual for army commanders in the field to allocate *timars* to replace cavalrymen who had died in battle or who were absent at the roll call, giving them sometimes to men who put themselves forward without a recommendation from a patron. In the seventeenth century, Kochi Bey was to point particularly to this category of *timar* holder as a cause of decline. In 1584, he wrote, Özdemiroghlu Osman Pasha, the commander in the Iranian campaign, began to give *timars* worth 3000 *akches* to 'outsiders', but only to men who had performed outstanding service. Thereafter, however, fiefs went, regardless of merit, 'to city lads and peasants', who had no entitlement by birth.

More important, however, in transforming the *timar* system was the increasing influence of the Palace. In the early sixteenth century, it was unusual for the palace, without a memorandum from a governor-general, to issue a decree allocating a *timar*. In fact, allocations of this kind were sufficiently rare to merit an explanatory note in the register. Later in the century, these notes disappear, suggesting that the Palace was beginning to exercise more control. By 1586, with the issue of a decree depriving governors-general of the right to allocate *zeamets*, that is fiefs worth more than 20 000 *akches* per year, this tendency became explicit. With these developments, the old system effectively collapsed.

These changes in the method of allocation brought with them new types of *timar* holder. What becomes particularly noticeable is the large number of *timars* that supported slaves or retainers of viziers, governors-general and other office holders, the registers noting such men as 'the follower of X', 'the man of Y' or 'attached to Z'. Such *timars* had always existed and, indeed, some time after 1541, Lutfi Pasha stated that grand viziers maintained their men with *timars*. In the late sixteenth century, however, the practice became more widespread and, in the seventeenth, became standard. A note in an early seventeenth-century register states as a rule: 'It is customary that *timars* of registered servants of a Vizier, in case of the death of the *timar* holder, be again given to his servant.'

It was not, however, only the retainers of viziers and governors who received *timars* in this way. By the late sixteenth century, men from the households of other members of the Imperial Council, such as the chancellor or chief treasurer, or the followers of palace officers, such as the head pantryman or head gardener, could also receive their pay in the form of *timars*. It was common, too, for even minor office holders, such as clerks in the chancellery or members of the Six Divisions to obtain *timars* for their servants. Princesses similarly acquired fiefs for their retinue, who clearly had no obligation to serve in the army. It became, in fact, customary to append lists of exempted *timar* holders to the muster rolls of cavalrymen, and dismissal for nonappearance on campaign was valid only if the missing man's name did not appear in the list of exemptees. Even then, if a person lost his *timar* because he had failed to appear at the roll call of the army, he could keep it if he could prove that he was a retainer of a great man.[55]

By the early seventeenth century, therefore, *timar*-holding had changed its character. Fewer fiefs supported cavalrymen, and more supported *office* holders and their followers. Some went to nominees whose sponsors pocketed the income, a practice which Murad IV formally abolished when, in 1631, he confiscated such timars and real-located them to fighting men. Murad's reforms did not, however, last. Records indicate that the changes in the *timar* system were perma-nent. From the late sixteenth century, the practice of drawing up detailed registers of *timars* in each district ceased. Instead, the Land Registry Office began to compile registers of households grouped into taxable units, together with other sources of government rev-enue. To maintain a record of *timars*, the government did, from the mid-seventeenth century, begin to keep summary lists, but the old system of detailed registers never revived. These new administrative procedures indicate that, by this time, *timars* were neither the major support for the army, nor the most important means of distributing revenue.

Accompanying the decline in *timar*-holding was a change in the sys-tem of provincial government. Until the late sixteenth century, the hierarchy of *timar* holder, *zeamet* holder, sanjak governor and gover-nor-general had also been one of military command. At the century's end, this too began to alter. With the chronic shortfall in treasury income, it became possible for tax farmers to acquire governorships, either for themselves or their nominees, on condition of increasing the revenues of the province or sanjak. For the same reason, it was no longer uncommon, as it had been, for a treasurer to receive the office of governor-general. With this development, provincial government began to lose its military character.[56]

There were other changes, too, in the mode of appointment to provincial government. Until the last decades of the sixteenth century, it was normal to appoint sanjak governors from the lower ranks of the provincial administration, so that, typically, a career might lead from a post in the Palace to a position in the registry or treasury of a province, and from there to a sanjak governorship. In the 1560s, about two-thirds of sanjak governors had received their posts by this route. It was normal, too, that a governor-general should have previously served as a sanjak governor. In 1570, about four-fifths of governors-general had come to their posts by this route. In 1580, however, this pattern began to change, with appointees from the Palace and, increasingly, from other great households, beginning to outnumber men with previous experience of provincial government. By 1630, only about a quarter of sanjak governors and governors-general had come to their position from an earlier provincial posting. At the same time, another change served to undermine the integrity of the old system of provinces and sanjaks.

From the 1580s, few sanjak governors served in a particular post for more than three years: by the 1630s, over half served less than a year, and about 90 per cent less than two. The same was true of governors-general. By the 1630s, over half served less than a year. This was a result, presumably of increasing competition for office, which had the effect not merely of shortening periods of service, but also of increasing the time spent out of office. Loss of position brought with it a loss of income and so, to compensate for this, it became common for the sultan to make lifetime grants of revenue, which served to maintain dismissed governors in the periods between appointments. Such grants had been less common in the earlier period, and had the effect of undermining the old system of provinces and sanjaks. Traditionally governors held their *hass*, the fief which produced their income, within their area of jurisdiction, whether this was a sanjak or a province. Life grants, however, meant that the lands or other revenue sources that formed a governor's permanent income lay outside his own area of government, producing a fragmentation of the old provincial system, at the expense particularly of the sanjaks. In the 1630s, too, some sanjaks, such as Bayburt in the Province of Erzurum or Smederovo in the province of Buda were abolished and assigned as revenue to the governor-general.[57]

By the mid-seventeenth century, therefore, Ottoman provincial government was very different from what it had been a century earlier. Most noticeable was the fall in the number of *timars*, and the assignment of *timars* as tax farms, or to non-military nominees of the palace or other great households. The changing nature of *timars* had its counterpart in the changing nature of provincial government. Until the end of the sixteenth century, provincial governors had also been military commanders. With the decline in the number of *timars* and the appointment of some governors with fiscal rather than military responsibilities, this ceased to be the case, except perhaps in border areas. This was a development which undermined sanjak governors in particular, whose main function had been to oversee the *timar* holders in their sanjaks and to command them on the battlefield. The increasing allocation of lifetime revenues from their district to men from outside the sanjak also tended to fragment their area of command, and to emphasise their loss of authority.

6 The Law

Legal communities

The Ottoman Empire was a Muslim polity, but one with a large non-Muslim population[1] which, in most districts of the European provinces, formed a majority of the population. The Muslim population itself was heterogenous. The Kurdish tribesmen on the eastern borderlands, the Turcoman of Anatolia, or the Bedouin of Syria, Egypt and the Arabian peninsula had little in common with the Muslim townsfolk. The shi'i and kizilbash communities found especially in central Anatolia, Iraq and the Lebanon professed a form of Islam at odds with the sunni orthodoxy of the Sultans.

The legal structure of the Empire reflected this diversity. There can be no doubt that tribesmen, villages in remote areas and the kizilbash populations that professed allegiance to the Safavid Shah rather than to the Ottoman Sultan followed their own customs in settling disputes and arranging their affairs. At the same time, Christian and Jewish communities enjoyed legal autonomy in intracommunal matters, under the aegis of their own religious leaders.[2] The sultans, however, maintained their authority over the non-Muslim communities through the system of appointments. Senior churchmen or rabbis held office by virtue of a royal warrant. This would probably involve a cash payment but, once appointed, the office holder gained tax exemptions and extensive legal and fiscal autonomy within his community, as a model warrant from the late fifteenth century for the appointment of a Greek Metropolitan demonstrates:

Because the bearer of this Noble Decree, the priest named X, has brought European florins as a gift to my Noble Treasury, I have granted him the Metropolitanship of Y. I have commanded that, in whatever way previous Metropolitans exercised their Metropolitanship over the priests, monks and

other Christians of that area, [he should do the same]; and whatever churches, vineyards and orchards they had the disposal of, he too should have the
disposal of them. He should be exempt from . . . taxes. The priests, monks
and other Christians should recognise him as their Metropolitan, and have
recourse to him in cases which pertain to the Metropolitanship.[3]

The heads of the Armenian and Jewish communities enjoyed a similar freedom in regulating the affairs of their communites. They exercised this power, however, by virtue of their appointment by the
sultan.

Ecclesiastical, Jewish and customary law were all, therefore, current within the Empire. Nonetheless, Islamic law always had precedence. From as early, presumably, as the fourteenth century, the
Ottoman sultans established a network of Islamic courts, so that
every town throughout the Empire had one to serve both the town
itself and the surrounding area. All the sultan's subjects therefore
came within the jurisdiction of an Islamic court. Muslims used these
courts exclusively, whether in cases which involved Muslims alone
or in those involving both Muslims and non-Muslims. However, the
courts were also open to non-Muslims who, as records testify, often
brought their affairs to be settled there, even in defiance of their own
religious authorities. Occasionally, for example, Jewish women
would take advantage of the more generous provisions of Islamic
law to claim their inheritance through the Islamic rather than
through the Jewish courts.[4] A Muslim, on the other hand, had no
access to a non-Muslim court, nor did a non-Muslim in any case
which also involved a Muslim. The Islamic courts were therefore, the
primary courts of the Empire. They existed in every district; they
were open to all, regardless of their religion; and for all mixed cases
and cases involving Muslims alone they were the only courts which
had official status.

The sacred law

Although the Ottoman sultans were the sponsors of Islamic law[5] – the
shari'a – they were not its originators. Islamic law was not the creation
of a Muslim state or sovereign, but rather the creation and common

property of the Muslim community, regardless of political divisions. Its origins lay in the eighth century in the discussions of jurists who formalised its basic concepts and terminology. By the tenth and eleventh centuries, it had achieved a classical elegance in its literary forms and subtlety and sophistication in its conceptual apparatus.

At the same time, the jurists had developed a theory of the origins of the law which gave it an unquestionable legitimacy. They located its source directly in Divine Revelation. God had made known His Eternal Word to mankind in the Quran, which He had revealed through the Prophet Muhammad. The Quran was therefore the first source of the law. The second was the record of the sayings and actions of the Prophet, whom God had chosen as an exemplar to mankind. The Quran is indeed the source for some statutes, such as the rule which allows a man to marry up to four wives, and the basis for some areas of the law, notably the rules for inheritance. The direct influence of the Quran is, however, limited. The Traditions of the Prophet were a more abundant source of legal authority. These probably in fact emerged in parallel with the law itself, and served to justify newly formulated doctrines by projecting them back to the time of the Prophet[6] but, whatever their origins, the study of Traditions became an important element in Islamic legal science. To supplement these divine sources, the jurists also recognised legal analogy, the unanimity of juristic opinion and custom as supplementary bases of the law.

The belief in the divine origins of the law gave it a prestige which raised it above the political authority of the moment. It was the ruler who brought the law to life by putting its ordinances into effect, but no ruler could alter its substance. The interpretation and transmission of the law always remained in the hands of scholars – the *ulema* – who, by virtue of their role as guardians of the tradition, always enjoyed a position of power in Islamic societies.

Islamic law was not, however, monolithic. There was a distinction between the law of the Sunnis and the law of the *Shi'is*, and sunni law itself, early in its history, divided into four Schools. These were the *Hanafi, Shafi'i, Maliki* and *Hanbali* Schools, each named after its supposed founder. The differences between the doctrines of the schools were not great but, once established, each school became virtually impervious to the influences of the others. Loyalty to a school became a characteristic of Islamic jurists, much of whose originality went into defending school doctrine. Here, for example, the *Hanafi* jurist Marghinani (d. 1198) is defending the *Hanafi* view that a gift becomes the property of the donee only after he or she has taken possession. He is refuting the *Maliki* opinion that offer and acceptance are alone enough to transfer ownership:

In the opinion of Malik, the [donee's] ownership of the property is established before he takes possession, by analogy with sale . . . But we [*Hanafis*] follow the Words of the Prophet – peace and blessings be upon him – : "Gift is not permissible before the gifted object has been taken into possession." The intention of this is to deny [that] ownership [is transferred] because the [mere] permissibility [of gift] is established without [taking possession. The *Hanafis* also stipulate taking possession] because making a gift is a voluntary act, and to establish ownership before [the donee] takes possession would make incumbent on a voluntary agent, something for which he has not volunteered, namely delivery [of the gift] . . .

School tradition became a distinguishing mark of *Hanafi* jurisprudence, and this also had an effect on the practice of law. Only in two cases, for example, do *Hanafi* jurists permit adherents of their school to have recourse to a non-*Hanafi* judge for the solution of problems. *Hanafi* law does not permit a woman whose husband has deserted her with no maintenance to seek a termination of her marriage, nor does it permit the dissolution of an oath. In these two case, however, *Hanafi* jurists allow *Hanafis* to seek a termination of the marriage or dissolution of an oath from a *Shafi'i* judge, since both these things are possible in the *Shafi'i* school. This, however, is a rare exception to the exclusivity of each school's doctrine and practice.

Contrary, perhaps, to expectations, the nearly impenetrable borders between the schools of law did not lead to excessive rigidity in legal thought or practice since, within itself, each school accommodates differences of opinion. Despite the theory of Divine Revelation as the source of law, the method which jurists normally in fact use to legitimise a doctrine is to attribute it to an earlier jurist of the school. The *Hanafis* typically attach legal opinions to the name of the school's founder, Abu Hanifa (d. 750), or to the names of his two disciples,

Abu Yusuf (d. 798) and al-Shaibani (d. 805). In *Hanafi* literature, it is common to find opposing opinions attributed to these figures, with each view representing a legitimate doctrine within the school. On the question, for example, of whether it is permissible for two non-Muslims to witness a marriage between a Muslim man and a non-Muslim woman, the jurist Quduri (d. 1037) writes: 'According to Abu Hanifa and Abu Yusuf, it is permissible; but Muhammad [al-Shaibani] said that it is not permissible.' On the question of whether the owner of a house or its current occupant pays blood money when a corpse is found on the premises and the killer is unknown, Abu Hanifa and al-Shaibani make the owner liable. Abu Yusuf, on the other hand, fixes liability on the current occupant. In both these cases, either doctrine is valid, and judges could choose which one to follow in a particular case. For each problem, therefore, unless it involved a fundamental doctrine, a school might offer two or more solutions, allowing for flexibility both in juristic debate and in legal practice.

In its contents, Islamic law covers all aspects of Islamic life. Any comprehensive legal text begins with the 'Acts of Worship', the ritual acts which mankind, as His slaves, owe to God. These are the laws which every Muslim must know at least in their fundamentals and which, in many ways, define Muslim life. Prayer, for example, is obligatory, and if the prayer is to be valid, the worshipper must be ritually pure. To achieve this state requires him to make a ritual ablution after most forms of bodily emission and even after sleep, with the consequence that mere physical existence serves as a constant reminder of God's command. The requirement to pray five times a day at set hours, to attend the communal prayer on Friday and to fast annually in Ramadan not only reminds Muslims of their obligations to God, but also defines their sense of the passing of time and, through the congregational prayer and universal fasting, create a sense of a religious community. The Friday prayer also had a political aspect. The law requires the prayer leader to be either the Muslim ruler himself, or the ruler's appointee, and hence it was through the obligatory congregational prayer that Muslim sovereigns broadcast their authority and the congregation signalled their obedience.

The longer section of a comprehensive manual of Islamic law regulates transactions between persons. It is here that the jurists discuss, for example, marriage, maintenance, divorce and inheritance or, in the fields of commerce and property rights, sale, pre-emption, hire, pledge and gift. In this section, too, the jurists lay down the rules for the foundation and maintenance of trusts, rules of evidence and procedure in court, and other matters important to the everyday life of the community. However, although this section of the law deals predominantly with secular affairs, ritual and religious considerations are always present. In the first section of his chapter on invalid sale, for example, Quduri reminds the reader that sale is invalid when 'one or both of the objects exchanged is [ritually] forbidden, such as the sale of carrion, blood, wine or pork', these being items which are forbidden to Muslims and so of no commercial value. Furthermore, the jurists included in the same section as covers the secular affairs of Muslims, chapters which relate more closely to an individual's relationship with God. Examples are the chapters on oaths, ritual slaughter, and religious taboos in hunting. In brief then, Islamic law is a religious law, and it is adherence to it that shapes and defines an Islamic society.

A further characteristic of Islamic law is its tendency to devote energy and space to discussions of cases which have no application in reality. Jurists frequently take a practical rule of law and then discuss its hypothetical ramifications in ever more minute detail. This concern with details which often have little or no bearing on reality is an important element in Islamic jurisprudence. Law, in fact, was seen only in part as offering a practical legal system. Taken as a whole, it represents God's will, or at least man's effort to discover God's will. It is therefore an act of piety to examine every tiny aspect of a legal rule, however remote from the real world, because it is by doing so that man comes to know God's infinity. There has never been an expectation that mankind can, in practice, conform to the law in every detail. This remains a pious aspiration, but never a present reality.

Another characteristic of the law is its conservatism[7] and, in places, even its archaism. This is most plainly visible in passages where the jurists retain from earlier texts rules which had no application in their own times, or words whose meanings they probably no longer understood. For example, when discussing the fixed sum compensation due for unintentional killing and injury, legal texts up to the nineteenth century persist in expressing the sum due in terms of different categories of camel, using the same technical vocabulary for camels as the founders of the school had used in the eighth and ninth centuries.

Archaism was not necessarily a barrier to the application of the law. In the case of compensation for death and injury, for example, it was possible to convert the tariff expressed in camels to a monetary or other value, so that the rules became applicable in practice. Nonetheless, the law remained conservative. Jurists continued to transmit the material, and indeed exact phrases and passages of text which they had inherited from their predecessors. Especially, they continued to work within the framework of concepts which the founders of the schools had established between the eighth and eleventh centuries.

This does not mean, however, that innovation was impossible. In Commentaries, in particular, by discussing hypothetical cases relating to a legal rule, jurists could develop sub-rules in almost infinite variety. Furthermore, manipulation of existing concepts could create new legal discussions and solutions. On the question of land and taxation, for example, the jurists treat land as a commodity in private ownership, whose tax status is dependent on what happened to the land at the time of the Islamic conquest. If it remained in the ownership of infidels, the land paid, and continued to pay, even if subsequently sold to a Muslim, a higher rate of tax than land whose ownership passed to one of the Islamic conquerors. This was a juristic fiction. In reality, much of the land in the mediaeval Islamic world was held by feudal tenure, whereby a ruler allocated the occupancy of the land to a soldier or tax farmer in return for military or fiscal service. Muslim jurists took note of this reality and attempted to describe feudal tenure. Nonetheless, they did so in terms borrowed from the classical laws of land and taxation, [8] which they continued to expound and discuss in detail. From the sixteenth century Ottoman jurists, too, attempted to explain the *timar* system within the framework of classical legal theory. The laws of homicide present another example of how jurists could manipulate existing rules to create a new solution. In cases of indirect killing, where A orders B to kill C, the law fixes liability on the contract killer, B. Unless A physically compelled B to carry out the act, he is not liable. In practice, however, a judge might consider A's intent to kill and his ordering B to do so, as culpable. Following the classical theory, he should fix liability on B, the actual killer. However, the law also allows judges or other authorities to impose punishments at their discretion, usually remaining vague as to the offences to which this applies, and to the level of punishment. The Judge could therefore invoke this power, and impose a discretionary punishment on the indirect killer, A. In this way, he could, by combining two available rules, satisfy the demands of justice without upsetting the conceptual structure of the law. This was, however, practical manipulation of the law, rather than a conceptual development.

Despite its conservatism, therefore, Islamic law, did provide the materials for a workable and fairly flexible legal system. However, in three areas in particular, it had a very limited application in practice. These were land tenure, taxation[9] and criminal law.[10] In the case of land tenure and taxation, the jurists did find ways of describing what was happening in practice, but what they were doing was to create legal fictions to describe an existing situation which they had not created and did not regulate. An Islamic notion of criminal law, however, scarcely exists.

Islamic law treats homicide and injury to the person as, in western terms, civil offences. It is the injured persons or relatives of the deceased, rather than the government authorities, who bring the claim against the accused. Only for five offences – fornication, false accusation of fornication, wine drinking, theft and highway robbery – does the law make the authorities responsible for prosecuting the case and demanding the fixed punishment. At the same time, however, it imposes so many procedural obstacles to successful conviction that the penalties for these offences remain symbolic rather than real. A prosecution for fornication which, if successful would require stoning to death or flogging, requires four male eyewitnesses to the act. A conviction for theft, which would entail the amputation of a limb, can be averted if the accused states simply that he thought that he was the owner of the stolen goods. The effect of these punishments is therefore rhetorical. They symbolise the enormity of the offence in the eyes of God, but are not real penalties for application in this world. In addition to these fixed punishments, the jurists recognised the right of the authorities to inflict penalties at their discretion, but never systematised the rules. The result was to pass responsibility for penal law to the secular government.

In practice, therefore, Islamic law has regulated religious rituals and most areas of secular life. However, in the fields of land tenure, taxation and criminal law, it is secular law that has dominated. This was as true for the Ottoman Empire as for other parts of the Islamic world.

The preservation, transmission and application of a body of law requires permanent institutions and offices. The origins of Islamic law lay perhaps in the debates among groups which gathered informally around scholars of distinction. From the eleventh century, however, the typical institution of Islamic learning was the college attached to a mosque and supported by a trust. From its eleventh-century origins in Iran and Iraq, the college became a characteristic institution throughout the entire Islamic world.[11] It was here that the professors taught the law and other Islamic sciences, and where some of them composed the manuals of law which preserved the tradition and served as text books for students. In the hierarchy of esteem, it was the writing jurist whose books present the law in its purest form that enjoyed the most revered position.

The colleges preserved and taught the law, but it was not they who put it into effect. This was the duty of muftis and Judges. The Mufti was a jurisconsult who offered authoritative opinions – fatwas[12] – on all questions of law which anyone, from the monarch to his humblest subject, might ask. In many parts of the Islamic world, he achieved his position informally through reputation for learning, although in the Ottoman Empire after the fifteenth century muftis were usually official appointees. It was the mufti who acted as mediator between the divine law and the affairs of mankind, and in this capacity occupied the next rung of esteem, below the writing jurist. Like the writing jurist, he had no executive powers. A fatwa is an opinion, not an edict, and to put it into effect requires its enactment by a judge or governor. The judge – or qadi – on the other hand had executive power. In theory, at least, the mufti owed his position to his knowledge of God's law, and was in principle superior even to the monarch, a concept which Ottoman ceremonial preserved by making the sultan stand in the presence of the chief mufti. The judge, on the other hand, was a royal appointee to whom the ruler had delegated authority, and it was by virtue of this delegation of power that his judgements in court were binding. They were not, however, valid as precedents. A judge's decree was effective only in the case to which it applied. An authoritative legal text or fatwa, on the other hand, was universally valid.

It was the figures of the writing jurist, the teacher, the mufti and the judge who preserved Islamic law and put it into effect in the Ottoman Empire, as they did throughout the Islamic world.

Colleges, muftis and judges

By the time of the establishment of the Ottoman Empire in the fourteenth century, Islamic law was fully formed, in both its substance and institutions, and it was perhaps this inheritance of law that, by imposing legal and religious norms, did more than anything else to determine the future shape of Ottoman society.

The Turks who, in the fourteenth century, made up the Muslim population of the Ottoman realms and of other western Anatolian principalities, were largely illiterate and ignorant of all but the rudiments of their faith. What they knew they seem to have acquired from their forebears' contact with Persian speaking Muslims in Iran and Seljuk Anatolia. The basic religious vocabulary of Turkish remains, to this day, Persian in origin. It is, however, clear from inscriptions on their buildings, and from translations and adaptations which they commissioned of Arabic and Persian works[13] that the fourteenth-century rulers of western Anatolia rapidly adopted the cultural and literary forms of the old Islamic world. They also adopted Islamic law, specifically the law of the *Hanafi* School, which had been current in Anatolia under the Seljuks and which, under the aegis of the Ottoman sultans, was to become the dominant school of Islamic law in the Middle East. To establish a legal system, however, demanded the foundation of colleges to train the professors, muftis and judges that were essential to its operation.

The chronicler Ashikpashazade credits Orhan (c.1324–62) with the foundation in Iznik of the first Ottoman college. He adds that he appointed Davud of Kayseri as the first professor. Of Davud, the sixteenth-century scholar Tashköprüzade writes:

He studied in his own land, and then journeyed to Cairo, to study Quranic Exegesis, Traditions [of the Prophet] and the Principles of Jurisprudence under its scholars. He distinguished himself in the rational sciences and acquired the science of mysticism . . . Sultan Orhan built a College in the city of Iznik. From what I have heard from reliable sources, this was the first College to be built in the Ottoman realms, and he appointed Davud of Kayseri to its Professorship.

Given the time lapse between the events described and the sources, it is not clear whether these stories are, in all respects, accurate. They are, however, plausible in detail and certainly accurate in a general sense.

In the first half century of the Empire's existence, there was no tradition of Islamic learning in Ottoman territory. It was necessary, therefore, to import teachers to staff the new colleges. The tradition makes Davud a native of Kasyseri, where he had also studied. This central Anatolian city had become a centre of learning and culture during the Seljuk era, and Davud's transfer to Iznik was therefore an example of how the Ottoman and other west Anatolian rulers transplanted the culture of the old Muslim world to the newly conquered territories in the west. It is significant, too, that Tashköprüzade should mention Davud's journey to Cairo to pursue his studies. Although Kayseri had been a Muslim city since the Seljuk conquest and settlement in the late eleventh and twelfth centuries, as a centre of learning it was insignificant in comparison with the great cities of the Muslim old world, such as Damascus or Cairo.

For scholars from Anatolia, learning journeys to these cities were part of their education. Davud of Kayseri's successor but one at the college in Iznik was Molla Alaeddin, known as Kara Hoja who, according to Tashköprüzade, 'went to the land of Persia and studied with its scholars' before his return to Anatolia and appointment to Iznik. One of Molla Alaeddin's pupils was Molla Shemseddin Fenari (1350–1431), whom Tashköprüzade reports as becoming 'Professor in

Bursa at the Monastery College, and Judge there, as well as Mufti in the Ottoman realms'. Fenari, too, after his study at Iznik, had travelled to Cairo to complete his education. So, too, did the jurist and mystic, Sheykh Bedreddin, who was to lead the rebellion against Mehmed I (1413–21) in 1416.[14] Some Anatolian scholars settled in the cities where they had studied, and made their careers there. An example in the first half of the fifteenth century is the jurist Ibn Humam (d. 1457), a native of the Anatolian city of Sivas.[15]

These journeys to the centres of learning in the old Muslim world were clearly essential to the transfer of Muslim law and culture to the early Ottoman Empire. Eventually, with the endowment of new colleges by the sultans and their wealthy followers, and with the annexation by conquest of the pre-Ottoman colleges in Anatolia, the Ottoman Empire itself had, by 1500, become an important centre of learning. Although journeys in quest of knowledge remained a feature of Muslim scholarly life, they were no longer a requirement for Ottoman students. Indeed, the prospects of sultanic patronage began to draw scholars from outside the Empire to the Ottoman capital.[16] Furthermore, the conquest of Syria and Egypt in 1516–17 brought the old centres of learning in Damascus and Cairo into the sultan's realms. By the second half of the fifteenth century and, especially during the sixteenth and seventeenth, it was scholars working in the Ottoman realms such as Molla Husrev (d. 1480), Ibrahim of Aleppo (d. 1549), Ibn Nujaym (d. 1563) or Timirtashi (d. 1595), who were producing the most highly regarded manuals of *Hanafi* law.

It was the system of colleges within the Empire that supported this growth in scholarly activity, as well as training new generations of teachers and muftis, and staffing the law courts with judges. Each college in the Empire was an independent foundation, with its own endowment, trustees and administrator. Nevertheless, by the first half of the sixteenth century, a hierarchy of colleges had developed with the salaries paid to professors and, to some degree, the books taught, determining a college's place within it. At the lowest level were those that paid their professor 20 akches daily; at the top, from the 1470s, were the Eight Colleges which Mehmed II (1451–81) had established around his mosque in Istanbul. After Süleyman I (1520–66) had completed the construction of the the Süleymaniye in

1557, the colleges attached to this mosque came to occupy a position equal to the eight colleges of Mehmed II. With the elaboration of this hierarchy, the sultans sought to control the progression of students and teachers through the colleges.

The so-called 'Law Book of Mehmed II', in this section perhaps dating from the early sixteenth century, lays out, in a highly idealised form, how a teaching career should progress. On graduating, a student should become a candidate for office, and then receive a professorship at 20 akches per day. He should then progress through the college system in steps of 5 *akches*, moving to a college paying 25 *akches* a day, then to a 30 *akche* college, and so on until he reached one of the eight colleges. This could be the first step to appointment as a Judge in a large city, earning 500 *akches* a day. From this position it was possible to become a military judge sitting on the Imperial Council.

The systematisation of the colleges also brought attempts to control the progress of students. A 'Law Book of Scholars', undated but presumably from the first half of the sixteenth century, tries in particular to ensure that students should continue to study the 'respected books' according to 'the old custom', and not to 'aim for quick promotion by petitioning'. Instead, each student, on completing a course with a professor should obtain a certificate stating how much of each book he had read, and the professor at the next grade should not accept him without examining this certificate. The Law Book also creates a rudimentary syllabus, by naming, in abbreviated form, the titles of the books which a student should study at each grade. In particular, professors at each stage should teach texts and commentaries on jurisprudence. The Law Book concludes with a statement that any professor or student not observing these regulations should suffer a severe punishment.

A second Law Book, which apparently went to the Inner Colleges of the Empire – that is, those in Istanbul and the old capitals of Bursa and Edirne – reiterates these rules. After a preamble, where the Sultan states that 'it has been heard that teaching and learning are in decay, . . . that the banners of science are broken . . . and the colleges empty of teaching and learning', the Law Book again insists that no student should begin a book until he has fully mastered the one which preceded it in the syllabus. Only when they have properly studied all the books at a particular level should they receive a certificate from the professor, permitting them to proceed to the next grade. In particular, the Law Book states, students have been reaching the highest grade in the Eight Colleges in a year, or even less. In future, students should read all the books required at each level and reach the Eight Colleges in no less than five years. The Law Book concludes by stating that the colleges would be under surveillance, and that any professor who disobeyed the command would suffer dismissal. At the turn of the seventeenth century, a decree of Mehmed III (1595–1606) repeated these edicts. [17]

Although they were nominally independent, the colleges came, during the sixteenth century, to form something approaching an imperial system, with appointments and syllabuses under the control of the sultan. They were, in fact, a vital element in Ottoman government, most obviously because they provided the legal training necessary for judges. They also provided career opportunities for native Muslims – mostly Turks in Anatolia and Rumelia, mostly Arabs in Syria, Egypt and Iraq – who found themselves excluded from the Palace Schools, and so from careers as provincial governors and viziers.

By the sixteenth century, a graduate of a college had a choice of three careers in particular. He could, with the right connections, join the scribal service, in the sultan's government or in a great household. Otherwise, he had the choice of a teaching career or a career as judge. In either case, he required, as a first step, the sponsorship of a senior member of the learned profession, who could nominate him as a candidate for office 'in attendance', nominally on the sultan, but in practice on one of the military judges who actually made the appointments. If a student came from one of the learned families that emerged during the sixteenth century and came to monopolise the higher offices in the learned profession, he could gain the sponsorship of a well positioned relative. Otherwise, he could seek the support of his teacher or other member of the profession, sometimes by providing a service, such as teaching assistant in a college or clerk in the office of a military judge.[18]

Until the 1530s, the system of sponsoring candidates was clearly haphazard. However, during his period as Military Judge of Rumelia between 1537 and 1545, the most renowned of Ottoman legal figures, Ebu's-su'ud (c. 1490–1574) reformed the system, following complaints from graduates that the MilitaryJudge of Anatolia, Chivizade Muhiyeddin, was preventing their enrolment as candidates for office. Henceforward, military judges were to keep special registers for enrolling candidates, while holders of high office had the right to nominate candidates at intervals of seven years. At the same time, Ebu's-su'ud fixed the number of candidates that holders of specified offices might nominate at ten each for military judges, five each for the judges of Istanbul, Edirne and Bursa, and three each for the judges of other important cities. In practice, the nomination of candidates seems to have happened at intervals of less than seven years, and it was customary for the sultans to decree ceremonial investitures on great occasions of state, or to honour the appointment of a new military judge or chief mufti. Nonetheless, the measures which Ebu's-su'ud introduced had the effect of controlling the intake of candidates into the learned professions and presumably of preventing the holders of the highest offices from monopolising the nomination of candidates.[19]

If a candidate chose to follow a career as teacher, he could expect an initial appointment in a provincial college with a low stipend. From here he could advance, with occasional periods out of office, through the hierarchy of colleges. The most successful could arrive eventually at one of the Eight Colleges or, after their completion in 1557, at one of the colleges of the Süleymaniye. It was above all a scholar's place in a particular college and the level of his stipend that determined his standing in the learned profession. This becomes clear from the collection of biographies by Nev'izade Atai (1583–1636), of scholars active between the reigns of Süleyman I (1520–66) and Murad IV (1623–40). Atai's biographies are usually little more than a record of what colleges each scholar had taught at, and what other offices he had held. For example, in his account of a certain Molla Mahmud, who flourished during the reign of Ahmed I (1603–17), he tells us only that the royal tutor, historian and chief mufti, Sa'deddin, had sponsored him for office; and that after he had reached the grade of a 40 *akche* college – the lowest grade which Atai considers worth recording – in 1605 he became Professor at the

Ibrahim Pasha College, and then, in 1608, at the Sinan Pasha College. In 1611, he moved to Edirne, where he died in the following year. For the more distinguished figures, Atai also gives anecdotes and perhaps also a list of their writings. Nonetheless, it is always progression through the hierarchy of colleges and offices that provides the outline of his account, indicating how firmly established the career structure in the learned profession had become.

A career as a judge followed a pattern similar to that of a college teacher. It is possible that, up until the first half of the fifteenth century, sanjak governors and other local authorities could appoint and promote judges. Certainly the 1431 cadastral survey of southern Albania shows that the Sanjak Governor granted an addition to the fief of the Judge of Kanina 'in accordance with the letter of [the Governor] Zaganoz Bey'. By the sixteenth century, however, an aspiring judge had first to seek the recommendation of a senior member of the learned hierarchy to become a candidate 'in attendance' on one of the military judges in Istanbul. An appointment as judge or deputy judge in one of the small towns of the Empire followed.[20]

In the early stages of their career, judges could earn more than professors in the colleges at an equivalent level. The lowest nominal salary that a judge received, whether paid in cash or held as a fief, was 25 *akches* per day, as against 20 *akches* for a novice teacher. In addition, he would receive fees and other emoluments. In another respect, however, the career had limitations. If a candidate chose initially to serve as a judge, rather than as a professor in a college, he would serve throughout his career in small towns and could never, as a rule, rise to become judge of a city. These positions – the great 'mollaships' – were the preserve of men who had risen through the colleges usually to become professor at the Eight Colleges or at the Süleymaniye. An example of this is the career of Ebu's-su'ud, whose first teaching appointment, in 1517, was to the 30 akche College at İnegöl. By 1525, he was at the Sultaniyye College in Bursa, a foundation of Mehmed I and, two years later, at one of the Eight Colleges. In 1533, Süleyman I appointed him Judge of Istanbul, effectively the senior judgeship in the Empire, and then, in 1537, Military Judge of Rumelia.[21]

A candidate, therefore, who set out on a career as judge would find that, at the highest level, his path was blocked and he could never rise to become Judge of Istanbul, Bursa, or Edirne, or of Cairo, Damascus or Baghdad. This career limitation did not, however, apply only to judges. Increasingly during the sixteenth century and more markedly during the seventeenth and eighteenth,[22] the highest judicial positions became the preserve of a few élite families, and a college professor from outside this circle had no more chance of a mollaship than did a small-town judge. It was presumably, therefore, to compensate frustrated aspirants to high positions that, during the late sixteenth century, it became possible, by enlarging the area of the court's jurisdiction, to designate minor judgeships as mollaships. Some of the new mollaships became permanent. Others were *ad hominem*. Atai records the career of a certain Molla Sinan, which provides an example. He had become a candidate for office after serving as a memorandum writer to the military judge, Abdurrahman (d. 1575), and then began a career as judge, serving in 'glorious towns, such as Tire and Alaşehir'. Then, through marriage, he became the protégé of a certain Ramazan Pasha, through whom he acquired a post as financial inspector and, with it, the opportunity to accumulate wealth. In view of his new position, he began to regard a small-town judgeship as too humble and to seek a mollaship. To this end, he attached himself to the following of the Grand Vizier, Ibrahim Pasha, commander of the army in Hungary. This must have been in 1599–1601. The Vizier, on his behalf, secured the elevation of the judgeship of Tire – a small town in western Anatolia – to a mollaship and its bestowal, in 1601, on Molla Sinan. The mollaships of the great cities, however, which secured access to higher office, remained the monopoly of the élite.

The judges were perhaps the most important figures in the day-to-day administration of the Ottoman Empire. Every city, town, village and settlement within the Empire came under the authority of a judge, and every individual within the judicial district, whatever his or her religion, had the right of recourse to the judge's court. Furthermore, the absence of lawyers and the fact that the public seem to have had access to the judge or his deputy at all hours, ensured that the courts dealt with business very quickly.[23]

The functions of the judge were also very wide. In the first place, he presided over his court, administering, in most parts of the Empire, *Hanafi* law, no matter what the religion or legal school of the parties concerned. His court was open to anyone who wished to bring a lawsuit or make a claim. Ottoman judges also acted as notaries, ensuring the observance of the proper legal forms and providing written records of acts such as, for example, marriage, divorce, the sale and purchase of real estate, or the foundation of trusts. A few entries from the register of the court of Ankara for two days in January 1583, give an impression of a judge's daily routine. A man demands the return of goods given as a pledge. Another seeks compensation from a man who has killed his packhorse. The manager of a trust demands ten gold coins owing to him. The Judge records that a village has paid 340 akches in lieu of barley to the agent who had come to collect barley for the Sultan's camels. A man records that he is no longer marrying his fiancée and that the parties had returned all goods exchanged in prenuptial arrangements. A man stands surety for another in a transaction concerning a horse. Claiming that her husband has divorced her, a woman demands that he pay her dower and also the maintenance due for the period during which she may not legally remarry. A villager complains about another who plays a musical instrument.

The court, it seems, would usually meet in the judge's house, where in all his functions, the judge had the assistance of a deputy, who could conduct proceedings in his absence, and a clerk or clerks who kept records, and could also carry out investigations outside the courtroom. The judges' registers also record, after each case, the names of a semipermanent group of 'witnesses to the proceedings'. Their function is not, however, clear. They seem to have acted as a collective memory of the court's proceedings, and might, for example, be asked to check the validity of documents. As people with a knowledge of the locality and its inhabitants, they perhaps also offered advice on cases, as well as keeping a check on the probity of the judge. A person bringing a matter to court would therefore encounter not only the judge or his deputy and the clerk of the court, but also a group of permanent witnesses.[24]

A judge's functions, however, were not all strictly legal. Court registers and records of the Imperial Council show that the sultan addressed commands to judges to perform a very wide range of duties. It was, for example, primarily the judges who were responsible for levying oarsmen to serve in the galleys of the imperial fleet, or to organise the collection of provisions along the army's route of march. A sampling of the decrees which the Imperial Council issued to judges in June and July 1564, gives a sense of the range of their duties. The Judge of Chernomen receives a command to levy for campaign the raiders of Rumelia, after their governor has reported that they have not mustered for duty. The Judges of Kilia and Akkerman were to oversee the sale of sheep to the drovers coming from Istanbul to bring them to supply the capital. The Sultan orders the Judges of Plovdiv and Sofia to allocate crafsmen and tradesmen – a butcher, a cook, a saddler, a cobbler and others – to the army of Rumelia, under the command of the Governor-General. The judges whose districts fall along this route are to secure provisions. The Judge of Antalya was to secure a galliot to ensure the speedy passage to Egypt of a messenger carrying an important decree from the Sultan to the Governor-General. It seems, in fact, to have been primarily the judges, in both their judicial and administrative functions, who provided support and continuity for the sultan's authority.

The role of muftis in the Ottoman legal establishment is more difficult to define. The Mufti of Istanbul rose during the sixteenth century to become not only the Chief Mufti, but also the senior figure in the religious and legal hierarchy.[25] Other muftis were not so prominent. It seems that in the fifteenth and sixteenth centuries, it was the college professors who acted as muftis. Bayezid II, for example, stipulated that the professor of the College which he founded in Amasya in 1486 should also function as mufti of the town.[26] Atai's biographies, however, give the impression that, from the mid-sixteenth century at least, the sultan also appointed salaried muftis to important towns and cities, such as Thessaloniki, Damascus or Rhodes. There seem, however, to be no surviving records of their activities, and appointments as mufti seem never to have formed the major part of a career. The muftiships that Atai records usually appear as interludes between postings as judge. Atai also makes it clear that college professors, officially or unofficially, continued to act as muftis. A Law Book of Aleppo, dated 1570, provides an example. The text records how a problem arose when a certain Mehmed Chelebi was making a new cadastral survey of the sanjak. During the course of his work a group of landowners and managers of trust land came to him to complain that their lands paid tithe, whereas other private and trust lands did not. 'If', they complained, 'it is lawful to levy tithe, why is it not taken from all [such lands]? And if it is contrary to the Noble Shari'a, we beg that it be abolished.' The reaction of the surveyor was to seek an opinion on the matter from the Professor of the Husrev Pasha College in Aleppo, who issued a fatwa ruling: 'The canonical tithe is binding on all of them.' The surveyor then forwarded this fatwa, as it was, to the palace and received a sultanic decree based on its ruling: 'You should collect the canonical tithe from all of them and take it for the Treasury.' This was a case of a government official seeking a fatwa from a mufti, which subsequently formed the basis of a decree. Judges could also consult muftis on questions of law, as could members of the public on any question whatsoever. In this respect, muftis played a vital part in adapting the inherited norms of Islamic law and religion to the problems of contemporary society.[27] From the Ottoman Empire, however, it is only the fatwas of the chief muftis – the Mufti of Istanbul – that have survived in large numbers. Of the provincial muftis, little is known, and service as mufti in the provinces seems never to have formed a distinct career, as did service as a judge or professor.

It seems that small-town judges and college professors in general remained within their own profession. Nonetheless, Atai's biographies record many cases of teachers receiving appointments as judges and vice versa. A certain Molla Abdullah, for example, entered the teaching profession as a candidate of the Chief Mufti, Zekeriyya Efendi (d. 1593). After progressing through the system, he became, in 1624, Professor at the Süleymaniye College in Iznik, with – undoubtedly as a consolation for a blocked career – 'the grade of the Eight Colleges'. In the following year, he left the college to become judge at Tire. A slightly earlier biography serves to show how a man could serve as teacher, mufti and judge during the course of a single career. Molla Ma'rifetullah began a teaching career as a candidate of 'some learned men'. By 1584, he was Professor at the College of Küçük

Çekmece near Istanbul. Five years later, he accepted a post as Mufti of Rhodes. Then, in 1590, he received a promotion to become Judge of Damascus, one of the great mollaships of the Empire. It was presumably the prestige of this post that led him to refuse what was in effect a demotion to the judgeship of Erzurum in 1595. Instead, he transferred to the college of Sultan Mehmed in Medina. He later transferred to the muftiship of Cyprus, then of Damascus, dying in Istanbul in 1606, while awaiting a new post.

In his biographies, Atai gives many examples of posts which carried an honorary rank during the incumbency of a particular individual, such as professorships held 'with the rank of the Eight Colleges', or small-town judgeships held as great mollaships. This indicates that, after the mid-sixteenth century, for most professors, judges and muftis, there was no hope of reaching the top of the profession, and that these ranks were consolation prizes.

There were three reasons for this. First, the positions at the top of the hierarchy were very few. During the sixteenth century, the Mufti of Istanbul emerged as the senior figure in the learned establishment, but this was only one post. The muftis in the provinces did not enjoy real prestige or influence. The senior judges of the Empire were the military judges who sat on the Imperial Council, but there were only two of these, and judgeships of the great cities – that is, mollaships that were not purely honorary – were few. There were only eight professorships at the Eight Colleges and, after the establishment of the Süleymaniye, a few more above this, but not enough to satisfy all aspirants. Furthermore, these élite colleges acted as a bottleneck. To become a judge of a great city, it was usually necessary to have served as a professor at the Eight Colleges. To become a military judge, it was in turn necessary to have served as judge of a great city, and the mufti of Istanbul had generally served as a military judge. Starting at the Eight Colleges, therefore, there was a strict control over who could occupy the senior teaching and judicial positions in the Empire. The second factor limiting a person's opportunity was overcrowding in the system. At the higher level, this led to fierce competition between candidates for posts, and very short periods of office. At the lowest level it led to the appearance in Anatolia of bands of college students who, with no prospects of employment, took to brigandage as a means of livelihood.[28] Finally, the ambitious would find that a few families already monopolised the top positions. This phenomenon became more pronounced from the late sixteenth century onwards. The occupants of the post of chief mufti serve as an example.

Ottoman tradition names Molla Shemseddin Fenari as the first to hold this office, between 1424 and 1431. His descendant, Fenarizade Muhiyeddin was to occupy the same position from from 1543 to 1545. By this time, however, the most powerful claimants to the post were were the two Military Judges, Ebu's-su'ud and Chivizade Muhiyeddin. Chivizade was the first to hold the muftiship, from 1539 until his removal four years later. His successor but one was his rival, Ebu's-su'ud, who remained in office until his death in 1574. His immediate successor, however, was Hamid Mahmud, the son-in-law of Chivizade. The rivalry between the two families clearly continued. Hamid Mahmud's successor but one was Ma'lulzade Mehmed, the son-in-law of Ebu's-su'ud and, on his departure in 1582, Chivizade's son, Hajji Mehmed assumed the office. He was the last of the family of Chivizade to occupy this position. Meanwhile, the fortunes of Ebu's-su'ud's family continued in his cousin's son, Sun'ullah, who was four times Chief Mufti between 1599 and 1608.[29] By this time, however, powerful rivals had emerged. In 1598, Mehmed III appointed his and his father's tutor, Sa'deddin, as Mufti. His period of office lasted only the year and a half to his death, but his descendants maintained a family claim for half a century. His elder son, Mehmed, was Chief Mufti between 1601 and 1603 and again between 1608 and 1615, while his younger son, Es'ad occupied the post between 1615 and 1622, 1623 and 1625, and finally between 1644 and 1646. Three year's later, Sa'deddin's grandson, Bahai Efendi was appointed Mufti. The most successful opponent to the aspirations of the Sa'deddin family was Zekeriyyazade Yahya. However, he was himself the son of a former chief mufti, Zekeriyya Efendi, who had occupied the post in 1592–3, so he too could lay a dynastic claim.[30]

From their positions as chief mufti or military judge, the successful members of the learned dynasties could use their patronage to promote their own relatives. Ebu's-su'ud's family provides an example.

Thanks to the influence of his father, Ebu's-su'ud's eldest son, Mehmed, received his first teaching appointment, at the Kasim Pasha College, at the age of thirteen, with the unusually high stipend of 50 akches per day. In 1551, at the age of about 26, he was professor at the Eight Colleges. His brother, Shemseddin Ahmed became, at the age of 17, professor at the college which the Grand Vizier Rüstem Pasha had recently founded in Istanbul. Both these sons died young, leaving Ebu's-su'ud with the burden of educating his grandsons. The elder of the two, Abdülkerim, became professor at the College of Mahmud Pasha, according to the biographer Manq Ali, 'in honour of his grandfather, and contrary to custom'. He died in 1573–4, having already in his twenties, become professor at one of the Colleges of the Süleymaniye. Ebu's-su'ud's other grandson, Abdulvasi, was, at the time of his grandfather's death, a professor at the Süleymaniye. However, with the death of his grandfather, he lost his source of patronage and, in Atai's words, 'the swift steed on the path of his prosperity stumbled on the stone of misfortune'. His career did not advance until, in 1580, he received the professorship at the new College of the Mosque of Sultan Selim II in Edirne. He died in this city a few years later. Ebu's-su'ud did not, however, bestow his patronage only on his sons and grandsons. As Military Judge of Rumelia in 1537, he was able to bring his cousin Ja'fer to Istanbul, where he embarked on a career which culminated in his six-year tenure of the military judgeship of Anatolia. Ja'fer's brother, Lutfullah, was professor at the Eight Colleges from 1562 until his death in 1568. His son Sun'ullah was to become Chief Mufti.[31] Ebu's-su'ud was in no way unusual in promoting his own family. Within a political system almost without corporate institutions and where power and patronage resided in families and households, this was the only way to advance a career.

Of the positions to which members of these learned families aspired, the judgeship of a great city did not, in essence, differ from the judgeship of a small town. The two military judges, however, were members of the Imperial Council and, as such, participated in government at the highest level, whether through the formal discussions of the council or through informal contacts with the palace and the great men of the Empire. On the council, they had particular responsibility for judicial business. This is clear from the notes which the clerks have appended to the drafts of sultanic decrees contained in the volumes which survive from the mid-sixteenth century onwards.

These show that the military judges were, in the first place, responsible for submitting to the Imperial Council letters and petitions for redress that they received from office holders and members of the public. In May 1560, for example, the Sultan – or rather the Imperial Council acting in the Sultan's name – issued a command to the Judge of Bursa to investigate and report on a complaint by the Armenian community against an individual who had been 'causing trouble' against two churches. The draft of the decree carries the note: 'The Military Judge [of Anatolia] submitted it.' In the same month, the council received a letter from the professor at the Mehmed Pasha College in Iznik, complaining that someone had unneccesarily built a bathhouse, which was diverting both water and cash from the bathhouses belonging to the trust which supported the college. In response, the Judge of Iznik received the command not to allow the construction of any new bathhouses in the town. The note attached to the draft indicates that the text of the decree incorporates the exact wording of the military judge's ruling: 'The Military Judge [of Anatolia] submitted [the letter]. Because he recorded his command on the petition, the decree has been written acordingly.' A similar note appears on a decree, also of May 1560, issued in response to a letter from the Sanjak Governor of Sultanönü, reporting on the suspects in a complex murder case. The decree, incorporating the ruling of the Military Judge, orders him and the Judge of Eskişehir to inflict 'the acceptable custom' – that is, torture – on the suspect, and to report what transpires. It adds emphatically that the suspect should not be killed. Another decree, this time of June 1560, and issued in response to a letter from the Judge of Beypazar, orders the execution of a roughneck for raping boys, and of his accomplices if they repeat the offence. The text carries the note: 'The Military Judge [of Anatolia] submitted [the letter], and the decree is registered incorporating his words.'

The military judges were also the main agents in fulfilling another of the Imperial Council's functions. From the late fifteenth century, the military class – that is, everybody who received a fief or a salary from the sultan – came under a separate jurisdiction from the rest of the sultan's subjects. In criminal matters, the local authorities forwarded the cases to the Imperial Council, where they came under the scrutiny of the military judges. In November 1559, for example, the Military Judge of Anatolia ordered the Judge of Iznik to execute the *subashi* – a *zeamet* holder with responsibility for maintaining order and inflicting punishments – in his district, after it had come to light that he was behind the murder of a group of women on the public road. In July 1560, after receiving a letter from the Judges of Ayazmend and Bergama, the Military Judge ordered the Sanjak Governor of Bursa to torture the subashi of Bergama, as he was under suspicion of murdering the warden of the castle at Bergama. In September 1560, the Military Judge of Rumelia ordered the Sanjak Governor and Judge of Vidin to investigate a case where one cavalryman in the sanjak was suspected of killing another. In all these cases, the executive authorities were to report what happened back to the Imperial Council.

In this sampling, it is only the clerks' notes on the draft decrees that make it clear that it was the military judges who presented the matter to the council and took the decision on what to do. The decrees themselves went out in the name of the sultan. The same sample, however, also suggests that the military judges could issue commands independently, in their own or in the sultan's name. A note appended to a draft decree of June 1560, records that 'a command written by the Military Judge [of Anatolia]' had been given to the same messenger as was carrying the sultan's decree. Furthermore, a Sultanic command to the Governor-General of Anatolia concerning the suspect 'in the case of the girl called Halime' notes that 'my Noble Command has been written to you by my Military Judge', suggesting that military judges could independently issue orders in the sultan's name.

In addition to their responsibility for judicial matters in the Imperial Council, it was the military judges who were responsible for appointing – again in the sultan's name – professors and judges from among the candidates for office who were 'in attendance' on them in the capital. The system of nominating candidates which Ebu's-su'ud introduced shortly after 1537 seems to have lasted into the seventeenth century.

As members of the Imperial Council, the two military judges occupied the highest executive positions in the learned and legal hierarchy. However, during the sixteenth century the chief mufti came to surpass them in rank and prestige. Tradition asserts that Molla Fenari between 1424 and 1431 was the first to hold this office, but it is difficult to trace with certainty even the names of his successors, suggesting that in the fifteenth century, the muftiship lacked the prestige which it was later to acquire. This was a phenomenon of the sixteenth century and later, and came about, it seems, partly as a result of the classical Islamic view of the moral superiority of the mufti over the judge, but mainly through the personal eminence of two of the greatest holders of the office. These were Kemalpashazade (1525–34) and Ebu's-su'ud (1545–74). The so-called Law Book of Mehmed II which, in this section, probably dates from the second half of the sixteenth century, states unequivocally that the chief mufti is head of the learned profession, and it was, by this time, normal for the mufti to have served previously as military judge.

Despite his eminence, the chief mufti possessed no executive powers, and was not a member of the Imperial Council. However, the office itself conferred prestige and the chief muftis moved in the highest political circles, often enjoying access to the sultan. Ebu's-su'ud, for example, was a confidant of Süleyman I. Sa'deddin had been the teacher of Murad III and Mehmed III and remained an advisor to both. His son Es'ad became father-in-law to Osman II (1618–22). With these connections, the muftis wielded influence in politics, but this was not their formal role. The public function of the chief mufti, like that of his more humble counterparts, was to issue fatwas in response to legal and other questions, which anyone from the sultan downwards might ask. His status as the most eminent interpreter of God's law was such that even the sultan had to defer to his opinion, and the authority of his fatwas was such that, from the time of Kemalpashazade's period in office, it became customary to select and issue them in edited anthologies. These volumes of fatwas served not only as edifying reading, but also to help judges and others who were seeking guidance in the solution of legal problems.

Before the Muftiship of Ebu's-su'ud, the process of writing fatwas was informal, as is evident from an account of the Chief Mufti, Ali Jemali

(1503–25) which appears in Tashköprüzade's volume of biographies of Ottoman learned men. 'He used', Tashköprüzade writes, 'to live on the top floor of his house, where he had a hanging basket. The questioner placed in it [his question written on a] piece of paper and agitated it. The said Molla would then pull up [the basket], write his answer and drop it down to him.' This and other informal procedures clearly limited the number of fatwas which the mufti could issue, and it was to speed up the process that Ebu's-su'ud, mufti from 1545 to 1574, reformed the system. From his time, until the abolition of the Fatwa Office in the twentieth century, the question no longer went straight to the mufti, but instead to the mufti's clerks, who were experts in law and the art of legal formulation. These rephrased the question according to a standard format and passed it to the mufti, who would write his answer below the question and add his signature, ready for the questioner to collect. Ebu's-su'ud's system speeded up the process to the extent that his clerk, Ashik Chelebi, was able to recall how '[Ebus-su'ud] began writing answers after the performance of the dawn prayer and was granted completion by the time of the call to afternoon prayer. He counted them and, on the first occasion, 1412 and, on the second occasion, 1413 fatwas were answered and signed'. In the following century, the system became more sophisticated as the skills of the clerks increased. By the end of the seventeenth century, it was normal to draft a question in such a way that it required no more than a 'yes' or 'no' answer, leaving the mufti to add no more than a 'yes' or a 'no' and his signature. Provided the clerks reliably sorted the fatwas into a 'yes' pile and a 'no' pile, he did not even have to read the question.[32] It was thus the permanent staff in the mufti's office, rather than the muftis themselves, who maintained standards and continuity in issuing fatwas, and who subsequently collected and arranged the fatwas in anthologies.

The chief mufti's office, like the judges' courts, was open to anyone who was physically able to present themselves with a question. However, since fatwas are, in principle, generalised statements of the law rather than judgements on particular cases, in format they are strictly anonymous with specific details of name, time or locality removed. This makes it difficult to guess who posed the original questions and in what circumstances. However, many must have come from members of the public, wishing to settle a query or dispute, or seeking a fatwa in order to strengthen a case which they were taking to court.[33] Others must have come from judges seeking guidance in settling a lawsuit or other problem. In the following fatwa, for example, Ebu's-su'ud seems to be answering the question of a private individual wishing to know the correct procedure for slaughtering animals, probably at the Festival of Sacrifice: 'When a slaughter animal has to be slaughtered, how many legs should be bound, and which should be left free? *Answer:* Three of its legs are bound. The right rear leg is left free, and it is laid on its left side.' The following, however, seems to have come to Ebu's-su'ud from a judge seeking a solution to a difficult problem: 'X produces evidence that A has been his wife since such-and-such a date. Y also produces evidence that she has been his wife since the same date. Which [piece of evidence] is acceptable? *Answer:* So long as the dates are the same, neither is acceptable. The [two pieces of] evidence contradict each other.'

The authority of the muftis was such that even sultans and men of state felt the need to consult them on the legality of certain political actions. There are fatwas, for example, which served to procure the execution of Sheykh Bedreddin in 1416, issued in this case by a Persian Molla;[34] or to justify the sixteenth-century wars against the Safavids; Süleyman I's execution of his son Bayezid; the attack on Cyprus in 1570, in breach of a peace treaty;[35] or the deposition of sultans in the seventeenth century. In these cases the fatwas have exactly the same format as those dealing with more trivial matters, with the questions and answers couched in the same anonymous language. There can, however, be no doubt that in these instances, the muftis knew exactly the reality of the situation on which they were delivering an opinion, and in almost all cases were prepared to give the sultan, or other authority, the answer he was seeking. The situation by the seventeenth century was that if they refused, they were likely to lose their position. 'But sometimes perhaps', the English Consul, Sir Paul Rycaut commented in the 1660s,

Queries are sent from the Grand Signior to the Mufti, which he cannot resolve with the satisfaction of his own conscience, and the ends of the Sultan; by which means affairs important to the well being of the State meet delays and impediments. In this case the Mufti is fairly dismissed from his infallible office, and another Oracle introduced, who may resolve the difficult demands with a more favourable sentence. If not, he is degraded like the former, and so the next, until one is found apt to prophesy according to what might best agree with the interest of his Master.

The secular law

From the fifteenth century and probably earlier, the sacred law – the *shari'a* – regulated most of the day-to-day affairs of Muslims in the Ottoman Empire, and many aspects too of the lives of non-Muslims. It was not, however, the only legal system in force in the Empire, but coexisted also with Ottoman secular law or *kanun*.

Kanun regulated areas where the provisions of the sacred law were either missing or too much at at odds with reality to be applicable. These, in the Ottoman Empire as in other Islamic polities, were above all in the areas of criminal law, land tenure, and taxation. The origins of the secular law lay in custom, and it was long usage that in the first place gave it legitimacy. The late fifteenth and sixteenth centuries, however, saw the sultans enact written versions of the law, and modify it through decrees, giving it a dual character of customary and sultanic law. By the sixteenth century, the consciousness of the disparity between the sacred and the secular law led Kemalpashazade and later, at royal command, Ebu's-su'ud to redefine and systematise the Ottoman laws of land and taxation in terms which they borrowed from the *Hanafi* jurists.[36] In doing this, they were following the tradition of their mediaeval predecessors who had also sought to explain the reality of feudal tenure and taxation using the terms and concepts of the classical law.[37] Also like their mediaeval predecessors, what they produced were legal fictions which satisfied pious aspirations without upsetting legal reality.

The basis of Ottoman secular law was the distinction between the sultan's tax-paying subjects, and his servants who received a salary either from a fief-holding or directly from the Treasury. The secular law determined the relationship between these two classes. This was quite different from the distinctions in the sacred law, where it is the classification as male or female, free or slave, Muslim, non-Muslim subject or non-Muslim enemy that determine a person's legal status and his or her rights and obligations. In the secular classification of Ottoman subjects, non-tax payers came to be known as the military – *askeri* – class. The adjective describes their function more or less accurately, since most members of the class were soldiers, either *timar*-holding cavalrymen, or else Janissaries and members of the Six Divisions of palace cavalry who received their salaries from the Treasury. However, in addition to these men and to the viziers and provincial governors, who served as army commanders, the military class also comprised courtiers in the palace and members of the religious, teaching and legal professions. The general term for a member of the tax-paying class was an Arabic term coming from the sacred law, *ra'iyyet* or, in the plural, *re'aya* ('flock'). The huge majority of these were peasant cultivators and, in its technical sense, the term *ra'iyyet* referred to a peasant who cultivated a plot of land by virtue of a contractual agreement with the fief holder as representative of the sultan. In a general sense, the term referred to all Ottoman subjects who were not members of the military class.

The formulation of a terminology to describe tax payers and non-tax payers is a result of attempts at the end of the fifteenth century to define their legal status. One of the things that had made this necessary was the establishment of a separate jurisdiction for the military class. This, if we are to believe a story which Spandounes tells us, happened on the order of Bayezid II (1481–12), and came about, like many institutional changes in the Ottoman Empire, by chance. Spandounes tells us how Bayezid appointed a sanjak governor as market inspector in Istanbul, in order to provide him with an income while he was out of office. As market inspector, he disobeyed a decree from the Judge of Istanbul, Yusuf Kirmasti (1494–8), claiming that, since he received his authority directly from the Sultan, the Judge had no jurisdiction. When, after a furious contretemps, the Judge tried to prosecute him, no one would give evidence against the market inspector, whereupon the Sultan 'deprived the said Judge of his office, and issued a command that no one should have power and authority over slaves who received a salary from the Sultan, and this command has been observed until today'. Spandounes adds that 'now, if anyone has a difference with a *timar* holder or a *subashi*, he makes them answer to the Sanjak Governor or, if they are in Istanbul, to the Agha [of the Janissaries] or to the Pashas [on the Imperial Council'.]

Bayezid II's decree placing the military class under a separate jurisdiction from ordinary tax payers required a clear definition of who belonged to which group. The distinction between the military class and tax-paying subjects must have emerged informally in the fourteenth century with the grant of lands and salaries to the sultan's followers. The compilation of the cadastral registers from the late fourteenth century onwards, which recorded revenues and their distribution among *timar* holders, provided a record of who belonged to the military class in each sanjak. They did not, however, provide a legal definition, nor were they comprehensive. In cases of dispute, it was presumably custom and local decision that determined a person's status as tax-payer or military. However, Bayezid's decree placing the military class under a separate jurisdiction made a definition imperative, and it was not long after this that a formulation appeared. The Law Book issued in 1499 at Bayezid's command defined who belonged to the military class:

The cavalryman who serves on Sultanic campaigns belongs to the military class, while in service and after retirement, so long as the retired [cavalryman] is not registered as a tax payer (*ra 'iyyet*) [belonging to] another person. The Sultan's male and female slaves, so long as they are married to one of the military class, [themselves] belong to the military class after manumission. Judges, Professors, Muftis and administrators and supervisors of trusts – that is, holders of offices that are given by attendance at the [Sultan's] Exalted Threshold – are [members of] the military class. The following also have military status: a son of a member of the military class, so long as he has a [recognised] status, and is not registered with anyone as a tax payer; his wives to whom he is currently married; slaves of a member of the military class, who serve the military class after manumission, whose livelihoods are from the military class, and who are not registered as anybody's *ra'iyyet*; the daughter of a cavalryman married to a cavalryman, so long as she is [currently] married to the cavalryman.

The legal and fiscal relationship between the military class and the taxpayers – mainly in practice, between *timar* holders and peasants – forms the main subject of the secular law. This emerged as a body of written codes during the reign, and at the command of Bayezid II. The earliest such code is the Law Book which forms the preface to the detailed cadastral survey of the Sanjak of Bursa, dated 1487. This lays out the taxes and fines which sanjak governors and fief holders may collect from the peasants and pastoralists, and the conditions on which the peasants may occupy the land. Its anonymous compiler tells us, in a rather convoluted pre amble, that his sources were the 'customary laws and rules for well established customary taxes', 'the [Ottoman] cadastral registers' and 'Sultanic decrees'. In so telling us, he provides an account not only of this code in particular, but of the secular law in general: its basis was established custom, as recorded in the cadastral registers and modified through royal commands. Another feature of this Law Book, which also came to typify the genre, is that it concentrates on details and exceptions, without first enunciating principles or explaining terms. The compiler does not, for example, lay out the rules for the inheritance of peasant holdings, but deals only with what had been controversial cases, such as the inheritance rights of widows and orphans. On orphans, the code states: 'To charge an orphan an entry-fine [for access to the land] is a rejected and forbidden innovation. His father's land is treated as heritable property. If the land left by the orphan's father is given to another on the ground that it is not cultivated, when the orphan comes of age, and if he demands the land, it should be returned to the orphan.' On widows, it states: 'A woman should not leave fallow the land of which she has the disposal. So long as she pays tithes and taxes, it is against the law to take it from her.'

The 1487 Law Book of Bursa provided a model for future codes.[38] Most of these were also Law Books for sanjaks, typically forming the preface to a district's cadastral survey by listing local taxes and other regulations. The basis of their statutes was local custom which, as the Slavonic, Hungarian, Greek and other non-Turkish technical vocabulary shows, was often pre-Ottoman.[39] The most striking example of the adoption of local practice appears, however, in the Law Books for the sanjaks of south-eastern Anatolia which Selim I had conquered between 1514 and 1516. The earliest Law Books for these sanjaks open with the statement that they are 'in accordance with the Law of Hasan Padishah', a reference to the Akkoyunlu ruler of the district, Uzun

Hasan, who had died in 1478. The compilers believed, therefore, that
they were restating Akkoyunlu law, and there seems to be no reason
to doubt their assertion, although some individual regulations clearly predate the Akkoyunlu period. The format of these Law Books is
to state what the Akkoyunlu regulations had been, noting whether
they had been confirmed or abolished, and converting the value of
money taxes into Ottoman coinage. A few clauses from the Law
Book for Ergani, dated 1518, provide an example: '. . . And from each
household they used to levy one day's labour . . . One sheep was
taken from each household as Festival Tax . . . And from each household, they used to take as *termürjik* tax, one *tenge*, which is two
Ottoman *akches* . . . The provisions given above have been confirmed
as they are.'

Much of Ottoman secular law, therefore, had its origin in local
practice and the laws of previous dynasties. Nonetheless, despite this
diversity, it tended over the decades to become more homogenous.
Total uniformity was not possible, given the diversity of peoples and
local economies within the Empire, but certain statutes, such as those
fixing the rate of the annual tax on peasant tenements, tithes on
crops, or incidental levies, such as bride tax, gradually came closer
together. This process was not haphazard. Although a sanjak might,
in the years following its conquest, have been subject to the laws of
the previous régime, the Law Books suggest that the compilers of
subsequent cadastral registers would bring land and tax regulations
more closely into agreement with what they regarded as 'Ottoman
law'. Indeed, on occasions this law came into force immediately after
the Ottoman conquest. The early registers for south-east Anatolia,
for example, preserve the texts of the Akkoyunlu 'Laws of Hasan
Padishah', but the registers themselves indicate that, in some areas,
the new Ottoman régime levied taxes not according to the 'Law of
Hasan Padishah', but according to 'Ottoman law'. Furthermore, in
this and other regions, the new Law Books compiled during the sixteenth century at the time of new land and tax surveys, sometimes
record a change in the rate or abolition of a tax, on the grounds that
the old tax was 'not Ottoman law'.

The notion of a specific 'Ottoman law' owes its origin to Bayezid
II. It was he who, shortly before 1500, issued a command to an

anonymous official to compile in a bound volume: '. . . all the Ottoman customary laws . . . which are the pole of the good order in the public affairs of all peoples'. The result of this command was the Law Book of 1499,[40] which has, as its major topic, the obligations of *timar* holders and tax payers in all parts of the Empire. In addition, the compiler added chapters which apply only to local groups, such as the Vlachs of the Balkan peninsula or the Turcomans of Anatolia. The work as a whole is a collage. As well as the clauses which the compiler seems to have composed himself, others clearly have their origins in sultanic decrees, fatwas, cadastral registers and the Law Books of sanjaks. The collection was a success, existing today in tens of copies, and going through several recensions until it reached its final form in about 1540. It provided, for the first time, a universally applicable code of secular law and a source of reference for defining 'Ottoman law'. Following its promulgation, it becomes common to find in the Law Books of sanjaks references to 'Ottoman law'. In the 1528 Law Book of the Sanjak of Kütahya, for example, the clause laying out the tax on vineyards and orchards begins: 'A tithe is taken from the produce of vineyards and orchards according to what is legal [in] Ottoman Law.' A clause specifying the rate of the sheep tax in a sixteenth-century Law Book of the central Anatolian Sanjak of Bozok reads: 'After lambing is finished in May, in accordance with Ottoman law, the sheep and lambs should be counted, and one akche taken per two animals. Nothing should be taken in addition . . .' Clauses such as these are evidence of the effect that Bayezid's code and its later recensions had on standardising the law.

Although the services due from *timar* holders and the taxes due from peasants form the main themes of Bayezid II's Law Book, the work in fact opens with what were originally two independent criminal codes. The first of these exists separately as the opening section in the misleadingly titled 'Law [Book] of Sultan Mehmed Khan', an unsystematic compilation, dating from about 1490. The second code, dealing primarily with capital offences,[41] seems to date from the late 1490s, since it has a clause indicating that the military class now came directly under the jurisdiction of the sultan and not of the judges. In later recensions of the Law Book, the compilers amalgamated the two codes into one. Criminal statutes also appear, rather haphazardly, in the Law Books of sanjaks. The 1487 Law Book of Bursa, for example, lays down: '150 akches is taken from someone who removes an eye, and 100 akches from someone who inflicts a headwound that lays bare the bone . . .' and so on. Similar clauses appear in the Law Books of other sanjaks. The reason for these penal statutes in the Law Books is that it was members of the military class, especially the *subashis*, who were responsible for the arrest and punishment of criminals, and who also pocketed fines as part of their income. The application of the criminal law was therefore an aspect of the relationship between the military class and the tax-payers.

The Law Books, however, tell us almost nothing about the procedures of the criminal law, more or less confining themselves to listing the tariff of fines and other punishments. It is difficult, therefore, to establish what was the legal process between arrest and punishment, and also whether the penal code in the Law Book of 1499 and its subsequent recensions were ever, in practice, effective.

On the question of capital offences, Spandounes in the early sixteenth century states unequivocally that the case had to come before a judge. 'No Sanjak Governor', he writes, 'for all the exalted nature of his office, can condemn to death without the permission of the Judge . . . A *subashi* arrests the malefactor, submits him to torture and elicits a confession of his crime, before taking him to take his stand before the Judge. If he is condemned, the *subashi* puts him to death.' Spandounes's statement confirms what appears in the 1487 Law Book for Bursa. This forbids the infliction of the death penalty before the miscreant's offences are proven 'in the presence of the Judge of the region'. It is probable, therefore, that, in principle, cases involving the death penalty came before a judge. Practice was probably a lot more variable. References to capital punishment are rare in the records of the judges' courts, and occasional clauses in the Law Books of sanjaks suggest that governors would sometimes, presumably for their own enrichment, commute the penalty for a fine. The Bursa Law Book, for example, forbids this practice. A similar clause appears in a Law Book of 1540 for the Boz Ulus, a tribal group in northern Syria and south-eastern Anatolia. This states that 'persons meriting capital punishment . . . should be executed. Not a farthing should be taken in lieu of capital punishment.' The fact that the same clause appears again in the 1570 Law Book for Aleppo suggests that it had been disregarded: 'Money in lieu of execution should not be accepted from persons worthy of capital punishment.' These clauses suggest that in capital cases the executive authorities tended either to bypass the courts, or at least to ignore their sentences.

Most lesser offences seem to have been the responsibility of the executive authorities. Certainly cases do occur in the judges' registers, but these usually record only the facts of the case and witness statements, without recording a verdict or punishment. These presumably were the province of the *subashi*. In many cases, however, it seems very likely that the *subashi* or other military authority was responsible for the entire process, from arrest – although this could be the responsibility of communities or private individuals – to punishment, bypassing the courts altogether. In the absence of records, however, this can only be speculation.

According to the criminal codes, punishment for non-capital offences consisted usually of strokes of the lash, fines, or a combination of both. Whether the authorities followed the code precisely is not certain. They must however have levied fines, as these formed part of the income of the military class, and one small piece of evidence does suggest that, at the time at least of its promulgation in the reign of Bayezid II, the provisions of the code were observed. For stabbing it prescribes an unusual punishment: '[The offender] should have knives stuck into his arms, and he should be paraded [in public.]' Spandounes provides evidence that this did indeed happen, when he notes: 'If a person draws a weapon against another, the Judge has him . . . stabbed in the flesh with five, six or seven knives . . . and led around all the public places in this way.'

7 The Army

The fourteenth century

The earliest accounts of Ottoman warfare survive in the Byzantine chronicles of Pachymeres and John Kantakouzenos. Neither author gives much detail, and Pachymeres is especially confusing. Nonetheless, he provides us with our only glimpses of Turkish warriors at the time of Osman (c.1324). Most of Osman's men were, it seems, mounted, and experts in ambushes and surprise attacks. Pachymeres describes, for example, an assault on a Byzantine force under a certain Mouzalon 'unexpectedly, while they were asleep'. In a later passage, he tells how Osman's men routed another Byzantine commander, Siouros, near a fortress called Katoika. Once again, it was surprise that overwhelmed the Greeks. 'They were attacked at night, by about five hundred of the enemy in full force, who had completely escaped detection and seized the roads to the fortress. More attacked from the other side.' The Turks cut down those who resisted, while 'women and children, an innumerable crowd, who tried to escape to the fortress were sitting targets for the enemy forces, who had occupied it first'.

In his description of the attack on Mouzalon, Pachymeres also hints at Osman's battle tactics. When the Byzantine forces had recovered their wits and tried to pursue the Turks, these retreated to the mountains and 'having found safety there, stopped and began to fire on the Byzantines, encircling them with shots from each side'. Taken together these passages suggest that Osman's forces consisted largely of mounted archers, whose offensive tactic was surprise, and whose defensive tactic was to retreat at speed to land which provided natural defences. It was an army, perhaps, of lightly armed but effective raiders. It is probable, however, that despite his victory over a smaller and apparently disorganised Byzantine force at Baphaeon, his men would not have been able to defeat a disciplined army in a formal encounter.

Nonetheless, it is clear from Pachymeres that Osman succeeded in gaining control of the countryside in Byzantine Bythinia. Villages and rural settlements had no defence against his raids. It was probably, too, his control of the countryside around, rather than a mastery of siege warfare that enabled him to capture at least the smaller Byzantine fortresses and towns. 'He used the fortresses', Pachymeres tells us, 'as places of safe-keeping for [his] treasures.'

The walled cities survived as Byzantine strongholds but not, Pachymeres implies, without suffering greatly. 'Prousas (Bursa)', he states, 'had the advantage of all these troubles' and, in his description of Pegai, he shows how even well defended towns suffered from their role as places of refuge from the countryside: 'Pegai, too, a coastal city, experienced these misfortunes. The surrounding population were confined inside the city and, for those who had escaped the sword, bad conditions produced an epidemic of the plague.' Nonetheless, they continued to resist. Pachymeres also records an attack on the city of Nikaia (Iznik). Osman, he reports, destroyed crops and vineyards, and then attacked the fortress of Trikkokia which guarded the approach to the city. Nikaia he besieged with his entire force and, filling in the defensive ditches with 'stakes, rocks, trees and rubble', attempted to storm the wall. The attack, in the end, failed. The survival of Nikaia and the other cities of Bithynia suggests that Osman's men lacked the discipline, the military skills and the material support to undertake long sieges of well defended places.

The picture of the earliest Ottoman warriors as, in essence, highly mobile raiders, also emerges from John Kantakouzenos's description of the battle of Pelekanon, fought in 1328 between Orhan (c.1324–1362) and the Byzantine Emperor, Andronikos III. Kantakouzenos describes Orhan's force as 'an army of infantry and cavalry', although the description which follows indicates that the majority fought on horseback. Part of his force he placed in ambush, with instructions to attack if the Greeks gained the upper hand. The main body of men Kantakouzenos describes as mounted archers with the swiftest horses. These Orhan instructed 'not to fight at close quarters, but to fall on the Emperor suddenly, retreat with a shower of arrows when the Byzantines counterattacked, and attack again as they withdrew'. The reserve forces he placed behind an area of broken ground which provided a natural defence.

Kantakouzenos gives the impression that Orhan's tactics did not work. When the Greeks counterattacked, his mounted archers could not halt the charge, and instead turned to flee until they reached the broken ground in the rear. In the end, however, the Emperor could not secure a victory 'for the Turks were surrounded by deep valleys, and the camp was protected by natural trenches. In these were stationed many archers, whose arrows impeded the Byzantine victory. The Emperor could not send in his army, because of the uneven terrain.' The details of this narrative recall Pachymeres's description of Osman's night attacks on Mouzalon and Siouros. Osman's forces, too, had consisted largely of mounted archers, and adopted ambush as a strategy. They too had proved unable to withstand a disciplined attack, but were able to avoid defeat by careful choice of defensive positions. It seems therefore that the use of mounted archers, ambushes and strategic retreats to rough ground were essential elements in the earliest Ottoman fighting technique.

This was a form of warfare more suited to raids than to field battles and sieges. Nonetheless, it was not until the late sixteenth century that it finally became obsolete. During the centuries of expansion, the Ottomans waged an almost continuous *kleinkrieg* along the frontiers of the Empire, which continued even during periods of formal peace. Characteristic of this mode of warfare were raids and counterraids across the frontier in pursuit of plunder, especially of slaves and animals. The same raiders might also go ahead of Ottoman armies on their formal campaigns in order to terrorise the enemy before the main onslaught. The tactics of the raiding troops were those of the followers of Osman and Orhan but, by the second half of the fourteenth century, their function was as auxiliaries, not as the main body of the army.

The creation of an army that was capable of conducting effective sieges and field-battles was the work of Orhan and Murad I (1362–89). It was during Orhan's reign that the great cities of Prousas (Bursa), Nikaia (Iznik) and Nikomedia (Izmit) fell, although in the case, at least of Prousas, a Greek Short Chronicle[1] indicates that it was starvation rather than assault that forced the city to surrender. With Orhan in command of the countryside, its eventual capitulation was inevitable. The same was undoubtedly true of the other Bithynian cities. However, the capture towards the end of Orhan's reign of Ankara in 1354 and Dimetoka in 1359 or 1360, suggest that by this time his troops had mastered the art of formal siege warfare. This becomes more evident during the reign of Murad I. Especially during his last decade, the conquest and control of castles and fortified towns became an essential element in Ottoman strategy. In Macedonia, Murad conquered Serrai in 1383 and Thessaloniki in 1387, after a siege of four years. As a prelude to an attack on southern Serbia, in 1386 he captured Nish in the Morava valley, in the version of the chronicler Neshri, after first establishing which part of the fortress was vulnerable to arrow shot. In 1388, Murad's vizier, Chandarli Ali, reduced Tsar Shishman to vassalage after a systematic campaign against his castles in eastern Bulgaria.[2]

It is clear, therefore, that during the course of the fourteenth century, the Ottomans learned how to conduct sieges. A few references from the last decade of the century indicate that they had mastered the techniques of blockade and battery, and of scaling walls. In 1394, Bayezid I (1389–1402) laid siege to Constantinople, first attempting to block access to the city by constructing a castle on the Asian shore of the Bosphorus, at its narrowest point. He then attacked the city, according to a Greek doxology to the Virgin, 'with innumerable engines of war'. What these were becomes slightly clearer from the account of John Chortasmenos, who writes: 'Now they brought up trebuchets for besieging the city . . . and made use of many machines, throwing down the walls of the city, and also storming the ramparts.' It seems that, by this time, the Ottomans also used siege towers. In his description of Bayezid's siege of Larende in 1398, Schiltberger tells how 'he constructed platforms' opposite the walls. These passing references to siege technology do not mention mining, but this probably reflects the inadequacy of the source materials rather than an absence of mines. Certainly, by 1422, mining had become part of Ottoman siegecraft. In his account of the siege of Constantinople in that year, the Greek, Kananos, describes how the attackers dug mines from behind their ramparts to the walls of the city and, 'as is the custom in

sieges', set fire to the wooden poles which supported the under-
ground chambers. As the mine collapsed, so too did a section of the
wall above the ground.

At the same time as they learned the art of siege warfare, the
Ottomans also became masters of battlefield tactics, as became clear
with Murad I's defeat of the two Serbian despots at the battle of the
Maritsa in 1371. In field battles, the sultan commanded what was overwhelmingly a cavalry army. From accounts of the battle of Nicopolis
against the Crusaders in 1396, it seems that the Ottoman cavalry
relied on its manoeuvrability, and continued, as in Osman's time, to
use the tactics of ambush and feigned withdrawal. It seems that, at
Nicopolis, the French heavy cavalry defeated the force that confronted it directly, but found that, in doing so, Bayezid had lured them into
an ambush by cavalry stationed on the flanks.[3]

Between 1300 and 1400, therefore, the Ottoman military had
changed from a force of raiders gathered around the ruler, to a disciplined army capable of undertaking sieges and formal battles. The
two institutions that underpinned this transformation were clearly
the two groups that are familiar from later centuries, the *timar* holding cavalry and the Janissaries. The establishment of the *timar* holders
was probably an early development, since similar institutions had
existed in the lands which the Ottomans had conquered. The institution must have been in existence by the reign of Murad I. The possession of a *timar* relieved each cavalryman from dependence on
plunder for a livelihood and, more importantly, created a contractual obligation to serve the sultan whenever he required. The Janissaries
were an infantry corps, perhaps established by Murad I, which not
only formed a unit in the army, but also acted as the sultan's personal bodyguard. As a standing force which fought together and trained
together in the use of weapons, they acquired an esprit de corps
which, from early in their history, made them outstandingly good
fighters. On the field of battle, they fought in the centre, around the
person of the monarch. In addition to these bodies of men, the sultan
could also call on the lightly armed raiders in Rumelia, and troops
from the vassal principalities who, like the cavalrymen and
Janissaries, had a contractual duty to serve.

By 1400, therefore, most of the troops in the Ottoman army served

on a contractual basis, allowing the sultan to levy a predictable number of reliable troops year after year. It was this, as much as anything
else that underpinned Ottoman military success.

1400 to 1590: troops

The military structure that emerged during the course of the fourteenth century remained, in its essence, intact until the end of the sixteenth, with the *timar*-holding cavalry and the Janissaries forming the
most significant bodies of fighting men.

Of these, the *timar* holders formed the overwhelming majority,
although the first reliable statement of their numbers does not
appear until 1525. A summary of the Empire's receipts and expendi-
tures in this year records 10 618 in the European provinces and 17
200 in Asia Minor and Syria. Each of these cavalrymen had to bring
a certain number of armed retainers, and this would have brought
the total numbers available up to about 50 000. Not all of these
would have served at any one time, but the number is high enough to
show that they formed the most important element in the Ottoman
army.[4]

More famous than the *timar*-holding cavalrymen but less numerous
were the Janissaries. At the time of its foundation in the second half of
the fourteenth century, the Janissary corps consisted of perhaps a few
hundred infantrymen, who served as the sultan's bodyguard. In this
role, they were an effective force and, having no other source of protection and patronage, reliably loyal to the sultan. In the closing stages
of the battle of Ankara in 1402, it was the Janissaries who remained
fighting around the sultan when the rest of the Ottoman army had
deserted or fled. At the battle of Varna in 1444, when a large part of the
cavalry army had left the field, it was the Janissaries who stood firm
around Murad II (1421–51) and, crucially, captured and killed the
Hungarian King.[5] Their numbers evidently increased during the
course of the fifteenth century. A Greek source from the early 1480s
reports that there were 5000 at the accession of Mehmed II (1451–81),
and that Mehmed doubled this number at the time of the wars with
Uzun Hasan in the early 1470s. Their number remained a bit above or
below 10 000 for much of the following century. Payroll figures show

10 156 Janissaries in 1514. In 1527, there were 7886 Janissaries and 3553 Novices; in 1567, there were 12 798 and 7745 respectively. Apart from these, there were Janissaries serving in garrisons in the provinces. In 1560, for example, there were 3377 in the fortresses of the province of Buda, on the frontier with Austria.[6]

Before the second half of the sixteenth century, the Ottoman government seems carefully to have restricted the numbers of Janissaries. This was partly, no doubt, a measure to control expenditure, and partly to accord with the maxim of Lutfi Pasha, Grand Vizier from 1539 to 1541, that: 'Troops should be few, but they should be excellent.' Another reason to restrict numbers was probably also to curtail their power. The Janissaries were an élite corps, and part of their effectiveness was the terror that they aroused in the enemy. But what was equally important was the fear that they inspired in the sultans. The loyalty of the corps to the Ottoman dynasty was never in doubt, but this did not preclude disloyalty to individual sultans. It was, in part, at least, a Janissary rebellion that forced the abdication of Mehmed II at the end of his first reign in 1446, and the return of his father Murad II to the throne. It was the Janissaries who forced the abdication of Bayezid II (1481–1512) in favour of Selim I (1512–20), and it was the Janissaries who murdered Osman II (1618–22), and brought Mustafa (1617–18; 1622–3) to the throne. In the short interregnum between the death of Mehmed II and the accession of Bayezid II, the Janissaries rioted and plundered parts of the capital. After the victory at Chaldiran in 1514, it was they who forced Selim I to retreat from Tabriz, and they rioted again in 1525. As an armed group stationed in Istanbul, the Janissaries were as powerful a force in the internal politics of the Empire as they were on the battlefield.

The *timar* holders and the Janissaries were the major, but not the only components of Ottoman battlefield armies. The élite Six Divisions of cavalry regulars recruited largely from the graduates of the Palace School accompanied the sultan on campaign, as well as on ceremonial occasions. It is impossible to establish the date of their foundation, but it is clear that they were in existence by the time of Mehmed II, when the Greek source gives their numbers as 600 Cavalrymen (*sipahis*), 600 Swordbearers (*silahdars*), 700 Stipendiaries (*ulufejis*) of the Left and of the Right, and 400 Strangers (*gureba*) of the

Left and of the Right. During the course of the sixteenth century, these numbers tripled. In 1527, they were 1993, 1587, 1007 and 415 respectively; and in 1567, 3331, 2785, 2546 and 2589. The increase in numbers was proportionately higher than that of the Janissaries, but they were still few in comparison with the *timar* holders from the provinces. By 1607, their numbers had increased still further, to 7805 Cavalrymen, 7683 Swordbearers, 3448 Stipendiaries and 1903 Strangers. By this time, however, the growth in Janissary numbers was much greater.[7]

Contrasting with the Janissaries were the *Azabs*. These too were infantrymen, recruited according to Iacopo di Promontorio in 1475 'from among craftsmen and peasants'. Ottoman chronicles refer to the existence of *Azabs* already in 1389, but this may be anachronistic. It is clear, however, that the Corps of *Azabs* was in existence at the time of the Hungarian wars in the 1440s,[8] and may well date from before 1400. The method of recruitment to the Corps, at least in the late fifteenth and early sixteenth centuries, is clear from Bayezid II's Law Book of 1499. This text suggests that the government made the levies mainly in towns, appointing the local judge and *subashi* to put it into operation, and demanding also the cooperation of the imam and another representative from each town quarter. Here they were to summon and inspect all the lads fit for war, rejecting any who were under age, disabled, too old, or slaves. From these they would select the *Azabs*. In addition to supplying these fighting men, the people of the quarter had to provide money for their expenses, up to a limit of 300 akches per *Azab*. The system for apportioning the levy of both men and cash was by number of households, as the Law Book explains: 'If, for example, it falls to twenty households to provide one *Azab*, from among the twenty people [provided by the twenty households] in that quarter, one suitable one should be enrolled for *Azab* service. Expenses for him should be collected from the remaining nineteen [households] . . .' Only if the appointed group of households could not provide a suitable lad, should those making the levy look elsewhere. They should also appoint a guarantor for each lad, so that if he absconded, it would be possible to recover his pay. Finally, in order to ensure the regularity of the procedures and to prevent a series of abuses which the Law Book enumerates, it was a requirement to make registers of the levy: 'From each judicial district where

Azabs are levied, there should be two registers. One should remain with the judges, and one should come to the Palace, so that when there is a roll-call of *Azabs*, or a guarantor is sought, it is possible to look either at the register which is with the judge, or at the register which has come to the Palace . . . and to take action accordingly.'

The *Azabs*, unlike the Janissaries, were not a corps of regular troops and, although Iacopo di Promontorio in 1475 estimated their strength at 6000, it is clear that their numbers in fact fluctuated according to military necessity. One account of the Chaldiran campaign in 1514, for example, states that there were 10 000 *Azabs* from Anatolia and 8000 from Rumelia serving in Selim I's army.[9] For the same campaign, Menavino puts their numbers even higher, at 30 000. Nor, unlike the Janissaries were the *Azabs* an élite corps. The *Azabs* were conscripts whose lives were expendable. Like the Janissaries, however, they served both on the battlefield and in fortresses. Spandounes in 1513 recorded the presence in garrisons of both *Azabs* and Janissaries, writing of the *Azabs*:

they are more numerous than the Janissaries, and if they are in a castle, the ones guard one fort and the others another; if they are garrisoning a town, the Janissaries will be in the citadel and the *Azabs* in the town, because the Janissaries are more capable and bold. If there are fewer *Azabs* than Janissaries, they could not last together. These *Azabs* have from three to six akches a day as wages, and are mostly from Anatolia.

Ottoman documents from throughout the sixteenth century continue to record both Janissaries and *Azabs* in fortresses.[10] From the second half of the sixteenth century, however, the *Azabs* seem to have lost their importance as battlefield troops. In the 1540s already, the Hospitaller Antoine Geuffroy commented: 'As for footsoldiers, [the Ottomans] have none apart from the Janissaries, at least none that are worth anything . . .'

The last important category of fighting men in the Ottoman army were the Raiders – *akinjis*. These were the lightly armed cavalry of Rumelia who, more than any other Ottoman soldiers, kept alive the fighting traditions of the the early fourteenth century. They emerged in the Balkan peninsula before 1400 as a distinctive body of soldiers, with their own hereditary leaders and structure of command. As

lightly armed raiders who fought outside the periods of formal campaigning, and independently of the main body of the army, their existence was symptomatic of the continuous *kleinkrieg* waged along the
borders of the Empire.

Constantine Mihailović, who fought with the Ottoman army
between 1453 and 1463, and Iacopo di Promontorio in 1475 provide
the earliest descriptions of these troops. Mihailović notes that 'they
live by means of livestock and raise horses'. He was probably right so
far as concerns horse breeding, since the Raiders provided their own
swift mounts, and later Spandounes was to remark how 'they are all
well mounted, because they have excellent horses'. Their main source
of living from the land seems, however, to have come from the cultivation of crops, on which the sultan exempted them from taxation.
Iacopo writes: 'They have the privilege of surviving on the holdings
of the Sultan, as much as two or three pairs of oxen can plough, without paying tithe.' A quarter of a century later, however, Spandounes
was to observe: 'They have no wages and, despite this, still pay the
tithes on their wheat and other food which they produce in the place
where they live with their family. Similarly, they pay the expenses of
the *timar* holder or garrison troops in their town.'

Most of their income, however, came from booty, whether they
collected it during formal campaigns, or from their independent
incursions across the frontier. Mihailović described their raids as:
'. . . like torrential rains that fall from clouds. From these storms
come great floods, until the streams leave their banks and overflow,
and everything this water strikes, it takes, carries away, and moreover
destroys . . . Thus also the Turkish raiders do not linger long, but
wherever they strike, they burn, plunder, kill and destroy everything,
so that for many years the cock will not crow there.' The few Turkish
accounts of incursions by the Raiders enthusiastically confirm
Mihailović's account. The chronicler Ashikpashazade served as a
Raider at Skopje during the 1430s and 1440s and, writing about the
aftermath of a raid across the Sava in 1440, he comments: 'I bought a
fine lad of six or seven years . . . and on that raid, I acquired seven
slaves and slave girls from the Raiders. It was such that, if the army
had moved off, the crowd of prisoners would have been more
numerous than the troops.'

These incursions by the Raiders served two purposes. From a military aspect, they aimed to terrify the enemy and weaken the opposition, especially in advance of a major campaign. However, during the campaign itself, the indiscipline of the Raiders could make them as much a hazard as an asset. A decree of 1560 illustrates this point. The sultan had ordered the commander of the Raiders, Turahan, to Azov in the Crimea, to guard the district against Russian attacks. Turahan, however found that the region was in the grip of a famine, with no opportunity for raiding or taking booty. In the circumstances, he could no longer control his men, and wrote to the Sultan: 'There is nowhere to plunder. The Raiders and their officers are people who are suitable only for plunder. They cannot endure staying still for four or five days, and cannot be disciplined.' Although effective within their own groups, they were not suitable for formal warfare. Apart from this military function, the booty which the Raiders took supplied the markets of the Empire, above all, with slaves. This traffic was also profitable to the sultans, who took a percentage of the prisoners as recruits for the Janissaries or the Palace Schools. In addition, probably from the end of the fourteenth century, they also levied a toll on these captives, as their owners ferried them across the Straits from Europe to Asia Minor.[11]

The form of warfare that the Raiders practised clearly went back to the beginnings of the Empire. However, it was probably not until Ottoman power became firmly established in the Balkan peninsula towards the end of the reign of Murad I that they emerged as a distinctive military organisation. With the annexation of the Bulgarian principalities in the 1390s and the establishment of the Danube as the frontier with Hungary, the organisation of the Raiders probably took the form which it was to keep for the next two centuries. During the fourteenth and fifteenth centuries, the marcher lords emerged as leaders of the Raiders. Particularly prominent in this respect was the Mihaloghlu family, who held hereditary lands at Vidin, a fortress on the Danube which looked across the river to the Kingdom of Hungary. Serving under these lords were officers, known as *dovijas*, and under them, the ordinary Raiders. When the sultan wished to levy them for a campaign, he would send, according to Spandounes in the early sixteenth century: 'one month before [the campaign], a messenger to warn them that they were to muster on such-and-such a day of the month, at such-and-such a place, where they would find a captain sent by the Sultan to lead them against the Christians.'

Service as a Raider was perhaps, in the early days, voluntary. By the sixteenth century, however, and probably much earlier, it had become customary to enrol and formally register the troops. A command to the sanjak governor of Vidin, undated, but probably from the sixteenth century, gives an idea of the procedure. The sanjak governor was to tour the towns and villages of Rumelia, and to conscript raiders who had a good horse, and weapons and armour suitable for campaign. He was also to levy the sons of dead and retired Raiders. As with the *Azabs*, the registers recording the levies contained the names not only of each Raider and his father, but also the name of a bailsman who would guarantee his appearance on campaign. At times of mobilisation, the conscripts were to appear with a turban or red headgear, armed with a sword and beflagged lance. The sanjak governor making the levy had presumably to forward a copy of the completed register to the Palace. This was certainly the case in a command of 1560, which informs the Sanjak Governor of Vulčitrn that a member of one of the palace cavalry divisions would be arriving to assist him in making a register of the Raiders, and ordering him to send it to the palace as soon as it was complete.[12]

Estimates vary on the total number of Raiders at the sultan's disposal. Iacopo di Promontorio in 1475 gives 8000, of which 6000 were available for campaign, while the other 2000 remained behind to guard the frontier. In Iacopo's time and earlier, there may well have been others in the personal following of the marcher lords. A sixteenth-century chronicle states that 20 000 accompanied Süleyman's first campaign in 1521, and this may have been a typical number for the century. Geuffroy in 1543 gives their number as 60 000. This figure, while probably an exaggeration, is perhaps not wholly fantastic, since it recalls what Kochi Bey was to write in the 1630s. Recalling the glorious sixteenth century, he notes that there used to be 20 000 registered Raiders, but that when there was a campaign, the commander of the Raiders crossed the Danube with 40–50 000 troops, some of these registered Raiders, and some of them volunteers and other auxiliary troops who were skilled in horsemanship.

Until the early decades of the sixteenth century, the Raiders most probably served on campaign under the marcher lords of Rumelia. By the mid-sixteenth century, their organisation was into two 'wings', the 'left wing' and the 'right wing', their attachment being according to the area in Rumelia where they lived. The names of the 'wings', however – 'the followers of Mihaloghlu' and 'the followers of Turahan' – show that the association with the marcher lords had continued at least in name.[13] The appearance in 1560 of a certain Turahan as a leader of the Raiders suggests[14] – if he was indeed a member of the Turahanoghlu dynasty – that a personal association between the Raiders and the old marcher families may have lingered into the late sixteenth century.

This was a time when the Raiders lost their importance as a military force. Until the end of the sixteenth century, the Raiders formed an important element in the Ottoman army, fighting in campaigns both in Europe and Asia. Their most significant role had been as border warriors, especially in making attacks across the river frontiers into the Kingdom of Hungary and, after the annexation of Bosnia in 1463, in launching raids from there into Venetian and Hungarian territory. Their raids north of the Danube and, in 1498, even into Poland, seem to have become particularly intense during the reign of Bayezid II, a period when the sultan undertook little formal warfare into Europe. In 1526, however, their role changed. The battle of Mohács brought to an end the independent kingdom of Hungary and, in 1541, Hungary, or that part of it under Ottoman suzerainty, became an Ottoman province. With the disappearance of the old Danube frontier, some of the functions of the Raiders seem also to have vanished. The new frontier with Austria seems to have been less vulnerable to raids than the old Hungarian frontier, especially with the construction of a line of effective border defences. Regular plundering raids, such as Mihailović had described in the fifteenth century came to an end. The Law Books for the Sanjak of Smederovo on the Danube provide an illustration of this change. In the version compiled in 1516, one clause lists the tolls levied at the quay of Smederovo on the categories of booty which the Raiders brought across the Danube after their razzias. In the version of 1560, this clause has disappeared.[15]

Nonetheless, even if the annual raids across the borders came to an end, the Raiders still kept their old function of harrying the enemy in advance of a campaign, and also of mounting punitive expeditions outside periods of formal warfare. When, for example, the Sultan received reports of Austrian attacks on Transylvania in 1565 – a year when the siege of Malta absorbed most of the Empire's military resources – he ordered the Sanjak Governor of Chernomen to go 'with the Raiders of the left wing, followers of Mihaloghlu', to Srem and to plunder the enemy's territory. He was to 'raid the abject infidels, enslave their children and wives, plunder and pillage their possesions and properties . . .', so that 'it would be a lesson to them'.[6] The same command orders him not to lose any regular troops, for whom the Raiders were, on this expedition, a substitute.

The end of the Raiders as an effective military force came in 1595. In this year, the Grand Vizier, Koja ('the Elder') Sinan Pasha, led his expedition into Wallachia. His army included a large contingent of Raiders and, as these waited to cross the Danube at Giurgiu, back into Ottoman territory, the Wallachian forces attacked and destroyed them almost to a man. 'Most of the Raiders', writes the Ottoman historian, Na'ima 'were on the opposite bank, and not a man of them escaped. At that moment, the root of the Raiders was cut off, and they became extinct.'[7] In fact, the remnants of the organisation lingered on. In the 1630s, Kochi Bey reported that there were 2000, but that the remainder had either renounced their status, or become absorbed into other army units. The demise of the Raiders' organisation does not, however, mean that the Ottomans ceased to harry enemy territory as a military tactic. It seems, however, that from the end of the sixteenth century, the Tatar troops attached to the Khan of the Crimea became more important in this role. They had participated in earlier campaigns, but not prominently. Indeed, in the mid-sixteenth century, Lutfi Pasha had warned against employing the Tatars. 'It is true', he wrote, 'that the Tatars are subjects of the Ottoman dynasty, but they are a refractory people, and cannot be obliged to serve on campaign.' With the end of the Raiders, however, their military importance increased.

Between the late fourteenth century, therefore, and the end of the sixteenth, the *timar*-holding cavalry, the Janissaries, the Six Divisions, the *Azabs* and the Raiders had been the most prominent contingents of Ottoman fighting troops. At the same time, the sultan maintained a body of non-combatants who acted as pioneers for the army. These were the Footmen – *yayas* – and the Exemptees – *müsellems*. It is possible that they originated in the fourteenth century as bodies of, respectively, infantry and cavalry, but that by the early fifteenth century they had lost their combatant role. Like the *timar*-holding cavalrymen, they received no pay from the Treasury. Instead, they raised the money for campaigns from within their own organisations. The sultan levied these men in Anatolia and Rumelia, and divided them into groups of thirty, allocating to each group a plot of land for cultivation, and exempting them from taxes on their produce and from extraordinary taxation. In each of these groups, five men were 'campaigners', who went to war in turn, and the rest were 'helpers', who were liable to pay 50 *akches* each for the maintenance of the campaigner. A Law Book of 1531 records that, until the time of Bayezid II, the helpers paid this amount each year, regardless of whether there was a campaign or not. To prevent disputes between the two groups, Bayezid decreed that, henceforth, the money was due only when there was a campaign.[18]

The organisation of these men resembled the organisation of *timar* holders under a sanjak governor. Both the Footmen and the Exemptees in a particular area came under the command of their own governor, rather than of the governor of the sanjak where they held their lands. Also like the *timar*-holding cavalrymen, a number of them served as officers, with the title 'troop commander' or 'infantry commander'. In Rumelia, the Turkish tribemen – the *yürüks* – performed the same duties as the Footmen in Anatolia, on the basis, it seems, of a similar organisation.

Altogether, these military auxiliaries were very numerous. In 1521 in Anatolia, there were officially 2584 groups of Exemptees and 7668 of Footmen. In Rumelia in 1552, there were 1377 groups of *yürüks* and 810 of Exemptees.[19] Their duties, according to Ayn Ali in the early seventeenth century, were in dragging cannon, clearing roads and bringing up provisions for the army. These were undoubtedly their most basic functions, but clearly their duties were in fact more varied. For example, a Law Book of Gallipoli, dated 1518, requires the mounted Exemptees, among other things, to keep watch on the coasts and harbours, and immediately to give notice to the villages and fortresses if they see any ship that might pose a danger. In addition, they had to perform heavy duties in the Gallipoli naval arsenal, such as dragging ships onto the dry land.

During the course of the sixteenth century, the organisation of Footmen and Exemptees seems to have become disordered and unreliable. Certainly, a command of 1540, ordering the conscription of new recruits and the proper registration of members and of the lands which they held,[20] suggests that desertion was common. In 1582, the sultan ordered the abolition of both groups. Immediately afterwards, he changed his mind and conscription began again.[21] By 1600, however, the two corps of Footmen and Exemptees no longer existed. Ayn Ali in 1609 noted that the former members had all been registered as ordinary tax-paying subjects.

1400–1590: weapons

The earliest Ottoman weapon of which there is a record was the Turkish bow, fired from horseback. This was a weapon which continued to play an important role in both land and sea battles into the sixteenth century, even if later warriors lost the skill of firing it from a galloping horse. At some stage, too, the Ottomans adopted the crossbow, perhaps mainly for use in fortresses. As late as the early seventeenth century, the 'Laws of the Janissaries' notes that the Janissary Corps still maintained a stock of these weapons.

In addition to bows, Ottoman troops carried a variety of weapons. Spandounes, for example, describes the *Azabs* as carrying 'bows, swords, shields and some [kind of] small axe'; the Raiders he describes as using 'swords, small shields and nothing else'. In the mid-sixteenth century, however, the Hungarian Bartholomaeus Georgevits equips them with 'lances, javelins, arrows and iron cudgels'. The *timar*-holding cavalrymen seem to have been, and to have remained until the eighteenth century, adept in the use of the short sword. These troops probably, in fact, used a great variety of weapons, since the law required them to bring their own equipment to battle. They would have had, therefore, to rely on what local craftsmen could produce, and what was available in local markets. A Law

Book of 1502, which regulates trading practices in the Rumelian capital, Edirne, lists bowmakers, arrow makers, and sword and dagger makers among the craftsmen of the city. It also, in specifying the minimum quality for categories of saddle, refers to a type called the 'Raider's saddle'. These clauses suggest that Raiders and *timar* holders bought their equipment in the city market. The law also required *timar*-holding cavalrymen to provide their own armour, in the form, it seems, of a helmet and light chain mail covering the upper body. A document of November, 1515,[22] ordering a review of troops in the following spring, threatens with decapitation or amputation of an arm, any soldier without a helmet or armlet respectively. The law also required the cavalrymen to provide their own horse-armour.[23]

The Janissaries and the cavalrymen of the Six Divisions, however, received their weapons and armour from a central supply. The manufacture and maintenance of these was the responsibility of the Corps of Armourers, a body of men which the sultan recruited through the Collection. The corps probably originated in the fifteenth century, and its numbers expanded to reflect the number of Janissaries and household cavalrymen. There were, it seems, about 500 armourers in the mid-sixteenth century, and almost 6000 in 1630. They maintained the supply of all kinds of equipment, including handguns and trenching tools for sieges.

The most important military development during the period of the rise of the Ottoman Empire was, however, the introduction of cannon and other firearms. These weapons came into use in western Europe during the course of the fourteenth century and, from there spread to the Balkan peninsula. By 1378, cannon were in position on the city walls of Dubrovnik and, during the next decade, came into regular use in the Kingdom of Bosnia and also, one may surmise, in Serbia. Ottoman troops may therefore have encountered them for the first time during raids and campaigns in the western Balkans during the 1380s.[24] However, the Ottomans themselves did not adopt cannon on a large scale until the following century. References to their use of gunpowder weapons during the reign of Bayezid I are untrustworthy. By the 1420s, however, they had begun to use cannon in sieges. Kananos, for example, in his account of the siege of Constantinople in 1422, refers to 'large bombards', which he reports as having had no effect. There are other isolated references to the Ottoman use of cannon in the first three decades of the fifteenth century, but they were not as yet an important factor in warfare.[25]

This changed with the Hungarian wars of the 1440s. During the campaigns of 1443–4, the Sultan's army had no field artillery. The Hungarians, by contrast, had developed battle tactics which they based on the *wagenburg*. This was a mobile fortress, consisting of carts chained together to provide a protective wall for troops carrying handguns, with cannon placed on the carts themselves or in the embrasures between the vehicles. The inability of the Ottoman cavalry to overwhelm these fortifications almost lost them the war. The effectiveness of this tactic is clear from the *Holy Wars of Sultan Murad*, an anonymous but contemporary Turkish account of the campaign. Here, the author makes Turahan advise the Sultan: 'My Padishah, command the troops of Islam to withdraw from the *wagenburg*, because if they do not, these ... infidels will fire their cannon and arquebuses and the army of Islam will be defeated.' In another passage, where he describes the bravado of a Turkish captive, the author has him say to the King of Hungary: 'You rely on your carts and hope that the House of Osman will attack them, and that you will repel them with cannon and arquebus. But you don't know that they have understood your trick ... They will not attack your carts. No, they will surround you at a distance the guns cannot reach.' The use of the *wagenburg* brought the Hungarians very close to victory. In 1443, it was the winter weather and the constriction of the army at the Zlatitsa Pass that prevented their further advance. At Varna in 1444, it was the stupidity of the King of Hungary in breaking loose from his army that led to the defeat.

It was, however, a tactic which the Ottomans themselves were very quick to adopt. When the Hungarians again encountered the Ottomans at the second battle of Kosovo in 1448, they found that the sultan had drawn up his ranks behind a 'castle-like' fortification of carts and spiked shields, which the Janissaries defended with guns.[26] Once the Ottoman army had begun to use this tactic, the Hungarians no longer enjoyed a strategic advantage, and the outcome of the battle was a decisive Ottoman victory.

During the Varna campaign, it was artillery that gave the

Hungarians battlefield superiority, although not ultimately victory. In another theatre of the war, however, artillery was crucial to the Hungarian defeat. In order to prevent Murad II's army from crossing into Europe to encounter the Hungarian invasion, the Christian allies had blocked the Straits. The Sultan, however, was able to bring his army across the Bosphorus at its narrowest point, despite the blockade by Burgundian ships. What frustrated the Burgundians, apart from the wind and strong current, were the guns which the Sultan had set up on both shores to cover his passage. The cannon on the Asian shore, the Ottomans themselves cast on the spot. The batteries on the European shore they acquired from the Genoese of Pera, who also provided Murad with guns for the coming campaign.[27]

In several respects, therefore, the Hungarian wars were crucial in Ottoman military development. They led to the adoption of battle-field artillery and the tactic of the *wagenburg*. Furthermore, Murad II's alliance with the Genoese opened a route for the transfer of military technology to the Ottomans. It was from this time that they adopted cannon on a large scale, and became experts in its manufacture. In one respect, however, the Ottomans did not take over the practices of the enemy. Some Ottoman accounts emphasise the effectiveness of Hungarian plate armour during the Varna campaign[28] and at the second battle of Kosovo,[29] but there is no evidence to suggest that this was something that the Ottomans adapted for their own use.

After 1444, however, cannon and later the arquebus came to play an increasingly important role in Ottoman warfare. In 1446, Murad II destroyed the Hexamilion wall across the isthmus of Corinth with gunfire. On this occasion, too, as at the Bosphorus in 1444, he transported gunmetal to the battle site and cast it on the spot. This was to remain an Ottoman practice until the late fifteenth century. In 1453, however, the Ottomans acquired what was probably their first permanent site for the manufacture of cannon. In this year, Mehmed II took the Genoese city of Pera, opposite Constantinople, and with it, its cannon foundry. This, with its buildings, material and craftsmen, almost certainly formed the nucleus of the Ottoman Imperial Cannon Foundry, part of which still stands today.[30]

The fall of Constantinople in 1453 is testimony to the effectiveness of Ottoman artillery in the years following the Hungarian wars: the city fell because Mehmed II's cannon were able to open a breach in the wall.[31] It also exemplifies the type of gun that the Ottomans favoured. What struck contemporary observers about these weapons was their size. The largest, according to the Florentine Tedaldi, threw 'a stone of eleven spans and three fingers in circumference, weighing nineteen hundred pounds', and required, according to the Greek chronicler, Doukas, a team of 60 oxen and 200 men to transport from Edirne to Istanbul. Doukas also reports that it was the work of the Hungarian cannon founder, Urban, who had left the service of the Emperor when the Sultan offered better pay. It was this cannon that destroyed the wall and allowed Ottoman troops to enter the city.

The effectiveness of this gun was clear to all observers, and it was perhaps this experience that encouraged the Ottomans to concentrate on the production of very large cannon for the rest of the century. After the failed siege of Jajce in 1464, for example, the Venetian Malipiero, reported that, before their retreat, the Ottoman besiegers threw five siege cannon, 'each seventeen feet long', into the river Vrbas to prevent their falling into the hands of the enemy. It was probably, too, the difficulty of transporting such large guns in one piece that led the Ottomans to continue the practice of casting cannon, apparently from scrap bronze, in the field. The monster gun for knocking down walls and terrorising the enemy was not, however, the only form of Ottoman artillery at this period. Descriptions of sieges record other types of artillery, notably mortars for firing into the air over fortress or city walls. It seems, too, that the Ottomans used field artillery which, by its nature, must be portable. It was, Ottoman sources convincingly claim,[32] artillery and arquebuses that secured the victory over Uzun Hasan in 1473. The use of large siege cannons was, however, a characteristic of Ottoman warfare.

By 1500, these huge guns were obsolescent. Although capable of inflicting great damage, they had two major disadvantages. First, the heat which a single shot generated limited the number of firings possible in a day. Second, the size and weight made it impossible, once it was in place, to move the cannon to a different section of the defences. These were problems which, in Europe, French artillerymen were to solve in the second half of the fifteenth century. Their solution was to use, instead of single large cannon, batteries of smaller guns. These could not deliver the huge projectiles of the monsters, but instead, by firing rapidly and in succession, could fling the same weight of shot against a defensive wall. Furthermore, this light artillery was easier to move, and so could be used against any point in the defence. The effectiveness of this new technique became clear when the French King, Charles VIII, invaded Italy in 1494.

The Ottomans soon learned of this strategy. In 1501, a French fleet sailed to the Aegean and laid siege to the fortress of Mitylene on Lesbos. The commander of the fleet, Philippe de Clèves, was a theoretician of war and, in particular, of the use of firearms on galleys. He was able therefore to disembark his troops successfully under the cover of galley fire and to bring up his artillery against the fortress. Here, the mobility and effectiveness of his cannon particularly impressed the two Ottoman authors of a report on the siege, who commented also on the French use of iron cannon balls. The siege in the end failed through poor organisation of the assaults rather than through deficiencies in artillery.[33]

The Ottomans very quickly learned the lessons of Charles VIII's Italian campaign and of the French assault on Mitylene. Within a decade they had abandoned the use of the monster gun as the mainstay of siege artillery and begun to adopt French techniques in the manufacture and use of cannon. Spandounes, writing in 1513, remarked on the change:

In the past, they had only large artillery, which they transported with the greatest trouble in the world. They carried the said pieces and recast them in the field where they happened to be. However, not long since, a large number of sailors and other men of war, even cannoneers and founders, have gone to Constantinople, and ever since King Charles came to Naples . . . these have shown them as much how to manufacture and mount artillery as to how to use it.

Other sources confirm what Spandounes says. A record of the Imperial Gun Foundry in Istanbul between 1522 and 1525 shows that 97 per cent of cannon – that is 1027 pieces – manufactured during these years were small to medium-sized guns. Similarly, an inventory of the weapons store at Belgrade in 1536 shows that, out of 485 guns, 82 per cent consisted of small cannon. The Ottomans did continue to manufacture and use large cannon – basilisks – but in small numbers relative to lighter pieces.[34] This is the impression, too, that emerges from the Savoyard Jean Maurand's account of the gun foundry in 1544. Here, outside the building, he saw 'a large number of cannon of all sorts: forked cannon, culverins, field pieces, basilisks, mortars and [the light cannon known as] *esmirigli* and *versi*.' It was, however, still the very large guns that impressed him most. He comments especially on the eleven basilisks, and on the mortars which the Ottomans had used in the siege of Rhodes twenty-two years earlier. These were so large that 'a man could enter the mouth cavity by kneeling'. By Maurand's time, however, Ottoman artillerymen used basilisks not as a main weapon, but as a supplement to the lighter batteries, to bring down already weakened walls. For example, at the siege of Famagusta in 1571, Pietro Bizari describes an Ottoman battery as 'having seventy-four battering guns, of which four were of terrifying and disproportionate size, known generally as basilisks'.

Spandounes attributes the Ottoman adoption of the French style of artillery to the import of foreign technicians. His observation must, in part at least, be true, given the ease with which military technology crossed cultural boundaries. The Ottomans had probably acquired their earliest knowledge of artillery in the Balkans, before contact with the Genoese had familiarised them with Italian techniques of manufacture and use. Mehmed II's cannon manufacturer, Urban, was Hungarian, practising a craft that had probably spread to Hungary from south Germany. In 1456, the German gun founder Jörg of Nuremberg entered the service of the King of Bosnia. When Mehmed II conquered Bosnia, he took Jörg prisoner and employed him as a cannon founder until his flight to Vienna in 1480. Spandounes indicates that this traffic in craftsmen continued in the late fifteenth and early sixteenth centuries, a point which Maurand confirms with his statement that there were forty or fifty Germans manufacturing artillery pieces in the Foundry. At about the same time as Maurand, the French ambassador D'Aramon claimed that many 'French, Venetians, Genoese, Spaniards and Sicilians', whom the Ottomans had captured on land and sea, worked in the gun foundry. In the mid-sixteenth century, too, the French traveller De

Nicolay made the claim that the Jews who had migrated to the Ottoman Empire after their expulsion from Spain, brought with them a knowledge of artillery manufacture.[35]

The importance of these foreign gun founders and artillerymen in the service of the sultan was that they represented a route for the transmission of technology: artillery manufacture and use was an international business. They were, however, a minority. Most of the men responsible for the manufacture, maintenance and use of artillery were members of the Corps of Gunners, a body which had perhaps come into existence in the mid-fifteenth century, when artillery came to form a regular and important element in siege and battlefield tactics. By the sixteenth century the main source of recruitment to this corps was through the Collection. Lists of gunners, however, also indicate the presence of native born Muslims and Christians, with a tendency, as the century progressed, for Muslims to outnumber Christians. The Corps of Gunners, therefore, provided a body of native expertise, while the employment of foreign technicians was a means for the acquisition of new technical knowledge.[36]

Most Ottoman cannon were cast from bronze. The transition from wrought iron which seems in the main to have occurred during the mid-fifteenth century, was, however, gradual. As late as 1514, in his enumeration of Ottoman cannon on the Chaldiran campaign, Menavino records 'two hundred large bronze bombards and one hundred iron ones'. The accounts, however, of the gun foundry in Istanbul from between 1522 and 1525 suggest that, by this time, Ottoman artillery pieces were exclusively bronze. This was still the case when when Evliya Chelebi described the foundry over a hundred years later, in the 1660s. Copper for making bronze was available from within the Empire, in particular from the mines in Kastamonu in northern Anatolia. The other component in the alloy, tin, seems to have been rarer, and some, at least, was imported. The foundry accounts, however, show that the manufacturers supplemented the supply of new ore with scrap bronze. This came to the foundry especially in the form of obsolete cannon, from the stock in the sultan's garden or directly to the foundry wharves. Other bronze items, such as old pitch cauldrons, supplemented the supply of obsolete and faulty guns.[37] Iron cannonballs, introduced probably after the French siege of Mitylene in 1501, the Ottomans manufactured not at the gun foundry in Istanbul, but at the centres of iron production, notably Samokov in Bulgaria.[38]

Similarly, it was the availability of saltpetre that seems to have determined the sites of the mills for producing gunpowder, with the main centres of production in the sixteenth and seventeenth centuries in Buda, Temesvár, Belgrade, Thessaloniki, Gallipoli and Istanbul in Europe, in Bor in Anatolia, in Aleppo, Baghdad and Yemen, and in Egypt. The Empire was, it seems, self-sufficient in saltpetre, except occasionally when hostilities were prolonged, such as during the war with Iran of 1578–90, or the Austrian war of 1593–1606. The Treasury attempted to monopolise production by ensuring that, whenever a new source of saltpetre came to light, it became part of the sultan's personal estate. Sulphur, on the other hand, was less abundant. The conquests of Süleyman I (1520–66) in eastern Anatolia brought the beds in the district of Van and Hakkari under Ottoman control, and further supplies were available from near the Dead Sea, and from Melos and Moldavia. Nonetheless, it was still necessary to import sulphur, especially from Iran. The third ingredient of gunpowder is charcoal. In most places this was easily available, but some areas of production were virtually treeless, forcing the manufacturers to find alternatives, such as shrub roots, mimosa and tamarisk in the Sinai peninsula. The process of refining saltpetre also consumed a huge amount of fuel, but for this, anything combustible would serve.[39]

1400–1590: tactics

The most typical forms of Ottoman warfare were sieges and skirmishes along the borders of the Empire. Field battles were rare, but when they happened they were often decisive. The battle of Varna, for example, in 1444 determined that it was the Ottomans and not the Hungarians who were to be the dominant power in the Balkan peninsula. The Ottoman conquest of Syria and Egypt in 1516 and 1517 was the outcome of the two battles at Marj Dabiq and Raydaniyya. It was the battle of Mohács in 1526 that put an end to the independent Kingdom of Hungary.

The formation of the Ottoman army in the field seems to have remained, in essence, unchanged between the late fourteenth and late sixteenth centuries. It was overwhelmingly a cavalry army with, as a rule, the Anatolian and Rumelian cavalry positioned separately on each wing. In the centre stood the Janissaries, who also guarded the sultan, if he was leading the army in person. Although they were infantrymen and few in number, it was the Janissaries who provided a stable core for the Ottoman battle line.

The near defeat which the Ottomans suffered in the Hungarian wars of the mid-fifteenth century spurred them to make greater use of firearms and to adopt the Hungarian tactic of the *wagenburg*. The disposition of the forces in the field, however, with the Janissaries in the centre and the cavalry on the wings, seems to have remained unchanged. The difference was that the centre of the field which the Janissaries occupied had become a strongly fortified position. It was probably, too, after the Hungarian wars that the Janissaries began to carry firearms These were to prove particularly effective in the wars against Uzun Hasan in the early 1470s. Lacking firearms himself, Uzun Hasan attempted but failed to obtain a supply from Venice[40] and, in his encounter with the Ottoman army, this lack was crucial. The Ottoman chronicler, Neshri, records that 'Uzun Hasan had never seen a battle with cannon and arquebus and so was powerless before the Ottomans.' The Venetian chronicle of Malipiero makes the same point: 'The Turks prevailed, because the Persian cavalry were not accustomed to artillery battles and fled before the beginning of the fight.' Bayezid II improved the quality of the Janissaries' arquebuses, following reverses in the war with the Mamluks in Cilicia between 1485 and 1490.

At this stage, it was only the Janissaries who carried firearms. Arquebuses were not practical on horseback, and the irregular infantry – the *Azabs* – probably did not serve long enough to learn the effective use of the weapon. It was only in the late sixteenth century that gunpowder weapons developed that were suitable for use on horseback, and only in the second half of the same century that firearms became sufficiently widespread to make it possible to recruit arquebusiers from among the general population. During the second half of the fifteenth century and for much of the sixteenth, therefore, handguns were an important element in Ottoman battlefield tactics, especially in defending the fortified position at the centre. Their use, however, was restricted in what was essentially a cavalry army.

Two accounts from the first half of the sixteenth century give a good picture of the Ottoman order of battle at this period. One of these appears in Selim I's victory proclamation following the battle of Marj Dabiq in 1516. The Sultan himself was at the centre of the battle line with his Janissary bodyguards. In the front were 10 000 infantrymen, including arquebusiers, presumably Janissaries. In front of these were 300 gun carts. On either side were horsemen from the Six Divisions, with the Crimeans and the *timar*-holding cavalry of Anatolia and Rumelia on each wing. Some years later, in about 1541, Paolo Giovo gave an account of the order of battle, which largely confirms, but with more detail, what appears in Selim I's proclamation. The Sultan, he said, took up his position in the centre, under the protection of the *solaks* – the inner group of Janissaries who acted as his bodyguard – and Janissaries. Most of these carried long arquebuses. On the right and left were the cavalry of the Six Divisions. In front of the Janissaries were the cannon and, further to the front, the *Azabs*. Another group of *Azabs* guarded the rear of the army. The Rumelian and Anatolian cavalrymen were ranged on either wing of the frontmost *Azabs*. Giovio also mentions the role of the Raiders. These rode in front of the army and lured the enemy into contact with the *Azabs*. These troops the Sultan probably regarded as largely dispensable. Already in 1475, Iacopo di Promontorio had commented: 'When it comes to an engagement, they are sent ahead like pigs, without any mercy, and they die in great numbers.' When the *Azabs* gave way and divided, the enemy next encountered the Ottoman artillery and then, behind the cannon, the Janissaries. The role of the cavalry on the wings was to encircle the enemy as they approached this fortified position in the centre of the Ottoman line.[41]

The commander of the Habsburg forces in Hungary between 1564 and 1568, Lazarus Schwendi, is a witness to the effectiveness of these tactics. He is emphatic that the Christian forces should not allow the Ottomans to lure them to within reach of the *wagenburg*, the mobile fortification in the centre of the line. He comments, too, on the excellence of the Janissaries as marksmen:[42] 'There are about 12 000

arquebusiers with long arquebuses which they manage excellently.'
Other Europeans, for example, at the Ottoman siege of Malta in 1565,
also comment on the accurate fire of the Janissaries. Schwendi, it
would seem, regarded the Ottomans as invincible on the battlefield
and during the summer, when they could mobilise a full army. He
advised instead that the Austrians attack border fortresses in winter,
when the Ottomans could not resist effectively, and that 'good and
well-equipped fortresses' were the best way to defeat the Turks.
Schwendi's attitude is defensive, indicating that Ottoman battlefield
tactics remained effective at least until the end of the wars of the
1560s.[43]

In identifying 'well-equipped fortresses' as the best weapon against
the Ottomans, Schwendi was also typifying the warfare of the period.
Sieges were more common than battles in the open field, and were a
form of warfare in which the Ottomans came to excel. In the early
fourteenth century, they had been able to reduce castles and fortified
towns only by starving them into submission. By the end of the century they had successfully adopted the equipment and techniques of
mediaeval siegecraft, using mangonels to hurl stones against and
over the walls, siege towers to give the attacking troops a fighting
platform from which to assault the defenders on the ramparts, and
mantlets to protect themselves from missiles. They had also learned
the art of mining. They continued to use these techniques for long
after the fourteenth century. In 1453, for example, it was cannon fire
that breached the walls of Constantinople, but cannon was only one
of the weapons which the Ottomans used to batter the city's
defences. The Ottoman chronicler, Tursun Bey, reports that Mehmed
II also brought up mangonels and sank mines beneath the walls. The
accounts of European defenders also refer to siege towers. These and
other 'obsolete' methods of siegecraft continued into the following
century. There are references to the use of mantlets at the siege of
Otranto in 1481, Malta in 1565 and Nicosia in 1570, and to the use of
mangonels at the siege of Rhodes in 1522. At Malta in 1565, the attackers constructed a siege tower which could hold five or six arquebusiers. Mining too remained a speciality of the Ottoman siege
engineers.[44]

Nonetheless, from the mid-fifteenth century, artillery came to be the crucial factor in sieges. The function of cannon was to destroy fortifications, but Ottoman ordnance from the mid-fifteenth century also included mortars for firing over the walls to demolish buildings and terrorise the population within. It seems, for example, to have been a giant mortar that destroyed the morale of the inhabitants at the Ottoman siege of Mitylene in 1462.[45]

Artillery was one element in siege warfare. Equally important was the work of sappers and miners in digging the approach trenches and constructing the earthworks which protected the besiegers and their artillery from enemy fire, and in undermining the walls of the fortress. These were arts in which the Ottomans excelled. There was, by the seventeenth century, a separate Corps of Sappers, but it is not clear when this came into existence. It is possible that such work had previously been the duty of the Exemptees and Footmen.

The first stage in a siege was to defeat any force that was outside the walls and to confine the enemy to the fortress. Then, under the cover of darkness, the sappers would dig the approach trenches at right angles to the walls. These were sinuous, to give protection from enemy shot, which otherwise would have gone straight from one end of the trench to the other. From these approaches, trenches radiated at right angles, parallel to the walls. Once these were complete, the Ottoman besiegers brought up artillery and gabions and, when these were in place, began the bombardment.[46] The gabions, which served to protect the sappers and soldiers in the trenches, drew the attention of the French traveller, De Nicolay, who witnessed them at the siege of Tripoli in 1551: 'The gabions are made of large planks, three inches thick ... When [the Turks] wish to attack some position, they set them up on the ground, in the form of a lozenge, hinging the planks one within the other. Then, when they have been placed in rows, they fill them with earth. This is a very useful invention, because the shot can only glance off them and do them no harm or damage.' As the trenches approached the ditch before the fort, the besiegers would often use the spoil from the excavation, or the rubble which the cannon had dislodged from the fortress, to level the ditch and approach the wall. In describing the siege of Famagusta in 1572, Bizari reports how 'the Turks had already thrown so much earth against the ditch that they had levelled the way up to the ramparts', and then 'put transverse joists and beams on both sides to serve as supports. These stretched right to the wall. And so that we could do no harm to them with our cannon, they protected them with wattle, sacks of wool and fascines.'

The trenches were the most essential element in siege works, as they provided cover, and it was through them that men and artillery approached the fortress. Ottoman siegecraft, however, also involved more elaborate undertakings. The fourteenth and fifteenth centuries sometimes saw the construction of blockading fortresses to prevent access to the place which was under siege. In the 1390s Bayezid I built a castle on the Asian shore of the Bosphorus to impede access to Constantinople as he brought the city under siege. For the same purpose, in 1452–3, Mehmed II built a second castle opposite Bayezid's, on the European shore. In 1440, Murad II opened his unsuccessful siege of Belgade with the construction of a blockading fort to the south of the city.

Most such works, however, the Ottomans constructed immediately outside the fortress or city under siege. For example, they opened the siege of Nicosia[47] in 1570[48] by constructing 'a fortress on the mountain which bears the name St Marina, a hundred and seventy paces distant from the bastions and boulevards of Podocattaro and Carrasa'. From here, they began to fire into the city, hitting houses and other buildings, but without causing much damage. They next set up a fort on 'a hill which the inhabitants call St George', firing at the roofs of the houses, but again without harming the defences. Two more forts followed, and only when they could knock down the defences of the city from these positions did the attackers move nearer. The next stage of the operation demonstrated how the Ottomans could also construct fortresses much closer to the city walls. When the besieging force approached the counterscarp of the ditch around the old city of Nicosia, 'they excavated and made terraces that were almost equal to our fortresses called Podoccattaro, Constantia, Anaba and Tripoli. Facing these, they built four fine fortresses, with great work and diligence, about fifty paces from our walls.' From these positions they were able to pound the walls. Similar works appeared at the siege of Famagusta in 1572. Bizari decribes how, at the beginning of the siege, 'the Turks began to set up platforms to place cannon for the bombardment, and to make casemates and bastions for arquebus fire'.

At the same time as the besieging forces constructed these earth and rubble fortifications above the ground, their miners would excavate below the earth. The original method was to construct a chamber beneath the fortress walls or towers, and to coat wooden props which supported the roof with pitch or other combustible material. The miners would then fire the props and withdraw. As the roof of the mine collapsed, so too would the masonry above the ground. In the sixteenth century, the use of gunpowder to fire mines increased the destructive effects of the technique. Gunpowder did, however, bring greater risks. At the siege of Famagusta, a large number of the besiegers lost their lives when an Ottoman mine exploded beneath their feet.

The final stage of the siege, when cannon fire and mining had reduced the fortification and gunshot and arrows decimated the defenders, was a general assault, when the besieging force attempted to enter through the breaches in the wall. Once an Ottoman army had entered a fortress, town or city, there was no hope of effective resistance.

After 1590: the military revolution

The success of the Ottoman armies in the last decades of the sixteenth century seemed to justify the caution which Schwendi had advised in the 1560s. Between 1570 and 1572, the Ottomans captured Cyprus. The war with Iran between 1578 and 1590 brought the Empire new territories in the Caucasus and Azerbaijan, and also demonstrated the Ottoman ability to keep an army in the field for over a decade.[49] When war with Austria broke out in 1593, twenty-seven years after Süleyman I's last Hungarian campaign, the Ottoman commander, Koja Sinan Pasha, could have had no doubts about Ottoman military superiority. What the war in fact revealed was that Ottoman military tactics were becoming obsolete.

In his account of the first year of the war, the Ottoman littérateur Ta'likizade, highlights an immediate obstacle that Sinan Pasha's army faced. He relates how, at Belgrade, the local people told the Ottoman commanders that, in the old days, if there were reports of a new Austrian fort in Hungary, the sultan would order its immediate destruction. However, engagement in Cyprus and against Iran had led to the neglect of the Hungarian frontier, giving the Austrians the opportunity to construct new fortifications.[50] This work took place from the late 1570s.

On the southern section of the border, between the middle Drava and the middle Sava, and through Croatia to the Adriatic, the mountains formed natural defences. The only large fortress which the Austrians constructed on this line was in the south, at Karlovac on the river Kupa. To protect the rest of the Croatian frontier, they constructed a chain of watchtowers, and the border southwards from the Drava they settled with Serbian and German mercenaries. In Hungary north of the Drava, the marshes provided some defence, but they were not enough to halt an advancing army. Furthermore, the Danube provided a river highway into Austria. It was in Hungary, therefore, that the Austrians concentrated their defences, building or rebuilding fortresses at Kanizsa in the south, and at Györ, Komaron, Ersekujvar and Eger in the north. They began also to strengthen large towns with bastioned defences. Positions which were not directly under imperial control, individual estate owners fortified with walls of compressed earth between heavy logs. The new and rebuilt fortresses were the work largely of Italian engineers, using the most modern design.[51]

It was not, however, the new defences that exposed Ottoman tactical weakness. Already in 1570, the capture of Nicosia had shown that Ottoman siegecraft was still effective against modern bastioned fortresses. The only technical problem that the besiegers encountered, according to Bizari, was that, at the beginning of the siege the earth ramparts, as they had been designed to do, absorbed the impact of the cannonballs, rendering them ineffective. During the war of Cyprus, the unmodernised fortress of Famagusta proved to be a far more serious obstacle than the modern fortifications of Nicosia. During the Austrian war, too, the Ottoman besiegers were able to reduce Györ in 1594, Eger in 1596, Kanizsa in 1600 and Esztergom in 1605, despite their improved design. It seems to have been the system of defences as a whole, and encounters outside the fortresses, rather than the modernised forts in particular that strained Ottoman resources.

The greatest problem for the Ottomans was not the new military architecture, but rather Austrian superiority in the field. This rested in the first place on the increased use of firearms. The war of 1593–1606 was not, in fact, the first occasion on which the Ottomans had encountered this problem. At the sea battle of Lepanto in 1571, superior firepower had been a factor in securing the victory of the Christian coalition. The Ottoman response to this had been to issue orders that the *timar* holders who were to serve in the fleet in the following year should learn the use of the arquebus or lose their *timars*, and to call up young men who did not belong to the military class, but who knew how to use handguns.[52] However, there was no systematic application of these measures in the next decade, and Ottoman commanders do not seem to have applied the lesson learned at sea to land armies. Furthermore, in the wars with Iran from 1578–90, the Ottomans were facing an enemy that was weak in artillery.

This was not the case in 1593, as both European and Ottoman records make clear. In 1594, Bernadino de Mendoça remarked how 'most of the victories in these times are as a consequence of artillery, or the skill of the arquebusiers', and Achille Tarducci commented in particular on the effectivenes of the Germans who had 'abandoned the old way of defensive wars to come to the offensive, in fortresses and in the field'. These new tactics gave the Austrians a new confidence which dismayed the Ottomans, leading one commentator, Hasan al-Kafi, to write: 'Through the use of certain weapons of war, the enemy is beginning to win victories over us ... The enemy has begun to get the upper hand through the use of certain war-materials, new kinds of weapon and cannon, which our soldiers have delayed in introducing.'[53] Of the new weapons to which Hasan al-Kafi alludes, three in particular seem to have impressed the historian Pechevi, who was a participant in these wars. The first two were the long-range cannon and the musket, which was heavier than the arquebus and required a support for the barrel. Both played their part in the near defeat of the Ottomans at Mezö-Keresztes. The other was the petard, a bomb for blowing in fortress doors or destroying walls.

New weapons required new tactics, and here, too, the Ottomans were slow to adapt. The most significant change was in the composition of the armies. Infantrymen carrying pikes and firearms came to outnumber cavalry, sometimes making up as much as three-quarters of the Austrian forces which confronted the Ottomans. Shortly after 1600, in a memorandum to the Grand Vizier, Yemishchi ('the Fruiterer') Hasan Pasha, the Ottoman commander in Hungary, Lala Mehmed Pasha, commented on how this had affected Ottoman fortunes: 'Most of the troops of these accursed ones are on foot and arquebusiers. Most of the troops of Islam are horsemen, and not only are their infantrymen few, but experts in the use of the arquebus are rare. For this reason, there is great trouble in battles and sieges.'

A result of the increased number of firearms and infantrymen was that warfare in the field became more static, with armies making greater use of earthworks and entrenched positions which cavalry could not easily overrun. Here too, as Pechevi's account of the war makes clear, the Ottomans were slow to adapt. It was the refusal of Janissaries and the Jelali troops to entrench, and their demand for cavalry reinforcements, that led to the disaster on Csepel island in 1603. The Austrian infantry was equally lethal outside its fortified positions, using the strategy which the Austrian commander, Basta, had devised to overcome the Ottoman cavalry. He recommended in particular that the musketeers and arquebusiers, under the protection of the pikemen, should fire at the advancing cavalry in controlled salvoes.[54] It seems to have been these pike squares, with arquebusiers at each corner or forming a sleeve on two sides, that allowed the Austrians at Mezö-Keresztes to advance almost unopposed to the Ottoman encampment. At Kanizsa in 1600, the Ottomans again fled before the Austrian gunfire, eventually winning a victory only because the Austrians believed their flight to be a trick.

The Ottoman response to Austrian tactics was to increase the number of infantrymen, by expanding the Janissary Corps, so that it numbered almost 40 000 by the end of the war, and by recruiting, for the space of a single campaign, men who knew how to use firearms. They also began to adopt new weapons, such as the petard from the Austrians. It is possible, too, that Lala Mehmed Pasha, the most successful Ottoman commander in the war, began to adopt the new battlefied tactics, since, as Pechevi implies, he was certainly aware of their significance.

The increased use of infantry had important consequences on and off the battlefield. Most significantly, the Janissary Corps ceased to be a military élite.[55] With increasing numbers, recruitment was widened to include Turks and other native Muslims. At the same time, to relieve the burden on the Treasury, Janissaries gained the right to earn a living outside the Corps. To pay such large numbers nonetheless required increased revenues, which the Treasury achieved partly by converting some *timars* to tax farms, and in so doing, altering the fiscal and administrative structure of the Empire. An effect of recruiting irregulars as infantrymen was also to put a strain on the Treasury. In the early seventeenth century, too, it fed the serious unrest in Anatolia. The demobbed infantrymen, proficient in the use of firearms, were a source of recruitment into the Jelali bands whose suppression was to require the full strength of the Ottoman army.

The increased use of infantrymen and the adoption of the new weapons allowed the Ottomans, in the end, to maintain their position in Hungary. Some military weaknesses, however, remained. The Ottoman army does not seem to have adopted the tactic, which Basta recommended, of firing in salvoes. In a Janissary formation, for example, it was only the front line that could use their weapons, and fire, even if accurate, was irregular. Furthermore, the production standard of Ottoman cannon, and the mathematical expertise of the gunners[56] seems to have fallen behind those of their European rivals. During the course of the seventeenth century[57], the habits of mind that produced the European 'scientific revolution' came increasingly to affect the conduct of war. This, however, was an intellectual current that did not cross the border into the Ottoman Empire, making it difficult for the Ottomans to grasp the theoretical principles which underpinned the new military sciences of fortress construction, sieges, battlefield tactics and gunnery. It was not, however, until the disastrous war of the Holy League from 1683 to 1699 that this became painfully apparent. On the eastern front, the

Ottomans were to suffer humiliations in the early seventeenth century at the hands of Shah Abbas. The Iranian victories did not, however, reflect any structural superiority. It was simply that Shah Abbas was as brilliant a military strategist as he was a master of politics, and able to exploit the engagement of the Ottomans in Austria and Anatolia, as well as their recurrent political crises and failures of leadership.

8 The Fleet

The Ottomans and the sea

In the century after the occupation of Gallipoli in 1354, the only sea passages that were vital to the integrity of the Ottoman Empire were at the Straits which divided its Asian and European territories. This situation changed with the conquest of Constantinople in 1453. The new Ottoman capital was a city whose existence depended on the supply of foodstuffs and other goods by sea, and this required a fleet to protect the ports and sea lanes from pirates and enemy action.[1] It was soon after 1453, too, that the Sultan began to use the fleet as an instrument of conquest, with Mitylene in 1462, and Negroponte in 1470, falling to amphibious assaults.

It was only in the last years of the fifteenth century, with actions against Venice in the Gulf of Corinth, and off the southern and western Peloponnesos that the Ottoman fleet began to operate outside the Aegean. In the second decade of the sixteenth century, however, two events occurred which made it necessary to extend the operating range of the fleet. The first of these was a land conquest.

In 1517 Selim I conquered Egypt and, in the next decade, the province became an important source of food for the capital and revenue for the sultan. Communication was practical only by sea, and it therefore became essential for the sultan to maintain a fleet that was able to protect shipping between Istanbul and Egypt. The need to keep this route free from marauders must have been a reason for the assault on the piratical Knights of Rhodes, in 1522. The conquest of Egypt also brought the sultan revenues from the trade between the Indian Ocean and the Mediterranean. This, however, involved a naval conflict with the Portuguese who, in the same decades, had established themselves in the Indian Ocean, and were attempting to divert trade from its old route through the Red Sea, and to gain a monopoly for their own vessels. The acquisition of the Holy Cities also made the sultan responsible for keeping safe, from the Portuguese and other predators, the Pilgrimage routes through the Red Sea from south Asia and Africa.

The second event encouraging the Ottomans to strengthen the fleet was the submission to the Sultan of Hayreddin Barbarossa, the ruler of Algiers. This extended Ottoman realms to the western Mediterranean and, in the Sultan, gave Algiers a protector against Spain. Later in the century, the conquests of Tripoli in 1551, Jerba in 1560 and Tunis in 1574 strengthened the Ottoman presence in North Africa but also, like the acquisition of Algiers, led to an inevitable naval rivalry with Spain, which was also seeking to establish strongholds on the North African coast. These factors made the possession of an effective fleet essential as much to the survival of the Empire as to its expansion.

Ships

Murad I (1362–89) may have built warships at Gallipoli after retaking the town and its harbour from the Byzantines in 1377, but the first reliable record of an Ottoman fleet dates from 1392, during the reign of Bayezid I (1389–1402). It was, however, Mehmed II (1451–81) who began to construct ships on a large scale for wars of conquest. Details of these early war fleets are lacking, but it is clear that, in building them, Ottoman shipwrights simply adopted the types of vessel that were common throughout the Mediterranean.[2]

The basic fighting vessel was the oared galley. In the form in which it had emerged during the Middle Ages, the galley was a narrow vessel, five to eight times as long as it was broad. A standard galley had twenty-four to twenty-six banks of oars on either side, with usually three oarsmen to each bench. A raised platform ran between the banks on either side. It carried a single mast with a lateen sail, and had a fighting platform at the prow. Light galleys, which corsairs especially favoured, had fewer than twenty-four rowing benches on each side, while heavy galleys, such as carried a fleet commander, had twenty-six or more. On the prow, they carried a ram which seems to have had the function of damaging the hulls of enemy ships and of pinning them down during hand-to-hand fighting.

The fundamentals of galley design did not change between the Middle Ages and the eighteenth century, when the galley finally disappeared from the Mediterranean. There were, however, some modifications over the centuries. The most important of these was the addition of artillery in the second half of the fifteenth century. Galleys carried their guns forward, allowing them to fire on the enemy before grappling and boarding. When the Ottoman fleet first used shipboard artillery is not clear, but certainly a Venetian woodcut depicting the battle off the Peloponnesos in 1499 shows the Ottoman galleys with a single large swivel cannon, mounted on a vertical post at the centre of the prow.[3] During the sixteenth century, as on land, bronze cannon replaced wrought iron ones, and the number of guns increased. The standard for Ottoman galleys in the sixteenth century was probably the same as Katib Chelebi specified as standard in the mid-seventeenth, that is a centre-line cannon, throwing a ball of about thirty pounds or more, flanked by two culverins.[4]

The addition of artillery was the most important development in galley design during the fifteenth century. Further modifications occurred during the sixteenth and seventeenth. Until the mid-sixteenth century, the standard galley had three oarsmen to a bench, with each oarsman pulling a separate oar, a system known in Italian as *alla sensile*. In the mid-century, all Mediterranean fleets seem to have converted to a system where the oarsmen on a single bench pulled a single oar, a system known as *al scaloccio*. The new arrangement made it possible to increase the number of oarsmen on a bench and reduced the number of skilled oarsmen required.[5] The Ottoman fleet, to judge from Venetian reports, adopted the *al scaloccio* system in about 1560. Another change came towards the end of the century, when standard galleys began to carry two rather than one mast.[6] Ottoman shipbuilders also made this modification. In the seventeenth century, too, they began to build galleys with a 'melon stern'; that is, a stern which was rounded and reinforced, to make it more resistant to the waves. A final small change came when the admiral, Ali Chelebi (held office 1617, 1618–19) abolished as superfluous the 'life-saver', a sail which crews used to help refloat galleys which had run aground.[7]

A more significant development in sixteenth-century galley design came about by accident. In 1570, when Venice began to construct a fleet to counter the Ottoman attack on Cyprus, the arsenal shipwrights converted ten merchant galleys into warships. This was an improvisation, but one that was highly successful. Merchant galleys were slower and more cumbersome than war galleys, but more capacious, and so allowed the shipbuilders to mount extra guns, including artillery that could fire broadsides. The extra height also allowed the vessels to dominate ordinary war galleys in battle.[8] The Spanish commander of the fleet of the Holy League, Colonna, certainly recognised the potential of these vessels when, in answering objections to his plan to pursue the Ottoman fleet in 1570, he noted that these Venetian 'galeasses were like fortresses towering over and firing down upon the enemy'.[9] The battle of Lepanto in the following year justified his optimism. The galeasses played a major role in the Holy League's victory over the Ottomans.

The technology of the galeass was, however, conservative, and it was a ship that the Ottomans could easily imitate. In the winter following the defeat at Lepanto, the Imperial Council instructed the chief shipwright of the arsenal to construct a ship, which should be 'propelled by oars and capable of firing guns from its stern, bow and sides', without harming the oarsmen. When the Admiral, Uluj Ali, had approved the plans, the arsenal at Sinop constructed three and the Istanbul arsenal one or two of the new vessels and, from 1572, galeasses formed a regular part of the Ottoman fleet.[10] Katib Chelebi records that, in the mid-seventeenth century, they carried twenty-four guns.[11]

The ease with which the Ottoman shipwrights imitated the Venetian galeass contrasts with their tardiness in introducing galleons, that is sailing vessels with high sides, and capable of firing broadsides. In this respect, however, they were typical of Mediterranean shipbuilders in general. The Venetians built a few warships of this kind in the late fifteenth century, inspiring Mehmed II to order a similar ship from the Istanbul arsenal. Mehmed's *bargia*, however, sank on launching,[12] and neither the Venetian nor the Ottoman arsenals continued to experiment with these vessels. The only exceptions were a pair of *coccas* that fought with the Ottoman fleet in 1499. These were hybrid vessels, with oars, but with the upperwork and sails of a galleon. Except, it seems, in this one year, the galley in its various forms was the only Ottoman fighting vessel.[13] This was also true of the other Mediterranean navies and, until the seventeenth century, put the Ottoman fleet at no disadvantage against its Mediterranean rivals.

The Ottoman Empire, however, was not solely a Mediterranean power and, in its encounters with the Portuguese in the Indian Ocean and the Gulf, the Ottoman galleys could not withstand the superior firepower of the Portuguese carracks, and were not suitable for navigation in the ocean. In the seventeenth century, they faced a similar problem in the Mediterranean. This century saw the appearance there of armed merchantmen from Holland, France and England. Since, in most circumstances, a galley was no match for a fully armed galleon, this changed the methods of Mediterranean warfare, and persuaded the Venetian arsenal to begin galleon construction. In consequence, when the Ottomans declared war on Venice in 1645, and launched an attack on Crete, they confronted a navy that was technologically superior to their own. To match the Venetian fleet, the Ottomans began to build galleons, with ten under construction in 1650. However, neither the ships themselves, nor the attempts to muster technically proficient crews were successful, and it was not until 1682 that the galleon became the standard warship in the Ottoman fleet. The North Africans, however, mastered the techniques of building and manning galleons well before the craftsmen and sailors of the Ottoman fleet. This was perhaps because the regencies of Algiers, Tunis and Tripoli attracted corsairs from northern Europe as well as from the Mediterranean, and it was perhaps these men who transferred the skills from the Atlantic seaboard.

This is not to say that the Ottoman naval arsenals produced no sailing ships at all. A document of 1487 records two sailing vessels – a *bargia* and a *gripar* – carrying respectively 83 and 45 guns.[14] These clearly were artillery transports, and it was as transport vessels that Ottoman *bargias* continued to function throughout the sixteenth century. One of these even accompanied a galley fleet to the Indian Ocean in 1564, but apparently carried only provisions and was not armed. In addition to *bargias*, other specialised vessels accompanied the Ottoman war fleets. Documents list, but do not describe, 'stone-ships', presumably for the transport of cannon balls or materials for the repair of harbours and fortifications, and 'horse ships'. These, according to a seventeenth century account, were square rigged vessels with a shallow draught for the transport of horses or artillery, with an opening at the poop to take on horses.[15] These were the ships that accompanied the Mediterranean fleet. Other specialised vessels served on the navigable rivers of the Empire.

Shipbuilding

The first and, for more than a century, the largest naval dockyard in the Ottoman Empire, was at Gallipoli. It was here at the end of the fourteenth century that Bayezid I built and repaired his fleet and, if we are to believe the report of the Aragonese ambassador to Timur who saw the ships in 1402, had a capacity for about 40 galleys.[16] It is quite probable that, already at this time, the captains and crews of the ships were permanent residents of the town. This was certainly the case by 1474, when their salaries appear in the first surviving register of government expenditure in Gallipoli. In this year there were 92 detachments of these seamen, each with a captain at its head,[17] with each detachment perhaps representing the crew of a single galley. This figure evidently remained constant until 1518, when there were 93 detachments.[18] As a yard for the construction of ships, however, Gallipoli seems to have expanded after 1518. In 1522, the year of the conquest of Rhodes, a Venetian *bailo* reported that more slipways were under construction. By 1530, there were 30, with further extensions in 1530 and 1565/6.[19]

The document of 1518 also records expenditure on the craftsmen who built and repaired the ships. These, it shows, fell into different categories. First, there were eight small groups of men who specialised in shipbuilding crafts – storekeepers, oarmakers, caulkers, pulley-makers and oakum workers – or in the maintenance and use of weapons – armourers, gunners and bombardiers. In all, these numbered only 81 men, the caulkers with 26 and the gunners with 28, forming the biggest group. The large number of caulkers suggests that their major task was the the maintenance rather than the construction of ships. The numbers went up slightly in subsequent years, reaching 127 in 1530, but were never great. The records show that many of these men were novice Janissaries, serving craft apprenticeships before enrolment in the Janissary Corps. The most numerous group of craftsmen, however, were temporary employees whom the arsenal hired, presumably from the neighbouring coastal districts, when work was in hand, and dismissed on its completion. For the unskilled but heavy tasks, such as dragging ships onto the land, the Footmen and Exemptees in the district of Gallipoli provided the labour.[20]

The naval Arsenal in Istanbul had a similar organisation. When Mehmed II conquered the Genoese town of Pera in 1453, he acquired with it the Genoese old arsenal, with its docks and slipways on the shore of the Golden Horn. He evidently expanded it during his reign, as he undertook the construction of large war fleets. It was not, however, until the sixteenth century that it surpassed Gallipoli as the main centre for shipbuilding and maintenance. Selim I (1512–20), according to the report of Lutfi Pasha, planned to construct 300 docks that would have stretched the entire length of the Golden Horn,[21] but he never completed the work. Nonetheless, by 1522, there were 114 docks, by 1557, 123, and this number seems to have remained steady until the mid-seventeenth century. In 1653, there were about 120.[22] Each dock had two covered slipways, where it was possible to build or house galleys, giving the Arsenal a capacity to construct or maintain about 250 galleys at one time. Between 1546 and 1549, the Admiral, Sokollu Mehmed, built a warehouse behind each dock, and walled off the entire area.[23]

As at Gallipoli, there were permanent and temporary craftsmen. The permanent employees in the Istanbul Arsenal were again novices, forming groups of caulkers, carpenters, oar makers, bombardiers, blacksmiths, 'repairers', pulley block makers and oakum workers. Their numbers were small, with the caulkers – 40 men in 1530 – making up the largest group of a total of 90 craftsmen. Most of the craftsmen, however, came from outside. They were mostly, according to a Venetian account, Greek shipwrights from Istanbul, Galata and the nearby islands; but when work was urgent, they would come from as far afield as Lesbos or Chios. The master shipwrights remain largely anonymous. In 1553, the Venetian *bailo* mentioned a Greek master,

whom he calls Michele Benetto, with three or four master shipwrights under his command. In 1562, another *bailo* reported that
there were Venetian shipwrights working in the arsenal, who had
greatly improved the standard of shipbuilding. Beyond this, there is
no information. It was again the Footmen and Exemptees who carried out heavy tasks in the Arsenal, serving terms of six months.[24]

By the early seventeenth century, the organisation of the craftsmen seems to have changed. There were far more permanent craftsmen – 838 in 1604 – representing a wider range of crafts, including
oarmakers and bronze casters, and recruitment was no longer exclusively, or even mainly, from the novices. Their total numbers, however, declined during the century, so that, by 1648, at the time of the
Cretan war, there were only 368.[25] It seems probable, therefore, that,
in order to save money, the government went back to the practice of
hiring the bulk of the labour force when the need arose. The number
of permanent employees seems, however, to have been much higher
than during the first part of the sixteenth century

Gallipoli and Istanbul were not the only shipbuilding sites in the
Empire. There were permanent installations at Izmit to the east of the
capital, at Sinop on the Black Sea, at Suez in the Red Sea and, for a
while during the sixteenth century, at Basra in southern Iraq.[26] To
build a galley hull, however, did not require a special dockyard and,
in years when need was pressing, as in 1571–2 after the loss of two
thirds of the fleet at the battle of Lepanto, the government would
order the construction of extra ships at specified points on the shores
of the Black Sea and Mediterranean, and the impressment of craftsmen to do the work. The winter of 1571–2 saw the completion of
more than 100 vessels outside Istanbul and Gallipoli.[27] The completed hulls had to go to the main arsenals only to receive their fittings
and artillery.

Of all the Mediterranean powers, the Ottoman Empire possessed
the most abundant resources for shipbuilding. Timber, in particular,
was available from the dense woodlands of north-western Anatolia,
near to the arsenals at Istanbul, Gallipoli and Izmit, and from the
forested slopes of the mountains along the southern shore of the
Black Sea. The supply was the envy of foreign observers in the sixteenth and seventeenth centuries, and did not show signs of exhaus-

tion until the late seventeenth and eighteenth centuries. Today, the area is largely treeless. Already in the sixteenth century, and probably earlier, the government had reserved tracts of forest for ships' timbers, appointing guards to protect the trees. The inhabitants of specified villages in these areas felled the timbers and cut them into shape, receiving a wage from the Treasury for their work. Since the forests were close to the sea, the next stage was to haul the timbers overland to the nearest port, and to transport them by ship to the arsenals. It seems that judges, and officials specially appointed when work was in hand, oversaw the operation.[28] In the seventeenth century, the same system continued, with some refinements. For the Istanbul arsenal, the Commissioner for Timber determined the amount of wood required from each area, and the specified number of villagers who would carry out the work. These, in turn, received their wages in the judge's court from the agent of the commissioner. The Treasury, however, met only one-fifth of the costs, the rest coming from extraordinary taxes levied in the timber producing districts. The arsenals could, when required, buy extra timber from merchants but, since the reserved timber was considerably cheaper, the wages and transport costs being below market rates, they clearly preferred not to do so.[29]

There was a similar continuity between the sixteenth and seventeenth centuries in the procurement of other materials. In the sixteenth century, the main areas for the supply of cloth for the sails and awnings of galleys were Gallipoli, southern Greece – especially Athens, Levadhia and Evvoia – and the Aegean region of Anatolia, although cloth could, as in 1560, come from as far away as Egypt and Aleppo. The organisation of the work had some resemblance to timber felling, with the local judge or a commissioner from Istanbul allocating the work between villages and overseeing production. Again, it was the weavers who had the responsibility for cutting and packing the finished cloth, before despatching it overland, or by sea, to the arsenals. In most cases, local revenues covered the costs of production and transport.[30] In the seventeenth century, the same system of production continued, in the same areas, although Gallipoli seems to have emerged as the most important supplier, especially of awnings. Consignments of sails and awnings from Egypt also became more regular. It was probably during the seventeenth century, too, that the system began of specifying exactly how much cloth each household was to produce, and of allocating specific parcels of local revenues to pay for production.[31]

The rigging and ropes for the fleet came from the areas of hemp production. In the sixteenth century, these were the Black Sea coasts of Anatolia to the west of Samsun, and the Bulgarian coastlands, with small amounts coming from Tire, inland from Izmir. Of these, Samsun was the most important. In 1539, the Istanbul Arsenal bought 156 tonnes from this area, as against about 20 tonnes from Bulgaria.[32] In the seventeenth century, Samsun became, if anything, even more important as a supplier of rope. In 1656, Katib Chelebi reported that each year the region produced 395 tonnes of hemp for use by the fleet.[33] The hemp was, as a rule, spun into rope in the area of production before despatch.

In both the sixteenth and seventeenth centuries, it was, above all, the mines and foundries of Samokov in Bulgaria that provided the nails, anchors and iron parts for the galleys. These usually came to the shipbuilding sites ready-made. The cost of transport was, however, enormous. In 1606–7, for example, the Istanbul Arsenal purchased 162 000 nails from Samokov for 198 608 akches. The cost of transport from Samakov to the port of Tekirdağı on the Sea of Marmara, and from there to Istanbul, was 188 014 akches, with additional costs of 29 451 akches to pay the wages of two clerks, a weigh-bridge clerk, and a master blacksmith.[34]

The ships' hulls, when complete, required pitch and oakum for caulking, and tallow or other grease for oiling below the waterline. There was an abundant supply of pitch from various parts of the Empire: Vlorë in Albania, Pazardzhik in Bulgaria, Mitylene, Thasos and the coasts of the north-western Aegean, and from near Samsun on the Black Sea.[35] These areas continued to supply the arsenals in the seventeenth century, when the government designated revenues from Durrës and Peć to pay for 115 tonnes each year from Vlorë, and the customs revenues of Mitylene to pay for an annual 17 or so tonnes from Lesbos.[36] These figures suggest that, as in the sixteenth century, Vlorë continued to be the most important source of supply. The oakum for caulking was available cheaply from throughout the

Empire, the major cost being for the transport rather than for the substance itself. The next process after caulking was to oil the hull, and this required tallow in huge quantities. To oil a galley required, according to Katib Chelebi, about 350 kilograms of tallow, and it was necessary to carry out the operation three times a year, once before leaving the Arsenal, and twice during the campaign.[37] Tallow also supplied the material for shipboard candles and for soap, especially necessary for the caulkers. The abundance of animals in the Empire seems, however, to have ensured that it was never in short supply, with consignments in the sixteenth and seventeenth centuries coming mainly, it appears, from Rumelia, Wallachia and Moldavia.[38]

Once a galley was complete, it received its cannon and its crew.

Admirals

The Admiral of the Mediterranean fleet – the *Kapudan Pasha* – was the senior figure in the Ottoman navy.[39] His post, however, emerged as a well defined office in the sultan's service only during the course of the sixteenth century. There is no record of the admirals before 1453, but after this date – and probably before – it became customary for the Sanjak Governor of Gallipoli to command the fleet, evidently because Gallipoli happened to be the most important naval base and fell within his sanjak. His command, however, was not automatic. In 1475, for example, it was the Vizier Gedik Ahmed Pasha who commanded the fleet which sailed against Azov and Caffa, and also the fleet which took the troops from Vlorë to Otranto in 1481. Nonetheless, it seems that, during the reign of Mehmed II, it was the Sanjak Governor of Gallipoli who was the fleet commander in principle, if not always in practice. An episode in the career of the Grand Vizier Mahmud Pasha illustrates this point. In 1469–70, Mehmed II dismissed him from his post as grand vizier, and appointed him instead to the Sanjak of Gallipoli. The reason for this apparent demotion was the projected attack on the Venetian island of Negroponte. This required a large fleet and, as sanjak governor, Mahmud had the task of constructing the ships and taking command of them when they put to sea. For that year at least, the governorship of Gallipoli had become one of the most important posts of the Empire, and required a man of Mahmud Pasha's abilities to fill it. After the fall of Negroponte, Mahmud returned to the vizierate.

As mere sanjak governors, the admirals did not occupy an important position in the Ottoman ruling establishment, except when a man of high personal standing occupied the post, as was the case during Mahmud Pasha's tenure, and also between 1506 and 1511, when Hersekzade Ahmed Pasha was admiral in the interval between two terms as grand vizier. It was only in 1533, during the reign of Süleyman I (1520–66) that the post of Admiral acquired both a clear definition and a high status. This was due in part to the increasing importance of maritime affairs, but especially to the illustrious reputation of the new Admiral.

In 1533, Süleyman bestowed the office on Hayreddin Barbarossa, the conqueror of Algiers. It was clearly unthinkable to make such a man a mere sanjak governor. Instead the appointment came with the governor-generalship of the new Province of the Archipelago, which the Sultan had created specially for Barbarossa by detaching the coastal sanjaks of Greece and western Turkey from the existing Provinces of Rumelia and Anatolia.

The Province of the Archipelago was thus an *ad hominem* creation, but one which nevertheless lasted. It was not, however, until after the reign of Süleyman I that the province came to exist permanently in its own right, with the admiral as its governor-general. When Barbarossa died in 1546, his successor was the sultan's head gate-keeper, Sokollu Mehmed, who held the admiralty as his first post outside the Palace. Given Sokollu's lack of distinction at this stage of his career, the Sultan clearly did not wish to appoint him as a governor-general. Instead, like the admirals before Barbarossa, he received the office with the sanjak governorship of Gallipoli. This was also true of his successor, Sinan Pasha. Sinan, however, was brother of the Grand Vizier, Rüstem Pasha, and it was probably at Rüstem's urging that Süleyman revived the defunct Province of the Archipelago and appointed Sinan as Governor-General. It is clear, however, that the sultan still regarded this as an *ad hominem* appointment, since Sinan's successor, Piyale, received the office of admiral as Sanjak Governor of Gallipoli. The sultan's warrant appointing him admiral in January, 1555, reads: 'I have increased my favours towards the *zeamet* of the

Head Gatekeper, Piyale and, with effect from . . . [8 January, 1555], the Admiralty and the Sanjak of Gallipoli, with its *hass* lands worth 550 000 akches has been bestowed on him . . .' Piyale received promotion to the governor-generalship of the revived Province of the Archipelago in 1558, after distinguishing himself in action against the Spaniards in North Africa.[40]

In 1566, on the accession of Selim II, Piyale received a promotion to the vizierate. His successor as admiral was the Agha of the Janissaries, Müezzinzade Ali. He received the admiralty with the Province of the Archipelago. This was probably in recognition of his existing status but, from the time of his appointment, the province was in continuous existence with the admirals as governors-general.

To become admiral did not require previous experience of the sea. The important fact in determining eligibility for the post was that the admiral was also a provincial governor, and appointments to the admiralty typically followed the pattern of appointments to the provinces. It is quite usual, therefore, in the sixteenth and seventeenth centuries, to find that admirals were graduates of palace service. Sokollu Mehmed and Piyale are both examples and, in the following century, things did not change. Katib Chelebi notes in his list of Admirals that, for example, 'Dervish Pasha' – later Grand Vizier – 'graduated from the Palace on . . . [18 January, 1606] while Head Gardener, with the post of Admiral'; or that 'Hafiz Ahmed graduated from the Palace and became Admiral in 1608'.[41] Some later admirals had also, like Müezzinzade Ali, served as Agha of the Janissaries or, like Jigalazade Sinan, who became admiral in 1591, as governors in the provinces. The lack of maritime experience did not necessarily lead to incompetence at sea, Piyale Pasha and Jigalazade Sinan, for example, being notably successful fleet commanders. However, this was not invariably the case, leading Katib Chelebi to state, as the first of thirty-nine principles for the effective management of the the fleet: 'If the Admiral himself is not a corsair, he should consult with corsairs concerning the sea and maritime war. He should listen, and not act on his own opinion.'[42]

Katib Chelebi's insistence on taking advice from 'corsairs' is an indication of the importance to the Ottoman fleet of the Muslim pirates of North Africa, whose predatory activities served in effect as a naval school in training seamen. On occasions, too, the North African corsairs provided the Ottoman fleet not only with galley captains, but also with admirals. The most famous of these was Hayreddin Barbarossa. The second such appointment was Uluj Ali, who succeeded to the Admiralty at a time of crisis following the battle of Lepanto. He began his career as an Algerian corsair, but in 1556 came to Istanbul to serve as a captain in the Ottoman fleet, with a daily salary that reflected his distinction. He later returned to Algiers as Governor-General, and it was as Governor-General that he fought at Lepanto. On the death in that battle of Müezzinade Ali, he succeeded him in the Admiralty.[43] His successor in 1588, Uluj Hasan Pasha, had been in his following and, like his patron, had lived as a corsair in Algiers. The last of Uluj Ali's followers to serve as admiral was Ja'fer Pasha, who held the office for two years from 1606. After this, the only nautical figure to occupy the office, in 1616–17, and again in 1617–19, was Chelebi Ali Pasha, the son of a governor-general of Tunis, originally from the Aegean island of Kos.[44] These figures, however, were exceptions in the series of landsmen who served as admirals.

The admiral of the Mediterranean fleet was the senior naval commander in the Empire. Besides him, however, there were captains of squadrons based outside Istanbul and Gallipoli, who were able to operate independently of his command. These flotillas and their captains first appear in records in the mid-sixteenth century, although they must have been in existence long before. Nearest to Istanbul was the Captain of Kavalla, who commanded a squadron of galleys patrolling the northern Aegean as far south as Lesbos. His most important function, at least according to records from the second half of the sixteenth century, was to escort, as far as the Dardanelles, ships carrying grain from northern and central Greece to the capital, guarding them from pirates, and also preventing the illegal sale of grain. At the same time, a smaller squadron, of only two galleys in 1566, operated under the command of the Sanjak Governor of Lesbos, guarding the island and nearby coastline. There was a larger fleet – ten galleys in 1566 – under the command of the Sanjak Governor of Rhodes. This island and its dependencies commanded the sea route between Egypt and Istanbul, and dominated the entrance to the Aegean and the eastern Mediterranean between southern Turkey and Cyprus. In view of its strategic position, Süleyman I must have established a fleet there immediately after its conquest in 1522.[45]

During the same period, governors of other sanjaks on the Aegean coast of Turkey sometimes received commands to patrol the seas off their sanjaks with one or more galleys. The only ships, however, on permanent station outside Istanbul and Gallipoli seem to have been those at Kavalla, Lesbos and Rhodes. After 1566, however, when the admiral's province of the Archipelago became a permanent institution, it became customary for eight of the sanjak governors in the province each to supply one or more ships to the imperial fleet when it put to sea, suggesting that the vessels were permanently on stand-by in the sanjaks.[46] During his periods as Admiral between 1616 and 1619, Chelebi Ali increased the number of such vessels, by requiring Chios, Naxos and Mahdia each to provide a ship.[47]

This network of small flotillas, concentrated especially in the Aegean, served both to provide reinforcements to the imperial fleet, and to defend the shipping lanes to the capital from pirates and enemy attack. There were further squadrons with independent captains outside this area. When he conquered Egypt in 1517, Selim I acquired two important harbours. The first of these was Alexandria, which the cartographer, Piri Reis, described in 1526 as 'a key port, especially for the Arab lands'.[48] The second was Suez, which provided a base for fleets in the Red Sea and Indian Ocean. It is most probable that Selim appointed an admiral in Egypt immediately after the conquest, although the first Ottoman record of the 'Admiral of Egypt' is from 1528. He was commander of both the Suez and Alexandria fleets until 1560, when the Sultan created a separate admiralty at Suez. The function of the fleet at Alexandria was to protect the eastern Mediterranean and the trade routes from Egypt, cooperating in this duty with the Sanjak Governor of Rhodes. The fleet at Suez was for the defence of the Red Sea and the Indian Ocean. The government, however, also recognised that the entry to the Red Sea at the Bab al-Mandab had great strategic importance and, probably a little before 1560, established a flotilla there under the command of the 'Captain of Yemen' or 'Captain of Mocha'. In 1565, this captain commanded a squadron of six galleys, equipped from Suez.[49] It is unlikely, however, given the vicissitudes of Ottoman rule in Yemen, that it survived for long.

These fleets in Egypt and the Red Sea were independent of the Admiral in Istanbul. So, too, were the ships that operated under independent captains on the Danube and its tributaries. The earliest such 'admiralty' was at Buda, where Süleyman I must have created a flotilla immediately after its annexation in 1541. One fleet, however, proved to be insufficient and, in 1560, the Sanjak Governor of Mohács petitioned the sultan for a new squadron in his district, since the enemy were attacking the islands in the Danube, at a point too far south for the ships to reach from Buda. References to the 'Captain of Mohács' in subsequent years show that the Sultan answered the request. The third Rumelian fleet was on the Sava, which joins the Danube at Belgrade. The first reference to a 'Captain of the Sava' dates from 1556, suggesting that the sultan perhaps also created this fleet after the annexation of Hungary.[50]

In addition to these permanently established flotillas under the command of captains or sanjak governors, the sultans sometimes created temporary commands for short-lived fleets. In the 1580s, for example, the creation of the office of 'Captain of the Caspian Sea' followed Ottoman conquests in the Caucasus.[51] The most important fleet outside Istanbul was, however, the fleet at Algiers. It was, above all, the Algerians who carried out the continuous raids against Christian shipping in the Mediterranean and beyond, and who also, when they fought under the command of their governor-general, formed the most effective contingent in the Ottoman fleet. Nonetheless, their participation in Ottoman warfare was, more or less, voluntary. In his decrees, the sultan could order the governor-general of Algiers merely to 'encourage' the corsair captains to join the fleet, but he could not exercise the direct control that he could over the other naval commanders in the Empire.

Captains and crews

Before 1533, the admirals most probably resided in Gallipoli, the site of the Arsenal and the chief town in their sanjak. From the appointment of Hayreddin Barbarossa in 1533, they resided in Galata – the old

Genoese town of Pera, and the site of the Imperial Arsenal – where they had jurisdiction, it seems, not only over the arsenal itself, but over the surrounding urban area as well. Under the admiral were the Commissioner – *emin* – and Warden – *kethüda* – of the arsenal. The Commissioner was responsible for financial control and administration, with departmental clerks working under his supervision. The Warden was the representative of the galley skippers and crews, and commanded a detachment of galleys when the fleet was at sea. Both posts presumably date from the mid-fifteenth century, when Mehmed II took over and extended the Genoese dockyards, and both lasted into the seventeenth. The normal route to the wardenship was, it seems, to have served as a galley skipper in the Arsenal at Galata.

The skippers of the galleys and other vessels in the imperial fleet were resident near the main arsenals at Gallipoli and Galata, each with a detachment of men known as *Azabs* in his following. These detachments, it seems, represented the crews of individual ships. The first record of them to survive comes from Gallipoli in 1474, but they had presumably been in existence for much longer. They survived until the late seventeenth century, when galleons finally displaced galleys as the main fighting vessels in the Ottoman fleet. Within these groups of *Azabs*, those with the senior position below the skipper had the title 'sailor' – *yelkenji* – or 'chamber-head' – *oda bashi* – and it tended to be these men who received a post as skipper when one fell vacant. What the rather laconic records do not, however, make clear is how the government recruited *Azabs*, or what their duties were.

A command to the Admiral in 1572 orders him to recruit 342 *Azabs* 'according to custom and law', and to enrol them from among men who were 'capable of combat and war', allocating their pay and sending the register of their names and salaries to the palace.[52] What the decree might be describing is a levy of young men in the provinces, similar to the levy of *Azab* infantrymen to the army. If this is the case, it is unlikely that the *Azabs* would be seamen by background, but rather would learn the trade through service on the ships, in such functions as overseer of oarsmen or helmsman. They also, it seems, carried weapons and, by the second half of the sixteenth century, were equipped with arquebuses.

Although each skipper and his detachment of *Azabs* seems, in principle, to represent the crew of a single vessel, such records as exist seem to show that there were usually more detachments than there were ships. There were 93 detachments in Gallipoli in 1518,[53] and it is unlikely that the dockyard had the capacity for this number of vessels. At Galata in 1571 there were 227 detachments, again probably rather more detachments than there were ships. In the same year, there were an additional 150 'skippers without a detachment', that is skippers who did not command a group of *Azabs*, but were in line to receive a command when there was a vacancy.[54] The same organisation continued into the seventeenth century. By this time, there were 440 detachments, including 34 at Gallipoli. In addition, there were, in 1604, 56 'captains without a detachment'.[55] By this time there were obviously more detachments than ships.

If the numbers of detachments increased in the seventeenth century, there was a decrease in the number of *Azabs* in each one. In Gallipoli in 1518, detachments were small, consisting usually of a skipper and three *Azabs*. A document of 1571, however, suggests that, by this time, there should be '12 *Azabs* in each of the 200 ships'.[56] In the seventeenth century, the number of *Azabs* in each detachment began to fall again. The number of 'skippers without a detachment' also fell from 56 in 1604 to 30 in 1608.[57] This suggests that an *Azab* detachment no longer represented the crew of a single galley or other vessel, as it evidently had done in the sixteenth century, but rather that the admiral simply began to distribute existing *Azabs* between existing skippers, regardless of whether they would serve under them at sea, and to save money by reducing their total numbers.

Throughout the age of galleys, therefore, skippers typically rose from the ranks of *Azabs*, receiving their promotion to command a vessel on the recommendation of the admiral, the warden of the Arsenal, or of any of the fleet commanders. In addition, the sultan sometimes appointed Muslim corsairs as galley skippers or, since seamanship is an international trade, foreigners.

The motive power for the ships came from sails and oars, and the men who tended these made up the majority of a galley's crew, with a standard galley requiring, according to Katib Chelebi, about 150 oarsmen and 20 riggers.[58] Both groups of men came from annual levies. A document of the 1530s records a levy of 57 riggers from Çeşme on the Aegean coast of Turkey.[59] From 1604, and probably earlier, a specified district in the Sanjak of Gallipoli provided riggers at a notional rate of one rigger for every seven households, the actual number varying according to demand. The arsenal could also, in case of need, hire riggers for a season.[60]

Tending the rigging and sails of a ship was a nautical skill, and the few records which survive suggest that the government levied riggers from coastal areas, presumably from among men with some knowledge of ships. To serve as an oarsman, however, the government regarded the only qualifications as health and strength, and called up most oarsmen from inland areas of Rumelia and Anatolia. In the mid-sixteenth century, some Europeans did comment on the inefficiency of Ottoman oarsmen but, given the numbers required – in 1539, for example, there were 23 538[61] oarsmen in a fleet of about 150 ships – it was clearly not practical to seek out experienced men.

According to Katib Chelebi, the practice of forcibly levying oarsmen for the fleet began in 1501.[62] However, the partial survival of a record showing a levy in 1499–1500, shows that he is not wholly accurate.[63] It is difficult, too, to imagine how Mehmed II could have manned his ships, in particular the enormous fleet that attacked Negroponte in 1470, without the forcible impressment of oarsmen. It is quite possible, however, that the levy did not become a regular event until the Venetian war of 1499–1503. The first extensive documentary evidence appears in the mid-sixteenth century.

This reveals that it was the Treasury that managed the levy, service on the galleys being essentially a form of taxation. About three months before the fleet was due to sail, decrees went out to judges in the areas which were to provide the oarsmen. If necessary, further urgent commands could follow ordering the governors-general and sanjak governors to assist the judges. The principles of the levy were the same as those that applied to the recruitment of *Azab* infantrymen. The judge divided his judicial district into quarters, villages, hamlets or communities and, within these divisions, a specified number of households had to produce an oarsman. Some time after 1541, Lutfi Pasha wrote that one in every four households had to send an oarsman, selected from 'the strong young men'.[64] In fact, the ratio varied according to the size of the fleet and the size of the area where the government made the levy. For example, in 1551, before the Tripoli campaign, the Treasury levied one oarsman per 23 households. In 1570–71, for the invasion of Cyprus, the rate was one in fifteen households. In the next year, after the catastrophe at Lepanto, it was one in seven or eight.[65] The oarsmen did receive pay, but the households within each group that did not provide the man had to provide the cash to cover his wages for one month. The rate was 106 akches for Muslims and 80 akches for non-Muslims.[66]

Galley service was obviously not popular, and orders to the judges require them to appoint guarantors for the appearance of the impressed men. Sometimes the name of a single bailsman appears against the name of the oarsman, sometimes a group, and sometimes 'all the inhabitants of the village/quarter.' These guarantors pledged their persons, property, or both. Once the levy was complete, the judge sent the men under guard to the Arsenal, or to whatever point they were to meet the ships. With them, he sent a register, which enabled the receiving authorities to check that all of them had arrived.

For the oarsmen, the journey to the coast must have caused almost as much hardship as service in the fleet. All districts in Turkey and the Balkan peninsula were liable for the levy, and not simply those that were close to the embarkation points, requiring the men to travel on foot from as far away as Albania or central Anatolia to Istanbul or other coastal sites. To man, for example, the fleet which was to besiege Chios in 1566, the Treasury called up oarsmen from the Provinces of Anatolia, Karaman and Rum in Turkey; from the districts of Albania, Epiros and Thrace in Rumelia; and from the islands and sanjaks in southern Greece that belonged to the Province of the Archipelago. These were oarsmen for the imperial fleet. The smaller squadrons in Egypt and elsewhere raised their complements locally.[67]

In the seventeenth century, the system for levying oarsmen remained essentially the same as it had been in the sixteenth. In one respect, however, it had become more systematic. From shortly after 1600, tax registers begin to show exactly which households in which sanjaks were liable for the levy. Most of these were in western and west-central Turkey. A register of 1640, for example, shows 62 946 households, producing 6634 oarsmen. This indicates that one household in every nine had to supply a man, with the remainder paying a tax to cover his wages and maintenance. The total number was enough to man 40 or more galleys.

This system, was clearly suitable for the first half of the seventeenth century, a period when there were no large scale naval expeditions and the annual needs of the fleet did not vary much. However, with the outbreak of the Cretan war in 1645, the demands of the fleet increased, and the government again began, as it had done in the sixteenth century, to levy oarsmen in central Anatolia and Rumelia. It also introduced an entirely new measure. From 1646, it began to raise oarsmen from Istanbul tradesmen – tavern keepers, keepers of *boza* shops, porters and watermen – and from the city's Greeks, Armenians and Jews. For this service they received exemptions from other war taxes. Apart from the watermen, these people did not have to serve in person. They had instead to raise the money to hire the oarsmen and to deliver them to the Arsenal, or else to pay a fine in lieu. In 1646, they raised 337 oarsmen; in 1656–7, after the disaster at the Dardanelles, 2108.[68]

Most of the oarsmen in the fleet were from the levy but, presumably from earliest times, there were alternative methods of recruitment. One way was to seek volunteers. References to these are few, but commands to the Judges of Izmit, Silivri and Zlatitsa from between 1571 and 1574 order them to hire oarsmen for 900 and 1000 akches, and in 1585, Arsenal accounts record 1139 oarsmen hired for 900 akches and 2475 for 1000. These numbers – if they do represent volunteers – are large and probably very unusual, since volunteers do not seem to have appeared again in any numbers until the Cretan war.[69]

Convicted criminals provided a more steady supply of oarsmen.[70] There was no legislation determining what offences were punishable by the galleys: decrees drafting criminals onto the ships state merely that the men should be, for example, 'criminal and seditious' or 'guilty of a grave offence, but not meriting capital punishment'. It is quite clear, in fact, that the criterion for inflicting this punishment was the needs of the fleet at any one time. In 1571–2, for example, after the battle of Lepanto, judges from every part of the Empire, from as far west as Buda to as far east as Van and Erzurum, received commands to send to the galleys in Istanbul all the prisoners in their districts, and all criminals arrested after the receipt of the command.[71] In 1648 and 1651, during the Cretan war, there were transfers of prisoners from the 'dungeon of Istanbul' to the Arsenal.[72] Prisoners, too, seem to have made up a large proportion of the oarsmen in local flotillas. It was, therefore, the circumstances of the Empire rather than the nature of the crime that led to punishment in the galleys. It was, however, the crime that determined the length of the sentence. The most serious offences were punishable by life, but for other offences, the oarsman – if he survived – gained his release after a minimum of six months. Since the Arsenal retained a copy of the entry in the judge's register relating to the accused, and issued a receipt to the man who delivered him, it was possible to keep track of the criminals in the galleys, and of how long they had served.[73]

Finally, prisoners-of-war were another source of manpower, but there appear to be no records of their numbers. It is clear, however, that most of the oarsmen came from within the Empire's borders.

Troops

Of the galley crews, only the *Azabs* were combatants. In addition to their crews, therefore, the galleys of the Ottoman fleet carried fighting troops. Venetian reports from the mid-sixteenth century estimate that the normal complement was 60 soldiers. After the defeat of 1571, the Imperial Council, presumably on the advice of the admiral, Uluj Ali, raised the number to 150.[74]

In calling up the troops, the Ottoman government did not distinguish between the land army and the fleet. Men liable for military duty could serve in either according to need. It is natural, therefore, that the majority of fighting men in the galleys were, as in the land army, *timar*-holding cavalrymen, together with a much smaller contingent of Janissaries. This was the pattern in the mid-sixteenth century, when records of the call-up become available, but it is unlikely that things had been different a century earlier. The records of the call-up for the campaigns of Jerba in 1560, Malta in 1565, Chios in

1566, and Cyprus in 1570–1, show that the *timar* holders who served in the fleet came from the provinces of Rumelia and the Archipelago, and from all the Provinces of western and central Turkey. As when they fought on land, they served in the fleet under the command of the governor and other officers from their sanjak. These, or indeed any of the fleet commanders, could recommend that they receive additions to their *timars* for outstanding service. Again, as on land, decrees calling up *timar* holders, require them to bring armed retainers, weapons, armour and provisions. The decrees also state where they were to join the ships. In the case of men from Anatolia, this was typically at the fortresses of the Dardanelles.

It seems that, for most of the sixteenth century, the overwhelming majority of troops in the fleet were *timar* holders. However, if numbers were insufficient, the Imperial Council might order the admiral, as it did before the Jerba campaign, to draft in fortress guards or, as before the siege of Malta in 1565, *Azabs* and volunteers. Local flotillas, especially the fleets in Egypt could raise troops from other sources, but these were few in comparison with the numbers of *timar* holders. It was the Imperial Council that issued the decrees calling up the men, but presumably after consultation with the admiral as to the numbers required and the points of embarkation.[75]

The system worked well until 1571. In this year, however, the defeat at Lepanto provoked a crisis of manpower and battle tactics. Many *timar* holders lost their lives in the battle, and the remainder were reluctant to serve in the fleet again. In 1572, the government was eventually able to raise only 4396 *timar* holders and 3000 Janissaries, against a total requirement of 15–20 000 combatants. There was therefore a severe shortage of manpower. There was also a crisis in weaponry.

It is clear that the Admiral attributed the defeat, in part at least, to the enemy's superiority in firepower and numbers of fighting men. To overcome this, the fleet which was to put to sea in 1572 was to carry between the benches of each galley two arquebusiers and a bowman. In order to achieve this, the decrees calling up *timar* holders to the campaign of 1572 require them and their retainers to bring to war arquebuses as well as bows, with one decree instructing a sanjak governor to make this announcement early in order to allow any *timar* holder 'who did not already know, to learn how to use the arquebus'. This did not, however, solve the problem. Even if the *timar* holders did learn to use firearms, the total number of arquebusiers would still have been inadequate. To make up the shortfall, the government raised an unprecedented number of volunteers. Each sanjak governor who received a command to levy *timar* holders, was also to levy volunteers, organise these into groups of ten men, and send them to the fleet, where they would receive an allocation of pay and biscuit. In Rumelia, governors received instructions to levy only 'volunteers', whereas governors-general and sanjak governors in southeast Turkey and Syria were to raise specifically 'Kurdish and other' volunteers, the Kurds being 'renowned for their valour'. All these men had to be proficient in the use of the arquebus. The sanjak governors at the same time received orders to buy arquebuses belonging to anyone who was not volunteering.[76]

The crisis after Lepanto does not seem to have brought about permanent changes in the way the government levied troops for the fleet, except perhaps in demanding proficiency in the use of the arquebus. In the seventeenth century, the majority of combatants were still the *timar* holders. The only change from the sixteenth century was a rationalisation in the area of the levy. After 1600, it seems that the *timar* holders who served in the fleet came usually from the Province of the Archipelago, whose ten sanjaks produced a notional 4500 men.[77] In addition to these, when the government abolished the Corps of Footmen and Exemptees in Anatolia, it reallocated their land as a notional 1039 *timars* assigned to the admiral,[78] enough to produce perhaps 3–4000 troops. Together with the men from the Archipelago, these were enough for a fleet of about 50 ships and, since there were no major naval campaigns between 1574 and 1645, this was sufficient to supply the imperial fleet for its annual tours in the eastern Mediterranean and the Black Sea during these years. As in the sixteenth century, a fluctuating number of Janissaries also served in the fleet.[79]

In addition to these fighting men, each galley carried two or three gunners – the galleasses which began to appear in the fleet after 1571 required more than this – and also armourers to maintain the weapons.

Tactics

The pattern of Ottoman, and indeed all Mediterranean naval warfare, was very similar to the pattern of war on land. The most typical form of combat was not the major fleet engagement, but rather a continuous *kleinkrieg* of attacks on enemy coasts and shipping. This was the form of warfare which Ottoman fleets engaged in between the late fourteenth and the mid-fifteenth centuries. It was plunder from Christian shipping and settlements that sustained the Ottoman provinces in North Africa, and in particular provided a source of wealth for the Ottoman outpost of Algiers. The Knights of St John played a similar role in the Christian Mediterranean, and it was against these and other Christian predators that the admiral made his annual tours, even during years of formal peace.[80]

When the Ottoman imperial fleet engaged in an action, it was typically an amphibious assault on a coastal or insular fortress, rather than a battle in the open sea. Almost all Ottoman naval victories, from the conquest of Mitylene in 1462 to the capture of Chania in 1645, were of this sort. Engagements between fleets on the open sea, like major field battles on land, were infrequent and, unlike field battles, rarely decisive in determining the course of events. The Venetian naval victory in 1416 was perhaps a factor in delaying the creation of an effective Ottoman war fleet until after 1450. The more famous victory at Lepanto did not, however, prevent the Ottoman conquest of Cyprus or the conquest of Tunis three years later. The Venetian victory outside the Dardanelles in 1656 caused severe problems for the Ottomans, but did not bring to an end the invasion of Crete. From the mid-fifteenth century, therefore, the most typical functions of the Ottoman fleet were sieges and raids on enemy shores. The fleet also served to protect Ottoman shipping and coastlines, and sometimes to restore the sultan's authority in outlying provinces.

The nature of the galley limited the Ottoman fleet's range of action. Galleys were long vessels, low in the water, with a shallow draught. They were not able to withstand heavy seas, and could not, therefore, put to sea in the winter, setting out in principle, if not often in practice, at the vernal equinox, and returning in October or early November. It was possible to risk keeping small flotillas or single vessels at sea during the winter, but not whole fleets. During the first half of the seventeenth century, Ottoman shipwrights started to build galleys broader and longer, with 'melon sterns' in order to withstand storms better,[81] but this did not prolong the campaigning season. The limited sailing season in turn limited the operational range of the fleet. The other constraint on the range of a galley was the size of its crew.

In 1656, Katib Chelebi estimated that a galley carried 330 men, including 196 oarsmen and 100 warriors. An Ottoman galeass, he says, carried a crew of 600, and a heavy galley a crew of 800.[82] In the previous century, numbers had been smaller, since galleys had three rather than four oarsmen to each bench, and 50 rather than 100 warriors, but numbers were still very large. At the same time, storage space on a galley was limited. It was not possible, therefore, to store on board more than about ten days' supply of food and water. Water was available from springs and rivers ashore, and knowledge of their location was presumably traditional within the Ottoman navy. In addition, the Mediterranean map of Piri Reis, completed in 1526, but still in use in the mid-seventeenth century, identifies water sources around the shores of the Mediterranean. Food supplies were a greater problem.

Since a galley could not carry victuals for a whole season, it was necessary to supply the fleet from prearranged points on the shore or, as at Malta in 1565, or Crete in 1651,[83] to transport food by ship. This required careful planning in advance. The basic, and probably the only food that the government supplied, was biscuit and the fleet's requirements were enormous. For example, the treasury accounts record 2305 tonnes of biscuit for the fleet which recaptured Herceg Novi in 1539.[84] To purchase the wheat, mill it, bake it into biscuit and transport it to the shore was therefore a major operation and a major expense. The Treasury raised the money locally, and distributed the work over a wide area. In 1566, for example, it ordered biscuit for the fleet from Arta, Patras, Navplion, Farsala, Trikkala and Gjirokastër in Albania and central and southern Greece, and from Thessaloniki in the north.[85] In the seventeenth century before 1645, when the size of the fleets was more predictable, Istanbul and Gallipoli were the major centres for baking, but the sixteenth-century practice of distributing the work around the provinces also continued. In this respect, Volos was particularly important. It served not only as the quay for the export of grain from central Greece, but also as a centre for the preparation of biscuit for the fleet. For example, in his tour of the Archipelago in 1618, Chelebi Ali took on a consignment of biscuit which had been baked at Volos and transported to Evvoia for collection by the fleet.[86]

A consequence of this need to take on food at frequent intervals was that galley fleets could not operate safely if they were far from their own shores or if the sea lanes were insecure. This, combined with the short campaigning season, limited their range. For this reason, the Ottoman fleet could not dominate the western Mediterranean without a base for the winter and a supply of provisions. This was possible only briefly when, in cooperation with the King of France, the Ottoman fleet, in 1543-4, was able to overwinter in Toulon. For the same reason, Christian galley fleets could not gain command of the eastern Mediterranean. Even after the great victory at Lepanto, the fleet of the Holy League had no choice but to return to its home bases before the onset of winter.

The galley determined the nature of Mediterranean warfare as much as it did the operating range of the fleets. As an oared vessel with a shallow draught, it did not rely on the wind and could operate close to the shore. For caulking, oiling or carrying out repairs, it was easy to pull ashore on a sandy beach. These characteristics made it especially useful as a pirate vessel, particularly on a windless day, when its prey might lie becalmed. Its ability to come close to the shore was also useful when bombarding coastal fortresses, one of the major functions of a galley fleet. Equally, if an enemy attacked such a fortress, an inshore squadron of galleys could provide a line of defence against the attacking fleet, while itself finding shelter beneath the guns of the fort.[87]

Before the introduction, some time in the late fifteenth century, of artillery, the basic method of galley warfare was ramming and boarding. Artillery did not change this practice. A galley carried cannon on its prow and approached the enemy head on, hoping to fire at least one salvo before the men on the forward fighting platform attempted to board. It was important not to allow the enemy to attack the sides of the vessel, where he could inflict the greatest damage. The vulnerability of the galley's flanks and the disposition of the guns gave commanders no choice but to adopt a line abreast formation, with all the ships' prows facing forward at the enemy fleet or fortress. Success depended on maintaining this formation and, when facing the enemy fleet, outflanking it and breaking its ranks. In 1656, Katib Chelebi described the ideal Ottoman battleline: 'In battle, the galleys should be arranged in rows. The Admiral's ship should be in the rear, with five vessels to accompany it, three in the rear and two in front.'[88]

The Ottoman fleet, therefore, from the late fourteenth century onwards, adopted the prevailing techniques of Mediterranean warfare. It seems, however, that Ottoman shipbuilders and seamen tended to be less competent than their western European rivals, notably the Venetians. In the fifteenth century, the fleets of Mehmed II, particularly the one which attacked Negroponte in 1470, relied on overwhelming superiority in numbers of ships, not on superior tactical skills. Even at the height of Ottoman naval power in the mid-sixteenth century, observers sometimes commented on the inadequacies of the Ottoman fleet. In 1558, for example, the Venetian *bailo* noticed a lack of skill, evidently by comparison with Venetian shipwrights, among the craftsmen in the Imperial Arsenal, and described the galleys themselves as 'not lasting more than a year, and when they come to disarm, it is pitiful to see them in a state of disrepair.'[89] Some Ottomans, too, were aware of shortcomings. Writing after 1541, Lutfi Pasha comments on the importance of maritime affairs, but also notes that 'in the organisation of naval expeditions, the Infidel is superior to us'.[90]

In the seventeenth century, too, Katib Chelebi mentions further problems, albeit ones that were probably common to all Mediterranean fleets. He warns in particular about the use of prisoners-of-war and convicts as oarsmen. These, he says, are liable to mutiny, and 'countless ships have been lost in this way'. The skippers should always mix prisoners with 'more reliable Turks' from the annual levy. In this respect, he commends Jigalazade Sinan Pasha, who was twice Admiral between 1591 and 1605, for placing every three prisoners with three 'Turks', so that the ships were safe.[91] He also gives advice on how to attack the enemy. A sea battle, he warns, is a 'death trap', and if the fleet attacks when it is inshore off the Ottoman coast, the troops on the galleys will swim ashore to escape the combat. The fleet should never give battle in these circumstances. If, on the other hand, the enemy is inshore off the Ottoman coast, then it is safe to attack, as the men cannot escape. The only way to save their lives was to stand and fight.[92]

The advantage which the Ottomans enjoyed in naval warfare was not, therefore, in shipbuilding, seamanship or fighting ability, but rather in the abundance of materials, money and men, which allowed the rapid construction of new fleets. It was perhaps, too, the ease with which they could replace ships that explains the apparently forlorn appearance of their galleys on their return from sea. It was an advantage which they enjoyed from the fourteenth to the late seventeenth centuries.

During the course of the fifteenth and sixteenth centuries, the Ottoman fleet had adopted the standard galley tactics of the Mediterranean. After 1600, it faced two new strategic problems. The first of these was temporary. The other was to render galley warfare obsolete.

The first problem was the appearance of Cossack raiders on the Black Sea, from which the Ottomans had excluded foreign fleets since the conquest of Caffa in 1475. From the late sixteenth century, the Cossacks on the Dniepr and the Don began to make frequent and destructive raids on coastal settlements and, to counter these, the Ottoman government fortified towns and villages along the coast, sent forces overland to engage the raiders, and sent the imperial fleet, or detachments of it, to encounter them at sea. In naval warfare, however, the Cossacks enjoyed an advantage. On their raids they used *shaykas*; that is, portable rowing boats with flat bottoms and no keel, which they could use in shallow waters and reed-beds. The Ottoman galleys also had a shallow draught, but far less so than the *shaykas*, and the Cossacks used this difference to their advantage. In 1614, ships of the imperial fleet pursued the Cossacks after these had attacked Sinop, but were unable to follow them down the Dniepr. In the following year, when the Admiral, Jigalazade Mahmud Pasha, attacked the *shaykas*, the Cossacks lured him towards the shore until his galleys ran aground. For this reason, Katib Chelebi advised that a galley fleet, in an encounter with the Cossacks, should always drive the *shaykas* out to sea, and should not attack close to the shore. In this case, the galleys would run aground. In the open sea, however, *shaykas* were no match for galleys.[93] The ability of *shaykas* to hide in reed beds also presented problems. The galleys could stand in deeper water and besiege them, but their bombardments were useless against an invisible enemy that could slip away in the darkness. To counter these tactics, from the 1630s, Ottoman fleets themselves began to use flat-bottomed rowing boats, carrying troops and artillery to send into the reeds. This was the tactic that the Warden of the Arsenal, Piyale, used in 1639 in his fight with the Cossacks in the Strait of Kerch. This tactic, together with the recapture of Azov in 1642 and the refortification of Ochakov at the mouth of the Dniepr eventually brought the Cossacks under control.[94]

In the long term, the more significant problem for the Ottoman fleet was the changing nature of naval warfare. For the first forty-five years of the seventeenth century, there had been no major wars in the Mediterranean, and the function of the Ottoman fleet had been to keep the Aegean and eastern Mediterranean free of predators and occasionally to suppress rebellions.[95] A galley fleet had been adequate for this task. It was during this period, however, that northern European ships began to appear in the Mediterranean in increasing numbers, and although their purpose was trade, they carried heavy armaments. The technique of casting iron cannon, which were cheaper than the bronze ordnance that they displaced, had made this possible. These vessels, with their high sides and the ability to fire heavy broadsides were superior in combat to the Mediterranean war galley.[96]

The Venetians, but not the Ottomans, had mastered the techniques of building and manning war galleons, with the result that when war broke out with Venice in 1645, the Venetian fleet enjoyed a clear advantage in battle. The only galleons in the Ottoman fleet came from Algiers which, in 1645, provided a squadron of 20 vessels. Apart from these, the Ottoman government also rented sailing vessels from the Dutch and, in the late 1640s, began to build their own. Katib Chelebi tells how the grand vizier took the decision after discussions with 'certain people' who told him that the enemy galleons could use the wind to run down the Ottoman fleet, forcing it to scatter. Equally, they could anchor outside the Dardanelles, preventing the exit of the Ottoman galleys. The galleons' firepower was clearly overwhelming. Katib Chelebi also records how, when discussions were in progress, the Chief Mufti Abdurrahim, had summoned him and asked him if the Ottoman fleet had used galleons in past naval wars. He had replied that, in large scale campaigns, it had used galleons for transport, but only galleys for combat. He added that building galleons was not a problem: the difficulty was to find skilled crews and gunners. Katib Chelebi reinforces his scepticism about the introduction of galleons by giving instructions on how a galley should fight a galleon, giving examples of successful engagements in the past.[97] A galley, he writes, should not immediately engage a galleon, but should first immobilise it by destroying its rudder and rigging, taking advantage of the fact that the broadside guns on a galleon had a shorter range than the artillery on a galley.[98]

Events were to prove Katib Chelebi right. The adoption of the galleon by the Ottoman fleet was not a success. The galleons in the fleet of 1656 could not prevent an overwhelming Ottoman defeat and, in 1662, the grand vizier brought the experiment to an end. In 1669, the Cretan war ended in victory for the Ottomans, but the inadequacy of the fleet had been a major factor in its prolongation.

Some Conclusions

The Ottoman Empire was a dynastic state, where the sultan, in appearance, enjoyed untramelled power. He was both the political leader and miltary commander in times of war. Every office holder in the Empire occupied his position by virtue of a warrant which bound him personally to the service of the sultan, who could promote, dismiss or execute him at will. The sultan was apparently all-powerful, and it has been customary, since the time of Machiavelli, to compare Ottoman absolutism with the position of monarchs in Europe, where the prerogatives of the nobility restricted the power of kings. This traditional picture is, however, an oversimplification.

The power of the sultan, especially between the mid-fifteenth and mid-sixteenth century, was indeed remarkable, but it was not unfettered, and its accretion had been a gradual process. The first two sultans had most probably shared authority with their brothers and sons, and it was only the practice of fratricide and the confinement of sons in provincial governorships that finally gave the ruling sultan unchallenged authority within the dynasty. This was a development probably of the reign of Murad I. Fratricide removed dynastic rivals, but did not make the sultan all-powerful. The absence of a nobility in the European sense did not mean an absence of territorial magnates, and a feature of the early Ottoman Empire is the emergence of the marcher lords and other dynasties with hereditary claims to land or office. The Evrenos dynasty of Macedonia and the vizieral family of Chandarli are examples. The early sultans could not ignore the claims of these families, who functioned as allies rather than as servants of the ruler. From the second decade of the fifteenth century, however, the sultans usually excluded the marcher lords from the central councils of the Empire, although not from army commands or provincial office, and no Chandarli served as vizier after 1500.

The diminished influence of these families enhanced the personal power of the sultans, but the expansion of the Empire in the fifteenth and sixteenth centuries inevitably increased the numbers of local lords and factions within its boundaries. The absorption of these into the Ottoman ruling élite was a feature especially, although not exclusively, of the years between about 1450 and 1520. Some local dynasts fled at the time of the Ottoman conquest, as some members of the Zenevis family had done when they settled in Corfu after the Ottoman conquest of their hereditary territory in 1418. Others, however, neither fled nor resisted, but instead entered the service of the sultan and received vizieral or provincial office. If they were Christians, conversion offered an immediate entry into the Ottoman governing class. In this way, they were able to retain or even enhance the social and political standing which they had enjoyed before the conquest, but their status, originally hereditary, had now become dependent on the patronage of the sultan. By these means, the sultan co-opted members of local dynasties to serve rather than to oppose his own interests. It was a system that increased the power of the sultan without recourse to brutal suppression. It was not a method, however, that worked throughout the Empire. Some local powers, such as the tribal chiefs in Kurdistan, were ineradicable. In these cases, the sultans tried to secure loyalty through negotiation and the bestowal of Ottoman titles.

The sultan probably enjoyed his greatest accession of power during the sixteenth century, precisely the period when the image of the Ottoman sultan as absolute ruler became fixed. It was at this period that the graduates of the Palace Schools, most of whom had entered royal service through the Collection, came to monopolise most of the governorships in the Empire, whether as viziers in the capital or as governors in the provinces. These were men with no power base outside the Palace, whose education was into the service of the dynasty, and whose career depended entirely on royal patronage. The system of marrying powerful viziers to Ottoman princesses was a means of ensuring their loyalty when they had left the Palace and established households of their own, by binding them to the imperial family.

Between the fourteenth and sixteenth centuries, the fundamental nature of the Empire had not changed. In the fourteenth century, the Ottoman Empire had been, in essence, a structure of personal alliances between the Ottoman ruler and the marcher lords and other magnates. Outside this inner core, the Ottoman sultans used marriage, force or other means to reduce independent dynasties on the borders of the Empire to the status of vassals or allies. The system was one which depended on personal ties between great families. In the sixteenth century, it was still personal ties that maintained the structure of the Empire. By this time, however, membership of the Empire's ruling class was no longer by virtue of a blood relationship to a powerful family, but by virtue of an education received as a member of the sultan's household. On assuming office and the income which office produced, the appointee would establish his own household, and with it, his own clients and followers, but ties of patronage would continue to bind him to the sultan. His relationship to the sultan was a personal one – this had not changed since the the fourteenth century – but the relationship was no longer as an ally, but as a client. This was a change that reflected the growing power of the sultan. It was presumably to keep office holders as clients and to prevent their establishing independent power bases that it became customary to move provincial governors at regular intervals from one locality to another.

Nonetheless, despite their growth in authority between the fourteenth century and the sixteenth, the power of the Ottoman sultans was never absolute, since there were checks, formal and informal, which limited their freedom of action. It was their adoption of Islam that imposed the formal limit. Before the twentieth century, Islam expressed itself, above all, through the law which, although very flexible in practice, was in its essence immutable. Furthermore, the interpretation of the law was the function not of monarchs, but of jurists. The Ottoman sultans could not create an independent body of law outside the areas of land tenure, taxation and criminal law, where Islamic law was in practice inoperative. In these areas, however, it tended to be custom rather than the will of the sultan that shaped the law. The prestige of Islamic law also created a privileged position within the Empire for the jurists who were its official interpreters. It was the sultans who appointed men to legal positions, but since, during the course of the sixteenth century, the senior posts in the legal establishment became the monopoly of a few families, his freedom of choice was very narrow. Furthermore, it was these senior legal figures who in practice appointed judges and other legal officers even if they did so in the sultan's name. The sultan did not, therefore, make or control the law. It did, however, form a part of his claim to legitimacy. From the early sixteenth century, as a response in particular to the 'heresy' of the Safavids, the Ottoman sultans began to portray themselves as the sole legitimate defenders of the Holy Law, and to claim that their rule was a precondition to its coming into effect. By the same token, however, the law could also justify their removal. The senior legal figures of the Empire played a major part in the deposition of both Mustafa I and Ibrahim, in both cases citing the Holy Law in justification for the act.

Although there were no formal checks on the sultan in his executive role, informally, there were many. The original role of the Ottoman ruler was as a leader in war. The early sultans led their armies in the field and, to judge from what Ashikpashazade tells us, seem to have known in person not only their commanders, but even many of their soldiers, and to have personally distributed rewards and punishments. With the gradual withdrawal of the sultans from public view, the era of face-to-face command came to an end. The sultans, however, continued to lead armies until the mid-sixteenth century and, although it is unlikely that they still had contact with common soldiers, they remained in charge of operations and, were able, if they wished, to intervene in appointments and promotions made during the campaign. From the late sixteenth century, with few exceptions, the sultan no longer went to war, and many of his powers passed in practice to the commander in the field. This, in effect, gave the army commander a major role in the government of the Empire. In non-military affairs, too, there were limits to the sultan's area of control. In the early days, the Ottoman rulers must have dealt personally with most affairs of state but, as the Empire expanded, the weight of government business made it impossible for the sultans even to be aware of all the decisions made in their name. What held the Empire together at this stage was not the sultan's direct control of all aspects of government, but rather the position of governors, army commanders and other authorities as his clients. The sultan retained control over the governing class rather than over individual acts of government. The frequent executions which remained a feature of Ottoman politics served as a constant reminder of this fact.

The sultan, therefore, had no authority over the Holy Law and in practice probably played little part in the day-to-day government of the Empire. The viziers, however, clearly referred major issues for the sultan's decision and, whenever he chose to intervene personally in government, his word was decisive. Nevertheless, there were again restrictions on what he might do. One permanent barrier to the sultan's unfettered power was the Janissary Corps. The original and, until the late sixteenth century, continuing function of this body was to protect the person and position of the monarch and, in fulfilling this role, was probably a force for political stability. Whatever crises the Empire or individual sultans faced, the dynasty itself was never under threat. The Janissaries, however, as an armed force, were also in a position to defend their own interests and secure their own political ends. In his *History of Mehmed the Conqueror* Tursun Bey tells a story of how this sultan beat the Janissary officers after the Corps had attempted to extract a bonus by threats of armed rebellion. Tursun's purpose in including the tale was to instruct future sultans in how to keep the Janissaries under control, but it had no effect. The demands of the Janissaries could be decisive in the accession and deposition of sultans, in the conduct of campaigns and in extracting money from the Treasury.

The Janissaries were a highly visible check on the sultan's personal authority. Less visible was the influence of his court. Decisions require information and consultation, and it was the courtiers who were best placed to inform and advise. In the fourteenth and early fifteenth centuries, the sultans seem to have presided in person at meetings of what was to become the Imperial Council and, on occasions, to have come into contact with their subjects. From the mid-fifteenth century, as they withdrew from council meetings and became less visible to the outside world, their circle of contacts narrowed, a tendency which became more pronounced from the mid-sixteenth century when they no longer, except on very rare occasions, went on campaign. This meant that whoever could gain the sultan's ear and control the information reaching him could influence his decisions. In Ottoman political doctrine, this was the duty of the grand vizier alone and, in a formal sense, this was true. The grand vizier was president of the Imperial Council which issued decrees in the sultan's name and, as such, he consulted with the sultan after each of its meetings. It is clear, however, that information could reach the sultan by other means, and that persons who were in attendance every day, such as the barber who tended his beard, the pages of the Privy Chamber or the senior eunuchs were as well placed to influence him as the grand vizier. It is difficult, however, to estimate the influence of courtiers, as these contacts have left few written records. Only a few figures, such as Sa'deddin, the royal tutor in the late sixteenth century, or Sultan Ibrahim's exorcist, Jinji Hoja, became well known sufficiently to receive the attention of Ottoman chroniclers. Ottoman advice writers claim that it was in the time of Murad III that courtiers and favourites began to acquire power, but this is probably an exaggeration. It is perhaps more true to say that they became more influential at this time than they had been in previous reigns.

Courtiers possessed no formal political authority, but were nonetheless in a position to influence the sultan. The same is true of the women of the Imperial Harem. Some, such as Mehmed II's stepmother, Mara, had exercised informal political power before the sixteenth century, but it was during the sixteenth century that the influence of the harem became quasi-institutional, with favourite concubines, and later queen-mothers, exercising an influence in dynastic and imperial politics. This was something which foreign ambassadors recognised, when they established informal contacts in the Harem in parallel to their formal relations with the viziers.

The degree to which a sultan allowed these constraints to limit his exercise of power depended to a large degree on his personality. The first ten Ottoman sultans clearly possessed the personal authority which allowed them to dominate politics and, to a degree, to keep political factions under control. The eleventh sultan, Selim II, clearly neglected affairs of state, and allowed much of his power to pass to his son-in-law, the Grand Vizier Sokollu Mehmed Pasha, who effectively governed on his behalf. In the early seventeenth century, however, there were no political figures whose personal authority allowed them to compensate for the weakness of the sultans and so to dominate rival factions, as Sokollu Mehmed had done during the reign of Selim II. In the Ottoman Empire, power was personal and rather than institutional and, to remain stable, the political system required a strong sultan or a commanding figure like Sokollu or the Köprülü viziers in the second half of the seventeenth century to act on his behalf.

Nonetheless, the Empire had a remarkable resilience. In 1402, the defeat at the battle of Ankara could have led to its dissolution. Instead, a hundred years later, it had begun its ascent to the status of world power, while the Empire of Bayezid's conqueror, Timur, had disappeared. At the beginning of the seventeenth century, the Ottoman Empire faced unsuccessful wars on two fronts, rebellion in Anatolia, weak sultans and unstable politics. It still survived. The reason for this capacity to weather crises probably lies in two institutions. First, the scribal service continued to work, ensuring that the daily functions of government such as taxation and the equipping of armies could continue despite rapid changes in the vizierate. In the late sixteenth and seventeenth centuries, too, the service adapted its accounting systems to accommodate the new ways of collecting taxes and recruiting troops. Second, the courts and the legal system continued to function and to keep the confidence of the sultan's subjects in regulating their affairs. It was, it seems, the continuity in these mundane functions of government that ensured the Empire's survival.

The Ottoman Empire was, above all, a military organisation. Even when the sultans no longer led their armies in person, they remained, in principle, leaders in war. The demand that Mehmed III accompany the army to Hungary in 1596 shows how the notion persisted that the presence of the sultan on the battlefield would bring success. There was no distinction between civil government and military command. The political structure of the Empire reflected the structure of army, with viziers and provincial governors acting also as commanders in war. The expansion of the Empire between 1300 and 1590 is a testimony to the effectiveness of the Ottoman military system. Several factors contributed to this success in arms. In the first place, the sultans had at their disposal an abundant supply of men and war materials, which few of their rivals could match. Second, from the late fourteenth century, the practice of registering the incomes and obligations of all *timar*-holding cavalrymen meant that the government had a permanent record of the troops at its disposal. At the same time, the establishment of the Janissaries and the Six Divisions created a small standing army, whose skill in arms and esprit de corps, acquired through living and fighting together, provided a stable centre to the Ottoman armies. Furthermore, all these troops had a contractual obligation to serve the sultan, with desertion or failure to appear on campaign resulting in the loss of livelihood. This made it possible for the sultan to levy at any time a predictable number of disciplined troops. Finally, until the end of the sixteenth century, the Ottomans had been proficient in developing weapons and tactics, and very quick to absorb lessons learned from their enemies. The mastery of the siege in the fourteenth century, and the adoption of artillery and the *wagenburg* in the fifteenth are evidence of this adaptability.

It became clear, however, during the Austrian war of 1593–1606 that the Ottoman army had lost its superiority both in weapons and tactics, and that it had the greatest difficulty in adapting to new methods, especially of warfare in the field. This loss of supremacy was to become even more evident in the wars of the late seventeenth and eighteenth centuries. Nonetheless, even during these times of trouble, the Ottoman ability to supply and maintain armies in the field was remarkable, a testimony to the resources and administrative system of the Empire, as much as to its military prowess.

Notes

1 Chronology (pp. 1–86)

1 Heath W. Lowry, 'When did the Sephardim arrive in Salonica?'; Minna Rozen, 'Individual and community in the Jewish society of the Ottoman Empire' both in Avigdor Levy, *The Jews of the Ottoman Empire* (Princeton, 1994), 203–13; 215–73.

2 On this phenomenon, see I. Metin Kunt, 'Ethnic-regional (*cins*) solidarity in the seventeenth century Ottoman establishment', *International Journal of Middle Eastern Studies*, 5 (1974), 233–9.

3 On the Turkish colonisation of Anatolia, see Speros Vryonis, *The Decline of Medieval Hellenism* (Berkeley and London, 1971); V.L. Ménage, 'The Islamisation of Anatolia', in Nehemia Levtzion (ed.), *Conversion to Islam* (New York, 1979), 52–67.

4 For pre-Ottoman Anatolia, see Claude Cahen, *Pre-Ottoman Turkey* (London, 1968).

5 For a chronological history of the Ottoman Empire to 1481, see Colin Imber, *The Ottoman Empire, 1300–1481* (Istanbul, 1990).

6 The foundation of the Ottoman Empire has been the subject of much argument. Contributions to this debate include F. Giese, 'Das Problem der Entstehung des osmanischen Reiches', *Zeitschrift für Semitistik*, 2 (1922), 246–71; M.F. Köprülü (trans. G. Leiser), *The Origins of the Ottoman Empire* (Albany, 1992); Paul Wittek, *The Rise of the Ottoman Empire* (London, 1938); R.P. Lindner, 'Stimulus and justification in early Ottoman history', *Greek Orthodox Theological Review*, 27 (1982), 207–24; R.P. Lindner, *Nomads and Ottomans in Medieval Anatolia*, (Bloomington, 1983); R.C. Jennings, 'Some thoughts on the gazi-thesis', *Wiener Zeitschrift für die Kunde des Morgenlandes*, 76 (1986), 151–62; Gy. Kaldy-Nagy, 'The Holy War (*jihad*) in the first centuries of the Ottoman Empire', *Harvard Ukrainian Studies*, 3/4 (1979), 462–73; Colin Imber, 'The legend of Osman Gazi' in Elizabeth A. Zachariadou (ed.), *The Ottoman Emirate (1300–1389)* (Rethymnon, 1993), 67–76; Colin Imber, 'What does *ghazi* actually mean?', in Ç. Balım-Harding and C. Imber (eds), *The Balance of Truth: Essays in Honour of Professor*

Geoffrey Lewis, (Istanbul, 2000), 165–78; Aldo Gallotta, 'Il "Mito Oguzo" e le origine dello stato ottomano: una riconsiderazione', in Elizabeth A. Zachariadou (ed.), *The Ottoman Emirate (1300–1389)*, 41–59; Cemal Kafadar, *Between Two Worlds: The Construction of the Ottoman State* (Berkeley, Los Angeles, London, 1995); Linda T. Darling, 'Contested territory: Ottoman Holy War in comparative context', *Studia Islamica*, XCI (2000), 133–69;

7 See Clive Foss, 'Byzantine Malagina and the Lower Sangarius', *Anatolian Studies*, XL (1990), 161–84.

8 Rudi P. Lindner, 'Springtime on the Sakarya'. I am grateful to Professor Lindner for allowing me to read his unpublished typescript.

9 On the growth of the Ottoman principality under Osman and Orhan, see Irène Beldiceanu-Steinherr, 'La conquête de la Bithynie maritime, étape décisive dans la fondation de l'État ottoman', in Klaus Belke, Friedrich Hild, Johannes Koder and Peter Soustal, *Byzanz als Raum* (Vienna, 2000), 21–36.

10 For details of the struggles for the succession to the Sultanate, see Chapter 2.

11 Elizabeth A. .Zachariadou, 'The conquest of Adrianople by the Turks', *Studi Veneziani*, XII (1970), 246–71.

12 Machiel Kiel, 'Mevlana Neşri and the towns of medieval Bulgaria', in C. Heywood and C. Imber (eds), *Studies in Ottoman History in Honour of Professor V.L. Ménage* (Istanbul, 1994), 165–88.

13 Stephen W. Reinert, 'From Niš to Kosovo Polje: reflections on Murad I's final years', in Elizabeth A. Zachariadou (ed.), *The Ottoman Emirate*, 169–211.

14 For the Battle of Kosovo and the growth of legends around it, see especially T.A. Emmert, *Serbian Golgotha: Kosovo, 1389*, (New York, 1990).

15 Elizabeth A. Zachariadou, 'Manuel Palaeologus on the strife between Bayezid I and Kadi Burhan al-Din Ahmed', *Bulletin of the School of Oriental and African Studies*, XLII (1980), 471–81.

16 His aim was perhaps to replace his rebellious vassal, Manuel II, with Manuel's rival, John VII. See Stephen W. Reinert, 'Political dimensions of Manuel II Palaiologos' 1392 marriage and coronation: some new evidence', in C. Sode and S. Takács (eds), *Novum Millenium: Studies on Byzantine history and culture dedicated to Paul Speck* (Aldershot, 2001), 291–303.

17 For Timur, see Beatrice Forbes Manz, *The Rise and Rule of Tamerlane* (Cambridge, 1989).

18 M.M. Alexandrescu-Dersca, *La Campagne de Timur en Anatolie (1402)* (Bucharest, 1942; repr. London, 1977).

19 G.T. Dennis, 'The Byzantine–Turkish Treaty of 1403', *Orientalia Christiana Periodica*, fasc. 1 (1967), 72–88.

20 Elizabeth A. Zachariadou, 'Süleyman Çelebi in Rumili and the Ottoman chronicles', *Der Islam*, 60 (1983), 268–96.

21 F. Babinger, 'Schejch Bedr ed-Din, der Sohn des Richters von Simaw' (Berlin and Leipzig, 1921); Michel Balivet, *Islam Mystique et Révolution Armée dans les Balkans Ottomans: Vie de Cheikh Bedreddîn, le 'Hallâj des Turcs' (1358/59–1416)* (Istanbul, 1995).

22 Pál Engel, 'Janos Hunyadi and the peace "of Szeged" (1444)', *Acta Orientalia* (Budapest), XLVII (1994), 241–257.

23 F. Babinger, 'Von Amurath zu Amurath: Vor- and Nachspiel der Schlacht bei Varna (1444)', *Oriens* (1950), 229–65.

24 On the reign of Mehmed II, see F. Babinger (trans. R. Manheim, ed. W. Hickman), *Mehmed the Conqueror and his Time* (Princeton, 1978).

25 J.R. Melville-Jones, *The Siege of Constantinople, 1453: Seven Contemporary Accounts* (Amsterdam, 1972); A. Pertusi, *La Caduta di Costantinopoli*, 2 vols (Milan, 1976); J.R. Jones, *Nicolô Barbaro: Diary of the Siege of Constantinople* (New York, 1969).

26 Halil İnalcık, 'The policy of Mehmed II toward the Greek population of Istanbul and the Byzantine buildings of the city', *Dumbarton Oaks Papers*, 23/24 (1969–70), 231–49.

27 John E. Woods, *The Aqquyunlu: Clan, Confederation, Empire* (Minneapolis, 1976).

28 For the reign of Bayezid II, see Robert Mantran (ed.), *Histoire de l'Empire Ottoman* (Paris, 1989): Chapter III 'L'ascension des Ottomans (1451–1512)' (Nicolas Vatin); Palmira Brummett, *Ottoman Seapower and Levantine Diplomacy in the Age of Discovery* (Albany, 1994).

29 N. Beldiceanu, 'Recherches sur la réforme foncière de Mehmed II', *Acta Historica*, 4 (1965), 27–39.

30 On Jem, see Nicolas Vatin, *Sultan Djem* (Ankara, 1997); on Rhodes and the Knights of St John, see Nicolas Vatin, *L'Ordre de St-Jean-de-Jérusalem, l'Empire Ottoman et la Méditérranée Orientale entre les Deux Sièges de Rhodes (1480–1522)* (Louvain, 1994).

31 On the Ottoman–Mamluk war, see Shai Har-El, *Struggle for Domination in the Middle East: the Ottoman–Mamluk War, 1485–1491* (Leiden, 1995).

32 See Hanna Sohrweide, 'Der Sieg der Safawiden in Persien und ihre Rückwirkung auf die Schiiten Anatoliens im 16. Jahrhundert', *Der Islam*, 41 (1965), 95–223.

33 R.M. Savory, *Iran under the Safavids* (Cambridge, 1988).

34 Quoted in Ş. Tekindağ, 'Şah Kulu Baba Tekeli isyanı', *Belgelerle Türk Tarih Dergisi*, vol. 3 (1967), 34–39; vol. 4 (1967), 54–9.

35 On Ottoman anti-Safavid propaganda, see Elke Eberhard, *Osmanische Polemik gegen die Safawiden im 16. Jahrhundert* (Freiburg, 1970).

36 Margaret L. Venzke, 'The case of a Dulgadir-Mamluk Iqta': a re-assessment of the Dulgadir principality and its position within the Ottoman–Mamluk rivalry', *Journal of the Social and Economic History of the Orient*, 43 (2000), 399–474.

37 On the conquest of Syria, see Herbert Jansky, 'Die Eroberung Syriens durch Sultan Selim I', *Mitteilungen zur Osmanischen Geschichte*, II (1923–6, repr. Osnabrück, 1972), 169–241.

38 S. Soucek, 'The rise of the Barbarossas in North Africa', *Archivum Ottomanicum*, III (1971), 238–50.

39 For Süleyman I's European wars and diplomacy, see Gy. Kaldy-Nagy, 'Suleimans Angriff auf Europa', *Acta Orientalia* (Budapest), XXVIII (2) (1974), 163–212. See also G. Veinstein, 'Suleyman I', in *Encyclopaedia of Islam*, 9 (1997).

40 Ferenc Szakály, 'Nándofehérvár: the beginning of the end of medieval Hungary', in Géza Dávid and Pál Fodor, *Hungarian–Ottoman Military and Diplomatic Relations in the Age of Süleyman the Magnificent* (Budapest, 1994), 47–76.

41 Nicolas Vatin, *L'Ordre de Saint-Jean-de-Jérusalem*, 341–60.

42 Colin Imber, 'The persecution of the Ottoman Shi'ites according to the *Mühimme Defterleri*, 1565–85', *Der Islam*, 56 (1979), 245–73; repr. in Colin Imber, *Studies in Ottoman History and Law* (Istanbul, 1996), 103–28.

43 Elke Niewöhner-Eberhard, 'Machtpolitische Aspekte des Osmanischen-Safawidischen Kampfes um Baghdad im 16/17. Jahrhundert', *Turcica*, VI (1975), 103–27.

44 Stéphane Yerasimos, *La Fondation de Constantinople et de Sainte Sophie* (Paris, 1990), 221.

45 Stéphane Yerasimos, 'Les relations franco-ottomanes et la prise de Tripoli en 1551' in Gilles Veinstein (ed.), *Soliman le Magnifique et son Temps* (Paris, 1992), 529–44.

46 Gilles Veinstein, 'Les préparatifs de la campagne navale franco-turque de 1552 à travers les ordres du Divan ottoman', in G. Veinstein, *État et Société dans l'Empire Ottoman, XVIe–XVIIIe Siècles* (Aldershot, 1994), VI.

47 On the Ottoman conflict with the Portuguese, see Salih Özbaran, *The Ottoman Response to European Expansion: Studies on Ottoman–Portuguese Relations in the Indian Ocean and Ottoman Administration of the Arab Lands during the Sixteenth Century* (Istanbul, 1994).

48 J. Richard Blackburn, 'The collapse of Ottoman authority in Yemen, 968/1560–976/1568', *Die Welt des Islams*, XIX (1979), 119–76.

49 On the Don–Volga project, see L. Tardy and I. Vásáry, 'Andrzej Taranowskis Bericht über seine Gesandschaftsreise in der Tartarei (1569)', *Acta Orientalia* (Budapest), XXVIII (2) (1974), 213–52.

50 Sir George Hill, *A History of Cyprus*: Vol. III *The Frankish Period* (Cambridge, 1948), 950–1040.

51 Bekir Kütükoğlu, 'Les relations entre l'Empire Ottoman et l'Iran dans la seconde moitié du XVIe siècle', *Turcica*, VI (1975), 128–45.

52 Palmira Brummett, 'Subordination and its discontents: Ottoman campaign 1578–80', in Caesar E. Farah (ed.), *Decision Making and Change in the Ottoman Empire* (Kirksville, 1993), 101–14.

53 Caroline Finkel, 'French mercenaries in the Habsburg–Ottoman war of 1593–1606: the desertion of the Papa garrison', *Bulletin of the School of Oriental and African Studies*, LV (1992), 451–71.

54 G. Bayerle, 'The compromise at Zsitvatorok', *Archivum Ottomanicum*, VI (1980), 5–53.

55 On the organisation and supply of the Ottoman armies during this war, see Caroline Finkel, *The Administration of Warfare: The Ottoman Military Campaigns in Hungary* (Vienna, 1988).

56 William J. Griswold, *The Great Anatolian Rebellion*, 1000–1020/1591–1611 (Berlin, 1983).

57 Dariusz Kolodziejcyk, *Ottoman–Polish Diplomatic Relations* (Leiden, 2000), 129–35.

58 Elke Niewöhner-Eberhard, 'Machtpolitische Aspekte'.

59 Madeline C. Zilfi, 'The Kadizadelis: discordant revivalism in seventeenth-century Istanbul', *Journal of Near Eastern Studies*, 45 (1986), 251–69.

60 Elke Niewöhner-Eberhard, 'Machtpolitische Aspekte'; Rhoads Murphey, *Ottoman Warfare, 1500–1700* (London, 1999), 115–22.

2 The Dynasty (pp. 87–127)

1 For a summary of Hanafi family law, see Joseph Schacht, *An Introduction to Islamic Law* (Oxford, 1964).

2 For the fullest account of the structure and politics of the Ottoman royal family, see Leslie P. Peirce, *The Imperial Harem: Women and Sovereignty in the Ottoman Empire* (Oxford and New York, 1993). For dynastic tables, see A.D. Alderson, *The Structure of the Ottoman Dynasty* (Oxford, 1956).

3 Franz Taeschner, 'Das Nilufer-Imaret in Isnik und seine Bauinschrift, *Der Islam*, 20 (1932), 127–37.

4 M.H. Yınanç, 'Bayezid I', in *İslam Ansiklopedisi*, 2, (Istanbul, 1949).

5 Petra Kappert, *Die Osmanischen Prinzen und ihre Fürstenresidenz Amasya im 15. und 16. Jahrhundert* (Leiden, 1976).

6 Leslie P. Peirce, *The Imperial Harem*; Leslie P. Peirce, 'The family as faction:

dynastic politics in the reign of Süleyman' in Gilles Veinstein (ed.), *Soliman le Magnifique et son Temps* (Paris, 1992), 105–16.

7   Leslie P. Peirce, 'The family as faction'; Alan Fisher, 'Süleyman and his sons', in Gilles Veinstein (ed.), *Soliman le Magnifique*, 117–26; Alan Fisher, 'The life and family of Süleyman I', in H. İnalcık and C. Kafadar (eds), *Süleyman II and his Time* (Istanbul, 1993), 1–19.

8   Maria Pia Pedani, 'Safiye's household and Venetian diplomacy', *Turcica*, 32 (2001), 9–32.

9   The popular designation for the period between the late sixteenth and mid-seventeenth century as 'The Sultanate of Women', is taken from a book of that title by the Turkish historian, Ahmed Refik (1880–1937).

10   For these marriages, see Leslie P. Peirce, *The Imperial Harem*; Colin Imber, *The Ottoman Empire, 1300–1481* (Istanbul, 1990).

11   A.A.M. Bryer, 'Greek historians on the Turks: the case of the first Byzantine–Ottoman marriage', in R.H.C. Davies and J.M. Wallace-Hadrill (eds), *The Writing of History in the Middle Ages* (Oxford, 1981), 471–93.

12   F. Babinger, 'Mehmed's II. Heirat mit Sitt Hatun', *Der Islam*, 29 (1950), 217–35.

13   F. Taeschner and P. Wittek, 'Die Vezirfamilie der Ğandarlyzade (14./15. Jahrhundert) und ihre Denkmäler', *Der Islam*, 18 (1929), 60–115.

14   For a case in the seventeenth century, see Robert Dankoff, 'Marrying a Sultana: the case of Melek Ahmed Paşa', in Caesar E. Farah (ed.), *Decision Making and Change in the Ottoman Empire* (Kirksville, 1993), 169–82.

15   İ. Artuk, 'Osmanlı Beyliğinin kurucusu Osman Gazi'ye ait sikke', in H. İnalcık and O. Okyar (eds), *Social and Economic History of Turkey (1071–1920)* (Ankara, 1980), 27–33.

16   Colin Imber, 'The legend of Osman Gazi', in Elizabeth A. Zachariadou (ed.), *The Ottoman Emirate (1300–1389)* (Rethymnon 1993), 67–75.

17   P. Fodor, 'Ahmedi's Dasitan as a source of early Ottoman history', *Acta Orientalia* (Budapest), XXXVIII (1984), 41–54, interprets 'brothers' as a metaphor, referring to the Muslim emirs of Anatolia.

18   Stephen W. Reinert, 'A Byzantine source on the battles of Bileća (?) and Kosovo Polje: Kydones' letters 396 and 398 reconsidered', in C. Heywood and C. Imber (eds), *Studies in Ottoman History in Honour of Professor V.L.Ménage* (Istanbul, 1994), 249–72.

19   Colin Heywood, 'Mustafa Čelebi, Düzme', in *Encyclopaedia of Islam*, 7 (Leiden, 1993).

20   Nicolas Vatin, *Sultan Djem* (Ankara, 1997) provides an outline of of the events of the civil war and of Jem's captivity in Europe; a full bibliography; the text and translation of the *Vâki'ât-i Sultan Cem*, a Turkish account

of the Prince's captivity; and translations of relevant passages from the *Oeuvres* of the Vice-Chancellor of Rhodes, Guillaume Caoursin.

21 Suha Umur, *Osmanlı Padişah Tuğraları* (Istanbul, 1980), 120.

22 Colin Imber, 'A note on "Christian" preachers in the Ottoman Empire', *Osmanlı Araştırmaları*, x (1990), 59–67; repr. in Colin Imber, *Studies in Ottoman History and Law* (Istanbul, 1996), 153–60.

23 Nicolas Vatin, 'Macabre trafic: la destinée *post-mortem* du prince Djem' in J.-L. Bacqué-Grammont and R. Dor (eds), *Mélanges offerts à Louis Bazin* (Paris, 1992), 231–39; repr. in Nicolas Vatin, *Les Ottomans et l'Occident* (Istanbul, 2001), 77–92.

24 The following account of the civil war and accession of Selim I summarises Çağatay Uluçay, 'Yavuz Sultan Selim nasıl Padişah oldu?', *Tarih Dergisi*, VI (1954), 53–90; VII (1954), 117–42; VIII (1955), 185–200.

25 The following account of the struggle for the succession summarises Şerafettin Turan, *Kanuni'nin Oğlu Şehzade Bayezid Vak'ası* (Ankara, 1961); 2nd edn as *Kanuni Süleyman Dönemi Taht Kavgaları* (Istanbul, 1997).

26 Colin Imber, 'Four letters of Ebu's-su'ud', *Arab Historical Review for Ottoman Studies*, 15/16 (1997), 177–83.

27 Colin Imber, 'The legend of Osman Gazi'.

28 Konrad Dilger, *Untersuchungen zur Geschichte des Osmanischen Hofzeremoniells im 15. und 16. Jahrhundert* (Munich, 1967) was the first to demonstrate that this work contains material which patently belongs to a period after the reign of Mehmed II.

29 E.J.W. Gibb, *A History of Ottoman Poetry* III (London, 1904, repr. 1965), 130–2, VI (1909, repr. 1963), 152–4.

30 Nicolas Vatin, 'Remarques sur l'oral et l'écrit dans l'administration ottomane au XVIe siècle', in Nicolas Vatin (ed.), *Oral et Écrit dans le Monde Turco-Ottoman* (Aix-en-Provence, 1996), 143–54.

31 Barbara Flemming, 'The reign of Murad II: a survey', *Anatolica*, XX (1994), 249–67.

32 Colin Imber, *Ebu's-su'ud: the Islamic Legal Tradition* (Edinburgh, 1997), ch. 4.

33 Nicolas Vatin, 'Aux origines du pèlerinage à Eyüp des sultans ottomans', *Turcica*, XXVII (1995), 91–9.

34 P. Wittek, 'Ayvansaray: un sanctuaire privé de son héros', *Annuaire de l'Institut de Philologie et d'Histoire Orientales et Slaves XI = Mélanges Henri Grégoire III*, Brussels (1951), 505–26; repr. Paul Wittek, ed. V.L. Ménage, *La Formation de l'Empire Ottoman* (London, 1982), v.

35 Konrad Dilger, *Untersuchungen*, provides an account of this process.

36 E.J.W. Gibb, *A History of Ottoman Poetry*, III, 151–5; VI, 157–61.

37 Gilles Veinstein, 'L'hivernage en campagne, talon d'Achille du système

militaire ottoman classique', *Studia Islamica*, LXVIII (1983), 109–48; repr. G. Veinstein, *État et Société dans l'Empire Ottoman, XVIe-XVIIIe Siècles* (Aldershot, 1994), V.

38 The following section summarises Colin Imber, 'The Ottoman dynastic myth', *Turcica*, XIX (1987), 7–27; repr. in Colin Imber, *Studies*, 305–22.

39 Colin Imber, 'What does *ghazi* actually mean?', in Ç. Balım-Harding and C. Imber, *The Balance of Truth: Essays in Honour of Professor Geoffrey Lewis* (Istanbul, 2000), 165–78.

40 Paul Wittek, 'Der Stammbaum der Osmanen', *Der Islam*, 14 (1925), 94–100.

41 Barbara Flemming, 'Political genealogies in the sixteenth century', *Osmanlı Araştırmaları*, VII–VIII (1987), 123–37.

42 Gülru Necipoğlu, 'Süleyman the Magnificent and the representation of power in the context of Ottoman-Hapsburg-Papal rivalry' in H. İnalcık and C. Kafadar (eds), *Süleyman the Second*, 161–94.

43 Anton C. Schaendlinger and Claudia Römer, *Die Schreiben Süleyman des Prächtigen an Karl V, Ferdinand I und Maximilien II* (Vienna, 1983), 11–18; Stéphane Yérasimos, *La Fondation de Constantinople et de Sainte Sophie* (Paris, 1990), 221.

44 Colin Imber, *Ebu's-su'ud*, ch. 3.

45 Markus Köhbach, 'Çasar oder Imperator? Zur Titulatur der römischen Kaiser durch die Osmanen nach dem Vertrag von Zsitva-Torok', *Wiener Zeitschrift für die Kunde des Morgenlandes*, 82 (1992), 223–34.

46 In his treatise on the Ottoman Caliphate, the former Grand Vizier, Lutfi Pasha, tried to prove that descent from the Quraish was not a necessary condition for the office of Caliph. H.A.R. Gibb, 'Lutfi Pasha and the Ottoman Caliphate', *Oriens*, 15 (1962), 287–95.

47 Colin Imber, *Ebu's-su'ud*, ch. 4.

3 Recruitment (pp. 128–42)

1 Colin Imber, 'The legend of Osman Gazi', in Elizabeth A. Zachariadou (ed.), *The Ottoman Emirate (1300–1389)* (Rethymnon, 1993), 67–76.

2 Colin Imber, 'Süleyman Pasha', *Encyclopaedia of Islam*, 9 (Leiden, 1997).

3 V. Demetriades, 'The tomb of Gazi Evrenos Bey at Yenitsa and its inscription', *Bulletin of the School of Oriental and African Studies*, 32 (1976), 328–32; V. Demetriades, 'Problems of land-owning and population in the area of Gazi Evrenos Bey's Wakf', *Balkan Studies*, 22 (1981), 43–57; V. Demetriades, 'Some thoughts on the origins of the devşirme in Elizabeth A. Zachariadou (ed.), *The Ottoman Emirate*, 23–34.

4   F. Babinger, 'Beiträge zur Geschichte des Geschlechtes der Malqoč-ogh-
    lus', *Annali. Istituto Orientale Universitario di Napoli*, n.s 1 (1940), 117–35.

5   F. Taeschner and P. Wittek, 'Die Vezirfamilie der Ğandarlyzade (14/15.
    Jahrhundert) und ihre Denkmäler', *Der Islam*, 18 (1929), 60–115.

6   S. Vryonis, 'Seljuk gulams and Ottoman devşirme', *Der Islam*, 41 (1965),
    224–52.

7   For example, see Elizabeth A. Zachariadou, 'Les "janissaires" de l'em-
    pereur byzantin', in Aldo Gallotta (ed.), *Studia Turcologica Memoriae Alexii
    Bombacci Dicata* (Naples, 1982), 591–7.

8   J. Schacht, *An Introduction to Islamic Law* (Oxford, 1964).

9   J.A.B. Palmer, 'The origin of the Janissaries', *Bulletin of the John Rylands
    Library*, 35 (1952–3), 448–81.

10 For these troops, see Chapter 7.

11 For the best account of this institution, see V.L. Ménage, 'Devshirme',
    Encyclopaedia of Islam, 2 (1965).

12 V.L. Ménage, 'Sidelights on the devshirme from Idris and Sa'duddin',
    Bulletin of the School of Oriental and African Studies, 18 (1956), 181–3; V.L.
    Ménage, 'Some notes on the devshirme', *Bulletin of the School of Oriental and
    African Studies*, 29 (1966), 64–78; R.C. Repp, 'A further note on the
    devshirme', *Bulletin of the School of Oriental and African Studies*, 31 (1968), 137–9.

13 S. Vryonis, 'Isidore Glabas and the Turkish devshirme', *Speculum*, XXXI
    (1956), 433–43.

14 V. Demetriades, 'Some thoughts on the origins'.

15 J.A.B. Palmer, 'The origins'.

16 İ.H. Uzunçarşılı, *Kapukulu Ocakları*, 1 (Ankara, 1943), 27–8.

17 I thank Dr Recep Çiğdem for showing me this entry in the register.

18 Noel Malcolm, *Bosnia: A Short History* (London, 1996), ch. 6.

19 On areas of collection, see also S. Vryonis, 'Seljuk gulams'.

20 For the Palace Schools, see Chapter 4.

21 Colin Imber, 'The Navy of Süleyman the Magnificent', *Archivum
    Ottomanicum*, VI (1980), 211–82; repr. Colin Imber, *Studies in Ottoman
    History and Law* (Istanbul, 1996), 1–70.

22 İdris Bostan, *Osmanlı Bahriye Teşkilatı: XVII. Yüzyılda Tersane-i Amire*
    (Ankara, 1992).

23 İ.H. Uzunçarşılı, *Kapukulu Ocakları*, 134.

24 For example, L. Fekete, *Die Siyaqat-Schrift in der Türkischen Finanzverwaltung*
    (Budapest, 1955), 146–63.

25 Gabor Ágoston, 'Habsburgs and Ottomans: defence, military change
    and shifts in power', *Turkish Studies Association Bulletin*, 22/1 (1998), 126–41.

26 For these changes in the composition of the army, see Chapter 7.

4 The Palace (pp. 143–76)

1   Clive Foss, 'Byzantine Malagina and the Lower Sangarius', *Anatolian Studies*, XL (1990), 161–84.

2   Kate Fleet, 'The Treaty of 1387 between Murad I and the Genoese', *Bulletin of the School of Oriental and African Studies*, LVI (1993), 13–33.

3   Rifat Osman (ed. S. Ünver), *Edirne Sarayı* (Ankara,1957).

4   This is the Topkapı Palace. For an account of the building history of the Palace, its ceremonial, and the structure of the Court, see Gülru Necipoğlu, *Architecture, Ceremonial and Power: The Topkapı Palace in the Fifteenth and Sixteenth Centuries* (Cambridge, Mass., 1991). See also Ahmet Ertuğ, Filiz Çağman, *Topkapı: The Palace of Felicity* (Istanbul, n.d.).

5   On Melek Ahmed Pasha, see Robert Dankoff (intro. Rhoads Murphey), *The Intimate Life of an Ottoman Statesman: Melek Ahmed Pasha (1588–1662)* (Albany, 1991).

6   Nicolas Vatin, *L'Ordre de St. Jean-de-Jérusalem, l'Empire Ottoman et la Méditerranée Orientale entre les Deux Sièges de Rhodes, 1480-1522* (Paris, 1994), 173.

7   Katib Çelebi, *Tuhfat al-Kibar fi Asfar al-Bihar* (Istanbul, 1911), 125.

8   On the Imperial Council in the sixteenth century, see Josef Matuz, *Das Kanzleiwesen Sultan Süleymans des Prächtigen* (Wiesbaden, 1974), 10–81.

9   Josef Matuz, *Das Kanzleiwesen*, 15.

10   Colin Imber, 'Molla Kabid', *Encyclopaedia of Islam*, 7 (Leiden, 1993).

11   Klaus Röhrborn, *Untersuchungen zur Osmanischen Verwaltungsgeschichte* (Berlin, 1973), 13–15; Klaus Röhrborn, 'Die Emanzipation der Finanzbürokratie im Osmanischen Reiche (Ende 16. Jahrhunderts)', *Zeitschrift der Deutschen Morgenländischen Gesellschaft*, 122 (1972), 118–39.

12   Klaus Röhrborn, 'Die Emanzipation'.

13   Paul Wittek, 'Notes sur la *tughra* ottomane', *Byzantion*, XVIII (1948), 311–34; *Byzantion*, XX (1950), 267–93; repr. Paul Wittek (ed. V.L. Ménage), *La Formation de l'Empire Ottoman* (London, 1982), VI.

14   Suha Umur, *Osmanlı Padişah Tuğraları* (Istanbul, 1980), pl. 60.

15   F. Taeschner and Paul Wittek, 'Die Vezirfamilie der Ğandarlyzade (14/15. Jahrhundert) und ihre Denkmäler', *Der Islam*, 18 (1929), 60–115; V.L. Ménage, 'Djandarli'. *Encyclopaedia of Islam*, 2 (1965).

16   F. Babinger, 'Von Amurath zu Amurath: Vor- und Nachspiel der Schlacht bei Varna (1444)', *Oriens*, 3 (1950), 229–65.

17   B. Krekić, *Dubrovnik (Raguse) et le Levant au Moyen Âge* (The Hague and Paris, 1958), no. 1364.

18   F. Babinger, 'Eine Verfügung des Paläologen Chass Murads', in F. Babinger, *Aufsätze und Abhandlungen* (Munich, 1962), 344–54.

19 H. İnalcık, 'Mesih Pasha', *Encyclopaedia of Islam*, 6 (1991).
20 H. Šabanović, 'Hersekzade Ahmed Pasha', *Encyclopaedia of Islam*, 3 (1971).
21 Hedda Reindl, *Männer um Bayezid* (Berlin, 1983), 333–4.
22 Hedda Reindl, *Männer um Bayezid*, 240–61.
23 F. Babinger, 'Piri Mehmed Pasha', *Encyclopaedia of Islam*, 8 (1995)
24 J.R. Blackburn, 'Othman Pasha Özdemir-oghli', *Encyclopaedia of Islam*, 8 (1995).
25 Christine Woodhead, 'Rustem Pasha', *Encyclopaedia of Islam*, 8 (1995).
26 P. Fodor, 'Sultan, Imperial Council, Grand Vizier: the Ottoman ruling élite and the formation of the Grand Vizieral *telkhis*', *Acta Orientalia* (Budapest), 47 (1994), 67–85.
27 Robert Dankoff, *The Intimate Life*.
28 See biographical details in İ.H. Danişmend, *Osmanlı Devlet Erkanları* (İstanbul, 1971).
29 Klaus Röhrborn, 'Die Emanzipation.'
30 Christine Woodhead, 'Ottoman *inşa* and the art of letter-writing: influences on the career of the *nişancı* and prose-stylist Okçuzade (d. 1630)', *Osmanlı Araştırmaları*, VII–VIII (1998), 143–59.
31 J.H. Mordtmann [V.L. Ménage], 'Feridun Beg', *Encyclopaedia of Islam*, 2 (1965).
32 Robert Dankoff, *The Intimate Life*.
33 Douglas Howard, 'The historical development of the Ottoman Imperial Registry (*Defter-i hakani*): mid-fifteenth to mid-seventeenth centuries', *Archivum Ottomanicum*, 11 (1986), 213–30.
34 Cornell Fleischer, 'Preliminaries to the study of the Ottoman bureaucracy', *Journal of Turkish Studies*, X (1986), 135–41.
35 Josef Matuz, *Das Kanzleiwesen*.
36 Nicolas Vatin, 'L'emploi du grec comme langue diplomatique par les Ottomans (fin XVe-début XVIe siècle)' in F.Hitzel (ed.), *Istanbul et les Langues Orientales* (Paris and Istanbul, 1997), 41–7; repr. Nicolas Vatin, *Les Ottomans et l'Occident (XVe-XVIe siecles)* (İstanbul, 2001), 105–11; Julian Raby, 'Mehmed the Conqueror's Greek scriptorium', *Dumbarton Oaks Papers*, 37 (1983), 15–34.
37 Christine Woodhead, 'Ottoman *inşa*'.
38 Compare also the career of the imperial historiographer, Ta'likizade, who began work as a scribe in the entourage of Prince Murad in Manisa. When the Prince ascended the throne as Murad III in 1574, Ta'likizade followed him to Istanbul, and enrolled in the Clerks of the Imperial Council. Christine Woodhead, 'From scribe to littérateur: the career of a sixteenth-century Ottoman *katib*', *British Society for Middle East Studies Bulletin*, 9 (1982), 55–74.

39 Christine Woodhead, 'Research on the Ottoman scribal service', in Christa Fragner and Klaus Schwarz (eds,), *Festgabe an Josef Matuz* (Berlin, 1992), 311–28; Cornell Fleischer, 'Between the lines: realities of scribal life in the sixteenth century', in C. Heywood and C. Imber (eds.), *Studies in Ottoman History in Honour of Professor V.L. Ménage* (Istanbul, 1994), 45–62.

40 Feridun Emecen, 'Ali'nin Aynı: XVII yuzyıl başlarında Osmanlı bürokrasisinde katip rumuzları', *Tarih Dergisi*, 35 (1984–94), 131–49.

41 Osmanlı Arşivi Daire Başkanlığı, *6 Numaralı Mühimme Defteri (972/1564–5)* (Ankara, 1995), no. 248.

42 Josef Matuz, *Das Kanzleiwesen*; Jan Reychman and Ananiasz Zajaczkowski, *Handbook of Ottoman Turkish Diplomatics* (The Hague and Paris, 1968); V.L. Ménage, 'On the constituent elements of certain sixteenth-century Ottoman documents', *Bulletin of the School of Oriental and African Studies*, 48 (1985), 283–304.

43 Cengiz Orhonlu, *Osmanlı Tarihine Aid Belgeler: Telhisler (1597–1607)* (Istanbul, 1970), no. 128.

44 Uriel Heyd, *Ottoman Documents on Palestine*, (Oxford, 1960), 3–31. William S. Peachy, 'Register of copies or collections of drafts? The case of four *mühimme* defters from the Archives of the Prime Ministry in Istanbul', *The Turkish Studies Association Bulletin*, 10 (1986), 79–85.

45 Suraiya Faroqhi, 'Das Grosswesir-telhis: eine aktenkundliche Studie', *Der Islam*, 45 (1969), 96–110.

46 Cengiz Orhonlu, *Telhisler*, no. 128.

5 The Provinces (pp. 177–215)

1 Uruj b. 'Adil (ed. F. Babinger), *Tevarih-i Al-i Osman* (Hanover, 1925), 12.

2 Petra Kappert, *Die Osmanischen Prinzen und ihre Residenz Amasya im 15. und 16. Jahrhundert* (Leiden, 1976).

3 Géza Dávid, 'Administration in Ottoman Europe' in I. Metin Kunt and Christine Woodhead (eds), *Süleyman the Magnificent and his Age* (London, 1995), 71–90.

4 Colin Imber, 'The navy of Süleyman the Magnificent', *Archivum Ottomanicum*, VI (1980), 211–82; repr. Colin Imber, *Studies in Ottoman History and Law* (Istanbul, 1996), 1–70.

5 Géza Dávid, 'Administrative strategies in western Hungary', in C. Heywood and C. Imber, *Studies in Ottoman History in Honour of Professor V.L. Ménage* (Istanbul, 1994), 31–43; repr. Géza Dávid, *Studies in Demographic and Administrative History in Ottoman Hungary* (Istanbul, 1997), 89–102.

6   G. Valentini, 'Dell'amministrazione Veneta in Albania' in A. Pertusi (ed.), *Venezia e il Levante fino al Secolo XV*, vol. 1 (Florence, 1973), 843–910.

7   Kenneth M. Setton, *The Papacy and the Levant (1204–1571)*, vol. II (Philadelphia, 1978), 219.

8   Tursun Bey (ed. A.M. Tulum), *Tarih-i Ebü'l-Feth* (Istanbul, 1977), 108.

9   For lists of provinces of the Empire, especially in the eighteenth and nineteenth centuries, see Andreas Birken, *Die Provinzen des Osmanischen Reiches* (Wiesbaden, 1976).

10 I. Metin Kunt, *The Sultan's Servants: The Transformation of Ottoman Provincial Government, 1550–1650* (New York, 1983), 26–8.

11 I.M. Kunt, *The Sultan's Servants*, 14–16.

12 M.M. İlhan, 'Some notes on the settlement and population of the Sancak of Amid according to the 1518 Ottoman cadastral survey', *Tarih Araştırmaları Dergisi*, XIV (1981–2), 415–36.

13 Halil İnalcık, 'Ottoman methods of conquest', *Studia Islamica*, II (1954), 104–29; repr. in Halil İnalcık, *The Ottoman Empire: Conquest, Organisation and Economy* (London, 1998), I.

14 Elizabeth A. Zachariadou, 'Lauro Quirini and the Ottoman sandjaks (c 1430)', *Journal of Turkish Studies*, 11 (1987), 239–47.

15 On the marcher lords, see I. Mélikoff, 'Ewrenos Oghullari', *Encyclopaedia of Islam*, 2 (Leiden, 1965); F. Babinger, 'Mikhal-oghlu', *Encyclopaedia of Islam*, 7 (1993).

16 V.L. Ménage, 'On the recensions of Uruj's History of the Ottomans', *Bulletin of the School of Oriental and African Studies*, XXX (1967), 314–22 shows how the story was spliced into the chronicler's narrative.

17 V. Demetriades, 'The tomb of Ghazi Evrenos Bey at Yenitsa and its inscriptions', *Bulletin of the School of Oriental and African Studies*, XXXIX (1976), 328–32.

18 Elizabeth A. Zachariadou, 'Lauro Quirini'.

19 Katib Çelebi, *Tuhfat al-Kibar fi Asfar al-Bihar* (Istanbul, 1911), 83–5.

20 Robert Dankoff, *Evliya Çelebi in Bitlis* (Leiden, 1990).

21 I. Metin Kunt, *The Sultan's Servants*, 16–26.

22 I. Metin Kunt, *The Sultan's Servants*, 23–6.

23 Klaus Röhrborn, *Untersuchungen zur Osmanischen Verwaltungsgeschichte* (Berlin, 1973), 107.

24 Colin Imber, 'Lutfi Pasha', *Encyclopaedia of Islam*, 5 (1986); Gilles Veinstein, 'Sokollu Mehmed Pasha', *Encyclopaedia of Islam*, IX (1997).

25 I. Metin Kunt, *The Sultan's Servants*, 56–67.

26 Klaus Röhrborn, *Untersuchungen*, 112–13.

27 On trust lands, see Colin Imber, *Ebu's-su'ud: the Islamic Legal Tradition* (Edinburgh, 1997), ch. 6.

28 Georg Ostrogorsky, *Pour l'Histoire de la Féodalité Byzantine* (Brussels, 1954). On the Byzantine *pronoia*, see Mark C. Bartusis, *The Late Byzantine Army: Arms and Society, 1204–1453* (Philadelphia, 1992).

29 Speros Vryonis, *The Decline of Medieval Hellenism in Asia Minor* (Berkeley, 1971), 468–70.

30 Irène Beldiceanu-Steinherr, 'Fiscalité et formes de possession de la terre arable', *Journal of the Economic and Social History of the Orient*, XIX (1976), 233–322.

31 M.M. İlhan, 'The process of Ottoman cadastral surveys during the second half of the sixteenth century', *Anuarul Institutului de Istoria și Arheologie A.D. Xenopol* (Iași) (1987), 17–25.

32 Douglas A. Howard, 'The historical development of the Ottoman Imperial Registry (*Defter-i hakanî*): mid-fifteenth to mid-seventeenth centuries', *Archivum Ottomanicum*, 11 (1986), 213–30.

33 I thank Professor V.L. Ménage for these references.

34 Tim Stanley, 'Men-at-arms, hauberks and bards: military obligations in the *Book of the Ottoman Custom*', in Ç. Balım-Harding and C. Imber (eds), *The Balance of Truth: Essays in Honour of Professor Geoffrey Lewis* (Istanbul, 2000), 331–63.

35 Fahir İz, *Eski Türk Edebiyatında Nesir* (Istanbul, 1964), 564–8.

36 Çiğdem Solas and İsmail Otar, 'The accounting system practiced in the Near East during the period 1220–1350 based on the book *Risale-i Felekiyye*', *The Accounting Historian's Journal*, 21 (1994), 117–35.

37 Text in Ö.L. Barkan, *Kanunlar* (Istanbul, 1943), I.

38 On the development of the Law Books, see Chapter 6.

39 For the development of this text, and a survey of manuscripts, see U. Heyd (ed. V.L. Ménage), *Studies in Old Ottoman Criminal Law* (Oxford, 1973), ch. 1.

40 Halil İnalcık, 'Ottoman methods of conquest', *Studia Islamica*, II (1954), 104–29; repr. Halil İnalcık, *The Ottoman Empire: Conquest, Organization and Economy* (London, 1978), I; Halil İnalcık, 'Timariotes chrétiens en Albanie au XVe siècle', *Mitteilungen des Österreichischen Staatsarchives* (Vienna), IV (1952), 120–8.

41 Irène Beldiceanu-Steinherr, 'Fiscalité'.

42 For the text and translation of a Law Book from the second half of the sixteenth century, laying out the rules for the assignment of *timars*, see Douglas A. Howard, 'Ottoman administration and the timar system: Kanunname-i Osmani Beray-i Timar Daden', *Journal of Turkish Studies*, 20 (1996), 46–125.

340 *Notes*

43 Klaus Röhrborn, *Untersuchungen*, 29–54. For the process of appointments to timars, see also Klaus Schwarz (ed. Claudia Römer), *Osmanische Sultansurkunden: Untersuchungen zur Einstellung und Besoldung Osmanischer Militärs in der Zeit Murads III* (Stuttgart, 1997), 94–117.

44 Prime Minister's Archive, Istanbul, Kamil Kepeçi, 223.

45 Ö.L. Barkan, *Kanunlar*, XXI, 79.

46 Ö.L. Barkan, *Kanunlar*, LXIV, 234.

47 Colin Imber, *Ebu's-su'ud*, ch. 5.

48 Machiel Kiel, 'Central Greece in the Suleymanic age', in Gilles Veinstein (ed.), *Soliman le Magnifique et son Temps* (Paris, 1992), 399–424. Studies of other areas of the Empire in the mid-sixteenth century confirm Kiel's picture of population growth and prosperity.

49 Halil İnalcık, 'Military and fiscal transformation in the Ottoman Empire', *Archivum Ottomanicum*, VI (1980), 283–337.

50 Douglas A. Howard, ' 'Ayn 'Ali Efendi and the literature of Ottoman decline', *Turkish Studies Association Bulletin*, 11 (1987), 18–20.

51 Mustafa Akdağ, 'Timar rejiminin bozuluşu', *Ankara Üniversitesi Dil ve Tarih-Coğrafya Fakültesi*, 3/4 (1945), 419–31.

52 G. Veinstein, 'L'hivernage en campagne: talon d'Achille du système militaire ottoman classique', *Studia Islamica*, LXVIII (1983), 109–48; repr. Gilles Veinstein, *État et Société dans l'Empire Ottoman, XVI–XVIIIe Siècles* (London, 1994), V.

53 Mehmet Ali Ünal, *Mühimme Defteri 44* (Izmir, 1995), 155.

54 Klaus Röhrborn, 'Die Emanzipation der Finanzbürokratie im Osmanischen Reiche (Ende 16. Jahrhunderts)', *Zeitschrift der Deutschen Morgenländischen Gesellschaft*, 122 (1972), 118–39.

55 Klaus Röhrborn, *Untersuchungen*, 64–84.

56 Klaus Röhrborn, *Untersuchungen*, 140–4.

57 I. Metin Kunt, *The Sultan's Servants*, 57–75.

6 The Law (pp. 216–51)

1 See essays in Benjamin Braude and Bernard Lewis (eds), *Christians and Jews in the Ottoman Empire*, 2 vols (New York, 1982).

2 On the Jewish legal system, see Joseph R. Hacker, 'Jewish autonomy in the Ottoman Empire: its scope and limits. Jewish courts from the sixteenth to the eighteenth centuries', in Avigdor Levy (intro. and ed.), *The Jews of the Ottoman Empire* (Princeton, 1994), 153–202; Aryeh Shmuelevitz, *The Jews of the Ottoman Empire in the Late Fifteenth and Sixteenth Centuries* (Leiden, 1984).

3 R. Anhegger and Halil İnalcık, *Kanunname-i Sultani ber Muceb-i'Örf-i Osmani* (Ankara, 1956), 65–6; A. Akgündüz, *Osmanlı Kanunnameleri*, 1 (Istanbul, 1990), 406–7; French trans. N. Beldiceanu, *Les Actes des Premiers Sultans* (Paris and The Hague, 1960), 139.

4 Aryeh Shmuelevitz, *The Jews of the Ottoman Empire*, 69.

5 For a brilliant short survey of the characteristics of Islamic Law, see Norman Calder, 'Feqh', *Encyclopaedia Iranica* IX (New York, 1999). See also Baber Johansen, 'The Muslim *fiqh* as a sacred law: religion, law and ethics in a normative system': Introduction to Baber Johansen, *Contingency in a Sacred Law* (Leiden, 1999).

6 Ignác Goldziher (ed. S.M.Stern), *Muslim Studies*, 2 (London, 1967).

7 Wael B. Hallaq and others have challenged this view. For example, Wael B. Hallaq, 'From *fatwas* to *furu*': growth and change in Islamic substantive law', *Islamic Law and Society*, I (1994), 29–65. On the problem of change, see Baber Johansen, 'Legal literature and the problem of change', in Chibli Mallat (ed.), *Islam and Public Law: Classical and Contemporary Studies* (London, 1993), 29–47; repr. in Baber Johansen, *Contingency*, 446–64.

8 Baber Johansen, *The Islamic Law of Tax and Rent* (London, 1988).

9 Baber Johansen, *The Islamic Law*.

10 Baber Johansen, 'Eigentum, Familie und Obrigkeit im hanafitischen Strafrecht', *Die Welt des Islams*, XIX (1979), 1–73; repr. Baber Johansen, *Contingency*, 349–420.

11 George Makdisi, *The Rise of Colleges: Institutions of Learning in Islam and the West* (Edinburgh, 1981).

12 M. Masud, D. Powers, B. Messick, 'Muftis, fatwas and Islamic legal interpretation', in Masud, Powers, Messick (eds), *Islamic Legal Interpretation: Muftis and their Fatwas* (Cambridge, Mass., 1996), 3–32. On Ottoman fatwas, see J.R. Walsh, 'Fatwa (ii. Ottoman Empire)', *Encyclopaedia of Islam*, 2 (Leiden, 1965).

13 These incuded legal texts. See, for example, the anonymous *Kitab-i Gunya* of 1379 and the anonymous, undated *Risaletü'l-islam*. Both were clearly intended for a relatively uneducated audience. Muzaffer Akkuş (ed.), *Kitab-i Gunya* (Ankara, 1995); Şinasi Tekin, 'XIV yüzyılda yazılmış Gazilik Tarikası 'Gaziliğin Yolları' adlı bir eski Anadolu Türkçesi metni', *Journal of Turkish Studies*, 13 (1989), 130–204. For an analysis of the latter text, see Colin Imber, 'Fiqh for beginners: an Anatolian text on *jihad*' in G.R. Hawting, J. Mojaddedi and A. Samely (eds), *Studies in Islamic and Middle Eastern Texts and Traditions in Memory of Norman Calder* (Manchester, 2000), 137–48.

14 Michel Balivet, *Islam Mystique et Révolution Armée dans les Balkans Ottomans: Vie du Cheikh Bedreddin, le "Hallâj des Turcs" (1358/9–1416)* (Istanbul, 1995).

15 Hakkı Aydın, *Sivaslı Kemaleddin Ibn-i Hümam ve Tahriri* (Sivas, 1993).

16 A famous example is the mathematician and astronomer Ali Kushchi of Samarkand. See A. Adıvar, 'Ali al-Kushdji', *Encyclopaedia of Islam*, 1 (1960).

17 İ.H. Uzunçarşılı, *Osmanlı Devletinin İlmiye Teşkilatı* (Ankara, 1965), 244–6.

18 R.C. Repp, *The Müfti of Istanbul* (Oxford, 1986), 51.

19 R.C. Repp, *The Müfti*, 52.

20 R.C. Repp, *The Müfti*. 56.

21 Colin Imber, *Ebu's-su'ud: the Islamic Legal Tradition* (Edinburgh, 1997), 12–13.

22 Madeline C. Zilfi, 'Élite circulation in the Ottoman Empire: great mollas of the eighteenth century', *Journal of the Economic and Social History of the Orient*, 26 (1983), 237–57.

23 R.C. Jennings, 'Limitations of the judicial powers of the kadi', *Studia Islamica*, L (1979), 151–184.

24 R.C. Jennings, 'Limitations'.

25 R.C. Repp, *The Müfti*.

26 R.C. Repp, *The Müfti*, 64.

27 M. Masud, D. Powers, B. Messick (eds), *Islamic Legal Interpretation*.

28 Mustafa Akdağ, *Celali İsyanları* (Ankara, 1963), 85–108.

29 Colin Imber, *Ebu's-su'ud*, 15–18.

30 See biographical notices in İ.H. Danişmend, *Osmanlı Devlet Erkanları* (Istanbul, 1971).

31 Colin Imber, *Ebu's-su'ud*, 17.

32 Uriel Heyd, 'Some aspects of the Ottoman *fetva*', *Bulletin of the School of Oriental and African Studies*, XXXII (1969), 35–56.

33 R.C. Jennings, 'Limitations'.

34 Michel Balivet, *Islam Mystique*, 87–96.

35 V.L. Ménage, 'The English capitulations of 1580: a review article', *International Journal of Middle Eastern Studies*, 12 (1980), 373–83.

36 Colin Imber, *Ebu's-su'ud*, ch. 5.

37 Baber Johansen, *The Islamic Law*.

38 Heath W. Lowry, 'The Ottoman Liva Kanunnames contained in the Defter-i Hakani', *Osmanlı Araştırmaları*, 2 (1981), 43–74.

39 B. Cvetkova, 'L'influence exercée par certaines institutions de Byzance du moyen-âge sur le système féodal ottoman', *Byzantinobulgarica*, I (1952), 237–57.

40 On the development of this text, see Uriel Heyd (ed. V.L. Ménage), *Studies in Old Ottoman Criminal Law* (Oxford, 1973), 14–37.

41 Uriel Heyd, *Studies*, 15–17.

7 The Army (pp. 252–86)

1 Peter Schreiner, *Die Byzantinischen Kleinchroniken*, I (Vienna, 1975), no.7/4; II (1977), 231–2.

2 Machiel Kiel, 'Mevlana Neşri and the towns of medieval Bulgaria', in C. Heywood and C. Imber (eds), *Studies in Ottoman History in Honour of Professor V.L. Ménage* (Istanbul, 1994), 165–87.

3 This is the impression given by Schiltberger and by Ashikpashazade. Schiltberger was taken prisoner in the battle, while Ashikpashazade took his account from Kara Timurtashoghlu Umur Bey, who had fought in the Ottoman ranks. The 'Monk of St Denis', whose main concerns are theological rather than military, nonetheless gives a similar narrative of the course of the battle. M.L. Bellaguet (ed.), *Chronique du Religieux de St. Denis*, 2 (Paris, 1839), 504–16.

4 Gy. Kaldy-Nagy, 'The first centuries of the Ottoman military organisation', *Acta Orientalia*, XXXI (Budapest) (1977), 147–83.

5 Halil İnalcık and M. Oğuz (eds), *Gazavat-i Sultan Murad b. Mehemmed Han*, (Ankara, 1978), 65–6.

6 Gy. Kaldy-Nagy, 'The first centuries'.

7 Gy. Kaldy-Nagy, 'The first centuries'.

8 See references in H. İnalcık and M. Oğuz (eds), *Gazavat.*

9 Gy. Kaldy-Nagy, 'The first centuries'.

10 See, for example, Asparuch Velkov and Evgenij Radushev (intro. Strashimir Dimitrov), *Ottoman Garrisons on the Middle Danube* (Budapest, 1996); Claudia Römer, *Osmanische Festungsbesatzungen in Ungarn zur Zeit Murad III* (Vienna, 1995).

11 İ.H. Uzunçarşılı, *Kapukulu Ocakları*, I (Ankara, 1943), 89–90.

12 Gy. Kaldy-Nagy, 'The first centuries'.

13 Gy. Kaldy-Nagy, 'The first centuries'.

14 Osmanlı Arşivi Daire Başkanlığı, 3 *Numaralı Mühimme Defteri (966–968 / 1558–1560)* (Ankara, 1995), no. 1393.

15 Colin Heywood, 'The evolution of the Ottoman provincial law-code (sancak kanun-name): the kanun-name-i liva-i Semendire', *Turkish Studies Association Bulletin*, 15 (1991), 223–51.

16 OADB, 6 *Numaralı Mühimme Defteri (972 / 1564–1565)* (Ankara, 1995), no. 318

17 Na'ima, *Tarih-i Na'ima*, 1 (Istanbul, 1864), 133.

18 Gy. Kaldy-Nagy, 'The first centuries'.

19 Gy. Kaldy-Nagy, 'The first centuries'.

20 Gy. Kaldy-Nagy, 'The conscription of müsellem and yaya corps in 1540',

in Gy. Kaldy-Nagy (ed.), *Hungaro-Turcica: Studies in Honour of Julius Németh* (Budapest, 1978), 275–281.

21 For documents, see Ahmet Refik, *Anadolu'da Türk Aşiretleri (966–1200)* (Istanbul, 1930), nos 87, 88.

22 Gy. Kaldy-Nagy, 'The first centuries'.

23 Tim Stanley, 'Men-at-arms, hauberks and bards: military obligations in the *Book of the Ottoman Custom'*, in Ç. Balım-Harding and C. Imber (eds), *The Balance of Truth: Essays in Honour of Professor Geoffrey Lewis* (Istanbul, 2000), 331–63; Alan Williams, 'Ottoman military technology: the metallurgy of Turkish armour', in Yaacov Lev (ed.), *War and Society in the Eastern Mediterranean, 7th–15th Centuries* (Leiden 1997), 363–97.

24 Djurdjica Petrović, 'Firearms in the Balkans on the eve of and after the Ottoman conquests', in V. Parry and M. Yapp (eds), *War, Technology and Society in the Middle East* (London, 1975), 164–94.

25 Ashikpashazade, who was born in about 1400 and lived into the 1480s, comments: 'It was in the time of Sultan Mehmed [II] son of Sultan Murad that the numbers of cannon increased.' See Ashikpashazde (ed. Ali), *Tevarih*, 66

26 Uruj b. Adil (ed. F. Babinger), *Tevarih-i Al-i Osman* (Hanover, 1925), 60.

27 Jehan de Wavrin (ed. N. Iorga), *La Campagne des Croisés sur le Danube* (Paris, 1927), 35.

28 H. İnalcık and M. Oğuz (eds), *Gazavat*.

29 Uruj b. Adil, *Tevarih*, 60.

30 Colin Heywood, 'Notes on the production of fifteenth century Ottoman cannon', *Islamabad: International Symposium on Islam and Science* (1980), n.d., 58–61.

31 Kelly DeVries, 'Gunpowder weapons at the siege of Constantinople, 1453' in Yaacov Lev (ed.), *War and Society*, 343–62.

32 Mehmed Neşri (ed. F.R. Unat and M.E. Köymen), *Kitab-i Cihan-nüma*, 2 (Ankara, 1957), 818–19.

33 Nicolas Vatin, 'Le siège de Mytilène (1501)', *Turcica*, XXI–XXIII (1992), 435–54; repr. Nicolas Vatin, *Les Ottomans et l'Occident* (Istanbul, 2001), 9–29.

34 Gábor Ágoston, 'Ottoman artillery and European military technology in the fifteenth and seventeenth centuries', *Acta Orientalia* (Budapest), XLVII (1994), 15–48.

35 Gábor Ágoston, 'Ottoman artillery'.

36 Gábor Ágoston, 'Ottoman artillery'. On the Corps of Gunners, İ.H. Uzunçarşılı, *Kapıkulu Ocakları*, 2 (Ankara, 1943), 36–93

37 Colin Heywood, 'The activities of the state cannon-foundry (tophane-i

amire) at Istanbul in the early sixteenth century', *Priloza za Orijentalna Filologija*, 30 (1980), 209–17.

38 Gábor Ágoston, 'Ottoman artillery'.

39 Gábor Ágoston, 'Gunpowder for the Sultan's army in the Hungarian campaigns of the sixteenth and seventeenth centuries', *Turcica*, XXV (1993), 75–96; Turgut Işıksal, 'Gunpowder in Ottoman documents of the last half of the sixteenth century', *International Journal of Turkish Studies*, 2 (1981/2), 81–91; V.J. Parry, 'Barud', *Encyclopaedia of Islam*, 1 (Leiden, 1960).

40 On Venetian attempts to supply Uzun Hasan with cannon, see the accounts of Ramusio and Barbaro in Charles Grey (ed.), *A Narrative of Italian Travels in Persia* (London, 1873).

41 V.J. Parry, 'La manière de combattre', in V.J. Parry and M. Yapp (eds), *War, Technology and Society*, 218–56.

42 For a decree of 1551, requiring the Janissaries to practise marksmanship, see Gy. Kaldy-Nagy, 'The first centuries'.

43 V.J. Parry, 'La manière'.

44 V.J. Parry, 'Hisar', *Encyclopaedia of Islam*, 3 (1971).

45 Archbishop Benedetto, ' Leonardo Chiensis (*sic*) de Lesbo a Turcis capta epistola Papae Pio II missa', in C. Hopf, *Chroniques Gréco-Romanes* (Berlin, 1873; repr. Brussels, 1966), 359–66.

46 V.J. Parry, 'Hisar'.

47 For a plan of the fortifications of Nicosia, see Christopher Duffy, *Siege Warfare: The Fortress in the Early Modern World* (London, 1996), 195.

48 For an account of the sieges of Nicosia and Famagusta, see Sir George Hill, *A History of Cyprus*, III (Cambridge, 1948), ch. XV.

49 On the logistics of Ottoman military campaigns, see Caroline Finkel, *The Administration of Warfare: The Ottoman Military Campaigns in Hungary, 1593–1606* (Vienna, 1988); Rhoads Murphey, *Ottoman Warfare, 1500–1700* (London, 1999).

50 Christine Woodhead, *Ta'likizade's Şeh-name-i Hümayun: A History of the Ottoman Campaign into Hungary 1593–94* (Berlin, 1983), 28.

51 Gábor Ágoston, 'Habsburgs and Ottomans: military change and shifts in power', *Turkish Studies Association Bulletin*, 22 (1998), 126–41; Christopher Duffy, *Siege Warfare*, ch. 8.

52 Colin Imber, 'The reconstruction of the Ottoman fleet after the battle of Lepanto' in Colin Imber, *Studies in Ottoman History and Law* (Istanbul, 1996), 85–101.

53 V.J. Parry, 'La manière'.

54 V.J. Parry, 'La manière'.

55 Rhoads Murphey, *Ottoman Warfare*, 53–9.

56 Cf. Rycaut's comments on Ottoman gunners: 'Few of them are expert and are ill practiced in the proportions and Mathematical parts of the Gunners mystery'. He refers to Ottoman naval gunners as being 'wholly ignorant of the art'. Sir Paul Rycaut, *The Present State of the Ottoman Empire* (London, 1668; repr. New York, 1971), 200, 215.

57 On Ottoman warfare in the seventeenth century, see especially Rhoads Murphey, *Ottoman Warfare*. Dr Murphey's well-documented work largely argues against the idea of the Ottomans failing to adapt to a 'military revolution'. See also Rhoads Murphey, 'The Ottoman attitude towards the adoption of western technology' in *Contributions à l'Histoire Sociale et Économique de l'Empire Ottoman* (Louvain, 1981), 287–98.

8 The Fleet (pp. 287–317)

1 Cf. Kemalpashazade's words to Selim I: 'My Sultan, you are resident in a city whose benefactor is the sea. When the sea is not secure, no ship can come, and when no ship comes, Istanbul cannot flourish.' Rudolf Tschudi (ed. and trans.), *Das Asafname des Lutfi Pascha* (Berlin, 1910), 32.

2 S. Soucek, 'Certain types of ship in Ottoman Turkish terminology', *Turcica*, VII (1975), 233–49.

3 J.F. Guilmartin, *Gunpowder and Galleys: Changing Technology and Mediterranean Warfare at Sea in the Sixteenth Century* (Cambridge, 1974), 296.

4 Katib Chelebi, *Tuhfat al-Kibar fi Asfar al-Bihar* (Istanbul, 1911), 156.

5 J.F. Guilmartin, *Gunpowder*, 226–8.

6 Colin Imber, 'The navy of Süleyman the Magnificent', *Archivum Ottomanicum*, VI (1980), 211–82; repr. Colin Imber, *Studies in Ottoman History and Law* (Istanbul, 1996), 1–69.

7 Katib Chelebi, *Tuhfat*, 153.

8 J.F. Guilmartin, *Gunpowder*, 233.

9 Sir George Hill, *A History of Cyprus*, III (Cambridge, 1948), 925.

10 Colin Imber, 'The reconstruction of the Ottoman fleet after the battle of Lepanto, 1571–1572' in Colin Imber, *Studies*, 85–101.

11 Katib Chelebi, *Tuhfat*, 152.

12 Katib Chelebi, *Tuhfat*, 13.

13 Katib Chelebi, *Tuhfat*, 18.

14 İ.H. Uzunçarşılı, *Merkez ve Bahriye Teşkilatı* (Ankara, 1948), 512–13.

15 Pantero Pantera, *L'Armate Navale*, 1 (Rome, 1614), 43.

16 C.R. Markham (trans.), *Narrative of the Embassy of Ruy Gonzalez de Clavijo to the Court of Timour at Samarkand* (London, 1859), 28.

17 Halil İnalcık, 'Gelibolu', *Encyclopaedia of Islam*, 2 (Leiden, 1965).
18 Fevzi Kurtoğlu, *Gelibolu ve Yöresi Tarihi* (İstanbul, 1938), 51–7.
19 Colin Imber, 'The navy'.
20 Ö.L. Barkan, *Kanunlar* (İstanbul, 1943), 241–2.
21 R. Tschudi (ed.), *Das Asafname*, 32.
22 İdris Bostan, *Osmanlı Bahriye Teşkilatı: XVII Yüzyılda Tersane-i Amire* (Ankara, 1992), 8.
23 Colin Imber, 'The navy'.
24 Colin Imber, 'The navy'.
25 İdris Bostan, *Osmanlı*, 66–78.
26 Colin Imber, 'The navy'. On the Basra arsenal, see S. Özbaran, 'The Ottoman Turks and the Portuguese in the Persian Gulf, 1534–1581', *Journal of Asian History*, 6 (1972), 45–87; repr. S. Özbaran, *The Ottoman Response to European Expansion* (İstanbul, 1994), 119–57.
27 Colin Imber, 'The reconstruction'.
28 Colin Imber, 'The navy'.
29 İdris Bostan, *Osmanlı*, 114–15.
30 Colin Imber, 'The navy'.
31 İdris Bostan, *Osmanlı*, 154–62.
32 Colin Imber, 'The navy'.
33 Katib Chelebi, *Tuhfat*, 155.
34 İdris Bostan, *Osmanlı*, 125–6.
35 Colin Imber, 'The navy'; Colin Imber, 'The reconstruction'.
36 İdris Bostan, *Osmanlı*.
37 Katib Chelebi, *Tuhfat*, 157.
38 İdris Bostan, *Osmanlı*, 133.
39 For a chronological list of the Kapudan Pashas, with biographical details, see İ.H. Danişmend, *Osmanlı Devlet Erkanı* (İstanbul, 1971).
40 Colin Imber, 'The navy'.
41 Katib Chelebi, *Tuhfat*, 141.
42 Katib Chelebi, *Tuhfat*, 159.
43 Colin Imber, 'The reconstruction'.
44 Katib Chelebi, *Tuhfat*, 140–2.
45 Colin Imber, 'The navy'.
46 Ayn Ali Efendi, *Kavanin-i Al-i Osman der Hulasa-i Mezamin-i Defter-i Divan* (İstanbul, 1863; repr. İstanbul, 1979), 20–1.
47 Katib Chelebi, *Tuhfat*, 147.
48 Piri Reis, *Kitab-i Bahriye*, 700.
49 Colin Imber, 'The navy'.
50 Colin Imber, 'The navy'.

51 Bekir Kütükoğlu, *Osmanli-İran Siyasi Münasebetleri, 1578–90* (Istanbul, 1962), 100.
52 İ.H. Uzunçarşılı, *Merkez*, 409 n.5.
53 Fevzi Kurtoğlu, *Gelibolu*, 51–7.
54 Colin Imber, 'The navy'.
55 İdris Bostan, *Osmanlı*, 51–64.
56 İ.H. Uzunçarşlı, *Merkez*, 409.
57 İdris Bostan, *Osmanlı*, 51–64.
58 Katib Chelebi, *Tuhfat*, 153.
59 Colin Imber, 'The navy'.
60 İdris Bostan, *Osmanlı*, 225–6.
61 Colin Imber, 'The costs of naval warfare: the accounts of Hayreddin Barbarossa's Herceg Novi campaign in 1539', *Archivum Ottomanicum* (1972), 204–16; repr. in Colin Imber, *Studies*, 71–84.
62 Katib Chelebi, *Tuhfat*, 22.
63 İdris Bostan, *Osmanlı*, 187.
64 Rudolf Tschudi (ed.), *Das Asafname*, 42–3.
65 İdris Bostan, *Osmanlı*, 188.
66 Colin Imber, 'The navy'.
67 Colin Imber, 'The navy'.
68 İdris Bostan, *Osmanlı*, 191–200.
69 İdris Bostan, *Osmanlı*, 204.
70 On punishment by the galleys, see U. Heyd (ed. V.L. Ménage), *Studies in Old Ottoman Criminal Law* (Oxford, 1973), 304–7; M. Ipşirli, 'XVI. asrın ikinci yarısında kürek cezas ile ilgili hükümler', *Tarih Enstitüsü Dergisi*, 12 (1982), 204–48.
71 Colin Imber, 'The reconstruction'.
72 İdris Bostan, *Osmanlı*, 218.
73 İdris Bostan, *Osmanlı*, 213–18.
74 Colin Imber, 'The reconstruction'.
75 Colin Imber, 'The navy'.
76 Colin Imber, 'The reconstruction'.
77 Ayn Ali Efendi, *Kavanin*, 69
78 Ayn Ali Efendi, *Kavanin*, 45–6.
79 İdris Bostan, *Osmanlı*, 235–41.
80 A.H. De Groot, 'The Ottoman Mediterranean since Lepanto (October 7th, 1571). Naval warfare during the seventeenth and eighteenth centuries', *Anatolica*, 20 (1994), 269–93.
81 Katib Chelebi, *Tuhfat*, 153.
82 Katib Chelebi, *Tuhfat*, 152–3.

83 İdris Bostan, *Osmanlı*, 259.
84 Colin Imber, 'The costs'.
85 Colin Imber, 'The navy'.
86 İdris Bostan, *Osmanlı*, 249.
87 J.F. Guilmartin, *Gunpowder*, 76–7.
88 Katib Chelebi, *Tuhfat*, 161.
89 Colin Imber, 'The navy'.
90 R. Tschudi (ed.), *Das Asafname*, 34.
91 Katib Chelebi, *Tuhfat*, 100.
92 Katib Chelebi, *Tuhfat*, 161.
93 Katib Chelebi, *Tuhfat*, 106–7.
94 Victor Ostapchuk, 'Five documents from the Topkapı Palace Archive on the Ottoman defence of the Black Sea against the Cossacks', *Journal of Turkish Studies*, II (1987), 49–104
95 A.H. De Groot, 'The Ottoman Mediterranean'.
96 J.F. Guilmartin, *Gunpowder*, 273.
97 Katib Chelebi, *Tuhfat*, 125.
98 Katib Chelebi, *Tuhfat*, 150.

Glossary

Note: for an extensive listing of Ottoman technical terms and titles, see Gustav Bayerle, *Pashas, Begs and Effendis: a Dictionary of Titles and Terms in the Ottoman Empire* (Istanbul, 1997).

Agha: 'master'; title given to the commander of the Janissary (*q.v.*) Corps and to other dignitaries

Akche: a silver coin, the standard Ottoman unit of account

Akkoyunlu: 'those of the White Sheep'; a confederation of Turcoman tribes which, under Uzun Hasan (1466–78) and Yakub (1478–90), established an Empire in eastern Anatolia, Iran and Iraq

Anatolia: (1) as a general term, Asia Minor, the area roughly corresponding with modern Turkey; (2) the Ottoman province of Anatolia (Ottoman: *Anadolu*) in western Turkey, with the Aegean and the Sea of Marmara forming its western border

Arquebus: a portable firearm

Azab: 'bachelor'; (1) an infantryman levied in Anatolia (*q.v.*) or Rumelia (*q.v.*), for service in a fortress or in the army; (2) a seaman, resident in Istanbul or Gallipoli, serving in a galley (*q.v.*) under a galley captain

Bargia: a type of small galleon used in the Mediterranean, primarily as a cargo vessel

Basilisk: the largest category of cannon

Boza: a drink made from fermented millet

Candidate (Ottoman: *mülazim*): a candidate for a post in the legal and learned professions

Chancellor (Ottoman: *nishanji*): the head of the sultan's scribal service, with a seat on the Imperial Council (*q.v.*)

Chief Mufti (Ottoman: *sheykhulislam, müfti el-enam*): the Mufti (*q.v*) of Istanbul, from the sixteenth century the highest legal and religious authority in the Ottoman Empire

Cocca: a type of small galleon used in the fourteenth and fifteenth centuries as a warship and as a merchant vessel

Collection (Ottoman: *devshirme*): the levy of Christian lads for service, after conversion to Islam, in the Janissary (*q.v.*) Corps, or in the Palace

College (Ottoman: *medrese*): a college for instruction in Law and the other Islamic Religious Sciences

Culverin: a type of cannon, long in proportion to its bore

Dovija: an officer of the Raiders (*q.v.*)

Emin: 'commissioner'; in the naval arsenal, the official charged with the finances and administration of the dockyard

Exemptee (Ottoman: *müsellem*): one of a class of men holding land in Rumelia (*q.v.*) and Anatolia (*q.v.*), in return for performing unskilled tasks, especially for the armed forces, or providing the maintenance for such a labourer. In origin, probably a cavalry force.

Fatwa: a legal opinion in answer to a question, issued by a competent authority

Footman (Ottoman: *yaya*): one of a class of men holding land in Rumelia (*q.v.*) and Anatolia (*q.v.*), in return for providing unskilled labour, especially for the armed forces, or providing the maintenance for such a man. In origin, probably an infantry force

Galleass: a heavy galley (*q.v.*), capable of firing broadsides

Galley: an oared fighting ship, firing cannon from the prow, with, on average, 25 benches on each side, with three oarsmen to a bench

Governor-General (Ottoman: *beylerbeyi*): a governor of a province

Grand Vizier (Ottoman: *sadr-i a'zam*): the chief vizier (*q.v.*) and president of the Imperial Council (*q.v.*)

Gureba: 'strangers'; a member of the Gureba of the Porte. The Gureba of the Left and Gureba of the Right formed two of the Six Cavalry Divisions (*q.v.*)

Hass: a fief worth 100 000 akches (q.v.) per year and above, allocated to the sultan, a vizier (q.v.) or provincial governor

Head Clerk (Ottoman: *reisü'l-küttab*): the chief clerk of the Imperial Council (q.v.)

Ilkhanids: the Mongol dynasty ruling in Iran from the mid-thirteenth to the mid-fourteenth century

Imam: 'leader'; (1) title of the caliph, as leader of the Muslim community; (2) a prayer leader in a mosque

Imperial Council (Ottoman: *divan-i hümayun*): the sultan's council, meeting in the Second Courtyard of the Palace under the presidency of the grand vizier

Janissary (Ottoman: *yenicheri*): a member of the Janissary Corps, a standing infantry corps, levied until the seventeenth century largely from prisoners-of-war or through the Collection (q.v.)

Judge (Ottoman: *kadi*): a legal officer presiding over a court, acting as both judge and notary, and also carrying out administrative functions in the area of his jurisdiction

Kanun: a secular law; secular law in general

Kapudan Pasha: the admiral of the Ottoman Mediterranean fleet. The title 'Pasha' (q.v.) dates from the mid-sixteenth century when the admirals began to hold the post together with the governor-generalship of the Archipelago

Kethüda: 'steward, representative'; in the naval arsenal, the officer in command of the galley (q.v.) captains

Kizilbash: 'red-head'; a follower of the Safavid (q.v.) religious order, so called from the order's distinctive red head-dress

Law Book (Ottoman: *kanunname*): a code of secular laws

Mamluks: 'things owned, slaves'; the succession of sultans, emerging from households of military slaves, who ruled Egypt and Syria between 1257 and 1517

Military class (Ottoman: *askeri*): the non-tax paying class, in receipt of fiefs or salaries from the sultan

Military Judge (Ottoman: *kadi'asker*): one of the two chief judges of the Empire, with a seat on the imperial council (q.v.)

Mufti: a religious authority qualified to issue fatwas (q.v.)

Musket: a heavy portable firearm, fired from a tripod

Müteferrika: member of a corps in the palace who acted as mounted escorts for the sultan

Pasha: a title bestowed on viziers and governors-general. Before the mid-fifteenth century, the use of this title was less well defined.

Professor (Ottoman: *müderris*): an instructor in a college, teaching law and the other Islamic religious sciences.

Raider (Ottoman: *akinji*): one of a body of soldiers settled in Rumelia (q.v.) and contractually obliged to make raids into enemy territory

Ra'iyyet (plural: *re'aya*): a tax-paying subject of the sultan

Rumelia: the European province of the Ottoman Empire, south of the Danube

Safavids: the dynasty ruling in Iran from 1501, descended and taking its name from Safi al-Din of Ardabil (d.1334), the founder of the Safavid religious order

Sanjak: 'banner'; subdivision of a Province, consisting of the *timars* (q.v) and *zeamets* (q.v.) within the sanjak boundaries

Seljuks: (1) The 'Great' Seljuks: a Turkish dynasty ruling in Iran, Iraq and Syria during the eleventh and twelfth centuries, (2) The Seljuks of Anatolia: a branch of the 'Great' Seljuk dynasty, ruling in central and eastern Anatolia (q.v.) from the late eleventh century to 1302. From the mid-twelfth century, the sultans ruled as vassals of the Ilkhanids (q.v.)

Shayka: a large, flat-bottomed rowing boat, with a shallow draught, used by the Cossacks in the Black Sea and the Ottomans on the Danube

Shi'i: a member of, pertaining to the branch of Islam that rejects the legitimacy of the first three caliphs – Abu Bakr, Umar and Uthman – and fixes the true succession to the Prophet in his son-in-law Ali and his descendants

Silahdar: 'weapons-bearer'; (1) One of the pages in attendance on the sultan; (2) a member of the Silahdars of the Porte, one of the Six Cavalry Divisions (*q.v.*)

Sipahi: 'cavalryman'; (1) a member of the Sipahis of the Porte, one of the Six Cavalry Divisions (*q.v.*); (2) a *timariot*, a cavalryman holding a timar (*q.v.*) in the provinces in return for military service

Six Cavalry Divisions (Ottoman: *alti bölük*): the six élite cavalry divisions, recruited largely from graduates of the Palace Schools, accompanying the sultan on campaign and in processions. Members of these Divisions also acted in official functions, notably as tax collectors

Solak: a member of the Janissary (*q.v.*) Corps, acting as a bodyguard of the sultan

Subashi: 'army-head'; holder of a *zeamet* (*q.v.*), often with responsibility for law and order in his district

Sunni: a member of, pertaining to, the branch of Islam that believes in the legitimacy of the first three caliphs to succeed the Prophet – Abu Bakr, Umar and Uthman

Tezkere: 'memorandum'; (1) a note written by a governor-general (*q.v.*) or other dignitary for the conferment of a timar (*q.v.*); (2) a summary of incoming correspondence for presentation to the imperial council (*q.v.*)

Timar: 'care, attention'; a military fief worth less than 20 000 akches (*q.v.*) per year, supporting a cavalryman and a specified number of armed retainers

Treasurer (Ottoman: *defterdar*): a finance officer, on the imperial council or in the provinces

Trust (Arabic: *waqf*, Ottoman: *vakf*): an endowment whose income is dedicated in perpetuity to the charitable purpose specified by its founder

Ulema (singular: *alim*): learned men; members of the learned class, educated in Islamic law and the other Islamic sciences

Ulufeji: 'stipendiary'; a member of the Ulufejis of the Porte. The

Ulufejis of the Right and Ulufejis of the Left were two of the Six Cavalry Divisions (*q.v.*)

Vizier: a minister of the sultan, exercising both political and military authority, and a member of the imperial council (*q.v.*)

Zeamet: a military fief worth 20 000 akches (*q.v.*) per year and above

Sources Quoted

Abdurrahman Pasha: 'Osmanlı kanunnameleri', *Milli Tetebbü'ler Mecmuası*, 1 (1913), 497–544.

Ahmedi: Ahmedi, 'Tevarih-i Müluk-i Al-i Osman', in Ç.N. Atsız, *Osmanlı Tarihleri* (Istanbul, 1949).

Anonymous author: ed. (Yaşar Yücel), *Kitab-i Müstetab* (Ankara, 1974).

Anonymous chronicle of 1485: Bodleian Library, Oxford, ms. Marsh 313. See V.L. Ménage, *Neshri's History of the Ottomans* (London, 1964) 11–14.

Ashikpashazade: Ashikpashazade (ed. Ali), *Tevarih-i Al-i Osman* (Istanbul, 1913–14); (trans. R. Kreutel), *Vom Hirtenzelt zur Hohen Pforte* (Graz, 1959).

Atai: Ata'i, *Hada'iq al-Haqa'iq fi Takmilat al-Shaqa'iq* (Istanbul, 1851–2).

Ayn Ali: Ayn Ali Efendi, *Kavanin-i Al-i Osman der Hulasa-i Mezamin-i Defter-i Divan* (Istanbul, 1863; repr. Istanbul, 1979).

Bassano: Luigi Bassano, *I Costumi e i Modi Particolari de la Vita de Turchi* (Rome, 1545).

Bihishti: *Tarikh-i Bihishti*, British Museum, Add ms. 7869. See Hedda Reindl, *Männer um Bayezid* (Berlin, 1983), 16–18.

Bizari: Pierre Bizari (trans. F. de Belle-Forest), *Histoire de la Guerre qui s'est Passé entre les Vénitienes et la Saincte Ligue contre les Turcs pour l'Isle de Chypre* (Paris, 1573).

Bobovi: C.G. Fisher (A.W. Fisher joint trans.), 'Topkapı Sarayı in the mid-seventeenth century: Bobovi's description', *Archivum Ottomanicum*, I (1985 [1987]), 5–81.

Bon: Ottoviano Bon (trans John Withers, ed. G. Goodwin), *The Sultan's Seraglio* (London, 1996).

Busbecq: Ogier Ghiselin de Busbecq (trans. E.S. Forster), *The Turkish Letters of Ogier Ghiselin de Busbecq* (Oxford, 1927), repr. 1968.

Cadastral survey of southern Albania: (ed. Halil İnalcik), *Suret-i Defter-i Sancak-i Arvanid* (Ankara, 1954).

Cadastral survey of Shkodër: (ed. Selami Pulaha), *Le Cadastre de l'An 1485 du Sandjak de Shkodër* (Tirana, 1974).

Campaign diary: Feridun Bey, *Munsha'at al-Salatin*, 1 (Istanbul, 1857), 584–98.

Chortasmenos: J. Bogdan, 'Ein Beitrag zur Bulgarischen und Serbischen Geschichtschreibung', *Archiv für Slavische Philologie*, XIII (1891), 481–543.

Chronology: Ç.N. Atsız, *Osmanlı Tarihine ait Takvimler* (Istanbul, 1961).

Chronology of Murad II: V.L. Ménage, 'The "Annals of Murad II" ', *Bulletin of the School of Oriental and African Studies*, XXXIX (1976), 570–84.

De la Brocquière: (trans. Galen R. Klein), *The Voyage d'Outremer by Bertrandon de la Broquière* (New York, 1988).

De Nicolay: Nicolas de Nicolay (ed. M. Gomez-Geraud and S. Yérasimos), *Dans l'Empire de Soliman le Magnifique* (Paris, 1989).

De Promontorio, Iacopo: (ed. F. Babinger), *Die Aufzeichnungen des Genuesen Iacopo de Promontorio de Campis über den Osmanstaat um 1475* (Munich, 1956).

De Wavrin: Jehan de Wavrin (ed. N. Iorga), *La Campagne des Croisés sur le Danube* (Paris, 1927).

Decree of Bayezid II: Irène Beldiceanu-Steinherr, 'En marge d'un acte concernant le pengyek et les aqinği', *Revue des Études Islamiques*, XXXVII (1969), 21–43.

Decrees of 1531–1536: M. Tayyib Gökbilgin, 'Kanuni Sultan Süleyman'ın timar ve zeamet tevcihi ile ilgili fermanlar', *Tarih Dergisi*, XVII (1967), 33–48; Irène Beldiceanu-Steinherr, 'Loi sur la transmission du timar (1536)', *Turcica*, 11 (1979), 78–102.

Decrees of the Imperial Council, 1558–1560: Osmanlı Arşivi Daire Başkanlığı, *3 Numaralı Mühimme Defteri* (Ankara, 1993).

Decrees of the Imperial Council, 1564–1565: Osmanli Arşivi Daire Başkanliği, *6 Numaralı Mühimme Defteri* (Ankara, 1995).

Dominic of Jerusalem: Domenico Hierosolimitano (trans. intro. and commentary by M.J.L. Austin, Geoffrey Lewis ed.), *Domenico's Istanbul* (Warminster, 2001.)

Doukas: Doukas (trans. H.J. Magoulias), *The Decline and Fall of Byzantium to the Ottoman Turks* (Detroit, 1975).

Doxology: P. Gautier, 'Récit inédit sur le siège de Constantinople par les Turcs (1394–1402)', _Revue des Études Byzantines_, XXIII (1965), 100–17.

Ebu's-su'ud: (ed. M.E. Düzdağ), _Şeyhülislam Ebussuud Efendi Fetvaları_ (İstanbul, 1972).

Evliya Chelebi: Evliya Çelebi, _Seyahatname_, 10 vols (İstanbul, 1896–1935).

Georgevits: Bartholomaeus Georgevits, _De Turcarum Ritu et Ceremoniis_ (Antwerp, 1544).

Geuffroy: Antoine Geuffroy, _Briefve Description de la Cour du Grant Turc_ (Paris, 1564).

Greek Short Chronicles: Peter Schreiner, _Die Byzantinischen Kleinchroniken_, 3 vols (Vienna, 1977–9).

Gregoras: Nikephoros Gregoras (ed. L. Schopen), _Byzantina Historia_, 3 vols (Bonn, 1829–55).

Holy Wars: (eds. H. İnalcık and M. Oğuz), _Gazavat-i Sultan Murad b. Mehemmed Han_ (Ankara, 1978).

Ibn Battuta: (trans. H.A.R. Gibb), _The Travels of Ibn Battuta_ (London, 1929).

Ibn Hajar: Ş. İnalcık, 'Ibn Hacer'de Osmanlılara dair haberler', _Ankara Üniversitesi Dil ve Tarih-Coğrafya Fakültesi Dergisi_, VI, 1948, 189–95.

Jelalzade: (intro. Petra Kappert), _Geschichte von Sultan Süleyman Kanunis von 1520 bis 1557 oder_ Tabakat ül-Memalik ve Derecat ül-Mesalik (Wiesbaden, 1981).

Kananos: (ed. I. Bekker), _Georgius Phrantzes. Ioannes Cananus. Ioannes Anagnostes_ (Bonn, 1836).

Kantakouzenos: John Kantakouzenos (ed. L. Schopen), _Historiae_, 3, vols (Bonn, 1828–32).

Katib Chelebi: Katib Çelebi, _Fezleke_, 2 vols (İstanbul, 1869–70); _Tuhfat al-Kibar fi Asfar al-Bihar_ (İstanbul, 1911).

Kemalpashazade: Ibn Kemal (ed. Ş. Turan), _Tevarih-i Al-i Osman_ (Ankara, 1957).

Kochi Bey: Koçi Bey (ed. A.K. Aksüt), _Koçi Bey Risalesi_ (İstanbul, 1939).

Law Book for the Inner Colleges: A. Akgündüz, _Osmanlı Kanunnamleri_, 4 (İstanbul, 1992), 665–9.

Law Book of Bayezid II: (ed. M. Arif), 'Kanunname-i Al-i Osman', _Tarih-i Osmani Encümeni Mecmuası_, supplement (1911).

Law Book for the Market of Edirne: Ö.L. Barkan, 'Suret-i Kanunname-i İhtisab-i Edirne', _Tarih Vesikaları_, 2 (1942–3), 168–77.

Law Book of Mehmed II: (ed. A. Özcan), 'Fatih'in teşkilat kanunnamesi ve nizami alem için kardeş katli meselesi', *Tarih Dergisi*, XXXIII (1982), 7–56.

Law Book of Scholars: A. Akgündüz, *Osmanlı Kanunnameleri*, 4 (Istanbul, 1992), 662–6.

Law Book of Sultan Mehmed Khan: (ed. and trans. F. Kraelitz-Greifenhorst), 'Kanunname Sultan Mehmeds des Eroberers', *Mitteilungen zur Osmanischen Geschichte*, I (1921; repr. Osnabrück, 1972), 13–49. Text and translation of criminal statutes in this Law Book and later recensions, U. Heyd (ed. V.L. Ménage), *Studies in Old Ottoman Criminal Law* (Oxford, 1973), ch. IV.

Law Books of Aleppo, Boz Ulus, Bozok, Bursa, Ergani, Gallipoli and Kütahya: Ö.L. Barkan, *Kanunlar* (Istanbul, 1943).

Laws of the Janissaries: *Kavanin-i Yeniçeriyan-i Dergah-i Ali*, in A. Akgündüz, *Osmanlı Kanunnameleri*, 9 (Istanbul, 1996), 127–367.

Leonard of Chios: 'Letter' in A. Pertusi, *La Caduta di Costantinopoli* (Milan, 1976), 120–71.

List of Provinces (1527): I. Metin Kunt, *The Sultan's Servants* (New York, 1983), 104–8.

Lutfi Pasha: (ed. and trans. Rudolf Tschudi), *Das Asafname des Lutfi Pascha* (Berlin, 1910).

Malipiero: Domenico Malipiero, *Annali Veneti* (Florence, 1843).

Manq Ali: Manq Ali, *Al-'Iqd al-Manzum fi Dhikr Afadil al-Rum* (Beirut, 1975).

Maurand: (ed. Léon Dorez), *Itinéraire de Jérome Maurand d'Antibes à Constantinople (1544)* (Paris, 1901).

Mehmed Pasha of Karaman: Karamanlı Mehmed Pasa, *Osmanlı Sultanları Tarihi*, in Ç.N. Atsız, *Osmanlı Tarihleri* (Istanbul, 1949), 323–69.

Memoranda: C. Orhonlu, *Telhisler (1597–1607)* (Istanbul, 1970).

Menavino: Giovan Antonio Menavino, *Trattato de Costumi et Vita de Turchi* (Florence, 1548).

Mihailović: Konstantin Mihailović (trans. B. Stolz, intro. and notes S. Soucek), *Memoirs of a Janissary* (Ann Arbor, 1975).

Neshri: Mehmed Neşri (ed. F.R. Unat and M.A. Köymen), *Kitab-i Cihan-nüma*, 2 vols (Ankara, 1949, 1957).

Pachymeres: George Pachymeres (ed. I. Bekker), *De Michaele et Andronico Palaeologo* (Bonn, 1835).

Palamas: (trans. Anna Philippidis-Braat), 'La captivité de Palamas chez les Turcs: dossier et commentaire', *Travaux et Mémoires*, 7 (1979).

Pechevi: Ibrahim Peçevi, *Tarih-i Peçevi* (Istanbul, 1866; repr. with intro. F.Ç. Derin and V. Çabuk; Istanbul, 1972).

Piri Reis: Piri Reis (intro. H. Alpagut, F. Kurtoğlu), *Kitab-i Bahriye* (Istanbul, 1935).

Postel: Guillaume Postel, *De la République des Turcs* (Poitiers, 1560).

Ramberti: Benedetto Ramberti, 'The Second Book of the affairs of the Turks' (trans. A.H. Lybyer), *The Government of the Ottoman Empire in the Time of Suleiman the Magnificent* (Cambridge, Mass., 1913), 239–61.

Rashid al-Din: Rashid al-Din, *Die Geschichte der Oğuzen des Rašid al-Din* (Vienna, 1969).

Register of the Court of Ankara, 1583: H. Ongan, *Ankara' nın İki Numaralı Şer'iye Sicili* (Ankara, 1974).

Rycaut: Sir Paul Rycaut, *The Present State of the Ottoman Empire* (London, 1668; repr. New York, 1971)

Schiltberger: (trans. J.B. Telfer), *The Bondage and Travels of Johann Schiltberger* (London, 1879).

Selaniki: Selaniki Mustafa (ed. M. Ipşirli), *Tarih-i Selaniki* (Istanbul, 1989).

Shukrullah: (ed. Th. Seif), 'Der Abschnitt über der Osmanen in Šükrullah's persischer Universalgeschichte', *Mitteilungen zur Osmanischen Geschichte*, II (1923–6; repr. Osnabrück, 1972), 63–128.

Spandounes: Italian version of 1513 (ed. Christiane Vilain-Gandoss), 'La cronaca italiana di Teodoro Spandugino', in C. Vilain-Gandossi, *La Méditerranée aux XIIe–XVIe Siècles* (London, 1983), III; French version, *Théodore Spandouyn Cantacasin* (ed. C.Schefer), *Petit Traicté de l'Origine des Turcqz* (Paris, 1896); recension of 1538, Theodoro Spandugino, 'De la origine deli Imperatori Ottomani', in C. Sathas (ed.), *Documents Inédits Relatifs à l'Histoire de la Grèce au Moyen-Âge*, 9 (Paris, 1890), 135–261. Partial English trans., Theodore Spandounes, trans. D. Nicol, *On the Origins of the Ottoman Emperors* (Cambridge, 1997).

Tashköprüzade: Tashköprüzade, *Al-Shaqa'iq al-Nu'maniyya* (Beirut, 1975).

Tedaldi: (ed. A.Pertusi). *La Caduta di Costantinopoli* 1 (Milan, 1976), 172–89.

Template decree: İ.H. Uzunçarşılı, *Kapukulu Ocakları*, 1 (Ankara, 1943), 92–4.

Trust Deed: İ.H. Uzunçarşılı, 'Gazi Orhan Bey'in vakfiyesi', *Belleten*, V/19 (1941), 489–514.

Tughi: (ed. Midhat Sertoğlu), 'Tuği Tarihi', *Belleten*, XI/43 (1947), 489–514.

Tursun Bey: Tursun Bey (ed. A.M. Tulum), *Tarih-i Ebü'l-Feth* (Istanbul, 1977).

Yazijioghlu: (ed. M.Th. Houtsma), *Histoire des Seldjoucides d'Asie Mineure d'après Ibn Bibi* (Leiden, 1902).

Bibliography

Note: this bibliography is not exhaustive and includes only works in English, French and German.

General Histories

Imber, C., *The Ottoman Empire, 1300–1481* (Istanbul, 1990).
İnalcık, H., *The Ottoman Empire: The Classical Age* (London, 1973).
Kreiser, K., *Der Osmanische Staat, 1300–1922* (Munich, 2001). This volume serves as a bibliographical guide.
Mantran, R. (ed.), *Histoire de l'Empire Ottoman* (Fayard, 1989).

Chronology

Alexandresca-Derscu, M.M., *La Campagne de Timur en Anatolie (1402)* (Bucharest, 1942; repr. London, 1977).
Babinger, F., *Schejch Bedreddin, der Sohn des Richters von Simaw* (Berlin and Leipzig, 1921).
Babinger, F., 'Von Amurath zu Amurath: Vor- und Nachspiel der Schlacht bei Varna (1444)', *Oriens*, 3 (1950), 229–65.
Babinger, F. (trans. R. Manheim, ed. W. Hickman), *Mehmed the Conqueror and his Time* (Princeton, 1978).
Balivet, M., *Islam Mystique et Révolution Armée dans les Balkans Ottomans: Vie de Cheikh Bedreddin, le Hallâj des Turcs (1358/59–1416)* (Istanbul, 1995).
Bayerle, G., 'The compromise at Zsitva-Torok', *Archivum Ottomanicum*, VI (1980), 5–53.
Beldiceanu-Steinherr, Irène, 'La conquête de la Bithynie maritime: étape décisive dans la fondation de l'état ottoman', in K. Belke, F. Hild, J. Koder, P.Soustal (eds), *Byzanz als Raum* (Vienna, 2000), 21–36.

Blackburn, J., 'The collapse of Ottoman authority in Yemen, 968/1560–976/1568', *Die Welt des Islams*, XIX (1979), 119–76.

Brummett, Palmira, *Ottoman Seapower and Levantine Diplomacy in the Age of Discovery* (Albany, 1994).

Cahen, C., *Pre-Ottoman Turkey* (London, 1968).

Darling, Linda, 'Contested territory: Ottoman Holy War in comparative context', *Studia Islamica*, XCI (2000), 133–69.

Dennis, G., 'The Byzantine–Turkish treaty of 1403', *Orientalia Christiana Periodica*, XXXIII, (1967), 72–88.

Eberhard, Elke, *Osmanische Polemik gegen die Safawiden im 16. Jahrhundert* (Freiburg, 1970).

Emmert, T., *Serbian Golgotha: Kosovo, 1389* (New York, 1990).

Engel, P., 'Janos Hunyadi and the peace "of Szeged"', *Acta Orientalia* (Budapest), XLVII (1994), 241–57.

Flemming, Barbara, 'The reign of Murad II: a survey', *Anatolica*, XX (1994), 249–67.

Giese, F., 'Das Problem der Entstehung des Osmanischen Reiches', *Zeitschrift für Semitistik*, 2 (1922), 246–71.

Griswold, W., *The Great Anatolian Rebellion* (Berlin, 1983).

Har-El, S., *Struggle for Domination in the Middle East: The Ottoman–Mamluk War, 1485–1491* (Leiden, 1995).

Heywood, C., 'Mustafa Čelebi, Düzme', *Encyclopaedia of Islam* (2nd edn), 7 (Leiden, 1993).

Imber, C., 'The persecution of the Ottoman Shi'ites according to the *Mühimme Defterleri*, 1565–85', *Der Islam*, 56 (1979), 245–73; repr. Colin Imber, *Studies in Ottoman History and Law* (Istanbul, 1996), 103–28.

Imber, C., 'The legend of Osman Gazi', in Elizabeth A. Zachariadou (ed.), *The Ottoman Emirate, 1300–1389* (Rethymnon, 1993), 67–76; repr. Colin Imber, *Studies*, 323–32.

Imber, C., 'What does ghazi actually mean?', in Ç. Balım-Harding and C. Imber (eds), *The Balance of Truth: Essays in Honour of Professor Geoffrey Lewis* (Istanbul, 2000), 165–78.

İnalcık, H., 'The policy of Mehmed II toward the Greek population of Istanbul and the Byzantine buildings of the city', *Dumbarton Oaks Papers*, 23/24 (1969–70), 231–49.

Jansky, H., 'Die Eroberung Syriens durch Sultan Selim I', *Mitteilungen*

zur Osmanischen Geschichte, II (1923–26; repr. Osnabrück, 1972),
169–241.

Jennings, R., 'Some thoughts on the gazi-thesis', Wiener Zeitschrift für die
Kunde des Morgenlandes, 76 (1986), 151–62.

Kafadar, C., Between Two Worlds: The Construction of the Ottoman State
(Berkeley, 1995).

Kaldy-Nagy, Gy., 'Suleimans Angriff auf Europa', Acta Orientalia
Budapest, XXVIII (1974), 163–212.

Kaldy-Nagy, Gy., The Holy War (jihad) in the first centuries of the
Ottoman Empire', Harvard Ukrainian Studies, 3/4 (1979), 462–73.

Kiel, M., 'Mevlana Neşri and the towns of medieval Bulgaria', in C.
Heywood and C. Imber (eds), Studies in Ottoman History in Honour of
Professor V.L. Ménage (Istanbul, 1994).

Kolodziejczyk, D., Ottoman–Polish Diplomatic Relations (15th–18th
Century) (Leiden, 1999).

Köprülü, M.F. (trans. G. Leiser), The Origins of the Ottoman Empire
(Albany, 1992).

Kunt, I.M., 'Ethnic-regional (cins) solidarity in the seventeenth century
Ottoman establishment', International Journal of Middle Eastern Studies,
5 (1974), 233–9.

Kütükoğlu, B., 'Les relations entre l'Empire Ottoman et l'Iran dans la
seconde moitié du XVIe siècle', Turcica, VI (1975), 128–45.

Levy, A., The Jews of the Ottoman Empire (Princeton, 1994)

Lindner, R.P., 'Stimulus and justification in early Ottoman history',
Greek Orthodox Theological Review, 27 (1982), 207–24.

Lindner, R.P., Nomads and Ottomans in Medieval Anatolia (Bloomington,
1983).

Manz, Beatrice, The Rise and Rule of Tamerlane (Cambridge, 1989).

Melville-Jones, J.R., The Siege of Constantinople, 1453: Seven Contemporary
Accounts (Amsterdam, 1972).

Ménage, V.L., 'The Islamisation of Anatolia', in Nehemia Levtzion
(ed.), Conversion to Islam (London, 1979), 52–67.

Niewöhner-Eberhard, Elke, 'Machpolitische Aspekte des
Osmanischen-Safawidischen Kampfes um Baghdad im 16/17
Jahrhundert', Turcica, VI (1975), 103–27.

Özbaran, S., The Ottoman Response to European Expansion (Istanbul,
1994).

Reinert, S., 'From Niš to Kosovo Polje: reflections on Murad I's final years', in Elizabeth A. Zachariadou, *The Ottoman Emirate*, 169–211.

Savory, R., *Iran under the Safavids* (Cambridge, 1965).

Sohrweide, H., 'Der Sieg der Safawiden in Persien und ihre Rückwirkung auf die Schiiten Anatoliens im 16. Jahrhundert', *Der Islam*, 41 (1965), 95–223.

Soucek, S., 'The rise of the Barbarossas in North Africa', *Archivum Ottomanicum*, III (1971), 238–50.

Szakály, F., 'Nándofehérvár: the beginning of the end of medieval Hungary', in G. David and P. Fodor, *Hungarian–Ottoman Military and Diplomatic Relations in the Age of Süleyman the Magnificent* (Budapest, 1994), 47–76.

Tardy, L. and Vásáry, I., 'Andrzej Taranowskis Bericht über seine Gesandtschaftsreise in der Tartarei (1569)', *Acta Orientalia* (Budapest), XXVIII (1974), 213–52.

Vatin, N. *L'Ordre de St. Jean de Jérusalem, l'Empire Ottoman et la Méditerranée entre les Deux Sièges de Rhodes (1480–1522)* (Louvain, 1994).

Vatin, N., *Sultan Djem* (Ankara, 1997).

Venzke, Margaret, 'The case of a Dulgadir–Mamluk iqta': a re-assessment of the Dulgadir principality and its position within the Ottoman–Mamluk rivalry', *Journal of the Social and Economic History of the Orient*, 43 (2000), 399–474.

Vryonis, S., *The Decline of Medieval Hellenism* (Berkeley, 1971).

Wittek, P. *The Rise of the Ottoman Empire* (London, 1938).

Woods, J., *The Aqquyunlu: Clan, Confederation, Empire* (Minneapolis, 1976).

Zachariadou, Elizabeth A., 'The conquest of Adrianople by the Turks', *Studi Veneziani*, XII (1970), 246–71.

Zachariadou, Elizabeth A., 'Manuel Palaeologus and the strife between Bayezid I and Kadi Burhan al-Din Ahmed', *Bulletin of the School of Oriental and African Studies*, XLII (1980), 471–81.

Zachariadou, Elizabeth A., 'Süleyman Çelebi in Rumili and the Ottoman chronicles', *Der Islam*, 60 (1983), 268–96.

The Dynasty

Alderson, A.D., *The Structure of the Ottoman Dynasty* (Oxford, 1956).

Babinger, F., 'Mehmed's II. Heirat mit Sitt Hatun', *Der Islam*, 29 (1950), 217–35.

Bryer, A.A.M., 'Greek historians on the Turks: the case of the first Byzantine–Ottoman marriage', in R.H.C. Davies and J.M. Wallace-Hadrill (eds), *The Writing of History in the Middle Ages* (Oxford, 1981), 471–93.

Dankoff, R., 'Marrying a Sultana: the case of Melek Ahmed Pasha', in Caesar E. Farah (ed.), *Decision Making and Change in the Ottoman Empire* (Kirksville, 1993), 169–82.

Fisher, A., 'Süleyman and his sons', in Gilles Veinstein (ed.), *Soliman le Magnifique et son Temps* (Paris, 1992), 117–26.

Fisher, A. 'The life and family of Süleyman I', in H. İnalcık and C. Kafadar (eds), *Süleyman II and his Time* (Istanbul, 1993), 1–19

Flemming, Barbara, 'Political genealogies in the sixteenth century', *Osmanlı Araştırmaları*, VII–VIII (1987), 123–37.

Gibb, H.A.R., 'Lutfi Pasha and the Ottoman Caliphate', *Oriens*, 15 (1962), 287–95.

Giese, F., 'Das Seniorat im osmanischen Herrscherhaus', *Mitteilungen zur Osmanischen Geschichte*, 2 (1923–6) (repr. Osnabrück, 1972), 248–56.

Heywood, C., 'Mustafa Çelebi, Düzme' in *Encyclopaedia of Islam* (2nd edn), 7 (Leiden, 1993).

Imber, C., 'The Ottoman dynastic myth', *Turcica*, XIX (1987), 7–27; repr. in Colin Imber, *Studies in Ottoman History and Law* (Istanbul, (1996), 305–22.

Kappert, Petra, *Die Osmanischen Prinzen und ihre Fürstenresidenz Amasya im 15. und 16. Jahrhundert* (Leiden, 1976).

Köhbach, M., 'Çasar oder Imperator? – Zur Titulatur der römischen Kaiser durch die Osmanen nach dem Vertrag von Zsitva-Torok', *Wiener Zeitschrift für die Kunde des Morgenlandes*, 82 (1992), 223–34.

Necipoğlu, Gülru, 'Süleyman the Magnificent and the representation of power in the context of Ottoman–Hapsburg–Papal rivalry', in H. İnalcık and C. Kafadar (eds), *Süleyman II*, 161–94.

Pedani, Maria P., 'Safiye's household and Venetian diplomacy', *Turcica*, 32 (2001), 9–32.

Peirce, Leslie P., 'The family as faction', in Gilles Veinstein (ed.), *Soliman le Magnifique et son Temps* (Paris, 1992), 105–16.

Peirce, Leslie P., *The Imperial Harem: Women and Sovereignty in the Ottoman Empire* (Oxford and New York, 1993).

Skilliter, S., 'Three letters from the Ottoman "Sultana" Safiye to Queen Elizabeth I', in S.M. Stern (ed.), *Documents from Islamic Chanceries* (Oxford, 1965), 119–57.

Skilliter, S. 'The letters of the Venetian "Sultana" Nur Banu and her Kira to Venice', in *Studia Turcologica Memoriae Alexii Bombaci Dicata* (Naples, 1982), 515–36.

Vatin, N., 'Macabre trafic: la destinée post-mortem du Prince-Djem', in J.-L. Bacqué-Grammont and Rémy Dor (eds), *Mélanges Offerts à Louis Bazin* (Paris, 1992), 231–9; repr. N. Vatin, *Les Ottomans et l'Occident* (Istanbul, 2001), 77–92.

Vatin, N., 'Aux origines du pèlerinage a Eyüp des Sultans ottomans', *Turcica*, XXVII (1995), 91–9.

Vatin, N., 'Remarques sur l'oral et l'écrit dans l'administration ottomane au XVIe siècle', in N. Vatin (ed.), *Oral et Écrit dans le Monde Turco-Ottoman* (Aix-en-Provence, 1996), 143–54.

Vatin, N., *Sultan Djem* (Ankara, 1997).

Wittek, P., 'Der Stammbaum der Osmanen', *Der Islam*, 14 (1925), 94–100.

Recruitment

Demetriades, V., 'Some thoughts on the origins of the devşirme', in Elizabeth A. Zachariadou (ed.), *The Ottoman Emirate (1300–1389)* (Rethymnon, 1993), 67–76.

Ménage, V.L., 'Sidelights on the devshirme from Idris and Sa'duddin', *Bulletin of the School of Oriental and African Studies*, XVIII (1956), 181–3.

Ménage, V.L., 'Some notes on the devshirme', *Bulletin of the School of Oriental and African Studies*, XXIX (1964), 64–78.

Ménage, V.L., 'Devshirme', *Encyclopaedia of Islam* (2nd edn), 2 (1965)

Palmer, J.A.B., 'The origin of the Janissaries', *Bulletin of the John Rylands Library*, 35 (1952–3), 448–81.

Papoulia, Basilike, *Ursprung und Wesen der Knabenlese im Osmanischen Reich* (Munich, 1963).

Repp, R.C., 'A further note on the devshirme', *Bulletin of the School of Oriental and African Studies*, XXXI (1968), 137–9.

Vryonis, S., 'Isidore Glabas and the Turkish devshirme', *Speculum*, XXXI (1956), 433–43.

Vryonis, S. 'Seljuk gulams and Ottoman devshirme', *Der Islam*, 41 (1965), 224–52.

Zachariadou, Elizabeth A., 'Les "janissaires" de l'empereur byzantin' in *Studia Turcologica Memoriae Alexii Bombacci Dicata* (Naples, 1982), 591–7.

The Palace

Dankoff, R. (intro. by R. Murphey), *The Intimate Life of an Ottoman Statesman: Melek Ahmed Pasha (1588–1662)* (Albany, 1991).

Ertuğ, A., Çağman, Filiz et al., *Topkapı: The Palace of Felicity* (Istanbul, n.d.)

Faroqhi, Soraya, 'Das Grosswesir-telhis: eine aktenkundliche Studie', *Der Islam*, 45 (1969), 96–110.

Fleischer, C., 'Preliminaries to the study of the Ottoman bureaucracy', *Journal of Turkish Studies*, X (1986), 135–41.

Fleischer, C., 'Between the lines: realities of scribal life in the sixteenth century', in C. Heywood and C. Imber (eds), *Studies in Ottoman History in Honour of Professor V.L. Ménage* (Istanbul, 1994), 45–62.

Fodor, P., 'Sultan, Imperial Council, Grand Vizier: the Ottoman ruling élite and the formation of the Grand Vizieral telkhis', *Acta Orientalia* (Budapest), 47 (1994), 67–85.

Foss, C., 'Byzantine Malagina and the lower Sangarius', *Anatolian Studies*, XL (1990), 161–84.

Matuz, J., *Das Kanzleiwesen Sultan Süleymans des Prächtigen* (Wiesbaden, 1974).

Ménage, V.L., 'On the constituent elements in certain sixteenth-century Ottoman documents', *Bulletin of the School of Oriental and African Studies*, XLVIII (1985), 283–304.

Miller, Barnette, *Beyond the Sublime Porte* (New Haven, 1931, repr. New York, 1970).

Miller Barnette, *The Palace School of Muhammad the Conqueror* (Cambridge, Mass., 1941; repr. NewYork: 1973).

Necipoğlu, Gülru, *Architecture, Ceremonial and Power: The Topkapı Palace in the Fifteenth and Sixteenth Centuries* (Cambridge, Mass., 1991).

Raby, J., 'Mehmed the Conqueror's Greek scriptorium', *Dumbarton Oaks Papers*, 37 (1983), 15–34.

Reindl, Hedda, *Männer um Bayezid* (Berlin, 1983).

Reychman, J. and Zajaczkowski, A., *Handbook of Ottoman Turkish Diplomatics* (The Hague and Paris, 1968).

Röhrborn, K., 'Die Emanzipation der Finanzbürokratie im osmanischen Reiche (Ende 16. Jahrhunderts)', *Zeitschrift der Deutschen Morgenländischen Gesellschaft*, 122 (1972), 118–39.

Röhrborn, K., *Untersuchungen zur Islamischen Verwaltungsgeschichte* (Berlin, 1973).

Taeschner, F. and Wittek, P., 'Die Vezirfamilie der Ğandarlyzade (14/15 Jahrhundert) und ihre Denkmäler', *Der Islam*, 18 (1929), 60–115.

Vatin, N., 'L'emploi du Grec comme langue diplomatique par les Ottomans (fin XVe-début XVIe siècle)' in F. Hitzel (ed.), *Istanbul et les Langues Orientales* (Paris and Istanbul, 1997), 41–7; repr. in N.Vatin, *Les Ottomans et l'Occident (XVe–XVIe siècles)* (Istanbul, 2001), 105–11.

Wittek, P., 'Notes sur la *tughra* ottomane', *Byzantion*, XVIII (1948), 311–34; *Byzantion*, XX (1950), 267–93; repr. in P. Wittek (ed. V.L. Ménage), *La Formation de l'Empire Ottoman* (London, 1982), VI.

Woodhead, Christine, 'From scribe to littérateur: the career of a sixteenth-century Ottoman katib', *British Society for Middle East Studies Bulletin*, 9 (1982), 55–74.

Woodhead, Christine, 'Research on the Ottoman scribal service', in Christa Fragner and Klaus Schwarz (eds), *Festgabe an Josef Matuz* (Berlin, 1992), 311–28.

Woodhead, Christine, 'Ottoman inşa and the art of letter-writing: influences on the career of the nişancı and prose-stylist Okçuzade (d. 1630)', *Osmanlı Araştırmaları*, VII–VIII (1998), 143–59.

The Provinces

Beldiceanu, N., 'Recherches sur la réforme foncière de Mehmed II', *Acta Historica*, 4 (1965), 27–39.

Beldiceanu, N., *Le Timar dans l'État Ottoman (début XIVe siècle–début XVIe Siècle)* (Wiesbaden, 1980).

Beldiceanu, N. and Beldiceanu-Steinherr, I., *Recherches sur la Province de Karaman au XVIe Siècle* (Leiden, 1968).

Beldiceanu-Steinherr, I., 'Fiscalité et formes de possession de terre arable', *Journal of the Economic and Social History of the Orient*, XIX (1976), 233–322.

Birken, A., *Die Provinzen des Osmanischen Reiches* (Wiesbaden, 1976).

Dankoff, R., *Evliya Çelebi in Bitlis* (Leiden, 1990).

David, G., 'Administrative strategies in western Hungary', in C. Heywood and C. Imber (eds), *Studies in Ottoman History in Honour of Professor V.L. Ménage* (Istanbul, 1994), 31–43; repr. Géza David, *Studies in Demographic and Administrative History in Ottoman Hungary* (Istanbul, 1997), 89–102.

David, G., 'Administration in Ottoman Europe', in I. Metin Kunt and Christine Woodhead (eds), *Süleyman the Magnificent and his Age* (London, 1995), 71–90.

Demetriades, V., 'The tomb of Ghazi Evrenos Bey at Yenitsa and its inscriptions', *Bulletin of the School of Oriental and African Studies*, XXXIX (1976), 328–32.

Fleischer, C., *Bureaucrat and Intellectual in the Ottoman Empire: The Historian Mustafa Âli (1541–1600)* (Princeton, 1986).

Howard, D.A., 'The historical development of the Ottoman Imperial Registry (*Defter-i hakanî*): mid-fifteenth to mid-seventeenth centuries', *Archivum Ottomanicum*, XI (1986), 213–30.

Howard, D.A., "Ayn 'Ali Efendi and the literature of Ottoman decline', *Turkish Studies Association Bulletin*, 11 (1987), 18–20.

Howard, D.A., 'Ottoman administration and the timar system: kanunname-i osmani beray-i timar daden', *Journal of Turkish Studies*, 20 (1996), 46–125.

İnalcık, H., 'Timariotes chrétiens en Albanie au XVe siècle', *Mitteilungen des Österreichichen Staatsarchiv* (Vienna), IV (1952), 120–8.

İnalcık, H., 'Military and fiscal transformation in the Ottoman Empire', *Archivum Ottomanicum*, VI (1980), 283–37.

İlhan, M.M., 'Some notes on the settlement and population of the Sancak of Amid according to the 1518 Ottoman cadasatral survey', *Tarih Araştırmaları Dergisi*, XIV (1981–82), 415–36.

İlhan, M.M., 'The process of Ottoman cadastral surveys during the second half of the sixteenth century', *Anuarul Institutului de Istoria si Arheologie A.D. Xenopol'* (Iaşi), XXIV (1987), 17–25.

İlhan, M.M., 'The Katif district (*liva*) during the first few years of Ottoman rule: a study of the 1551 cadastral survey', *Belleten*, LI (1987), 781–800.

İnalcık, H., 'Ottoman methods of conquest', *Studia Islamica*, II (1954), 104–29; repr. Halil İnalcık, *The Ottoman Empire: Conquest, Organisation and Economy* (London, 1998), I.

Kiel, M., 'Central Greece in the Suleymanic age', in Gilles Veinstein (ed.), *Soliman le Magnifique et son Temps* (Paris, 1992), 399–424.

Kunt, I.M., *The Sultan's Servants: The Transformation of Ottoman Provincial Government, 1550–1650* (New York, 1983).

Röhrborn, K., *Untersuchungen zur Osmanischen Verwaltungsgeschichte* (Berlin, 1973).

Schwarz, K. (ed. Claudia Römer), *Osmanische Sultansurkunden: Untersuchungen zur Einstellung und Besoldung Osmanischer Militärs in der Zeit Murads III* (Stuttgart, 1997).

Stanley, T., 'Men-at arms, hauberks and bards: military obligations in the *Book of the Ottoman Custom*', in Ç. Balım-Harding and C. Imber (eds), *The Balance of Truth: Essays in Honour of Professor Geoffrey Lewis* (Istanbul, 2000), 331–63.

Zachariadou, Elizabeth A., 'Lauro Quirini and the Ottoman sanjaks (c. 1430)', *Journal of Turkish Studies*, 11 (1987), 239–47.

The Law

Calder, N., 'Al-Nawawi's typology of *muftis* and its significance for a general theory of Islamic law', *Islamic Law and Society*, 3 (1996), 137–64.

Calder, N., 'Feqh', *Encyclopaedia Iranica*, IX (New York, 1999).

Cohen, A., 'Communal legal entities in a Muslim setting: the Jewish community in sixteenth century Jerusalem', *Islamic Law and Society*, 3 (1996), 75–90.

Cvetkova, B., 'L'influence exercée par certaines instititutions de Byzance du moyen-âge sur le système féodal ottoman', *Byzantinobulgarica*, I (1952), 237–57.

Gerber, H., *State, Society and Law in Islam: Ottoman Law in Comparative Perspective* (Albany, 1994).

Gerber, H., 'Rigidity versus openness in late classical Islamic law: the case of the Palestinian mufti Khayr al-Din al-Ramli', *Islamic Law and Society*, 5 (1998), 165–95.

Gerber, H., *Islamic Law and Culture, 1600–1840* (Leiden, 1999).

Gradeva, R., 'Orthodox Christians in the kadi court: the practice of the Sofia sheriat court', *Islamic Law and Society*, 4 (1997), 37–69.

Hacker, J., 'Jewish autonomy in the Ottoman Empire: its scope and limits. Jewish courts from the sixteenth to the eighteenth centuries', in Avigdor Levy, *The Jews of the Ottoman Empire* (Princeton, 1994).

Heyd, U., 'Some aspects of the Ottoman *fetva*', *Bulletin of the School of Oriental and African Studies*, XXXII (1968), 35–56.

Heyd, U. (ed. V.L. Ménage), *Studies in Old Ottoman Criminal Law* (Oxford, 1973).

Heywood, C., 'The evolution of the Ottoman provincial law code (sancak kanunname): the kanun-name-i liva-i Semendire', *Turkish Studies Association Bulletin*, 15 (1991), 223–51.

Imber, C., 'Zina in Ottoman law', *Contributions à l'Histoire Sociale et Économique de l'Empire Ottoman* (Louvain, 1981), 59–92; repr. Colin Imber, *Studies in Ottoman History and Law* (Istanbul, 1996), 175–206.

Imber, C., 'The status of orchards and fruit trees in Ottoman law', *Tarih Enstitüsü Dergisi*, 12 (1982), 763–74; repr. C. Imber, *Studies*, 207–16.

Imber, C., 'Involuntary annulment of marriage and its solutions in Ottoman law', *Turcica*, XXV (1993), 39–73; repr. C. Imber, *Studies*, 217–52.

Imber, C., *Ebu's-su'ud: The Islamic Legal Tradition* (Edinburgh, 1997).

Imber, C., '*Fiqh* for beginners: an Anatolian text on *jihad*', in G.R. Hawting, J. Mojaddedi, A. Samely (eds), *Studies in Islamic and Middle Eastern Texts and Traditions in Memory of Norman Calder* (Manchester, 2000), 137–48.

Jennings, R., 'Limitations of the judicial powers of the kadi', *Studia Islamica*, L (1979), 151–84.

Jennings, R., *Studies on Ottoman Social History in the Sixteenth and Seventeenth Century: Women, Zimmis and Shariah Courts in Kayseri, Cyprus and Trabzon* (Istanbul, 1999).

Johansen, B., *The Islamic Law of Tax and Rent* (London, 1988).

Johansen, B., *Contingency in a Sacred Law* (Leiden, 1999).

Lowry, H., 'The Ottoman Liva Kanunnames contained in the Defter-i Hakani', *Osmanlı Araştırmaları*, II (1981), 43–74.

Repp, R.C., *The Müfti of Istanbul* (Oxford, 1986).

Schacht, J., *An Introduction to Islamic Law* (Oxford, 1964).

Tucker, Judith, *In the House of the Law: Gender and Islamic Law in Ottoman Syria and Palestine* (Berkeley, 1998).

Zilfi, Madeline, 'Élite circulation in the Ottoman Empire: great mollas of the eighteenth century', *Journal of the Economic and Social History of the Orient*, 26 (1983), 237–57.

Zilfi, Madeline, ' "We don't get along": women and *hul* divorce in the eighteenth century', in Madeline C. Zilfi (ed.), *Women in the Ottoman Empire* (Leiden, 1997), 264–96.

The Army

Ágoston, G., 'Gunpowder for the Sultan's army in the Hungarian campaigns of the sixteenth and seventeenth centuries', *Turcica*, XXV (1993), 75–96.

Ágoston, G., 'Ottoman artillery and European military technology in the fifteenth and seventeenth centuries', *Acta Orientalia* (Budapest), XLVII (1994), 15–48.

Ágoston, G., 'Habsburgs and Ottomans: military change and shifts in power', *Turkish Studies Association Bulletin*, 22 (1998), 126–41.

Ágoston, G., '*Merces prohibitae*: the Anglo-Ottoman trade in war materials and the dependence theory', *Oriente Moderno*, XX (LXXXI)/1 (2001), 177–92.

Brummett, C., 'Subordination and its discontents: the Ottoman campaign, 1578–80', in Caesar E. Farah (ed.), *Decision Making and Change in the Ottoman Empire* (Kirksville, 1993), 101–14.

DeVries, Kelly, 'Gunpowder weapons at the siege of Constantinople', in Yaacov Lev (ed.), *War and Society in the Eastern Mediterranean, 7th–15th centuries* (Leiden, 1997), 343–62.

Finkel, Caroline, *The Administration of Warfare: The Ottoman Military Campaigns in Hungary, 1593–1606* (Vienna, 1988).

Fodor, P. 'Bauarbeiten der Türken an den Burgen in Ungarn im 16.–17. Jahrhundert', *Acta Orientalia* (Budapest), XXXV (1981), 55–88.

Heywood, C., 'Notes on the production of fifteenth century Ottoman cannon', *Islamabad: International Symposium on Islam and Science* (1980) (Islamabad, n.d.), 58–61.

Heywood, C., 'The activities of the state cannon-foundry (tophane-i amire) at Istanbul in the early sixteenth century', *Priloza za Orijentalna Filologija*, 30 (1980), 209–17.

Işıksal, T., 'Gunpowder in Ottoman documents of the last half of the sixteenth century', *International Journal of Turkish Studies*, 2 (1981/2), 81–91.

Kaldy-Nagy, Gy., 'The first centuries of the Ottoman military organisation', *Acta Orientalia* (Budapest), XXXI (1977), 147–83.

Kaldy-Nagy, Gy., 'The conscription of müsellem and yaya corps in 1540', in Gy. Kaldy-Nagy (ed.), *Hungaro-Turcica: Studies in Honour of Julius Németh* (Budapest, 1978), 275–81.

Murphey, R., *Ottoman Warfare, 1500–1700* (London, 1999)

Parry, V., 'Barud', *Encyclopaedia of Islam* (2nd edn), 1 (1960).

Parry, V., 'Hisar', *Encyclopaedia of Islam* (2nd edn), 3 (1971).

Parry, V., 'La manière de combattre', in V.J. Parry and M.E. Yapp (eds), *War, Technology and Society in the Middle East* (London, 1975), 218–56.

Petrović, Djurdjica, 'Firearms in the Balkans on the eve of the Ottoman conquest', in V.J. Parry and M.E. Yapp (eds), *War, Technology and Society*, 164–94.

Römer, Claudia, *Osmanische Festungsbesatzungen in Ungarn zur Zeit Murad III* (Vienna, 1995).

Vatin, N., 'Le siège de Mitylène, 1501', *Turcica*, XXI–XXIII (1992), 454; repr. Nicolas Vatin, *Les Ottomans et l'Occident* (Istanbul, 2001), 9–29.

Veinstein, Gilles, 'L'hivernage en campagne, talon d'Achille du système militaire ottoman classique', *Studia Islamica*, LXVIII (1983); repr. Gilles Veinstein, *État et Société*, v.

Veinstein, Gilles, 'Some views on provisioning the Hungarian campaigns of Süleyman the Magnificent', in H.G. Majer (ed.), *Osmanistische Studien zur Wirtschafts- und Sozialgeschichte in Memoriam Vanco Boškov* (Wiesbaden, 1986), 177–85; repr. Gilles Veinstein, *État et Société dans l'Empire Ottoman, XVIe–XVIIe siècles* (Aldershot, 1994).

Velkov, A. and Radushev, E., *Ottoman Garrisons on the Middle Danube* (Budapest, 1996).

Williams, A., 'Ottoman military technology: the metallurgy of Turkish armour', in Yaacov Lev (ed.), *War and Society*, 363–97.

The Fleet

De Groot, A., 'The Ottoman Mediterranean since Lepanto (October 7th, 1571): Naval warfare during the seventeenth and eighteenth centuries', *Anatolica*, 20 (1994), 269–93.

Fleet, Kate, 'Early Turkish naval activities', *Oriente Moderno*, xx (LXXXI)/1 (2001), 129–38.

Guilmartin, F., *Gunpowder and Galleys: Changing Technology and Mediterranean Warfare at Sea* (Cambridge, 1974).

Hess, A.C., 'The evolution of the Ottoman seaborne Empire in the age of the oceanic discoveries', *American Historical Review*, 75 (1970), 1892–1919.

Imber, C., 'The costs of naval warfare: the accounts of Hayreddin Barbarossa's Herceg Novi campaign in 1539', *Archivum Ottomanicum* (1972), 204–16; repr in C. Imber, *Studies*, 71–84.

Imber, C., 'The navy of Süleyman the Magnificent', *Archivum Ottomanicum*, vi (1980), 211–82; repr. Colin Imber, *Studies in Ottoman History and Law* (Istanbul, 1996), 1–69.

Imber, C., 'The reconstruction of the Ottoman fleet after the battle of Lepanto', in Colin Imber, *Studies* (1996), 85–101.

Ostapchuk, V., 'Five documents from the Topkapı Palace Archives on the Ottoman defence of the Black Sea against the Cossacks', *Journal of Turkish Studies*, ii (1987), 49–104.

Ostapchuk, V., 'The human landscape of the Ottoman Black Sea in the face of the Cossack naval raids', *Oriente Moderno*, xx (LXXXI)/1 (2001), 23–95.

Soucek, S., 'Certain types of ship in Ottoman terminology', *Turcica*, vii (1975), 233–49.

Veinstein, G., 'Les préparatifs de la campagne navale franco-turque de 1552 à travers les ordres du Divan ottoman', *Revue de l'Occident Musulman et de la Méditerranée*, 39 (1985), 35–67; repr., Gilles Veinstein, *État et Société*, vi.

Yérasimos, S., 'Les relations franco-ottomanes et la prise de Tripoli en

1551', in Gilles Veinstein (ed.), *Soliman le Magnifique et son Temps* (Paris, 1992), 529–44.

Zachariadou, Elizabeth A., 'Holy War in the Aegean during the fourteenth century', *Mediterranean Historical Review*, 4 (1989), 212–25.

Zachariadou, Elizabeth A. (ed.), *The Kapudan Pasha and his Domain*, Rethymnon, forthcoming.

Index

Printed in the United States
118425LV00001B/13-30/A